How to
Program and Interface
the 6800

by
Andrew C. Staugaard, Jr.

Howard W. Sams & Co., Inc.
4300 WEST 62ND ST. INDIANAPOLIS, INDIANA 46268 USA

Copyright © 1980 by Andrew C. Staugaard, Jr.

FIRST EDITION
THIRD PRINTING—1982

All rights reserved. No part of this book shall be reproduced, stored in a retrieval system, or transmitted by any means, electronic, mechanical, photocopying, recording, or otherwise, without written permission from the publisher. No patent liability is assumed with respect to the use of the information contained herein. While every precaution has been taken in the preparation of this book, the publisher assumes no responsibility for errors or omissions. Neither is any liability assumed for damages resulting from the use of the information contained herein.

International Standard Book Number: 0-672-21684-1
Library of Congress Catalog Card Number: 80-50050

Printed in the United States of America.

Preface

In the past few years, we have experienced a revolution in electronic computer technology that began with the introduction of the first microprocessor in 1971. This revolution was made possible by an integrated-circuit technology called large scale integration (LSI), which is the ability to pack thousands of transistor devices within a small silicon "chip." As a result of this technology, we have seen circuit complexity and capability double each year with this pace expected to continue for the foreseeable future by the introduction of circuits utilizing very-large scale integration (VLSI) and super-large scale integration (SLSI). These new integration technologies have not only increased circuit capabilities, but have surprisingly and dramatically reduced circuit costs. Products such as appliances, instrumentation, toys, games, etc., which could never possess a computer "intelligence" because the cost was prohibitive, are now being marketed with *microcomputer* control at minimum cost. One of the first microprocessor applications was the electronic calculator industry. In the past years, we have seen calculator capabilities go up and cost come down. Not only are microprocessors finding widespread use in these products, but they have also spawned a hobby computer market. Full computer systems are now available for less than half the price of a new automobile—something unheard of 10 years ago.

After the introduction of the first microprocessor chip by the Intel Corporation, many semiconductor companies introduced their own microprocessors. Three leading chips emerged: the Motorola 6800, Intel 8080, and Zilog Z-80. Each of these is an 8-bit central processing unit (CPU) that requires external memory and i/o circuitry to function as a microcomputer. However, we are now witnessing a surge of "computer-on-a-chip" devices that contain all the logic, memory, and i/o capability for a small microcomputer in one integrated circuit package.

Motorola, at the time of this writing, is the only company that has developed these new chips around its standard 6800 architecture.

The 6800 "family" now ranges from an advanced microprocessor, the 6809, to a *complete* single-chip microcomputer, the 6801. This broad range of software compatibility, which is not currently available within the 8080 and Z-80 chip families, is highly desirable since it permits one to meet a wide variety of application requirements. This was one of the important reasons for the decision by General Motors and the Ford Motor Co. to incorporate the 6800 family of microprocessors/microcomputers into their new cars.

In this book, we will provide you with an introduction to the world of microprocessors/microcomputers via the Motorola 6800. It begins with microprocessor/microcomputer concepts and, therefore, assumes the reader has a basic understanding of number systems and digital electronic concepts. However, this prerequisite material is presented in Appendix A and Appendix B for the reader who might need some "brushing-up" or is not familiar with these concepts. The first chapters of the book discuss the 6800 internal structure, instruction set, and programming techniques. The final chapters are devoted to the 6800 hardware and interfacing techniques.

The book is meant to be a tutorial type of text for an introduction to the 6800 or microprocessors/microcomputers in general. Review questions and answers are provided after each chapter. In addition, there are over 30 "hands-on" experiments provided throughout the text that demonstrate "real-world" applications. The experiments are written around the Heath ET3400 microcomputer learning system and the Motorola MEK6800D2 evaluation kit. Applications are stressed throughout the text and are especially evident in the chapters on interfacing where the reader learns how to construct a minimum workable 6800 system and interface that system to switches, keyboards, displays, digital-to-analog converters, and analog-to-digital converters.

Finally, I would like to express my appreciation to Dave Larsen of Virginia Polytechnic Institute and State University whose encouragement to write on the Motorola chip line led to this book and to Jon Titus of Tychon, Inc., whose many suggestions have contributed to the final product. In addition, I must thank my wife, Janet, for her talent with a typewriter and to one of my students, Sandy Trentini, whose talent at the drawing board is evident in most of the text illustrations.

ANDREW C. STAUGAARD, JR.

To my wife Jan, she believes in me.

Contents

CHAPTER 1

FUNDAMENTAL MICROPROCESSOR CONCEPTS 9

Introduction – Objectives – Microprocessor/Microcomputer Basics – Basic 6800 Chip Structure – 6800 Fetch and Execute – Review Questions – Answers

CHAPTER 2

HEATH ET3400 AND MOTOROLA MEK6800
MICROCOMPUTER LEARNING SYSTEMS 27

Introduction – Objectives – Heath ET3400 Microcomputer Learning System – Motorola MEK6800D2 Evaluation Kit – Experiment Instructions and Format – Experiments

CHAPTER 3

6800 ARITHMETIC, LOGIC, AND DATA-HANDLING INSTRUCTIONS . 52

Introduction – Objectives – 6800 Data Transfer – 6800 Arithmetic Instructions – 6800 Logic Instructions – Review Questions – Answers – Experiments

CHAPTER 4

CONDITION CODE REGISTER AND DATA
SHIFTING/COMPARING/TESTING 84

> Introduction–Objectives–Condition Code Register–Data Shifting, Rotating, Comparing, and Testing–Review Questions–Answers–Experiments

CHAPTER 5

6800 BRANCHING, INDEXING, AND STACKS 113

> Introduction – Objectives – Branching – Branch Instructions – Index Register and Addressing–Stacks and Stack Pointer–Subroutines–Review Questions–Answers–Experiments

CHAPTER 6

6800 INPUT/OUTPUT 144

> Introduction–Objectives–General I/O Concepts–Decoding–I/O Techniques–6800 Interrupts–Pin Assignments–Review Questions–Answers–Experiments

CHAPTER 7

INTERFACING WITH MEMORY 178

> Introduction – Objectives – Memory Technology – Interfacing With Read/Write Memory–MCM6810 R/W Memory–2112 R/W Memory–Interfacing With Read-Only Memory (ROM)–MCM68708 (Intel 2708) EPROM–Review Questions–Answers–Experiments

CHAPTER 8

THE 6820/6821 PERIPHERAL INTERFACE ADAPTER 208

> Introduction–Objectives–6821 Functional Description–PIA Interfacing and Addressing–PIA Initialization and Servicing–Review Questions–Answers–Experiments

CHAPTER 9

6800 SYSTEM INTERFACING 240

Introduction — Objectives — Interfacing With Switches — Interfacing With Keyboards — Interfacing With Displays — Interfacing With Digital-to-Analog Converters — Interfacing With Analog-to-Digital Converters—Review Questions—Answers—Experiments

APPENDIX A

DIGITAL REVIEW 279

Basic Logic Gates—Flip-Flops

APPENDIX B

NUMBER SYSTEMS AND COMPUTER ARITHMETIC 285

Number Systems—Digital Computer Arithmetic

APPENDIX C

6800 INSTRUCTION SET 297

Symbol Definitions and Nomenclature—Executable Instructions

APPENDIX D

SPECIFICATION SHEETS 340

MC6800/MC6800C—MCM6810A/MCM6810C—MC6820/MC6820C—MCM6830A—MCM68708/MCM68A708—2112—MC1508/MC1408—NE5018—ICL7109

INDEX 411

CHAPTER 1

Fundamental Microprocessor Concepts

INTRODUCTION

In this chapter we will begin by discussing the fundamental differences between a microprocessor chip, a microcomputer chip, and a microcomputer system. This will then lead to a discussion of chip families, specifically the Motorola 6800 family. Once the decision to purchase a particular microprocessor or microcomputer chip is made, the purchaser is really committed to a chip family. The family will consist of all the external support chips required to make a workable system. Such support chips include read/write memory, read-only memory, peripheral interface chips, peripheral controllers, etc. If a manufacturer maintains family compatibility for future chip design, even the newer-generation microprocessors and microcomputer chips can be part of the same basic family. This is the case with the Motorola 6800 chip line. All of the newer-generation chips such as the 6802, 6809, and 6801 are *software,* and to some extent *hardware,* compatible with the 6800. Therefore, we include them as part of the 6800 family.

We will then take a closer look at the 6800 chip which can be divided into three functional regions: *address, data,* and *control.* We will discuss the internal registers that make up each functional region. This will be the beginning 6800 structure (architecture) which will be completed in Chapter 3. You will become familiar with the 6800 instruction format. A simple program will then be written to add two numbers and the program execution will be traced through the internal structure of the 6800.

Finally, in order to understand digital computers, it is necessary to know the binary number system. Since the learning systems used with the experiments employ the hexadecimal (hex) number system and all of the programs will be written in hex, it is especially important to understand this number system as well as how to convert between hex and other number systems such as binary and decimal. It might be helpful to review number systems in Appendix B prior to reading this chapter.

OBJECTIVES

At the end of this chapter you will be able to do the following:

- Understand the difference between a microprocessor and microcomputer.
- Know some microprocessor chip families and microcomputer systems and their applications.
- Distinguish between read/write and read-only memory.
- Understand the basic internal structure of the 6800.
- Distinguish between microcomputer instructions written in binary code, hexadecimal code, or mnemonic code.
- Understand and trace a simple program through the 6800 chip.

MICROPROCESSOR/MICROCOMPUTER BASICS

Let us start by making a distinction between the terms *microprocessor* and *microcomputer*. A *microprocessor* is usually only a single integrated circuit, or "chip," and it is generally thought of as a Central Processing Unit (CPU). It does not contain any permanent memory or convenient input/output (i/o) features. Many of these chips do not include a clock for the timing of operations and none of them include a power supply. The first- and second-generation chips such as the Motorola 6800 and 6802; the Intel 8008, 8080, and 8085; and the Zilog Z-80 are truly microprocessors. They are the result of Large Scale Integration (LSI) which can integrate 500 to 10,000 transistors and associated components on a 100-mil × 100-mil silicon chip. These chips are not "stand-alone" computers and may require anywhere from 3 to 300 additional digital chips and i/o devices to achieve a workable system, depending on the application. However, these microprocessor chips sell for under $20.00 and represent as much computing power as many of the larger computers of the mid-1960s. Present applications of these devices are calculators, tv games, "smart" toys, appliances, home and small-business computing systems, industrial process controls, and automobiles. The largest future applications are seen to be in homes, automobiles, appliances, and industrial controls. Because of the low cost of these devices, almost any mechanical or electrical product has the potential of utilizing a programmed intelligence.

A microcomputer, on the other hand, is virtually a total computer system. It can be as large or small as the application requires. The microcomputer can be broken down into two categories: the microcomputer chip and microcomputer system. The microcomputer chip is a result of third-generation technology that utilizes VLSI (*Very-Large Scale Integration*) which integrates from 10,000 to 50,000 transistors and associated components per chip. This 40-pin chip will typically contain a small amount of read-only and read/write memory, a clock, possibly a serial communications interface capability or an internal analog-to-digital converter, and other i/o features. The Motorola 6801 and Intel 8748 are products of this technology. These chips are "stand-alone" computers for many small applications, such as appliances and industrial controls. They will be used for future applications essentially in the same manner as the microprocessor chip. The Motorola 6801 microcomputer chip layout is shown in Fig. 1-1.

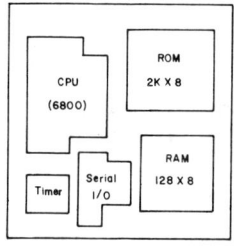

Fig. 1-1. Motorola 6801 microcomputer chip layout.

The second category of microcomputers is the microcomputer system. This system is built around the microprocessor or microcomputer chip. Such systems usually contain the following, external to the chip itself.

1. *Read-Only Memory* (ROM) for operation control.
2. *Read/Write* (R/W) memory for data storage.
3. CRT and keyboard for convenient user input/output.
4. Floppy disk or cassette recorder for mass data storage.

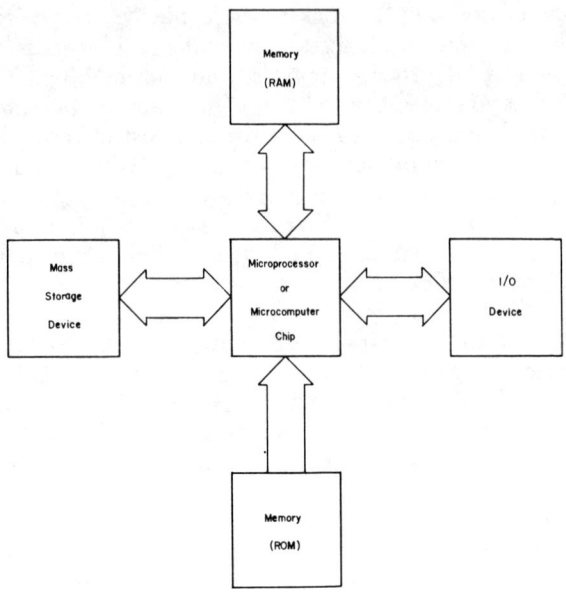

Fig. 1-2. Microcomputer system block diagram.

Examples of such systems are the Radio Shack TRS-80, Heathkit H-8, IMSAI 8080, Altair 8800, and Cromemco Z-2. These systems are relatively inexpensive and rival many minicomputers in their capabilities. They can be used for industrial process control, data acquisition, and personal and small business computing. They are also a very popular hobby item. A microcomputer system block diagram is shown in Fig. 1-2. Note that the microprocessor/microcomputer chip is at the "heart" of the system.

Before we begin with a detailed discussion of the 6800 chip, let us look at some microprocessor and microcomputer chip families.

Manufacturers of microprocessor chips, such as Motorola, Intel, Zilog, and RCA, have each marketed a complete series of external chips that can be used with their microprocessor. Remember, the beauty of a microcomputer system is that it can be as large or as small as the application requires. Therefore, once a particular microprocessor is purchased, almost any number of chips within the family of that microprocessor can be added to obtain the desired system. All chips within a family are compatible, which means that they typically use the same supply voltages, have the same size data words, etc. The 6801 we referred to earlier is considered part of the 6800 chip family since it uses the 6800 as its Central Processing Unit (CPU). See Fig. 1-1. The same is true of the Motorola 6802, 6803, and 6809 microcomputer chips. We intend to study the 6800 in detail because it is the basic hardware and software model for almost all of Motorola's chip line. All of the Motorola microcomputer chips, such as the 6801, 6802, 6803, and 6809, utilize the 6800 as their CPU and many future Motorola chips will be software and hardware compatible with the 6800. Fig. 1-3 shows the 6800 chip family. There are many chips within the family other than the ones indicated in Fig. 1-3. For a complete listing and description of all the 6800 family, consult *The Complete Motorola Microcomputer Data Library*, available from Motorola Semiconductor Products, Inc., Box 20912, Phoenix, Arizona 85036. We will cover some of these chips in more detail when we discuss interfacing.

BASIC 6800 CHIP STRUCTURE

We will begin with a description of only those functional parts of the 6800 that will permit us to program simple operations. Then,

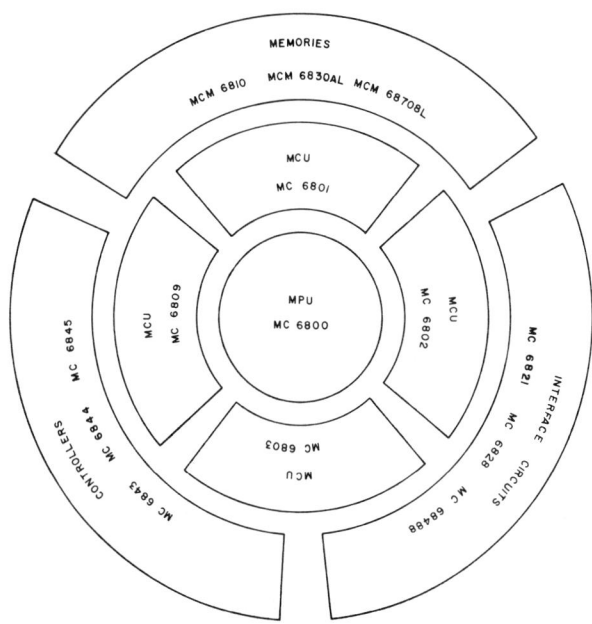

Fig. 1-3. Motorola 6800 chip family.

later on, we will complete the 6800 architecture with the addition of some special functions to make the 6800 a very powerful processing unit. Fig. 1-4 represents the beginning of our 6800 structure.

First, note that the chip is divided into two distinct sections, *address* and *data/control*. On the surface it would seem that these sections are unconnected and unrelated. However, both sections are connected to an external memory. The address section is used to

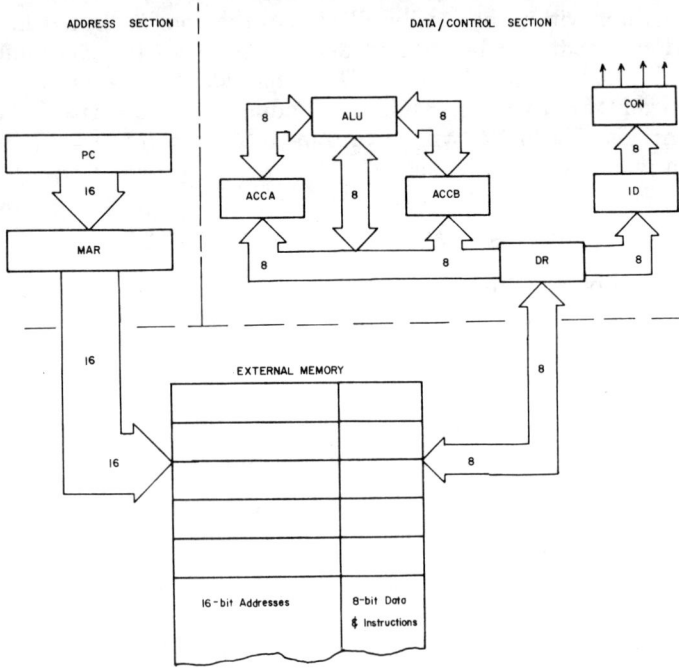

Fig. 1-4. 6800 functional chip structure.

fetch program instructions and data from memory and the data/control section is used to interpret these instructions and *execute* the program commands. Therefore, the sections are related and interact with each other via an external memory.

Second, note that broad arrows connect the various blocks. These are internal *buses* (conductor paths) that transmit binary information from one area to another. The arrow indicates the direction of information flow. Note that some of the buses are bidirectional. The number within the bus indicates the size of the bus in binary bits. Therefore, by observation, the address section utilizes 16-bit buses while the data/control section uses 8-bit buses. Now let us look at each functional block in more detail.

Program Counter

The Program Counter (PC) is simply a 16-bit binary counter. The PC is capable of counting from $0000\ 0000\ 0000\ 0000_2$ to $1111\ 1111\ 1111\ 1111_2$ or 0000_{16} to $FFFF_{16}$. When the counter is clocked by CON, it will be incremented by one binary digit. The count in the PC will represent an address in memory. In fact, it is always the memory address of the *next* program instruction to be performed.

Memory Address Register

The Memory Address Register (MAR) is a 16-bit storage register. It receives a 16-bit memory address from the PC. It will then pass the address to the external memory to "fetch" the next program instruction to be performed.

External Memory

This memory is external to the 6800 chip. It is a Random-Access Memory (RAM). A RAM can be thought of as a Read/Write (R/W) memory, i.e., information can be read from the memory and information can also be written into the memory. Each location in memory contains an 8-bit word; therefore, all information in the memory is ordered in 8-bit blocks, or *bytes*, as shown in Fig. 1-4. This is why the 6800 data bus in Fig. 1-4 is an 8-bit bus.

Each byte of information must have an address so that it can be located. The address is a 16-bit (2-byte) word and this is the reason that the 6800 address bus is a 16-bit bus. Since our address is a 16-bit word, there are 2^{16} possible addresses. Therefore, we say that the 6800 is capable of addressing 65,536 locations in memory. More will be said about memory later.

Data Register

The Data Register (DR) is an 8-bit temporary storage register which receives 8-bit information from memory. If the 8-bit memory information is a program instruction, the DR will pass it to the instruction decoder. If the information is to be processed, rather than used to indicate an operation, the DR will pass it to one of the accumulators or the Arithmetic Logic Unit (alu), depending upon the previous program instruction command. The DR directs the information and is, therefore, sometimes referred to as a Data Direction Register (DDR).

Instruction Decoder

The *I*nstruction *D*ecoder (ID) is exactly what the name implies. It decodes, or interprets, 8-bit instructions received from memory. It will then direct the chip to "execute" the instructions through the controller/sequencer.

Controller/Sequencer

The *CON*troller/Sequencer (CON) receives the decoded instructions from the instruction decoder and enables and disables the other parts of the chip to carry out these instructions. Therefore, it controls and sequences all of the operations within the chip.

Accumulators

The 6800 contains two accumulators, *ACC*umulator *A* and *ACC*umulator *B* (ACCA and ACCB). These are 8-bit storage registers that are used to hold operands before they are used in an operation and are also used to hold the results of operations after they have been performed. Operands are data to be used as part of an operation.

Example 1-1: Use of Instructions and Operands

ADD ⟶ Instruction
2 ⟶ Operand

The operand is the number used in the operation. In this case, we are adding two. ADD is the instruction, while 2 is the operand.

Arithmetic Logic Unit

The alu is the heart of the 6800 microprocessor chip. It performs all of the arithmetic and logic operations. The results of these operations are stored in one of the accumulators. Typical operations are adding, subtracting, ANDing, ORing, or XORing.

6800 FETCH AND EXECUTE

Before we trace a simple operation through the chip, let us look at a typical instruction format. Instructions in the 6800 can be one, two, or three bytes in length. As shown in Example 1-2, the first byte is always the command. The second byte can be a memory address or data. The third byte is always part of a memory address or a second data byte. Some commands require a second or third byte while others do not.

In writing a series of instructions, the mnemonic of the command is listed then the second and third bytes in hex are shown, if they are required. Since hexadecimal is used as a standard number sys-

Example 1-2: 6800 Instruction Format

1st byte	8-bit command
2nd byte	address or data
3rd byte	optional address or date

NOTE: Since our command byte is eight bits, there are 2^8, or 256, different commands possible with an 8-bit chip such as the 6800.

tem, all numbers in the program listings will be hex unless otherwise indicated with a subscript.

A mnemonic is simply a representation for a command that is easily understood and remembered by the programmer. An op code is the 8-bit binary or 2-digit hex representation for the mnemonic which resides in memory.

Now let us look at the following program listing.

Example 1-3: 6800 Sample Program Listing

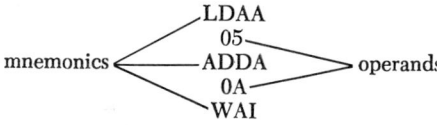

The first command is to LoaD Accumulator A with 5. The second command tells the computer to ADD 0A to the contents of accumulator A. The third instruction tells the computer to WAIt or halt its operation.

The second bytes of the first two instructions are operands and *not* addresses; neither of the instructions require a third byte. In fact, the WAI instruction does not require a second or third byte.

Note that in the preceding description of the program, we have capitalized each letter that forms the mnemonic of the instruction. This will be done throughout the text when new instruction mnemonics are introduced.

Once the program is loaded into memory, it is ready to go. The memory structure for this program is represented by Fig. 1-5 which is the actual binary memory structure. However, for ease of diagramming, hexadecimal is used to represent memory addresses and information as shown in Fig. 1-6. Note that the LDDA, ADDA and WAI instructions are represented by their respective op codes.

Now, we will trace the program through the 6800 chip and external memory. Our explanation will use Figs. 1-7 through 1-11.

Figure 1-7

The first instruction (LDAA) is *fetched* and decoded.

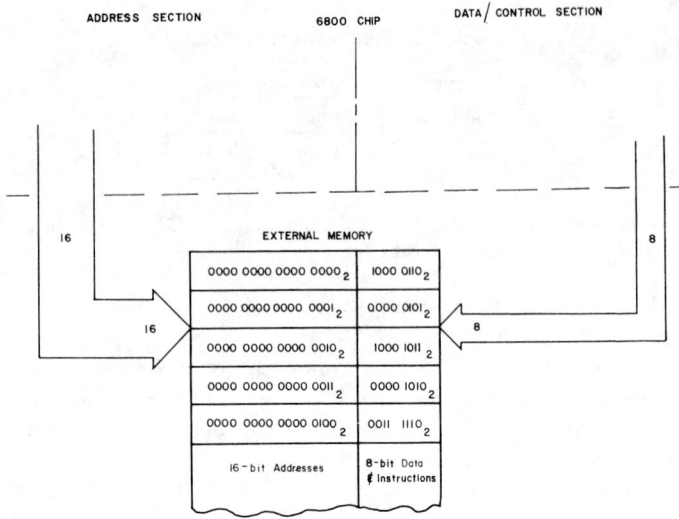

Fig. 1-5. Binary representation of "ADD" program in memory.

Explanation

Since the LDAA instruction is located at address 0000, this address must appear on the address bus for LDAA to be fetched. The PC is

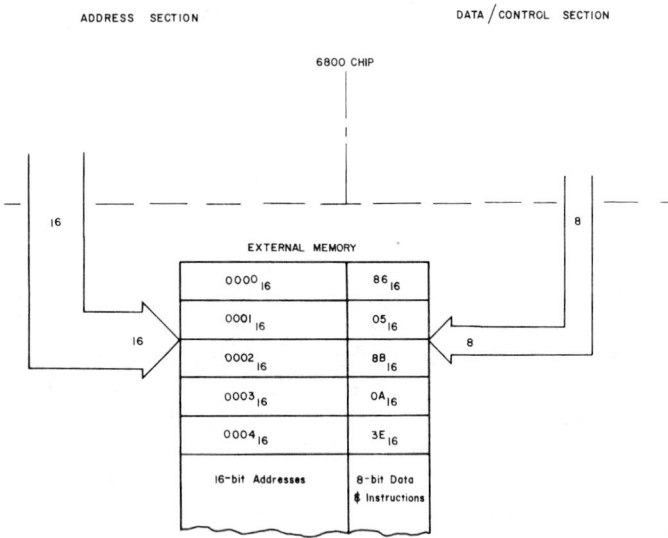

Fig. 1-6. Hexadecimal representation of "ADD" program in memory.

set to the beginning address of our program, 0000 in this case. Since program execution begins at address 0000, the 6800 expects to find an instruction op code there and not data. If data is stored there, it is treated as an instruction op code. The CON (controller/sequencer) section of the 6800 then enables the PC to transfer its count to the MAR (memory address register). Immediately after the transfer, the PC is clocked and its count is incremented by one. The MAR is then

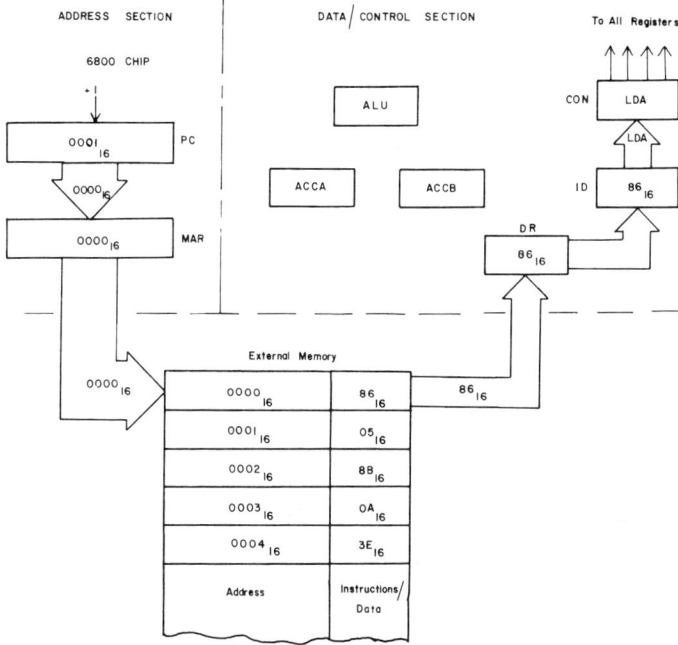

Fig. 1-7. LDA fetched and decoded.

enabled to transfer 0000 to the external memory. When memory location 0000 is accessed, its contents (86) are placed onto the data bus. This information is received by the DR (data register) then transferred to the ID (instruction decoder) for interpretation (decoding). Once the instruction is decoded, the CON provides the proper signals to execute the instruction. Observe the present register contents of the address section (Fig. 1-7). The PC contains 0001, which is the *next* memory location in be accessed. The MAR contains 0000, which is the address of the *present* memory location being accessed.

Figure 1-8

The operand (05) for the first instruction is fetched and loaded into accumulator A.

Explanation

The program count (0001) is transferred to the MAR and the PCs count is incremented. The MAR then places 0001 onto the address

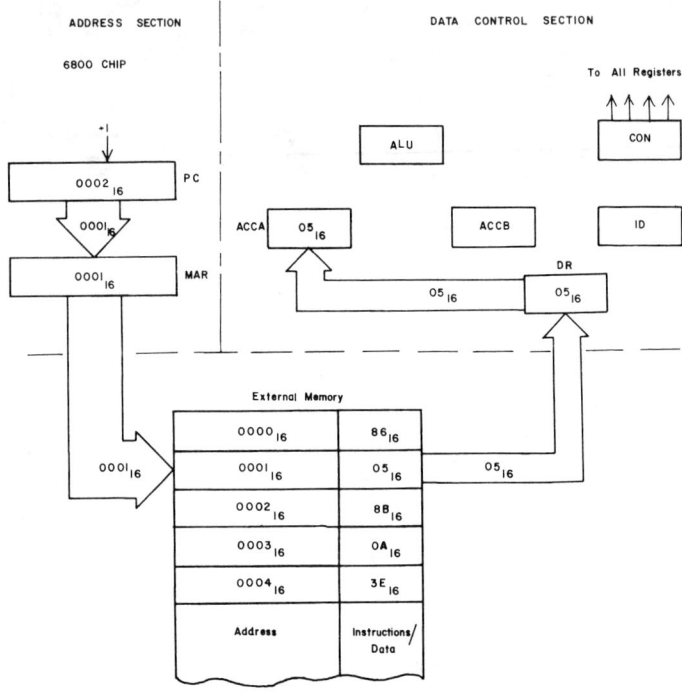

Fig. 1-8. LDA execution.

bus to be transferred to external memory. Memory location 0001 is accessed and its contents are placed on the data bus. The DR receives 05 and loads it into accumulator A.

How did the DR know that its incoming information was an operand and not another instruction to be decoded?

After the LDA instruction was decoded, the CON signaled the other registers that the byte of information in the next memory location was an operand to be loaded into accumulator A.

Figure 1-9

The ADDA instruction is fetched and decoded.

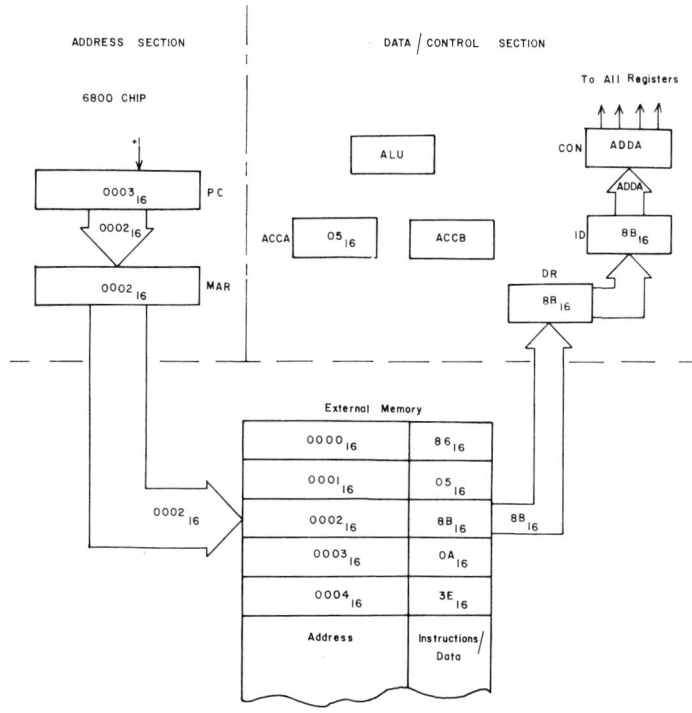

Fig 1-9. ADDA fetched and decoded.

Explanation

Address 0002 is placed on the address bus and the PC is incremented as before. The op code 8B is then accessed and placed on the data bus. The DR receives the instruction and passes it to the ID for decoding. The CON section then signals the other registers that the *next* byte in memory is an operand to be added to the contents of accumulator A and the sum is to be stored *back* into accumulator A.

Figure 1-10

The value 0A is added to 05 with the results being placed in accumulator A.

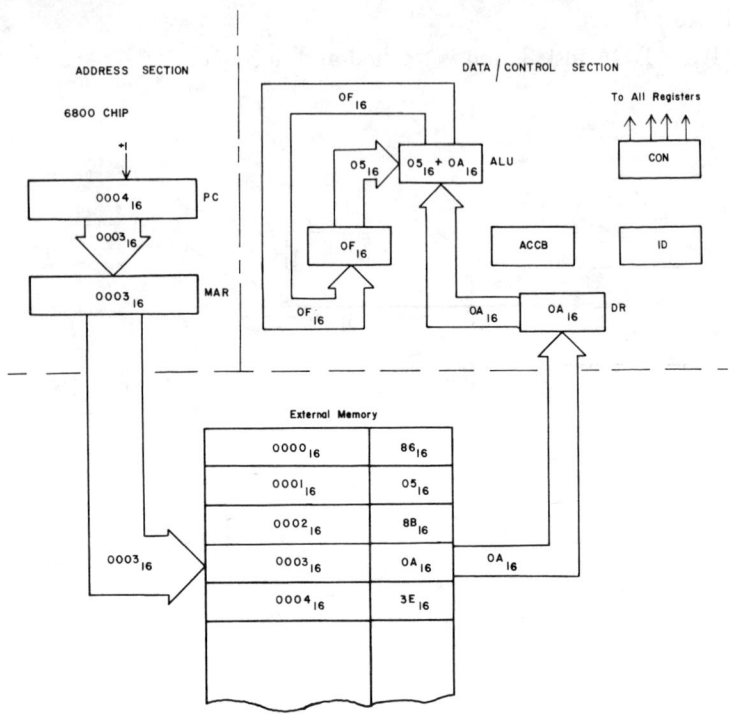

Fig. 1-10. ADDA execution.

Explanation

Address 0003 is placed on the address bus as before and the operand 0A is accessed and placed on the data bus. The DR sends 0A to the alu. At about the same time, the CON section indicates to accumulator A that it is to send its contents to the alu. The alu then adds the two operands and places the result (0F) back in accumulator A. We will see later that once the result of an operation is in one of the accumulators, it can then be stored in memory, used in another operation, or transferred to an i/o device.

Figure 1-11

The WAIt instruction is fetched and executed.

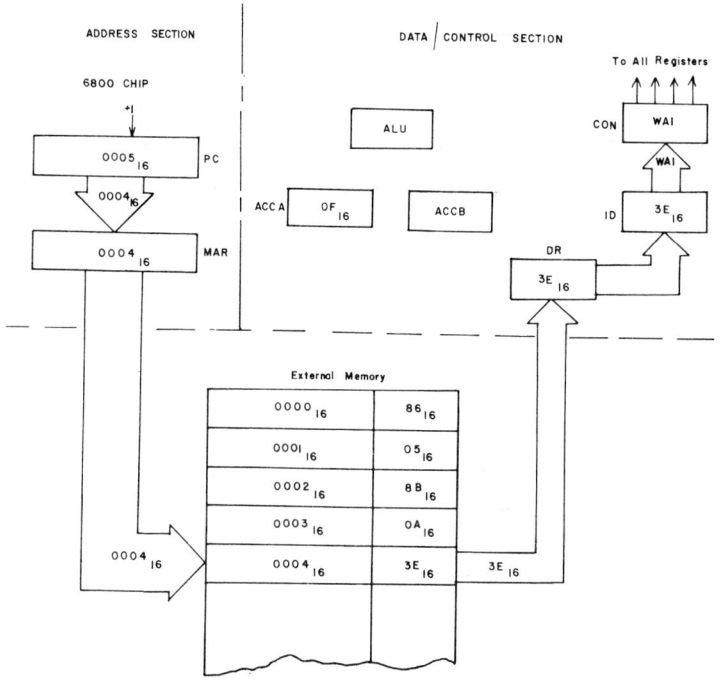

Fig. 1-11. WAI fetched and executed.

Explanation

The instruction is accessed and decoded as before. The CON section indicates to the other registers that they are to wait or halt operation until further notice. Note that the result of the addition, 0F, remains in accumulator A (ACCA).

REVIEW QUESTIONS

1. What is a digital computer?

2. What number system does a digital computer utilize?

3. What is meant by base 10, base 2, base 16?

4. Define the following terms:
   a. bit

   b. byte

   c. word

5. Which of the following is a byte?
   a. 1101

   b. 1101111

   c. 11011111

   d. 1000101011100111

6. State the difference between a microprocessor and microcomputer.

7. What is meant by the term LSI?

8. Identify the following instructions as to whether they are binary code, hexadecimal code, or mnemonic code.
   a. WAI

   b. 11010011_2

   c. 1101_{16}

   d. LDA

   e. 1101_2

   f. $0FC9_{16}$

9. State the difference between RAM and ROM.

10. Which of the following is a microcomputer system?
    a. 6800

    b. TRS-80

    c. 8080

    d. Z-80

11. What is meant by a chip family?

12. The 6800 uses a _____-bit data bus.

13. The PC is a _____-bit counter.

14. The MAR is a _____ register.

15. The _____ performs all arithmetic and logic operations.
16. The 6800 contains how many accumulators? What are they named?

17. Instructions can be _____ bytes in length (how many?).

18. The 6800 is capable of addressing _____ memory locations.

19. The results of an arithmetic or logic operation are always placed in the _____.

20. With reference to the instruction being executed, the PC always contains the address of the _____ program instruction.

21. A synonym for decoding is _____.

ANSWERS

1. A computer that utilizes on/off states (binary) to represent numbers and make decisions.
2. Binary, base 2.

3. Base 10 means decimal number system.
   Base 2 means binary number system.
   Base 16 means hexadecimal number system.

4. a. A binary digit (1 or 0).
   b. 8 bits.
   c. Any number of bits, depending on how it's used.

5. c.

6. A microcomputer is a fully operational digital computer that is based on a microprocessor.

7. Large Scale Integration—500-20,000 transistors and associated components per chip.

8. a. mnemonic
   b. binary
   c. hexadecimal
   d. mnemonic
   e. binary
   f. hexadecimal

9. RAM is random access memory (ROM is read-only memory).

10. TRS-80

11. Generally, a group of chips designed to be compatible with a specific microprocessor chip.

12. 8

13. 16

14. storage or buffer, 16-bit

15. arithmetic logic unit (alu)

16. Two—ACCA and ACCB.

17. one, two or three

18. $65,536_{10}$ (64K)

19. accumulator

20. next

21. interpret

CHAPTER 2

Heath ET3400 and Motorola MEK6800D2 Microcomputer Learning Systems

INTRODUCTION

In the chapters that follow, the Heath ET3400 or Motorola MEK-6800D2 learning systems will be used to demonstrate the concepts of microcomputer programming and interfacing. This chapter will familiarize you with the layout of each system and prepare us to use them properly to perform the experiments. It is assumed that the microcomputer system that will be used has already been properly assembled and tested and is in satisfactory working order. The programming experiments are designed to be used on either system. However, the interfacing experiments in Chapters 6 through 9 are *only* designed for the Heath ET3400 system. The interfacing experiments cannot be easily performed on the Motorola MEK6800D2 system since the data, address, and control signals are not made *conveniently* available and no solderless breadboarding region is supplied.

In order to complete all of the interfacing experiments, the following parts must be available in addition to the basic ET3400 training system:

One 7400 digital IC (2-bit NAND—Heath #443-1
One 74LS30 digital IC (8-bit NAND)—Heath #443-732
One 74LS27 digital IC (3-bit NOR)—Heath #443-800
One 7475 digital IC (Dflip-flop)

One 6820 or 6821 PIA—Heath #483-843
Two 2112 256 × 4 R/W memory chips—Heath #443-721
One TIL-312 7-segment display—Heath #411-831
One solderless connector block—Heath #432-875
Four push-button switches—Heath #64-724, 64-725, 64-726, 64-727
One Motorola MCM6810 128 ×8 R/W memory chip
Two 74154 one-of-sixteen decoders
Five 1000-ohm ¼-watt resistors
No. 20—No. 22 wire cut to 3", 6", and 9" lengths (approximately 25 of each length)

OBJECTIVES

At the end of this chapter you will be able to do the following:

- Describe the characteristics of each major functional area of the learning system.
- Identify the input/output parts of the system.
- For the ET3400, demonstrate the operation of the eight binary switches and LEDs.
- For the ET3400, demonstrate the operation of the DO, EXAM, FWD, AUTO, BACK, CHAN, SS, ACCA, ACCB, and PC keys on the keyboard.
- For the MEK6800D2, demonstrate the operation of the N, V, M, E, R, anid G keys on the keyboard.
- Load and execute a simple microcomputer program on each system.
- Trace a program through the 6800 chip with each system.

HEATH ET3400 MICROCOMPUTER LEARNING SYSTEM

The ET3400 is truly a *student-oriented* learning system. It is well designed to provide the student with an efficient learning experience in microcomputer architecture, programming, and interfacing. And yet, it is a powerful and versatile microcomputer. The system can be purchased from Heath in kit form for under $200.

A composite pictorial view of the learning system is shown in Fig. 2-1. This system can be broken down into two major areas as follows:

1. Those regions used for actual computation, memory, and i/o (Fig. 2-2).
2. Those regions which allow us to access different parts of the system and to breadboard external circuits to the system (Fig. 2-3).

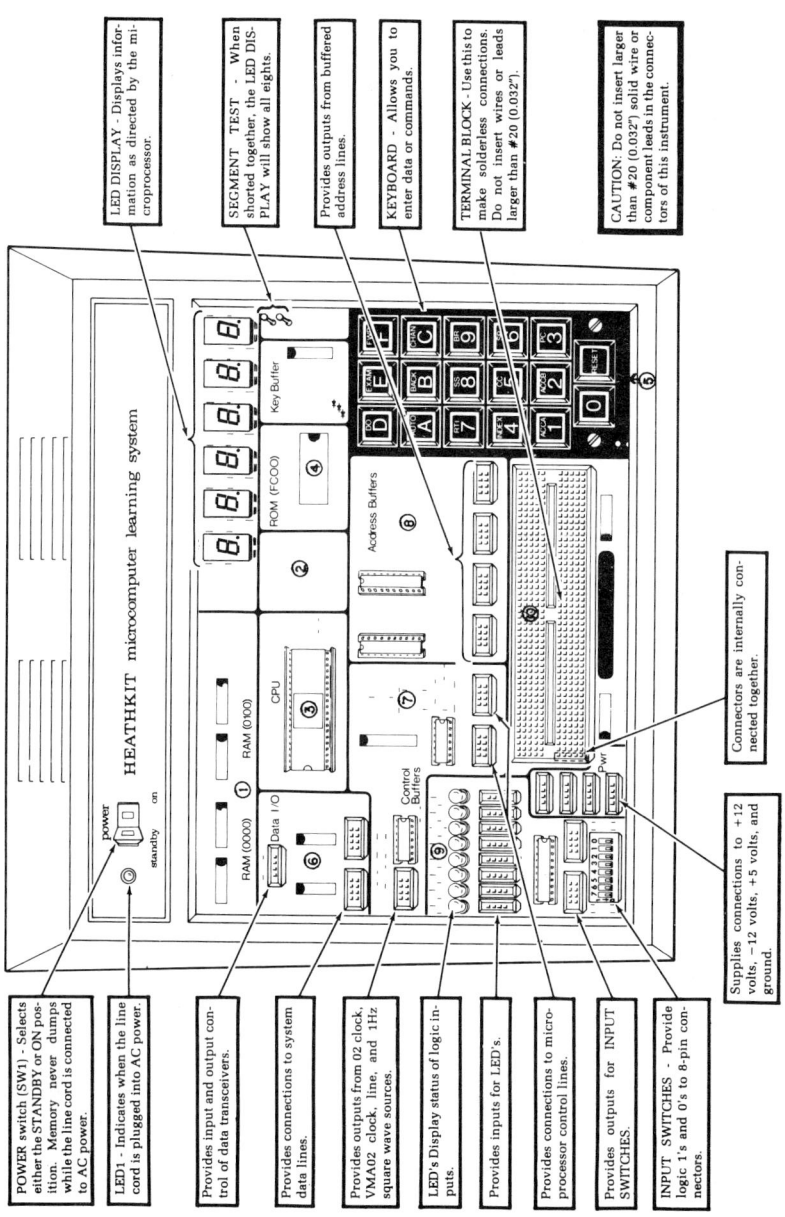

Fig. 2-1. Pictorial view of Heath ET3400 Microcomputer Learning System.

Functional Operating Regions

Refer to Figs. 2-1 and 2-2 which use numbered references. An explanation of each number reference follows.

1. *RAM*—Random Access or read/write Memory. This is the region where information can be stored and retrieved. It consists of 2 pairs of RAM chips. Each pair consists of two 256 by 4-bit

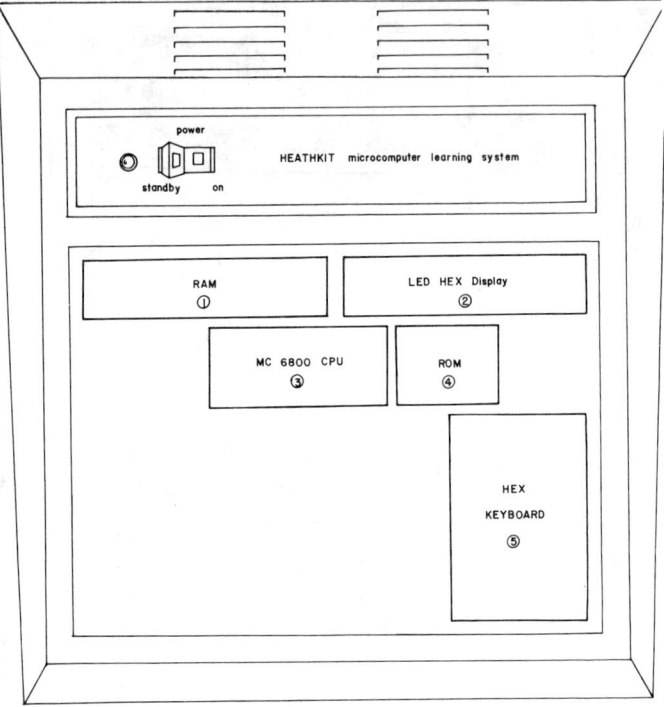

Fig. 2-2. Functional operating regions of Heath ET3400 Microcomputer Learning System.

(256×4) chips, which means that 256 4-bit words per chip or 256 8-bit words for each pair of chips can be stored. Since we have 2 pairs, the system is capable of storing 512 8-bit words in RAM. One pair comprises memory locations 0000_{16} through $00FF_{16}$ (256 locations) and the other pair starts at memory location 0100_{16} and ends with $01FF_{16}$ (256 locations) for a total of 512 8-bit read/write memory locations.

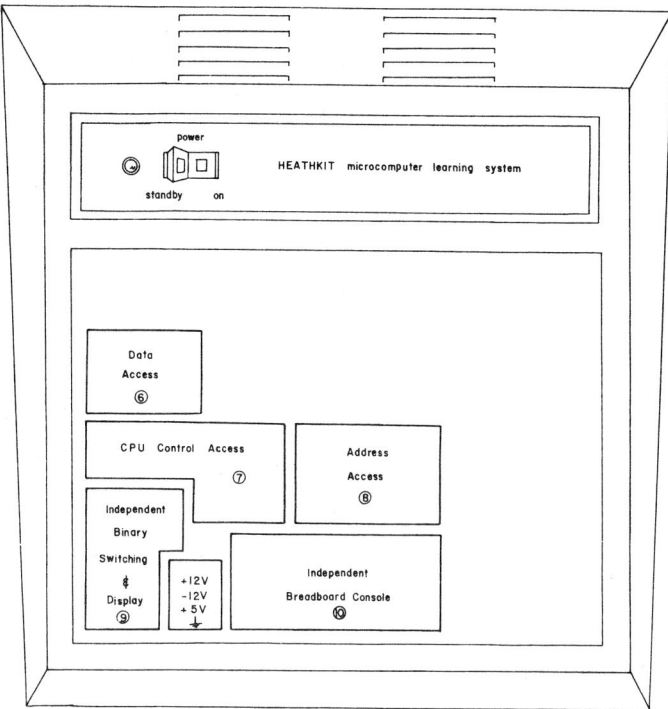

Fig. 2-3. Access and breadboarding regions of Heath ET3400 Microcomputer Learning System.

2. *LED Hex Display*—This is an output display that consists of six 7-segment LED displays. The system will display information on these displays in hexadecimal as directed by the microprocessor.
3. *MC6800 CPU*—The microprocessor chip which performs all computation and control functions.
4. *ROM*—Read-Only Memory is a memory chip that has been preprogrammed to make the system much more convenient to use. It contains a program which allows the use of hex rather than binary. It also permits you to do many other convenient things that will become valuable as the experiments are performed. This chip contains 1024 8-bit memory locations which begin at address $FC00_{16}$. This area of memory *cannot* be used for your program.
5. *Hex Keyboard*—Allows you to enter data or commands in hexadecimal. Each key except for 0 and RESET is a dual-function key. The functions of each key are described in Fig. 2-4.

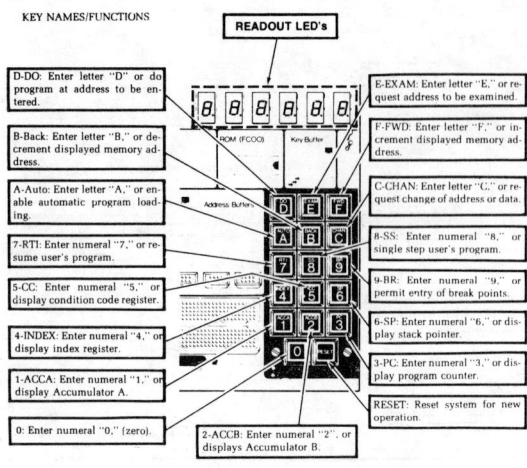

Courtesy Heath Co.

Fig. 2-4. Keyboard layout and key functions of Heath ET3400 Microcomputer Learning System.

Access and Breadboarding Regions

Refer to Figs. 2-1 and 2-3 using the numbered references.

6. *Data Access*—At the top of this region is a connector block for data i/o control. At the bottom of the region are eight dual-inline solderless breadboard sockets for access to each of the eight data bus lines (D0-D7).
7. *CPU Access*—The three solderless connector blocks in this region provide a direct connection to the various control pins on the 6800. More will be said about these later.
8. *Address Access*—This area consists of 16 dual-inline solderless breadboard sockets for access to each of the 16 address bus lines (A0-A15).
9. *Binary Switches and Displays*—This section is independent from the other regions of the system. It consists of eight microswitches (0-7) to provide logic ones and zeros to the dual-inline eight-pin connectors located just above the switches. It also consists of eight LED display indicators (0-7) to monitor logic status, which are connected through the dual-inline eight-pin connectors located just below the LEDs.
10. *Breadboard Console*—The breadboard is also independent from the other regions of the system. It is designed to accommodate the many experiments that will be performed in subsequent chapters. Integrated-circuit chips, resistors, capacitors, and wires

can all be connected in the solderless breadboard sockets. Do not use wires or leads larger than AWG#20 (.032″).

MOTOROLA MEK6800D2 EVALUATION KIT

The MEK6800D2 evaluation kit, marketed by Motorola, is a 6800-based system very much like the Heath ET3400 system. It is designed for the engineer, technician, or experimenter who wants to familiarize himself with the 6800 CPU. The system is not as well documented as the Heath ET3400 and the individual is more or less left "hanging" as how to program and interface it. By following this and subsequent sections, you should become much more familiar with the use of the MEK6800D2 system. The kit is available from Motorola for less than $200 with a student discount.

The MEK-6800D2 consists of two main printed-circuit boards connected by a flex cable as shown in Fig. 2-5. A functional layout of each board with numbered references is provided in Figs. 2-6 and 2-8. An explanation of each number reference follows.

Keyboard/Display Module

1. *Hex Keyboard*—This allows the operator to enter data in hexadecimal (white keys) and system commands (blue keys). All of the keys are single function and are described in Fig. 2-7.
2. *LED Hex Display*—This is an output display which consists of six 7-segment LED displays. The system will display information on these displays in hexadecimal as directed by the microprocessor.

Microcomputer Module

3. *MC6800 CPU*—The microprocessor chip which performs all computation and control functions.
4. *Clock*—A square-wave generator that provides synchronization pulses for the 6800 CPU.
5. *JBUG ROM*—Read-Only Memory that has been preprogrammed by Motorola to make the system much more convenient to use. For one, it contains a program which allows the use of hexadecimal rather than binary. It also allows you to enter and examine programs more conveniently. You will realize the value of JBUG as the experiments are performed.
6. *Optional ROM*—These two sockets are provided so that you may expand the system to add your own programmed ROMs. These can be Programmable *ROMS* (PROMS), Electrically Alterable *ROMS* (EAROMS), or Erasable *PROMS* (EPROMS).

Courtesy Motorola Semiconductor Products Inc.

Fig. 2-5. Pictorial view of Motorola MEK6800D2 Evaluation Kit.

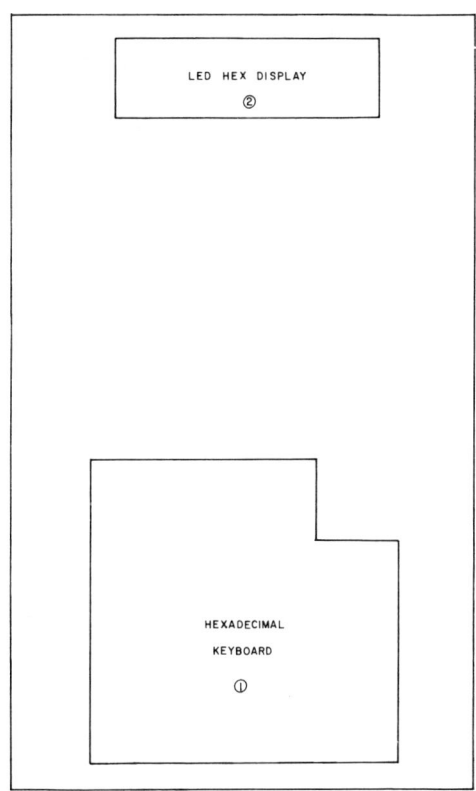

Fig. 2-6. Keyboard/display module of Motorola MEK6800D2 Evaluation Kit.

7. *RAM*—Random-Access or read/write Memory. This is the region where information can be stored and retrieved. The basic kit consists of three RAM chips. Each chip is a 128 by 8-bit (128×8) chip; which means that 128 8-bit words can be stored per chip. Two of the chips are available to the user, with the third chip being reserved for use by the JBUG ROM program. Therefore, with the two chips provided for the user, 256 8-bit words can be stored in RAM.
8. *Optional RAM*—These two sockets are provided so that the "on-board" RAM capability may be expanded to 512 bytes.
9. *ACIA*—Asynchronous Communications Interface Adapter. The basic function of ACIA is to provide serial/parallel data conversions. It will take parallel data bus information and convert it to serial data to be transmitted to some i/o device. It will also ac-

cept serial data from an i/o device and convert it to parallel data to be used by the CPU. The main applications of the ACIA would be in interfacing the MEK6800D2 system to some serial device such as a cassette, teletype, printer, or telephone line (modem).
10. *PIA*—Peripheral Interface Adapter. This is a programmable device which is used to provide basic input and output interface

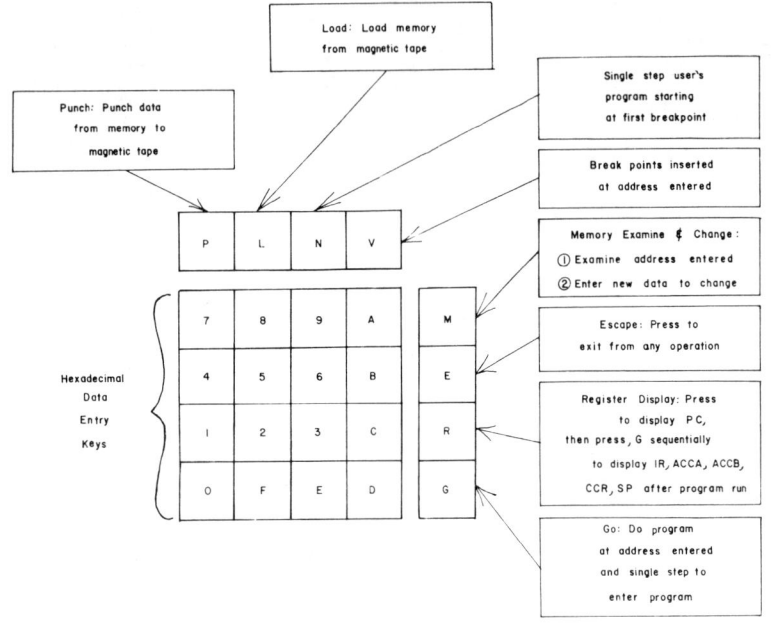

Fig. 2-7. Keyboard layout and key functions for Motorola MEK6800D2 Evaluation Kit.

for 8 bits of parallel data. Each PIA contains two 8-bit channels (ports) which can be used for either input or output. The PIA in the upper right corner of Fig. 2-8 is used by the MEK6800D2 system to interface the keyboard/display module to the microcomputer module. The PIA below this one is available for parallel interfacing. More information about this device is contained in Chapters 8 and 9.
11. *RESET*—Reset system for new operation.
12. The large open area in the lower right-hand corner of Fig. 2-8 is provided for user-designed circuitry to be added to the system.

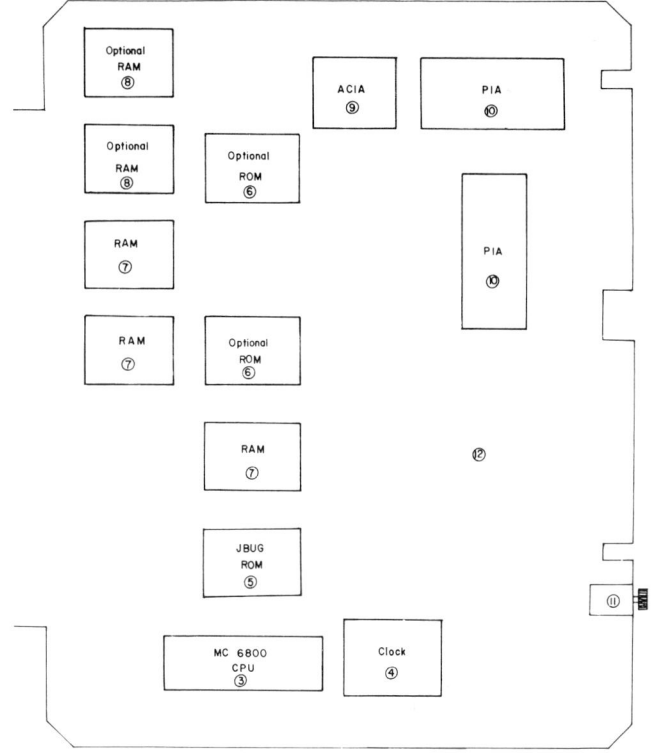

Fig. 2-8. Microcomputer module of Motorola MEK6800D2 Evaluation Kit.

EXPERIMENT INSTRUCTIONS AND FORMAT

The instructions for each experiment are presented in the format described below.

Purpose

The material under this category states the intended purpose of the experiment. Keep this purpose in mind as you conduct the experiment.

Equipment

This category will list the equipment required to complete the experiment including any external integrated circuits, transistors, resistors, capacitors, etc. There will be two listings: one of the equipment required for the Heath ET3400 trainer and the other of the equipment required for the Motorola MEK6800D2 system.

Schematic Diagram

A schematic diagram of the completed circuit to be used in the experiment is provided. The user should make an effort to follow the diagram and understand the circuit before doing the experiment.

Program

The hexadecimal microcomputer program to be loaded into RAM at the indicated memory addresses will be provided.

Procedure

A sequential step-by-step procedure for completing the experiment will be provided. In some cases, the procedure will be divided into two sections, one for the ET3400 trainer and the other for the MEK-6800D2 trainer.

Conclusions

Space will be given at the end of each experiment to form conclusions. Questions will be asked in an attempt to guide your thinking. Try to sincerely answer these questions. Ask yourself: What *concepts* are being demonstrated?

EXPERIMENT 2-1

Purpose

To provide power to the microcomputer system and prepare the system for operation.

Equipment

ET3400

MEK6800D2
5-volt dc power supply

Procedure

| ET3400 |

Step 1
Plug in the system and turn the power switch to "on."

Step 2
Press the RESET button on the keyboard and the hex display should indicate "CPU UP."

Step 3

Answer the questions at the end of this experiment and draw your conclusions.

MEK6800D2

Step 1

Apply +5 volts dc to point A of the J1 connector located on the microcomputer module.

Step 2

Apply ground ($\perp$) to point $\overline{C}$ of the J1 connector located on the microcomputer module.

Step 3

Press the RESET button (S1) located on the microcomputer module. The hex display should show a dash "–" on the first 7-segment LED (U1). All the other displays should be blank.

Step 4

Answer the questions at the end of this experiment and draw your conclusions.

Conclusions

Was the proper display achieved? If not, why?

If the proper display was not achieved, repeat the procedure. If it fails again, test and troubleshoot the system until this experiment can be successfully completed.

For the Heath ET3400, what caused the display to show "CPU UP" after the RESET button was pressed?

For the Motorola MEK6800D2, what caused the display to show "–   " after the RESET button was depressed?

What is the function of the RESET?

EXPERIMENT 2-2

Purpose

To demonstrate the method of program entry into RAM.

Equipment

ET3400   MEK6800D2
                          +5-volt dc power supply

Program

Hex Address	Hex Contents	Mnemonics/ Contents	Operation
0000	86	LDA	
0001	05	05	05 → ACCA
0002	8B	ADDA	
0003	0A	0A	(05 + 0A) → ACCA
0004	3E	WAI	Stop

Procedure

| ET3400 |

Step 1

Press RESET then AUTO. The display should show "----Ad."

Step 2

Press 0000 for the first address then 86 for the first op code. The display should now indicate "0001   ." Note that it has automatically incremented to the next address.

Step 3

Enter the operand—05.

Step 4

Continue to enter the rest of the program.

Step 5

Press RESET. The program is now entered in RAM and the display should indicate "CPU UP."

Step 6

Answer the questions at the end of this experiment and draw your conclusions.

| MEK6800D2 |

Step 1

Press the RESET button on the microcomputer module board. The display should show "_   ."

Step 2

Enter 0000 for the first address then press M.

Step 3

Enter 86 for the first op code. The display should now show "0000 86."

Step 4

Press G and enter 05 for the operand. The display should now show "0001 05." Note that the address incremented by one when the G key was pressed.

Step 5

Press G and enter the next op code and continue until the entire program is loaded.

Step 6

Press E. The program is now entered in RAM and the display should indicate "_   ."

Step 7

Answer the questions at the end of this experiment and draw your conclusions.

Conclusions

Why did you have to enter the first address and none of the other addresses?

What caused the address to automatically increment?

Why did you have to RESET the system after program entry?

EXPERIMENT 2-3

Purpose

To examine RAM contents, specifically the program entered in Experiment 2-2. Also, to change the contents of a memory location.

Equipment

ET3400　　　　　　　　　　MEK6800D2
　　　　　　　　　　　　　　+5-volt dc power supply

Program

Hex Address	Hex Contents	Mnemonics/ Contents	Operation
0000	86	LDA	
0001	05	05	05 → ACCA
0002	8B	ADDA	
0003	0A	0A	(05 + 0A) → ACCA
0004	3E	WAI	Stop

Procedure

| ET3400 |

Step 1

Enter the above program into RAM. Press RESET and then EXAM. The display should show "----Ad."

Step 2

Press 0000 for the first address of your program. The display should show the contents of memory location 0000 which should be 86.

Step 3

Press FWD and the display should show the contents of memory location 0001.

Step 4

Continue to press FWD to examine each subsequent memory location. Verify that your program entry was correct.

Step 5

Now suppose we wish to change memory location 0003 from 0A to 0B. Press EXAM and then the address to be changed which is 0003.

Step 6

Press CHAN and then the new contents, 0B.

Step 7

Re-examine the program to verify the change has been made.

NOTES:
1. You may examine any specific location by pressing EXAM and then the address.
2. While examining a program, a change may be made at any time by pressing CHAN and then entering the new contents.
3. You may also backstep through the program with the "BACK" key.

Step 8

Answer the questions at the end of this experiment and draw your conclusions.

```
MEK6800D2
```

Step 1

Enter the program into RAM. Press the E key and then 0000 for the first address in your program.

Step 2

Press M and the display should show the contents of address 0000 which should be 86.

Step 3

Press G and the display should show the contents of memory location 0001.

Step 4

Continue to press G to examine each subsequent memory location. Verify your program entry was correct.

Step 5
Now suppose we wish to change memory location 0003 from 0A to 0B. Press E and then the address to be changed which is 0003.

Step 6
Press M and then the new contents—0B.

Step 7
Re-examine the program to verify the change has been made

NOTES:
1. You may examine any specific memory location by pressing E and then the address followed by M.
2. While examining a program, a change my be made at any time by simply entering the new contents.

Step 8
Answer the questions at the end of this experiment and draw your conclusions.

Conclusions
When should a program be examined?

With the Heath ET3400 system, what are the relationships between the EXAM and FWD keys?

With the Motorola MEK6800D2 system, what are the relationships between the M and G key?

With the Heath ET3400, what is the function of the BACK key?

EXPERIMENT 2-4

Purpose

To execute a simple program and verify its results. Also, to examine the program counter and accumulator contents at each step of a program.

Equipment

ET3400   MEK6800D2
                                  +5-volt dc power supply

Program

Hex Address	Hex Contents	Mnemonics/ Contents	Operation
0000	86	LDA	
0001	05	05	05 → ACCA
0002	8B	ADDA	
0003	0A	0A	(05 + 0A) → ACCA
0004	3E	WAI	Stop

Procedure

```
ET3400
```

Step 1

Enter and examine the above program for proper entry. *Always* examine your program after entry.

Step 2

Press RESET and then DO. The display should show "----do."

Step 3

Enter the starting address of your program (0000). The display should go blank, indicating that your program has been executed.

Step 4

The program adds 05 + 0A and stores the results (0F) into ACCA. Press RESET then ACCA and observe the results. The display should indicate "Acca 0F." If it does not, re-examine your program, make any required changes, re-execute and verify the proper results in ACCA.

Step 5

Now you will step through the program, observing the contents of PC and ACCA at each step.

Step 6

Press PC and change its contents to 0000 by using the CHAN key. This tells the computer to start single stepping at 0000.

Step 7

Press SS. The display should show the *next command* instruction which is 8B located at address 0002.

Step 8

Press ACCA and observe its contents. It should be 05 since to this point you have only executed the first instruction which loads 05 into accumulator A.

Step 9

Press PC and observe its contents. It should be 0002 which is the *address* of the *next* instruction to be executed.

Step 10

Press SS. This display should indicate "0004 3E" which is the *next* command instruction to be executed. You have just executed the ADDA instruction.

Step 11

Press ACCA and observe its contents. This should be 0F since 0A has been added to 05, with the sum (0F) stored in accumulator A.

Step 12

Press PC and note that it contains the *address* of the *next* instruction to be performed (0004).

Step 13

Press SS and note that the display does not change. This is because the next instruction was a stop command and control of the system by the SS key is stopped at this point.

Step 14

Change memory location 0003 to 0B and repeat the above procedure. This time, the result in accumulator A should be 10.

Step 15

Answer the questions at the end of this experiment and draw your conclusion.

| MEK6800D2 |

Step 1

Enter and examine the program for proper entry. *Always* examine your program after entry.

Step 2

Press E and then enter the starting address of your program (0000).

Step 3

Press G. The display should go blank, indicating that your program has been executed.

Step 4

The above program adds 05 + 0A and stores the result (0F) into ACCA. To observe the contents of ACCA, press E then R, and then press the G key *twice* and observe the display. The display should show "0F ." If it does not, re-examine your program, make any required changes, re-execute, and verify the proper results in ACCA.

Step 5

Now we will step through the program, observing the PC and ACCA contents at each step. Press E to reset the system.

Step 6

Enter the starting address of your program followed by V. This enters a "breakpoint" at address 0000, which allows you to start single stepping through the program at this point.

Step 7

Press G. The program will Go to the first breakpoint and then stop. By pressing the G key two more times, you can display the contents of ACCA. It should be a random number since no data has been loaded into the accumulator at this point.

Step 8
Now press the N key. This will single step the program and cause the first instruction to be executed. The display should show 0002 8B. The contents of the PC is 0002, which is the *address* of the *next* instruction to be performed.

Step 9
Press the G key twice and observe the accumulator contents. It should be 05, since at this point we have only executed the first instruction which loads 05 into accumulator A.

Step 10
Press N. This will single step the program again and cause the second instruction to be executed. The display should show 0004 3E. The contents of the PC is 0004, which is the address of the *next* instruction to be performed.

Step 11
Press the G key twice and observe the accumulator contents. It should be 0F since 0A has been added to 05 with the sum stored in accumulator A. The N key can now be used to single step as many instructions as desired.

> NOTE: If the E key is pressed at any time, the breakpoint will be removed. The breakpoint must be re-installed if it is desired.

Step 12
Change memory location 0003 to 0B and repeat the above procedure. This time, the result in accumulator A should be 10.

Step 13
Answer the questions at the end of this experiment and draw your conclusions.

Conclusions
In what part of the 6800 did the addition take place?
Where was the sum stored?
Why would it not be advisable to use the accumulator as a permanent storage register?   Where might it be better to store an operation result?

Why does the PC always indicate the address of the *next instruction* to be performed?
What controls the single-step routine of your trainer?

EXPERIMENT 2-5

Purpose
To store an operation result in memory.

Equipment
ET3400   MEK6800D2
                                    +5-volt dc power supply

Program

Hex Address	Hex Contents	Mnemonics/ Contents	Operation
0020	C6	LDB	
0021	05	05	05 → ACCB
0022	CB	ADDB	
0023	0A	0A	(05 + 0A) → ACCB
0024	D7	STAB	
0025	50	50	ACCB + → M$_{50}$
0026	3E	WA1	Stop

The above program loads ACCB with 05 then adds 0A to 05. The sum is placed in ACCB then the STAB stores the sum into memory location 50. (STAB means *ST*ore Accumulator *B* at the specified memory location.)

Procedure

| ET3400 |

Step 1

Enter the above program into memory beginning with address 0020.

Step 2

Examine the program and make any required changes.

Step 3

Execute the program. (Remember, the program begins at address 0020.)

Step 4

Observe the contents of ACCA. It should be some random number or the result of the last experiment, since this program uses ACCB.

Step 5

Observe the contents of ACCB by using the ACCB key. The display should be "ACCB 0F," indicating the sum of 05 + 0A.

Step 6

The program should have stored this sum in memory location 50. Examine this memory location. The display should show "0050 0F."

Step 7

Step through the program and observe the PC and ACCB contents at each instruction step. (Reference Experiment 2-4.)

Step 8

Change the program to add $44_{10} + 48_{10}$ and store the results at memory location 252_{10}.

Step 9

Execute the program and verify your results.

MEK6800D2

Step 1

Enter the above program into memory beginning with address 0020.

Step 2

Examine the program and make any required changes.

Step 3

Execute the program. (Remember, the program begins at address 0020.)

Step 4

Observe the contents of ACCA by pressing E, R, and then the G key twice. The display should indicate some random number since this program uses ACCB.

Step 5

Observe the contents of ACCB by pressing the G key one more time. The display should be "0F ," indicating the sum of 05 + 0A.

NOTE: After pressing E and then R, the display will show the PC contents. Then, sequencing G twice will show ACCA contents. Sequencing G three times will show ACCB contents.

Step 6

The program should have also put this sum at memory location 50. Examine this memory location. The display should show "0F ."

Step 7

Step through the program and observe the contents of the PC and ACCB at each instruction step. (Reference Experiment 2-4.)

Step 8

Change the program to add $44_{10} + 48_{10}$ and store the results at memory location 252_{10}.

Step 9

Execute the program and verify the results.

Conclusions

Why would you want to store the results of an operation in memory?

What would be the highest memory location available for storage with your system?

Was there any noticeable difference in using ACCB rather than ACCA? If so, what?

Can you think of a case where you might want to use both ACCA and ACCB in the same program? (Explain.)

CHAPTER 3

6800 Arithmetic, Logic, and Data-Handling Instructions

INTRODUCTION

Now we are ready to begin studying the 72 fundamental instructions utilized by the 6800 microprocessor. These instructions, along with their various *addressing modes*, make up the total 6800 *instruction set* of 197 instructions. With this instruction set you will form programs that make the 6800 a very powerful microprocessor. These programs make up the *software* part of a microcomputer system. Software is what makes the system so flexible, since it takes the place of digital logic gates. Given a specific application involving a decision-making problem, a conventional digital design approach could be used. This design might consist of anywhere from one to one thousand digital logic gates. However, with a microprocessor-based design the logic gates are replaced with software instructions. Now suppose that you wish to change the application. In most cases, the conventional design would require a complete redesigning and rebuilding of the system. However, with the microprocessor-based design only the program needs to be changed to change the application. This flexibility at minimal cost is what has made the microprocessor so valuable.

The 6800 instruction set can be broken down into seven general categories as follows:

1. arithmetic
2. logic
3. data handling
4. data test
5. condition code
6. index register and stack pointer
7. jump and branch.

In this chapter we intend to discuss the first three categories in part. Since the 6800 chip uses binary data internally and the arithmetic instructions involve binary arithmetic, it might be helpful to review *Digital Computer Arithmetic* in Appendix B, prior to reading this chapter.

OBJECTIVES

At the end of this chapter you will be able to do the following:

- Write a simple arithmetic or logic program for the 6800.
- Define Inherent, Immediate, Direct, and Extended Addressing.
- Know when to use or when not to use a particular addressing mode.
- Add, subtract, and perform logic operations on binary numbers the way the 6800 does.
- Interpret simple 6800 arithmetic and logic instruction mnemonic and op-code listings.
- Represent negative numbers using the twos-complement number code.
- Define a status byte and a mask byte.
- Explain how logical instructions can be used to determine the status of an external device.
- Explain how logical instructions can be used to determine any change in the state of an external device.

6800 DATA TRANSFER

Load Accumulators (LDAA, LDAB)

As discussed in Chapter 1, the 6800 has two 8-bit accumulators, A and B. These accumulators are used as temporary storage registers for operands and operation results. The LDAA (*LoaD Accumulator A*) and LDAB (*LoaD Accumulator B*) instructions allow you to load data into either accumulator *immediately* from the byte that immediately follows the instruction or *directly* from a memory location. The experiments in Chapter 2 used this instruction to load data *immediately;* that is, the data to be loaded followed the instruction as an operand. This is referred to as *immediate addressing.* Another way to load data into the accumulator is from a memory location. When this method of loading the accumulator is desired, the address of the memory location that contains the operand must be specified. In this case, the byte or bytes that follow the LDA instruction will represent an address rather than the actual data that is to be used in the operation. This mode is referred to as *direct addressing.* When an address is specified following an instruction, it can be either one or two bytes depending upon the type of addressing that is to be used. A one-byte address may be used to specify any address from location 00_{16} to FF_{16} or a two-byte address may be used to specify an address from locations 0000_{16} to $FFFF_{16}$. When two address bytes

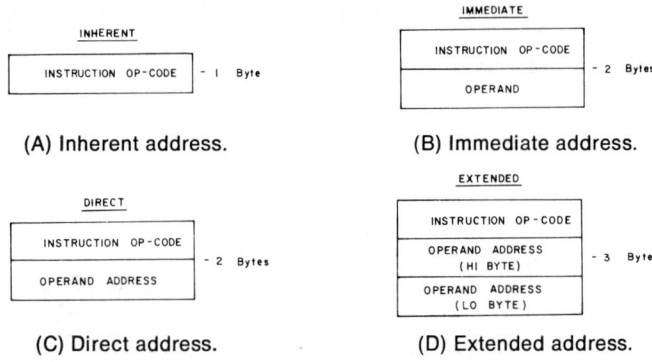

Fig. 3-1. Addressing modes.

are used following an instruction, the mode is referred to as *extended addressing.* When extended addressing is used, the first byte is called the *high address byte,* representing the upper eight bits of an address, and the second byte is referred to as the *low address byte,* representing the lower eight bits of an address. The instruction formats for the above addressing modes are shown in Fig. 3-1.

Question

How does the 6800 know which type of addressing is being used?

Answer

There are three separate op codes for the load accumulator instruction to designate either the immediate, direct, or extended mode of addressing. For example, the LDAA instruction utilizes the following op codes:

LDAA (*LoaD* Accumulator *A*) $M_x \rightarrow$ ACCA

Immediate 86 DATA	The byte *immediately* following the op code is the *operand* to be loaded into ACCA.
Direct 96 LO ADDR	The byte following the op code is the *address* of the operand to be loaded into ACCA (No HI ADDR)
Extended B6 HI ADDR LO ADDR	The next *two* bytes is the *address* of the operand to be loaded into ACCA.

The same is true for the LDAB instruction.

LDAB (*LoaD* Accumulator *B*) $M_x \rightarrow$ ACCB

Immediate C6 DATA	The byte immediately following the op code is the operand to be loaded into ACCB.
Direct D6 LO ADDR	The byte following the op code is the address of the operand to be loaded into ACCB. (No HI ADDR)
Extended F6 HI ADDR LO ADDR	The next two bytes is the address of the operand to be loaded into ACCB.

When either of the preceding instructions are used, the previous contents of the accumulator are lost but the contents of the memory location (if any) that was addressed are not affected. Also, note the operation symbols used. For example, ACCA$\rightarrow M_x$ is the notation we will use to indicate that Accumulator A is being stored to memory location x (M_x). We will use similar operation symbols throughout the text and their meaning should be an obvious result of the operation involved.

Question

When data is to be loaded from a memory location, why not use the extended mode all the time?

Answer

The extended mode utilizes three instruction bytes which occupies more memory space and it takes more time to process than would the two-byte instructions. Time is critical in a computer system. Therefore, always use direct addressing if the operand is located at an address of 00FF or below.

Store Accumulators (STAA, STAB)

The accumulators are only temporary storage registers, so their contents must be stored in memory if a result is to be permanently saved and the accumulators used for other purposes. This is the function of the store-accumulator instructions. Since the destination of the data is *always* an address in memory, these instructions utilize direct and extended addressing but not immediate addressing. The contents of the accumulator are not affected by the store-accumulator instruction but are "copied" into the memory location. The previous content of the memory location is "lost."

STAA (ST*ore* Accumulator A) ACCA → M_x

Direct 97 LO ADDR	Store the contents of ACCA at the memory location specified by the next byte. (No HI ADDR)
Extended B7 HI ADDR LO ADDR	Store the contents of ACCA at the memory location specified by the next *two* bytes.

STAB (ST*ore* Accumulator B) ACCB → M_x

Direct D7 LO ADDR	Store the contents of ACCB at the memory location specified by the next byte. (No HI ADDR)
Extended F7 HI ADDR LO ADDR	Store the contents of ACCB at the memory location specified by the next *two* bytes.

Again, to save computer time, use the direct addressing mode when possible.

Transfer Accumulators (TAB, TBA)

There are situations when it is desirable to transfer the contents of one accumulator into the other. These instructions do not require an operand or an address since no data is involved in the instruction itself. Therefore, they are simple one-byte instructions. One-byte instructions that require no subsequent operand or address bytes are referred to as *inherent* or *implied* instructions, since the instruction can perform only one type of operation upon a known address, register, or piece of information. Thus, the data or address is an *inherent* part of the op code.

TAB (*T*ransfer from accumulator *A* to accumulator *B*) ACCA → ACCB

Inherent Moves the contents of ACCA to ACCB.
16

NOTE: The former contents of ACCB are lost but the present contents of ACCA are not affected.

TBA (*T*ransfer from accumulator *B* to accumulator *A*) ACCB → ACCA

Inherent Moves the contents of ACCB to ACCA.
17

NOTE: The former contents of ACCA are lost but the present contents of ACCB are not affected.

Clear Accumulator and Memory (CLRA, CLRB, CLR)

We may clear either accumulator with a one-byte instruction (inherent addressing). Clearing a memory location requires three bytes, the clear instruction op code plus a two-byte address (extended addressing). When a register is cleared, its contents are replaced with zeros.

CLRA (*CL*ea*R* accumulator *A*) 00 → ACCA

Inherent Replace the contents of ACCA with zeros.
4F

CLRB (*CL*ea*R* accumulator *B*) 00 → ACCB

Inherent Replace the contents of ACCB with zeros.
5F

CLR (*CL*ea*R* the specified memory location) 00 → M_x

Extended Replace the contents of the specified memory
7F   location with zeros.
HI ADDR
LO ADDR

Wait (WAI)

This inherent instruction tells the 6800 to stop until further notice. It will usually be used at the end of your program.

WAI (*WAI*t)

Inherent   Stop
3E

Since we are using different addressing modes, we will distinguish one from the other in the mnemonic listing as follows:

a. mnemonic followed by # → immediate addressing
b. mnemonic followed by $ → direct addressing
c. mnemonic followed by $$ → extended addressing
d. mnemonic followed by nothing → inherent addressing

Example 3-1: Swapping Accumulator Data

The following program can be used to "swap" the accumulator contents.

Hex Address	Hex Contents	Mnemonics/ Contents	Operation
0000	97	STAA $	
0001	5B	5B	ACCB → M_{5B}
0002	17	TBA	
			ACCB → ACCA
0003	D6	LDAB $	
0004	5B	5B	M_{5B} → ACCB
0005	3E	WAI	STOP

First, store the contents of accumulator A at any available location using direct addressing. We chose to use memory location 5B. Then, transfer the contents of accumulator B to accumulator A with an inherent instruction (TBA). Next load accumulator B direct with the contents of accumulator A which were stored at memory location 5B. Finally, stop the program execution with the WAI instruction. Why wouldn't the following program accomplish the transfer?

> TBA
> TAB
> WAI

Because the contents of accumulator A would be lost during the first transfer. When you write into a register, its previous contents are always lost; therefore, you must store the register contents into memory prior to the operation if you wish to save the data. Reading from a register will not destroy the contents of that register.

Example 3-2: Clearing Accumulators A and B

The following program can be used to clear accumulators A and B.

Hex Address	Hex Contents	Mnemonics/ Contents	Operation
0000	4F	CLRA	00 → ACCA
0001	16	TAB	ACCA → ACCB
0002	3E	WAI	STOP

This is a very simple program utilizing inherent instructions that can be used to clear both accumulators. Simply clear accumulator A, which will place all zeros in that accumulator. Then transfer these zeros to accumulator B. The zeros in A will *not* be lost in this transfer since you are reading from the accumulator. The program is terminated with the WAI instruction.

Can you think of any different programs that would accomplish this same task?

6800 ARITHMETIC INSTRUCTIONS

Add (ADDA, ADDB)

These instructions are used to add an operand to one of the accumulators using immediate addressing or to add the contents of a specified memory location to one of the accumulators using direct or extended addressing. The sum always remains in the accumulator that you are working with. The former contents of the accumulator are lost.

ADDA (*ADD* to accumulator *A*) ACCA + M_x → ACCA

Immediate 8B DATA	Adds the byte immediately following the op code to the contents of ACCA and places the sum in ACCA.
Direct 9B LO ADDR	Adds the contents of the memory location specified by the next byte to ACCA and leaves the sum in ACCA. (NO HI ADDR)
Extended BB HI ADDR LO ADDR	Adds the contents of the memory location specified by the next two bytes to ACCA and leaves the sum in ACCA.

ADDB (*ADD* to accumulator *B*) ACCB + M_x → ACCB

Immediate CB DATA	Adds the byte immediately following the op code to the contents of ACCB and places the sum in ACCB.
Direct DB LO ADDR	Adds the contents of the memory location specified by the next byte to ACCB and places the sum in ACCB. (No HI ADDR)
Extended FB HI ADDR LO ADDR	Adds the contents of the memory location specified by the next two bytes to ACCB and places the sum in ACCB.

Add Accumulators (ABA)

This is an inherent instruction that adds together the contents of the A and B accumulators and places the sum in ACCA. The previous contents of ACCA are lost but the contents of ACCB are not affected.

ABA (*Add* accumulator *B* to accumulator *A*)
  ACCA + ACCB → ACCA

Inherent $1B_{16}$	Adds ACCB to ACCA and places the sum in ACCA.

Subtract (SUBA, SUBB)

These instructions are used to subtract an operand from one of the accumulators using immediate addressing, or to subtract the contents of a specified memory location from one of the accumulators using direct or extended addressing. The difference is always placed in the accumulator that you are working with. The former contents of the accumulator are lost.

NOTE: The 6800 microprocessor utilizes twos-complement arithmetic to perform this operation.

SUBA (*SUB*tract from accumulator *A*) ACCA − M_x → ACCA

Immediate 80 DATA	Subtracts the byte immediately following the op code from the contents of ACCA and places the difference in ACCA.
Direct 90 LO ADDR	Subtracts the contents of the memory location specified by the next byte from ACCA and places the difference in ACCA. (No HI ADDR)

Extended   Subtracts the contents of the memory location
B0   specified by the next two bytes from ACCA and
HI ADDR   places the difference in ACCA.
LO ADDR

SUBB (SUBtract from accumulator B) ACCB − M_x → ACCB

Immediate   Subtracts the byte immediately following the op
C0   code from the contents of ACCB and places the
DATA   difference in ACCB.

Direct   Subtracts the contents of the memory location
D0   specified by the next byte from the contents of
LO ADDR   ACCB and places the difference in ACCB. (No
                    HI ADDR)

Extended   Subtracts the contents of the memory location
F0   specified by the next two bytes from the con-
HI ADDR   tents of ACCB and places the difference in
LO ADDR   ACCB.

Subtract Accumulators (SBA)

Similar to the ABA instruction, this is an inherent instruction that subtracts the contents of ACCB from ACCA and places the difference in ACCA. The previous contents of ACCA are lost, but ACCB is not affected.

SBA (Subtract accumulator B from accumulator A)
ACCA − ACCB → ACCA

Inherent   Subtracts ACCB from ACCA and places the dif-
10_{16} ference in ACCA.

Increment (INC, INCA, INCB)

These instructions will increment (add 1) to a specified memory location or to either accumulator.

INC (INCrement the specified memory location) M_x + 1 → M_x

Extended   Add one to the memory location specified by the
7C   next two bytes.
HI ADDR
LO ADDR

INCA (INCrement accumulator A) ACCA + 1 → ACCA

Inherent
4C   Add one to ACCA.

INCB (*INC*rement accumulator *B*) ACCB + 1 → ACCB

Inherent
5C   Add one to ACCB.

Decrement (DEC, DECA, DECB)

These instructions will decrement (subtract 1) from a specified memory location or either accumulator.

DEC (*DEC*rement the specified memory location) $M_x - 1 \rightarrow M_x$

Extended
7A   Subtract 1 from the memory location specified
HI ADDR   by the next two bytes.
LO ADDR

DECA (*DEC*rement accumulator *A*) ACCA − 1 → ACCA

Inherent
4A   Subtract 1 from ACCA.

DECB (*DEC*rement accumulator *B*) ACCB − 1 → ACCB

Inherent
5A   Subtract 1 from ACCB.

Example 3-3: Adding Numbers Immediately

This program uses the immediate addressing mode for adding numbers.

Hex Address	Hex Contents	Mnemonics/ Contents	Operation
0000	86	LDAA #	
0001	01	01	01 → ACCA
0002	8B	ADDA #	
0003	02	02	ACCA+02 → ACCA
0004	8B	ADDA #	
0005	03	03	ACCA+03 → ACCA
0006	8B	ADDA #	
0007	04	04	ACCA+04 → ACCA
0008	B7	STAA $$	
0009	50	50	ACCA → M_{5000}
000A	00	00	
000B	3E	WAI	STOP
5000	—	—	RESULT

This program adds four numbers (01, 02, 03, 04) using the immediate addressing mode. Recall that when a number is added to the accumulator, the result is placed in the accumulator. Usually, when the operation is completed, you will want to save your result and free the accumulator to perform other operations. Therefore, in this example we have stored the final result of the addition in memory location 5000 using extended addressing. How would this program change if these numbers were located in memory?

Example 3-4: Subtracting Numbers from Memory

This program uses the direct addressing mode since the operands are located in external memory.

Hex Address	Hex Contents	Mnemonics/ Contents	Operation
0000	96	LDAA $	
0001	50	50	$M_{50} \rightarrow ACCA$
0002	90	SUBA $	
0003	51	51	$ACCA - M_{51} \rightarrow ACCA$
0004	97	STAA $	
0005	52	52	$ACCA \rightarrow M_{52}$
0006	3E	WAI	STOP
0050	05	05	Data
0051	03	03	Data
0052	—	—	Result

The above program subtracts three from five and stores the result in memory location 52. The direct addressing mode must be used since the operands (05 and 03) are located in memory. First the ACCA is loaded with the first operand (05) located in memory location 50 and then the second operand (03) located in memory location 51 is subtracted. Finally the result is stored in memory location 52 and the program stops. Rewrite the above program using immediate addressing. How would this program change if the operands were located in *high memory* (above location 00FF)?

Example 3-5: Subtracting Numbers from Memory

The following program would accomplish the same result as in Example 3-4.

Hex Address	Hex Contents	Mnemonics/ Contents	Operation
0000	96	LDAA $	
0001	50	50	$M_{50} \rightarrow ACCA$
0002	D6	LDAB $	
0003	51	51	$M_{51} \rightarrow ACCB$
0004	10	SBA	$ACCA - ACCB \rightarrow ACCA$
0005	97	STAA $	
0006	52	52	$ACCA \rightarrow M_{52}$
0007	3E	WAI	STOP
0050	05	05	Data
0051	03	03	Data
0052	—	—	Result

Here, each accumulator is loaded with an operand and then the accumulators are subtracted with the inherent instruction SBA. Again, the result is stored in memory location 52.

Example 3-6: Decrementing to Zero

This program can be used to decrement an accumulator to zero.

Hex Address	Hex Contents	Mnemonics/ Contents	Operation
0000	C6	LDAB #	
0001	05	05	05 → ACCB
0002	5A	DECB	ACCB−1 → ACCB
0003	5A	DECB	ACCB−1 → ACCB
0004	5A	DECB	ACCB−1 → ACCB
0005	5A	DECB	ACCB−1 → ACCB
0006	5A	DECB	ACCB−1 → ACCB
0007	3E	WAI	STOP

The above program loads accumulator B with 05 and then decrements it down to zero. Many times, during microcomputer programming and interfacing, it becomes necessary to create time delays within the system. Since each decrement instruction requires a precise amount of time to be executed, the total time delay will be a function of the size of the number to be decremented to zero. Naturally, more delay requires more decrement instructions. A more efficient time-delay method, called *looping*, will be presented in Chapter 5.

Could the same result be obtained using the increment instruction? How?

6800 LOGIC INSTRUCTIONS

Ones Complement (COM, COMA, COMB)

With these instructions you generate the ones complement of any specified memory location or either of the accumulators.

COM (*COM*plement the specified memory location) $\overline{M}_x \rightarrow M_x$

Extended
73 Complement the contents of the memory loca-
HI ADDR tion specified by the next two bytes.
LO ADDR

COMA (*COM*plement accumulator *A*) $\overline{ACCA} \rightarrow ACCA$

Inherent
43 Complement ACCA.

COMB (*COM*plement accumulator *B*) $\overline{ACCB} \rightarrow ACCB$

Inherent
53 Complement ACCB.

Twos Complement (NEG, NEGA, NEGB)

Remember that the 6800 microprocessor uses a twos-complement representation for positive and negative. Therefore, these instructions will be used to make a positive number negative or, conversely, to make a negative number positive. We can negate the contents of a specified memory location or the contents of either accumulator.

NEG (*NEG*ate the specified memory location) $00 - M_x \to M_x$

Extended
70   Take the twos complement of the memory loca-
HI ADDR   tion specified by the next two bytes.
LO ADDR

NEGA (*NEG*ate accumulator A) $00 - ACCA \to ACCA$

Inherent
40   Take the twos complement of ACCA.

NEGB (*NEG*ate accumulator B) $00 - ACCB \to ACCB$

Inherent
50   Take the twos complement of ACCB.

AND (ANDA, ANDB)

These instructions will perform a logical AND operation between the contents of either accumulator and an operand immediately following the instruction or an operand in a specified memory location. The result of the operation is left in the respective accumulator.

ANDA (*AND* accumulator A) $ACCA \cdot M_x \to ACCA$

Immediate
84   AND the operand immediately following the op
DATA   code with ACCA and place the results in ACCA.

Direct
94   AND ACCA with the contents of the memory lo-
LO ADDR   cation specified by the next byte and place the
                results in ACCA. (No HI ADDR)

Extended
B4   AND ACCA with the contents of the memory lo-
HI ADDR   cation specified by the next two bytes and place
LO ADDR   the results in ACCA.

ANDB (AND accumulator B) ACCB · M$_x$ → ACCB

Immediate
C4
DATA
   AND the operand immediately following the op code with ACCB and place the results in ACCB.

Direct
D4
LO ADDR
   AND ACCB with the contents of the memory location specified by the next byte and place the results in ACCB. (No HI ADDR)

Extended
F4
HI ADDR
LO ADDR
   AND ACCB with the contents of the memory location specified by the next two bytes and place the results in ACCB.

OR (ORAA, ORAB)

The OR instructions will perform a logical OR operation between the contents of either accumulator and an operand immediately following the instruction or the contents of a specified memory location. The result is always left in the respective accumulator.

ORAA (*OR Accumulator A*) ACCA + M$_x$ → ACCA

Immediate
8A
DATA
   OR the operand immediately following the op code with ACCA and place the results in ACCA.

Direct
9A
LO ADDR
   OR ACCA with the contents of the memory location specified by the next byte and place the results in ACCA. (No HI ADDR)

Extended
BA
HI ADDR
LO ADDR
   OR ACCA with the contents of the memory location specified by the next two bytes and place the results in ACCA.

ORAB (*OR Accumulator B*) ACCB + M$_x$ → ACCB

Immediate
CA
DATA
   OR the operand immediately following the op code with ACCB and place the results in ACCB.

Direct
DA
LO ADDR
   OR ACCB with the contents of the memory location specified by the next byte and place the results in ACCB. (No HI ADDR)

Extended　　　OR ACCB with the contents of the memory loca-
FA　　　　　　tion specified by the next two bytes and place
HI ADDR　　　the results in ACCB.
LO ADDR

XOR (EORA, EORB)

The XOR instructions allow you to perform a logical XOR operation between either accumulator and an operand immediately following the instruction or the contents of a specified memory location. Again, the result is always placed in the respective accumulator.

EORA (Exclusive OR accumulator A) ACCA $\oplus$ M_x → ACCA

Immediate
88　　　　　　XOR the operand immediately following the op
DATA　　　　code with ACCA and place the results in ACCA.

Direct　　　　XOR ACCA with the contents of the memory lo-
98　　　　　　cation specified by the next byte and place the
LO ADDR　　results in ACCA. (No HI ADDR)

Extended　　XOR ACCA with the contents of the memory lo-
B8　　　　　　cation specified by the next two bytes and place
HI ADDR　　　the results in ACCA.
LO ADDR

EORB (Exclusive OR accomulator B) ACCB $\oplus$ M_x → ACCB

Immediate
C8　　　　　　XOR the operand immediately following the op
DATA　　　　code with ACCB and place the results in ACCB.

Direct　　　　XOR ACCB with the contents of the memory lo-
D8　　　　　　cation specified by the next byte and place the
LO ADDR　　results in ACCB.

Extended　　XOR ACCB with the contents of the memory lo-
F8　　　　　　cation specified by the next two bytes and place
HI ADDR　　　the results in ACCB.
LO ADDR

Logic instructions allow you to determine if external devices are on or off. You can also determine if specific events have occurred or not with the use of these instructions. When performing logical operations, you will logically compare a mask byte to a status byte. The *status byte* represents the unknown condition of the external device.

For example, suppose that you have eight external devices that will exhibit either an off or on state. You can let a "1" represent an on state and "0" represent an off state. Thus, you can represent all of the device states with an 8-bit status byte. The *mask byte* represents a known condition. Masking is a logical technique in which certain bits of a multibit word are blanked out. A mask in a computer operation covers some or most of the bits in a status byte, leaving only those bits which are important to the operation. ANDing the status and mask bytes can determine device conditions.

Example 3-7: Determining Device Condition

Suppose that you have eight external devices (device 0 through device 7) represented by status byte bits D_0 through D_7. Given the following status byte, you conclude that devices 1, 2, 4, 5, and 7 are on while devices 0, 3, and 6 are off.

$$\text{Status byte} - 1011\ 0110$$

Now, suppose that you were only interested in the status of device 2. Then, to determine its status, you would form a mask byte as follows:

$$\text{Mask byte} - 0000\ 0100$$

Note that each device bit is "masked-out" with a zero except device 2. If you now perform an ANDing operation between the status and mask bytes, the result will indicate the device 2 status:

```
1011 0110—status
0000 0100—mask
───────────
0000 0100—shows device 2 is on
```

To determine if a device has changed state, i.e., on to off or off to on, you will use an XOR routine.

Example 3-8: Determining Device Change of State

Suppose that a device status byte of 1011 0110 was previously read into the computer. Now the computer reads a current device status byte of 0101 0101. Which devices have changed state from the previous to the current condition? The answer may be found by XORing the two bytes as shown below:

```
      1011 0110—previous status byte
XOR.  0101 0101—current status byte
      ─────────
      1110 0011
```

You conclude that devices 0, 1, 5, 6, and 7 have changed state.

REVIEW QUESTIONS

1. Define each of the following:
    a. Inherent Addressing

Table 3-1. Alphabetical Mnemonic Listing of Instructions Presented in This Chapter

Mnemonic	Addressing Modes				Operation
	Immediate	Direct	Extended	Inherent	
ABA	—	—	—	1B	A+B→A
ADDA	8B	9B	BB	—	A+M→A
ADDB	CB	DB	FB	—	B+M→B
ANDA	84	94	B4	—	A·M→A
ANDB	C4	D4	F4	—	B·M→B
CLR	—	—	7F	—	00→M
CLRA	—	—	—	4F	00→A
CLRB	—	—	—	5F	00→B
COM	—	—	73	—	M̄→M
COMA	—	—	—	43	Ā→A
COMB	—	—	—	53	B̄→B
DEC	—	—	7A	—	M−1→M
DECA	—	—	—	4A	A−1→A
DECB	—	—	—	5A	B−1→B
EORA	88	98	B8	—	A + M→A
EORB	C8	D8	F8	—	B + M→B
INC	—	—	7C	—	M+1→M
INCA	—	—	—	4C	A+1→A
INCB	—	—	—	5C	B+1→B
LDAA	86	96	B6	—	M→A
LDAB	C6	D6	F6	—	M→B
NEG	—	—	70	—	00−M→M
NEGA	—	—	—	40	00−A→A
NEGB	—	—	—	50	00−B→B
ORAA	8A	9A	BA	—	A+M→A
ORAB	CA	DA	FA	—	B+M→B
STAA	—	97	B7	—	A→M
STAB	—	D7	F7	—	B→M
SBA	—	—	—	10	A−B→A
SUBA	80	90	B0	—	A−M→A
SUBB	C0	D0	F0	—	B−M→B
TAB	—	—	—	16	A→B
TBA	—	—	—	17	B→A
WAI	—	—	—	3E	STOP

b. Immediate Addressing

c. Direct Addressing

d. Extended Addressing

2. When would you use direct rather than extended addressing?

3. Explain what each of the following instructions do.
   a. 7C

      00

      50

   b. 7C

      C5

      50

   c. 10

   d. DA

      10

   e. BB

      20

4. Perform the indicated *logic* operation.
   a. 01101011 + 10110001

   b. 01001000 · 10011110

   c. 10111111 ⊕ 11001010

5. What would be the 8-bit binary and corresponding hexadecimal representation of the following *decimal* numbers?
   a. −10

   b. −125

   c. −77

6. Using twos-complement numbers, what decimal number would the 6800 interpret the following to be?
   a. $1000\ 1010_2$

b. 1011 0010$_2$

c. 0101 1011$_2$

d. 0111 1111$_2$

e. 1000 0000$_2$

7. Given: A status byte of 1010 1101 and a mask byte of 1111 1111. What would the ANDing of the two bytes show?

8. Given: A previous status of 0111 0101 and a current status of 1011 0001. What would the XORing of the two bytes show?

ANSWERS

1. a. A one-byte (self-contained) instruction.
   b. A two-byte instruction where the second byte is the operand.
   c. A two-byte instruction where the second byte is the *address* of the operand.
   d. A three-byte instruction where the second and third bytes form the address of the operand.
2. For addresses below 00FF.
3. a. Increment memory location 50.
   b. Increment memory location C550.
   c. Subtract ACCB from ACCA and place the results in ACCA.
   d. OR ACCB with the contents of memory location 10.
   e. This is an invalid instruction since BB is the op code to add the contents of a specified memory location using *extended* addressing. Only one byte of address is provided and extended addressing requires two bytes.
4. a. 1111 1011
   b. 0000 1000
   c. 0111 0101
5. a. 1111 0110$_2$ = F6
   b. 1000 0011$_2$ = 83
   c. 1011 0011$_2$ = B3
6. a. -118_{10}
   b. -78_{10}
   c. $+91_{10}$
   d. $+127_{10}$
   e. -128_{10}

7. If in the unknown status byte a one implied a device was on and a zero implied a device was off, the ANDing operation would show which devices were on and which were off.

8. This operation would show which devices have changed state (on to off or off to on) from the previous status. A one would indicate a device changed state while a zero would indicate a device has not changed state.

EXPERIMENT 3-1

Purpose

To add three numbers from memory and demonstrate the use of the direct addressing mode.

Equipment

ET3400   MEK6800D2
                          +5-volt dc power supply

Program

Hex Address	Hex Contents	Mnemonics/ Contents	Operation
0000	96	LDAA $	
0001	50	50	$M_{50} \rightarrow ACCA$
0002	D6	LDAB $	
0003	51	51	$M_{51} \rightarrow ACCB$
0004	1B	ABA	$ACCA + ACCB \rightarrow ACCA$
0005	9B	ADDA $	
0006	52	52	$ACCA + M_{52} \rightarrow ACCA$
0007	97	STAA $	
0008	53	53	$ACCA \rightarrow M_{53}$
0009	4F	CLRA	$00_{16} \rightarrow ACCA$
000A	7F	CLR $$	
000B	00	00	$00_{16} \rightarrow M_{50}$
000C	50	50	
000D	7F	CLR $$	
000E	00	00	$00_{16} \rightarrow M_{51}$
000F	51	51	
0010	7F	CLR $$	
0011	00	00	$00_{16} \rightarrow M_{52}$
0012	52	52	
0013	3E	WAI	Stop
0050	01	01	Data
0051	02	02	Data
0052	03	03	Data
0053	—	—	Results

This program adds three numbers from memory by first loading the two accumulators with the first two operands. Then the two accumulators are added with the result stored in ACCA. Then, the third operand is added to ACCA. Following this operation, the result is finally stored in memory location M_{53} and the contents of ACCA and memory locations M_{50}, M_{51}, and M_{52} are cleared.

Procedure

| ET3400 | | MEK6800D2 |

Step 1
Load and execute the program. Do not forget to load the three operands in memory locations M_{50}, M_{51}, and M_{52}, respectively.

Step 2
Examine the contents of ACCA and ACCB.

ACCA = _____   ACCB = _____

You should observe that ACCA is cleared and the second operand (02) is in ACCB.

Step 3
Examine the contents of M_{50}, M_{51}, M_{52}, and M_{53}.

M_{50} = _____ M_{51} = _____
M_{52} = _____ M_{53} = _____

You should observe that memory locations 0050, 0051, and 0052 are cleared with the result (06) in memory location 0053.

Step 4
Revise the program to add five numbers from memory. Load the program and execute it. Then, verify the results of the program.

Conclusions

Which of the instructions uses direct addressing?

Which of the instructions uses extended addressing?

Why couldn't direct addressing be used instead of extended in the CLR memory instructions for this program?

Explain the final contents of ACCB.

EXPERIMENT 3-2

Purpose

To demonstrate the use of the DECA, NEGATE, and SUBA instructions. To demonstrate the addition of signed numbers.

Equipment

ET3400   MEK6800D2
                          +5-volt dc power supply

Program

Hex Address	Hex Contents	Mnemonics/ Contents	Operation
0000	96	LDAA $	
0001	50	50	$M_{50} \to$ ACCA
0002	4A	DECA	ACCA $-$ 1 $\to$ ACCA
0003	4A	DECA	ACCA $-$ 1 $\to$ ACCA
0004	4A	DECA	ACCA $-$ 1 $\to$ ACCA
0005	4A	DECA	ACCA $-$ 1 $\to$ ACCA
0006	4A	DECA	ACCA $-$ 1 $\to$ ACCA
0007	4A	DECA	ACCA $-$ 1 $\to$ ACCA
0008	9B	ADDA $	
0009	51	51	ACCA + $M_{51} \to$ ACCA
000A	3E	WAI	Stop
0050	03	03	Data
0051	05	05	Data

This program will decrement $+3_{16}$ to -3_{16} and then add $5 + (-3)_{16}$ which should result in 02_{16} being in ACCA.

Procedure

ET3400

Step 1

Load the above program and single step through it, observing the contents of ACCA at each step. Verify that these contents are correct by referring to the operation listing provided with the program. Remember that negative numbers are represented using twos-complement code.

Step 2

Revise the program by replacing the six DECA instructions with one NEGA instruction.

Step 3

Single step the program and examine ACCA at each step. Is the final result the same as obtained in Step 1?

Step 4

Revise the program to perform the same operation (subtract three from five) using the SUBA instruction. Load and execute the new program. The result in ACCA should be the same (02).

Conclusion

Three methods were used to subtract three from five. Discuss the advantages and disadvantages of each.

Where might the program using the DECA routine be advantageous?

EXPERIMENT 3-3

Purpose

The purpose of this experiment is to determine which of the following eight devices are on. A logic one will indicate a device is on, and a logic 0 will indicate that device is off. The input of an 8-bit status byte representing the device states will be simulated by the LDAA immediate instruction.

Bit 0: frequency measuring device
Bit 1: temperature measuring device
Bit 2: flow measuring device
Bit 3: voltage measuring device
Bit 4: current measuring device
Bit 5: velocity measuring device
Bit 6: pressure measuring device
Bit 7: thickness measuring device

Equipment

ET3400   MEK6800D2
                               +5-volt dc power supply

Program

Hex Address	Hex Contents	Mnemonics/ Contents	Operation
0000	86	LDAA #	
0001	55	55	$55_{16} \rightarrow$ ACCA (load status byte)
0002	84	ANDA #	
0003	FF	FF	$55 \cdot FF \rightarrow$ ACCA (AND status and mask bytes)
0004	97	STAA $	
0005	50	50	ACCA $\rightarrow M_{50}$ (store result)
0006	3E	WAI	Stop

The status byte in this program is $55 = 0101\ 0101_2$. The mask byte is $FF = 1111\ 1111_2$. The status and mask bytes are ANDed together with the result being stored in memory location 50.

Procedure

| ET3400 | | MEK6800D2 |

Step 1

Load and execute the program.

Step 2

Examine memory location 50. Which of the simulated devices are on?

We conclude that the frequency, flow, current, and pressure measuring devices were on; all other devices were off.

Step 3

Substitute the status byte 3F and execute the program. Now what devices are on?

Step 4

Substitute the status byte 04 and execute the program. Now, what devices are on?

Conclusion

Given an 8-bit status byte representing eight external devices, how could we check status of just four of the devices?

How could we check status of just one device?

EXPERIMENT 3-4

Purpose

The purpose of this experiment is to determine if a particular device is on or off. The status word will represent the same devices as in Experiment 3-3.

Equipment

ET3400   MEK6800D2
                             +5-volt dc power supply

Program

Hex Address	Hex Contents	Mnemonics/ Contents	Operation
0000	C6	LDAB #	
0001	5A	5A	5A → ACCB (load status byte)
0002	C4	ANDB #	
0003	02	02	5A·02 → ACCB (AND status and mask bytes)
0004	D7	STAB $	
0005	50	50	ACCB → M_{50} (store result)
0006	3E	WAI	Stop

This program loads the status byte into ACCB. You want to know if the temperature measurement device is on or off. Therefore, you will mask $02 = 0000\ 0010_2$ with the status byte since this device uses position Bit 1. If the operation produces 02, then you know the temperature device is on. If it produces 00, it must be off. The results of the operation are being stored in memory location 50.

Procedure

| ET3400 | | MEK6800D2 |

Step 1
Load and execute the above program.

Step 2
Examine memory location 50. Is the temperature measuring device on or off?

Step 3
Using the same status byte, revise the program to check the status of the frequency measuring device.

Step 4
Repeat step 3 for each of the measuring devices.

Conclusion

Explain the procedure for checking status of a particular device.

How do you think you might determine if a device has changed status from the last time its on/off status was checked?

EXPERIMENT 3-5

Purpose

To determine if an external device changed state from the last time its on/off status was checked. The status word will represent the same devices as in Experiment 3-3.

Equipment

ET3400
MEK6800D2
+5-volt dc power supply

Program

Hex Address	Hex Contents	Mnemonics/ Contents	Operation
0000	C6	LDAB #	
0001	5A	5A	5A → ACCB (load old status byte)
0002	D7	STAB $	
0003	20	20	ACCB → M_{20} (store old status byte)
0004	86	LDAA #	
0005	42	42	42 → ACCA (load new status byte)
0006	98	EORA $	
0007	20	20	ACCA⊕M_{20} → ACCA (XOR old and new status bytes)
0008	97	STAA $	
0009	50	50	ACCA → M_{50}
000A	3E	WAI	Stop
0020	—	—	Old Status Byte
0050	—	—	Result

Given two status bytes, one previous (5A) and one current (42), this program stores the previous byte in M_{20}. It then XORS the current byte with the previous byte and places the result in M_{50}. XORing will show which devices have changed state. A "1" in the result will indicate a change of state while a "0" indicates the device did not change state.

Procedure

| ET3400 | | MEK6800D2 |

Step 1
Load and execute the program.

Step 2
Examine memory location 50. Which devices have changed state?

We conclude the voltage and current measuring devices have changed state.

NOTE: $5A \oplus 42 = (0101\ 1010_2) \oplus (0100\ 0010_2)$
$= 0001\ 1000_2$
current bit — voltage bit

Step 3
Suppose a new status byte of AB is transmitted to the 6800. Revise the program to determine which devices have changed state with this new byte and the previous byte.

Step 4
Which devices have changed state?

We conclude that the frequency, voltage, velocity, pressure, and thickness devices have changed.

Conclusion

Explain the procedure for keeping track of new and old status and determining which devices have changed status.

EXPERIMENT 3-6

Purpose

To determine, once a device has changed state, whether it has changed from off to on or on to off. The status word will represent the same devices as in Experiment 3-3.

Equipment

ET3400

MEK6800D2
+5-volt dc power supply

Program

Hex Address	Hex Contents	Mnemonics/ Contents	Operation
0000	C6	LDAB #	
0001	5A	5A	5A → ACCB (load old status byte)
0002	D7	STAB $	
0003	20	20	ACCB → M_{20} (store old status byte)
0004	86	LDAA #	
0005	C7	C7	C7 → ACCA (load new status byte)
0006	97	STAA $	
0007	30	30	ACCA → M_{30} (store new status byte)
0008	98	EORA $	
0009	20	20	ACCA + M_{20} → ACCA (XOR old and new status bytes)
000A	97	STAA $	
000B	40	40	ACCA → M_{40} (store result)
000C	94	ANDA $	
000D	20	20	ACCA · M_{20} → ACCA (AND result with old status byte to get on to off result)
000E	97	STAA $	
000F	50	50	ACCA → M_{50} (store on to off result)
0010	43	COMA	$\overline{ACCA}$ → ACCA (complement accumulator A)
0011	94	ANDA $	

0012	40	40	ACCA·M_{40} → ACCA (AND M_{40} with ACCA to get off to on result)
0013	97	STAA $	
0014	51	51	ACCA → M_{51} (store off to on result)
0015	3E	WAI	Stop
0020	–	–	Old status byte
0030	–	–	New status byte
0050	–	–	Result
0051	–	–	Result

The results of this operation are found in memory locations 50 and 51. Memory location 50 will determine on to off changes while 51 will determine off to on changes. They can be summarized as follows:

Memory Location 50 (on to off changes)

- a "0" will indicate a device did not go from on to off.
- a "1" will indicate a device changed from on to off.

Memory Location 51 (off to on changes)

- a "0" will indicate a device did not go from off to on.
- a "1" will indicate a device changed from off to on.

Procedure

| ET3400 | MEK6800D2 |

Step 1

Load and execute the program.

Step 2

Examine memory location 0050 to determine which devices have changed from on to off.

We conclude that the voltage and current measuring devices changed from on to off.

Step 3

Examine memory location 0051 to determine which devices have changed from off to on.

We conclude that the frequency, flow, and thickness measuring devices have changed from off to on.

Step 4

Revise the program using two different status bytes and repeat.

Conclusion

Explain the procedure for determining if a status bit has changed. Has it changed from 0 to 1 or 1 to 0?

Can this procedure be accomplished another way?

CHAPTER 4

Condition Code Register and Data Shifting/Comparing/Testing

INTRODUCTION

In the last chapter, we dealt with the 6800 arithmetic, logic, and data-handling instructions. In performing these operations, we can generate conditions or results in the accumulators that the 6800 should be capable of detecting. To keep track of such conditions, the 6800 contains an internal register called the Condition Code Register (CCR). The CCR actually consists of six *flag* bits. These flag bits are used to represent operation-result conditions. When a flag is *set*, the flag bit is at logic 1; when a flag is *reset* or *cleared*, the flag is at logic 0. The flag bits are

Carry
Overflow
Zero
Negative
Interrupt
Half Carry

The ability to make decisions is the main reason for the "intelligence" of a microprocessor. However, decisions must be made based on given conditions. Such conditions exist in the microprocessor as the result of arithmetic and logic operations, and are represented by the condition code flags. For example, decisions could be made to alter the program execution if an operation result is zero, positive, negative, etc.

Data bytes or bits may also be tested and the CCR used to represent the results of the test. For example, suppose that you wish to compare two bytes of data. Using a *compare* instruction, you will see that the *zero* flag will be set if the bytes are identical and the flag will be cleared if they are not identical. The 6800 can then make a decision based on the zero flag status. Instructions such as the *compare* instruction are called *data test* instructions and will be discussed in detail in this chapter. Each CCR flag will be discussed in detail along with the *condition code* instructions which allow the flags to be manipulated.

OBJECTIVES

At the end of this chapter you will be able to do the following:

- Define the functions of the H, I, N, Z, V, and C flags in the condition code register.
- Be familiar with the condition code register instructions.
- Be familiar with all the 6800 data shifting, rotating, comparing, and testing instructions.
- Define twos-complement overflow.
- Write a program to "pack" bcd numbers.
- Define multiple-precision arithmetic and explain how to add and subtract multiple-byte numbers using the instruction set for the 6800.
- Explain the difference between data testing and comparing instructions and standard arithmetic and logic instructions.
- Utilize instructions directly related to the 6800 condition code register.
- Write a program to add bcd numbers and to obtain a result in bcd format.
- Multiply or divide a number by two.

CONDITION CODE REGISTER

The condition code register is an 8-bit storage register which is internal to the 6800 microprocessor chip. This register is structured as shown in Fig. 4-1. The bits within the register are sometimes referred to as *flags*. These flags indicate that a certain condition has resulted from an arithmetic or logical operation in the computer program or from a data transfer to one of the accumulators. We will see that the flags become a very important part of the decision-

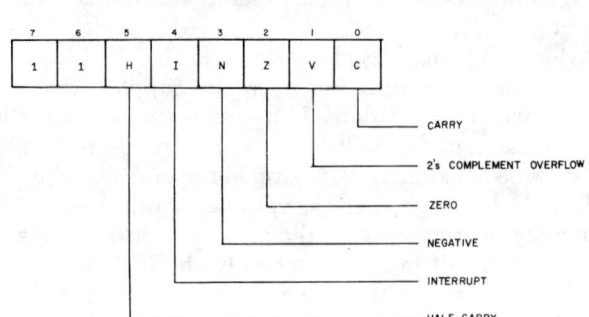

Fig. 4-1. Condition code register.

making ability of the 6800. For example, we might want to test for a result being zero, positive, or negative. Then, depending on the test, the 6800 could make a decision to *branch* or not to *branch* to another part of the program.

Carry Flag (Bit 0)

The carry flag is set (1) whenever there is a "last" carry generated by the eighth bit column in an arithmetic operation, or, as we will see later, whenever data is "moved" or rotated within the accumulators. The carry bit can sometimes be thought of as a "ninth bit" on the accumulator.

Example 4-1: Generating a Last Carry

$$\begin{array}{r} \boxed{01011111} = 5F \\ +(\text{PLUS}) \quad \boxed{11010110} = D6 \\ = \boxed{1} \quad \boxed{00110101} = 35 \end{array}$$

C Flag Set ⎯⎯⎯⎯⎯⎯⎯⎯⏋   Accumulator
Indicating a last carry   Results

Overflow (*V*) Flag (Bit 1)

The V flag is set whenever a twos-complement overflow occurs. This condition is a result of twos-complement arithmetic. If you add two positive numbers, you would expect to obtain a positive result. If you add two negative numbers, you would expect to obtain a negative result. Bit 7 in twos-complement arithmetic indicates the sign of the number. If a twos-complement overflow occurs, then a carry from the D6 column was generated into the D7 column, causing the overflow.

Example 4-2: Generating a Twos-Complement Overflow (Case P

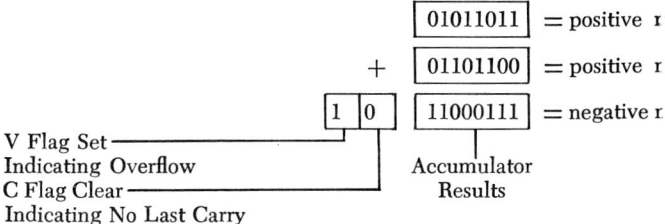

V Flag Set ─────
Indicating Overflow
C Flag Clear ─────
Indicating No Last Carry

Example 4-3: Generating a Twos-Complement Overflow (Case N

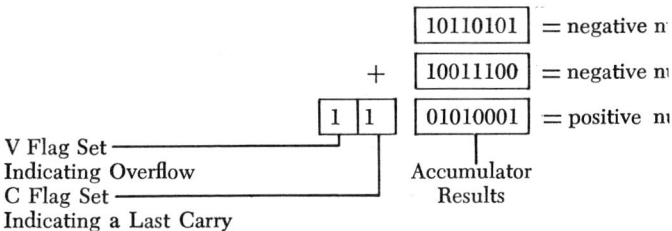

V Flag Set ─────
Indicating Overflow
C Flag Set ─────
Indicating a Last Carry

Zero Flag (Bit 2)

The Z flag is set (1) whenever the accumulator become as the result of an operation or a data transfer. It can also b to *reflect* the equal or nonequal condition between two data that are being compared. If the bytes are identical, the Z fla set.

Example 4-4: Setting the Z Flag as the Result of an Arithmetic Oper

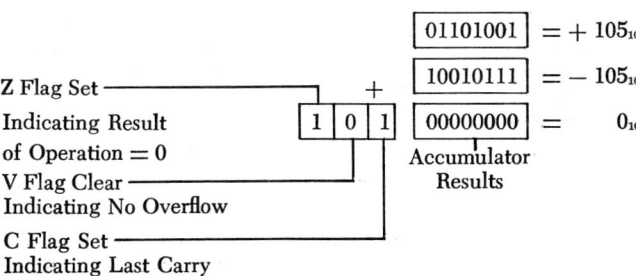

Z Flag Set ─────
Indicating Result
of Operation = 0
V Flag Clear ─────
Indicating No Overflow
C Flag Set ─────
Indicating Last Carry

Example 4-5: Setting the Z Flag as the Result of a Compare Operation

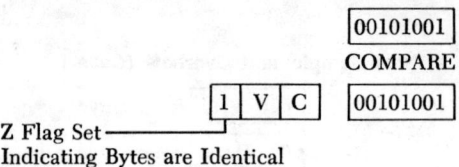

Z Flag Set
Indicating Bytes are Identical

Negative Register (Bit 3)

The N flag is used to indicate a negative result and is connected directly to bit 7 of the result. A one indicates a negative result and a zero indicates a positive result. Therefore, bit 7 of the accumulator can be tested very easily for one or zero status. It is the *only* bit of the accumulator that has its status reflected directly in the condition code register. This idea will be used later when we need to check the status of i/o devices.

Example 4-6: Generating a Negative Result

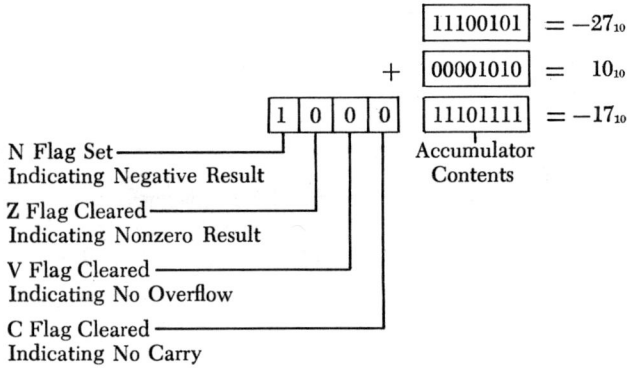

N Flag Set
Indicating Negative Result

Z Flag Cleared
Indicating Nonzero Result

V Flag Cleared
Indicating No Overflow

C Flag Cleared
Indicating No Carry

Interrupt Flag (Bit 4)

This flag is used in conjunction with external i/o device interfacing and it will be discussed in detail later. Briefly, when this flag is set, it will not allow the 6800 to be interrupted by an external device.

Half-Carry Flag (Bit 5)

The half-carry flag is used to indicate a carry from bit 3 to bit 4 in the accumulator. It will be set if a carry from the bit-3 column to the bit-4 column took place during an arithmetic operation. The 6800 uses this flag to implement the decimal-adjust instruction that allows it to operate on bcd values. (This operation will be discussed subsequently.) Bits 6 and 7 of the condition code register are not used and are permanently set to logic one.

Condition Code Register Operations

Now, with the following set of inherent instructions, we can clear or set the C, V, and I flags. We may also transfer the contents of accumulator A to the condition code register or vice versa.

CLC (*CL*ear *C*arry) 0 → C

   Inherent   Clears the C Flag
   0C

SEC (*SE*t *C*arry) 1 → C

   Inherent   Sets the C Flag
   0D

CLV (*CL*ear o*V*erflow) 0 → V

   Inherent   Clears the V Flag
   0A

SEV (*SE*t o*V*erflow) 1 → V

   Inherent   Sets the V Flag
   0B

CLI (*CL*ear *I*nterrupt) 0 → I

   Inherent   Clears the I Flag
   0E

SEI (*SE*t *I*nterrupt) 1 → I

   Inherent   Sets the I Flag
   0F

TAP (*T*ransfer *a*ccumulator *A* to *P*rocessor CCR) ACCA → CCR

   Inherent   Transfers bits 0 through 5 of ACCA to bits 0
   06   through 5, respectively, of the CCR. Bits 6 and 7 of the accumulator have no effect since bits 6 and 7 of the CCR are permanently set to one.

TPA (*T*ransfer *P*rocessor condition code register to accumulator *A*) CCR → ACCA

Inherent　　　　　Transfers bits 0 through 7 of CCR to bits 0
07　　　　　　　　through 7, respectively, of ACCA. Note that bits
　　　　　　　　　6 and 7 will always transfer as ones.

DATA SHIFTING, ROTATING, COMPARING, AND TESTING

The following instructions are used in connection with the various CCR flags in performing both arithmetic and logic operations.

A series of *data-handling* instructions will be used to shift and rotate data within the accumulator. In these operations the C flag acts as a ninth bit, or memory, thereby allowing us to test each data bit using this flag. The 6800 has the ability to alter (*branch*) its program execution based on the C-flag status.

A series of *data test* instructions utilize the Z and N flags to compare or test data prior to a decision-making process. Finally, arithmetic operations can be performed on bcd numbers without special conversion routines by using a *decimal-adjust* instruction which utilizes the H flag.

Shift Left—Arithmetic (ASL, ASLA, ASLB)

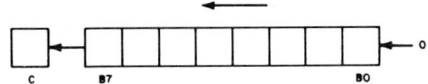

These instructions can be used to shift all of the bits in the accumulators, or a specified memory location, one place to the left. Bit 7, the *M*ost *S*ignificant *B*it (MSB), will be shifted into the C bit of the condition code register and a 0 will be placed in bit 0, the *L*east *S*ignificant *B*it (LSB).

ASL (Arithmetic Shift Left)

Extended　　　　All bits in the specified memory location are
78　　　　　　　shifted left one position. MSB → C, 0 → LSB
HI ADDR　　　　Note that this instruction does not affect the
LO ADDR　　　　accumulators.

ASLA (Arithmetic Shift Left—accumulator A)

Inherent　　　　　All bits in ACCA are shifted left one position.
48　　　　　　　　MSB → C, 0 → LSB

ASLB (Arithmetic Shift Left—accumulator B)

Inherent All bits in ACCB are shifted left one position.
58 MSB → C, 0 → LSB

Shift Right—Arithmetic (ASR, ASRA, ASRB)

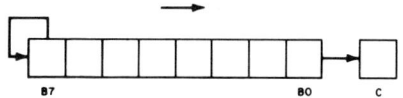

These instructions are used to shift all of the bits in a specified memory location, or in either accumulator, one place to the right. Again, as in the shift-left instructions, the C bit of the condition code register is used as a ninth bit. However, with the shift-right instructions, bit 0 (LSB) will be loaded in the C bit and the contents of bit 7 (MSB) will not change. Note that B7 → B6; however, B7 remains unchanged (B7 → B7).

ASR (Arithmetic Shift Right)

Extended All bits in the specified memory location are
77 shifted right one position. MSB → MSB, LSB
HI ADDR → C
LO ADDR The accumulators are not affected.

ASRA (Arithmetic Shift Right—accumulator A)

Inherent All bits in ACCA are shifted right one position.
47 MSB → MSB, LSB → C

ASRB (Arithmetic Shift Right—accumulator B)

Inherent All bits in ACCB are shifted right one position.
57 MSB → MSB, LSB → C

Shift Right—Logic (LSR, LSRA, LSRB)

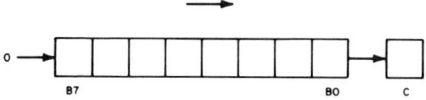

This instruction is similar to the arithmetic shift except that the MSB (bit 7) is loaded with a zero.

LSR (Logic Shift Right)

Extended	All bits in a specified memory location are shifted right one position.
74	
HI ADDR	$0 \rightarrow$ MSB, LSB $\rightarrow$ C
LO ADDR	The accumulators are not affected.

LSRA (Logic Shift Right—accumulator A)

Inherent	All bits in ACCA are shifted right one position.
44	$0 \rightarrow$ MSB, LSB $\rightarrow$ C

LSRB (Logic Shift Right—accumulator B)

Inherent	All bits in ACCB are shifted right one position.
54	$0 \rightarrow$ MSB, LSB $\rightarrow$ C

Rotate Left (ROL, ROLA, ROLB)

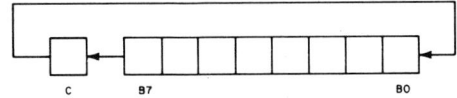

Rotate Right (ROR, RORA, RORB)

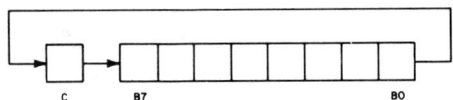

These instructions make a closed loop of a specified memory location or either accumulator. Rotate Left (ROL) will move all bits to the left by one position, with the C bit moving to the LSB (bit 0) and the MSB (bit 7) moving into the C bit. In effect, we have a clockwise rotation of the bits, again considering the C bit as the ninth data bit. Rotate Right (ROR) will provide a counterclockwise movement of data, with the LSB (bit 0) moving into the C-bit position and the C bit moving into the MSB (bit 7) position.

ROL (ROtate Left)

Extended	All bits in the specified memory location are rotated left by one position.
79	
HI ADDR	MSB $\rightarrow$ C, C $\rightarrow$ LSB
LO ADDR	The accumulators are not affected.

ROLA (ROtate Left—accumulator A)

Inherent
49

All bits in ACCA are rotated left by one position.
MSB → C, C → LSB

ROLB (ROtate Left—accumulator B)

Inherent
59

All bits in ACCB are rotated left by one position.
MSB → C, C → LSB

ROR (ROtate Right)

Extended
76
HI ADDR
LO ADDR

All bits in the specified memory location are rotated right one position.
C → MSB, LSB → C
The accumulators are not affected.

RORA (ROtate Right—accumulator A)

Inherent
46

All bits in ACCA are rotated right one position.
C → MSB, LSB → C

RORB (ROtate Right—accumulator B)

Inherent
56

All bits in ACCB are rotated right one position.
C → MSB, LSB → C

Example 4-7: Multiplying by Two

Suppose that accumulator A contains the binary number $0011\ 0110_2$ when an ASLA instruction is encountered. After ASLA is executed, the new accumulator contents will be $0110\ 1100_2$. Let us see what has happened to the accumulator data:

$0011\ 0110_2 = 54_{10}$
$0110\ 1100_2 = 108_{10}$

Notice that by shifting left one time, the contents are multiplied by two. To multiply by four, you would shift left twice. However, you must be careful because the 6800 could interpret the number as negative if a one is shifted into bit 7. Also, you will start running out of shifting locations as the number gets larger. To extend the shifting range, the C flag can be used as a ninth bit.

Example 4-8: Dividing by Two

A number may be divided by two using the logic-shift-right instruction (LSR). If an LSR instruction is executed on the contents, $0011\ 0110_2 = 54_{10}$, the result would be $0001\ 1011 = 27_{10}$ with the cleared C flag indicat-

93

ing no remainder. Another shift right operation would produce 0000 1101 = 13_{10} with the carry flag set. In this case, the C flag would indicate a remainder. Another shift right would produce 0000 0110 with the C flag set, indicating 6_{10} with remainder 1. The shifting can continue until a zero result is obtained.

Add and Subtract With Carry (ADCA, ADCB, SBCA, SBCB)

The add and subtract with carry instructions allow the C bit and any specified memory location to be added to or subtracted from the contents of either accumulator A or accumulator B. The operation will place the result in the accumulator that was involved in the operation. If a carry is generated as a result of this operation, the *new* carry will be represented in the carry bit (C) of the CCR.

ADCA (*AD*d to *C* bit and accumulator *A*) ACCA + M_x + C → ACCA

Immediate　　　Add the C bit and the byte immediately fol-
89　　　　　　　lowing the op code to ACCA.
DATA

Direct　　　　　Add the C bit and the contents of the memory
99　　　　　　　location specified by the next byte to ACCA.
LO ADDR　　　 (No HI ADDR)

Extended　　　 Add the C bit and the contents of the memory
B9　　　　　　　location specified by the next two bytes to
HI ADDR　　　 ACCA.
LO ADDR

ADCB (*AD*d to C-bit and accumulator *B*) ACCB + M_x + C → ACCB

Immediate　　　Add the C bit and the byte immediately follow-
C9　　　　　　　ing the op code to ACCB.
DATA

Direct　　　　　Add the C bit and the contents of the memory
D9　　　　　　　location specified by the next byte to ACCB.
LO ADDR　　　 (No HI ADDR)

Extended　　　 Add the C bit and the contents of the memory
F9　　　　　　　location specified by the next two bytes to
HI ADDR　　　 ACCB.
LO ADDR

SBCA (*SuB*tract from accumulator *A* with *C*arry) ACCA−M_x−C
→ ACCA

Immediate 82 DATA	Subtract the C bit and the byte immediately following the op code from ACCA.
Direct 92 LO ADDR	Subtract the C bit and the contents of the memory location specified by the next byte from ACCA. (No HI ADDR)
Extended B2 HI ADDR LO ADDR	Subtract the C bit and the contents of the memory location specified by the next two bytes from ACCA.

SBCB (Su*B*tract from accumulator *B* with *C*arry) ACCB−M_x−C → ACCB

Immediate C2 DATA	Subtract the C bit and the byte immediately following the op code from ACCB.
Direct D2 LO ADDR	Subtract the C bit and the contents of the memory location specified by the next byte from ACCB. (No HI ADDR)
Extended F2 HI ADDR LO ADDR	Subtract the C bit and the contents of the memory location specified by the next two bytes from ACCB.

Example 4-9: Adding With the Carry Bit

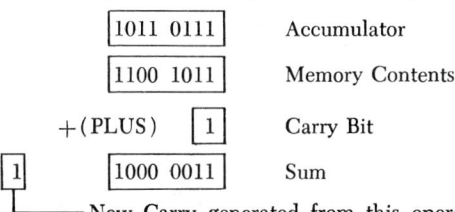

The preceding diagram shows how the ADC instruction would be executed. One of the main uses for this instruction is when we represent larger numbers using multiple bytes. Adding or subtracting multiple-byte numbers is referred to as *multiple precision arithmetic*. Refer to Experiment 4-3 for examples of multiple precision arithmetic.

Data Comparing (CMPA, CMPB, CBA)

These instructions are used solely for the purpose of setting or clearing the condition code register bits. Although they are used to compare data bytes, the *only* effect is that they set or clear the CCR flags accordingly. You can compare an immediate data byte with the contents of ACCA or ACCB. You can also compare the contents of a specified memory location wtih ACCA or ACCB, or compare the contents of ACCB with ACCA. When comparing a memory location to one of the accumulators, the contents of the memory location are subtracted from the respective accumulator with the N, Z, V, and C flags being set or cleared accordingly. Neither the contents of the memory location or the accumulator contents are affected. You can also compare the contents of the two accumulators. To do this, the 6800 subtracts ACCB from ACCA and sets the N, Z, V, and C flags according to the result. Again, the original contents of ACCA and ACCB are not affected.

CMPA (*CoMP*are to accumulator *A*) ACCA − M_x

Immediate
81
DATA

The byte immediately following the op code is subtracted from ACCA with the N, Z, V, and C bits being set or cleared accordingly. The contents of ACCA are not affected.

Direct
91
LO ADDR

The contents of the memory location specified by the next byte are subtracted from ACCA, with the N, Z, V, and C bits being set or cleared accordingly. The contents of ACCA are not affected.
(No HI ADDR)

Extended
B1
HI ADDR
LO ADDR

The contents of the memory location specified by the next two bytes are subtracted from ACCA, with the N, Z, V, and C bits being set or cleared accordingly. The contents of ACCA are not affected.

CMPB (*CoMP*are to accumulator *B*) ACCB − M_x

Immediate
C1
DATA

The byte immediately following the op code is subtracted from ACCB, with the N, Z, V, and C bits being set or cleared accordingly. The contents of ACCB are not affected.

Direct D1 LO ADDR	The contents of the memory location specified by the next byte are subtracted from ACCB, with the N, Z, V, and C bits being set or cleared accordingly. The contents of ACCB are not affected. (No HI ADDR)
Extended F1 HI ADDR LO ADDR	The contents of the memory location specified by the next two bytes are subtracted from ACCB, with the N, Z, V, and C bits being set or cleared accordingly. The contents of ACCB are not affected.

CBA (Compare accumulator B to A) ACCA − ACCB

Inherent 11	The contents of ACCB are subtracted from ACCA, with the N, Z, V, and C bits being set or cleared accordingly. The contents of ACCA and ACCB are not affected.

Example 4-10: Executing a Compare Instruction

```
                    00110010      Accumulator
                    COMPARE
                    01001101      Memory Contents
                NO RESULT GENERATED
         H  I  N  Z  V  C
CCR ——  [X][X][1][0][0][1]
```

With the compare operation, the memory contents are subtracted from the accumulator contents; however, no result is generated. The only effect is to set or clear the CCR flags. Note in this example that the memory contents are larger than the accumulator contents; therefore, the N flag is set. The Xs in the H and I flags indicate a "don't care" state which means they are not affected by the operation.

Data Testing (BITA, BITB, TST, TSTA, TSTB)

The data testing instructions only affect the N and Z bits of the condition code register. The contents of the registers involved in the operation are not affected. Therefore, you can use these instructions to determine whether the contents of ACCA, ACCB, or any memory location are positive, negative, or zero without affecting the contents of the respective register. These instructions will normally be used to test for a condition prior to branching within a program.

BITA (*BI*t *Test*—accumulator A) ACCA · M_x

Immediate
85
DATA
    The byte immediately following the op code is ANDed with ACCA setting or clearing the N and Z bits accordingly. The contents of ACCA are not affected.

Direct
95
LO ADDR
    The contents of the memory location specified by the next byte are ANDed with ACCA, with the N and Z bits being set or cleared accordingly. The contents of the ACCA are not affected. (No HI ADDR)

Extended
B5
HI ADDR
LO ADDR
    The contents of the memory location specified by the next two bytes are ANDed with ACCA, with the N and Z bits being set or cleared accordingly. The contents of ACCA are not affected.

BITB (*BI*t *Test*—accumulator B) ACCB · M_x

Immediate
C5
DATA
    The byte immediately following the op code is ANDed with ACCB setting or clearing the N and Z bits accordingly. The contents of ACCB are not affected.

Direct
D5
LO ADDR
    The contents of the memory location specified by the next byte are ANDed with ACCB, with the N and Z bits being set or cleared accordingly. The contents of ACCB are not affected. (No HI ADDR)

Extended
F5
HI ADDR
LO ADDR
    The contents of the memory location specified by the next two bytes are ANDed with ACCB, with the N and Z bits being set or cleared accordingly. The contents of ACCB are not affected.

TST (*TeST* the specified memory location) $M_x - 00$

Extended
7D
HI ADDR
LO ADDR
    The value 00 is subtracted from the memory location specified by the next two bytes, with the N and Z bits being set or cleared accordingly. The contents of M_x are not affected.

TSTA (TeST accumulator A) ACCA − 00₁₆

Inherent
4D

The value 00 is subtracted from ACCA with the N and Z bits being set or cleared accordingly. The contents of ACCA are not affected.

TSTB (TeST accumulator B) ACCB − 00

Inherent
5D

The value 00 is subtracted from ACCB, with the N and Z bits being set or cleared accordingly. The contents of ACCB are not affected.

Example 4-11: Executing a Test Instruction

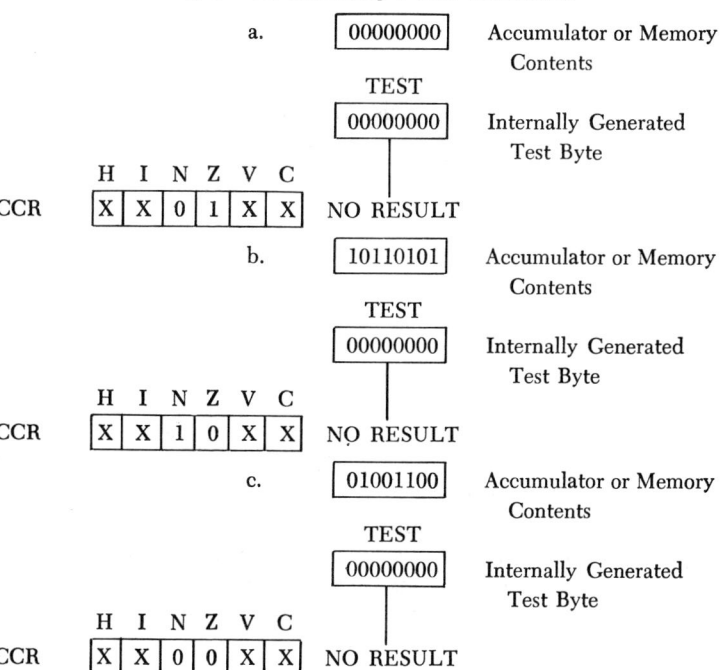

Notice the status of the CCR in each example. In Example 4-11a the Z flag is set indicating the byte tested was zero. In Example 4-11b the N flag is set indicating the byte tested was negative. Finally, in Example 4-11c the byte tested was positive and both the N and Z flags are cleared. The other CCR flags are not affected by this operation.

Binary Coded Decimal Instructions (DAA)

The 6800 can add binary coded decimal (bcd) numbers directly with the use of the decimal adjust accumulator (DAA) instruction. It is used in conjunction with the ADD and ADC instructions and allows you to add bcd numbers directly without a conversion routine. The DAA instruction tells the 6800 that two bcd numbers are being added and to convert the result to bcd. It must be used directly after an ADD or ADC instruction and *cannot* be used to simply convert binary to bcd. (See Appendix B for a discussion of the bcd number system.)

DAA (Decimal Adjust Accumulator)

Inherent Converts binary addition of bcd characters into
19   bcd format.

Example 4-12: Using the Decimal Adjust Instruction

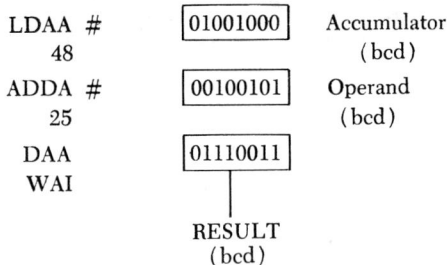

```
LDAA #      01001000      Accumulator
  48                        (bcd)
ADDA #      00100101      Operand
  25                        (bcd)
DAA         01110011
WAI
              |
           RESULT
            (bcd)
```

Example 4-12 shows how the DAA instruction can be used to add two bcd numbers. Notice that DAA is placed *immediately after* the add instruction. When this is done, the 6800 assumes the numbers being added are bcd and will generate a bcd result. Without DAA, the 6800 would add the numbers as straight binary and obtain a result of 0110 1101$_2$. This instruction proves to be very valuable in interfacing since many instruments communicate in bcd.

REVIEW QUESTIONS

1. How many bits are contained in the CCR?

2. How many bits in the CCR are utilized by the 6800?

3. The C flag can be thought of as the _____ bit of the accumulator.

4. The _____ flag is connected directly to B7 of the accumulator.

Table 4-1. Alphabetical Mnemonic Listing of Instructions Presented in This Chapter

Mnemonic	Addressing Modes				Operation
	Immediate	Direct	Extended	Inherent	
ADCA	89	99	B9	—	A+M+C→A
ADCB	C9	D9	F9	—	B+M+C→B
ASL	—	—	78	—	See Text
ASLA	—	—	—	48	See Text
ASLB	—	—	—	58	See Text
ASR	—	—	77	—	See Text
ASRA	—	—	—	47	See Text
ASRB	—	—	—	57	See Text
BITA	85	95	B5	—	A·M
BITB	C5	D5	F5	—	B·M
CBA	—	—	—	11	A−B
CLC	—	—	—	0C	0→C
CLI	—	—	—	0E	0→I
CLV	—	—	—	0A	0→V
CMPA	81	91	B1	—	A−M
CMPB	C1	D1	F1	—	B−M
DAA	—	—	—	19	See Text
LSR	—	—	74	19	See Text
LSRA	—	—	—	44	See Text
LSRB	—	—	—	54	See Text
ROL	—	—	79	—	See Text
ROLA	—	—	—	49	See Text
ROLB	—	—	—	59	See Text
ROR	—	—	76	—	See Text
RORA	—	—	—	46	See Text
RORB	—	—	—	56	See Text
SBCA	82	92	B2	—	A−M−C→A
SBCB	C2	D2	F2	—	B−M−C→B
SEC	—	—	—	0D	1→C
SEI	—	—	—	0F	1→I
SEV	—	—	—	0B	1→V
TAP	—	—	—	06	A→CCR
TPA	—	—	—	07	CCR→A
TST	—	—	7D	—	M−00
TSTA	—	—	—	4D	A−00
TSTB	—	—	—	5D	B−00

5. When is the H flag set?

6. Explain the difference between the SUBA and CMPA instructions.

7. If B2 is added to 97 what CCR flags would be set?

8. Define twos-complement overflow.

9. Explain the difference between a logic and arithmetic shift right.

10. Rotate left moves accumulator data _____.

11. Explain the difference between a compare and bit-test instruction.

12. The instruction that converts binary add of bcd characters into bcd format is the _____ instruction.

13. Using the ASLA instruction four successive times would multiply ACCA contents by _____.

14. The _____ and _____ instructions, respectively, are used to add and subtract multibyte numbers, respectively.

15. Define multiple-precision arithmetic.

ANSWERS

1. Eight
2. Six
3. ninth
4. N
5. When there is a carry from bit column 3 (B3) to bit column 4 (B4) during an arithmetic operation involving one of the accumulators.
6. Both instructions subtract an operand from ACCA; however, SUBA generates a result and places it in ACCA. The CMPA instruction does not generate any result. It simply sets or resets the flags according to the operation and the contents of ACCA are not affected.
7. C and V
8. When, during an arithmetic operation, a carry modifies the value of the most significant bit (Bit 7) which results in a sign error in the result.
9. With an arithmetic shift right, bit 7 remains unchanged. A logic shift right will cause a 0 to be placed in bit 7.

10. clockwise

11. A compare subtracts an operand from the specified accumulator and sets the CCR accordingly. A bit-test instruction ANDs an operand with the specified accumulator and sets the CRR accordingly.

12. DAA (decimal adjust accumulator)

13. 16

14. ADC (add with carry) and SBC (subtract with carry)

15. This is an arithmetic operation performed on multiple-byte numbers.

EXPERIMENT 4-1

Purpose
To determine the various conditions that set and clear the C, V, N, and Z flags.

Equipment
ET3400   MEK6800D2
                 +5-volt dc power supply

Program
This program illustrates Examples 4-1 through 4-6 in their respective order. Refer to the examples to check your results.

Hex Address	Hex Contents	Mnemonics/ Contents	Operation
0000	4F	CLRA	00 → ACCA
0001	06	TAP	ACCA → CCR
Example 4-1			
0002	86	LDAA #	
0003	5F	5F	5F → ACCA
0004	8B	ADDA #	
0005	D6	D6	ACCA + D6 → ACCA
Example 4-2			
0006	86	LDAA #	
0007	5B	5B	5B → ACCA
0008	8B	ADDA #	
0009	6C	6C	ACCA + 6C → ACCA
Example 4-3			
000A	86	LDAA#	
000B	B5	B5	B5 → ACCA
000C	8B	ADDA#	
000D	9C	9C	ACCA + 9C → ACCA

Example 4-4

000E	86	LDAA#		
000F	69	69	69 → ACCA	
0010	8B	ADDA #		
0011	97	97	ACCA + 97 → ACCA	

Example 4-5

0012	86	LDAA#		
0013	29	29	29 → ACCA	
0014	81	CMPA#		
0015	29	29	ACCA − 29	

Example 4-6

0016	86	LDAA#		
0017	E5	E5	E5 → ACCA	
0018	8B	ADDA #		
0019	0A	0A	ACCA + 0A → ACCA	
001A	3E	3E	STOP	

Procedure

| ET3400 | | MEK6800D2 |

Step 1

Load the program and single step the first instruction. (Refer to Experiment 2-4 for the single-stepping procedure.)

Step 2

Examine the contents of ACCA. You should observe 00.

Step 3

Single step the program again. Examine the contents of the condition code register.

a. With the ET3400 system, press the CC key. The display will then show the H, I, N, Z, V, and C flags in that order. Note that the displays are labeled to indicate their respective flags.
b. For the MEK6800D2 system, press the G key four times after single stepping (N key) to display the contents of the condition code register in hexadecimal.

None of the flags should be set since the TAP instruction transferred the cleared accumulator contents into the CCR.

Step 4 (Reference to Example 4-1)

Single step the program again and examine ACCA and the CCR. The contents of ACCA should be 5F and none of the CCR flags should be set.

Step 5

Single step the program again and examine ACCA and the CCR. ACCA should show 35 which is the result of our addition. The CCR should show only the H and C flag set since the addition resulted in a carry from bit column 3 to bit column 4 and a last carry was generated.

Step 6 (Reference to Example 4-2)

Single step again and examine ACCA and CCR. ACCA should show 5B which we loaded and the CCR should show the C flag and H flag set. Why?

The H and C flags are still set from the previous operation and will not change until the alu performs another operation. Simply loading a quantity in ACCA does not cause the alu to perform an operation.

Step 7

Single step again. Now ACCA should show the result of the operation and the CCR should show the H, N, and V flags set.

Step 8 (Reference to Example 4-3)

Single step the program through the instructions related to Example 4-3. Examine ACCA and the CCR. Refer to the example in each case to check your results. Explain to yourself why a particular flag is set or cleared in each case.

Step 9 (Refer to Examples 4-4 through 4-6)

Repeat Step 8 for each one of the referenced examples.

Conclusions

What is the relationship between each flag and the contents of the accumulator?

When are the CCR flags not affected by a program instruction?

EXPERIMENT 4-2

Purpose
To investigate some applications of the shift instructions.

Equipment
ET3400 MEK6800D2
+5-volt dc power supply

Program No. 1

Hex Address	Hex Contents	Mnemonics/ Contents	Operation
0000	86	LDAA #	
0001	09	09	09 → ACCA
0002	48	ASLA	
0003	48	ASLA	Shift ACCA left
0004	48	ASLA	arithmetic three times
0005	3E	WAI	STOP

This program arithmetically shifts the contents of the accumulator three times to the left. Each time we shift left, we are multiplying the contents by two. Therefore, by shifting left three times we multiply the number by 2^3 or 8.

Program No. 2

Hex Address	Hex Contents	Mnemonics/ Contents	Operation
0010	86	LDAA #	
0011	09	09	09 → ACCA
0012	47	ASRA	
0013	47	ASRA	Shift ACCA right
0014	47	ASRA	arithmetic three times
0015	3E	WAI	STOP

This program arithmetically shifts the contents of the accumulator three times to the right. Each time we shift, we divide the accumulator contents by two.

Program No. 3

Hex Address	Hex Contents	Mnemonics/ Contents	Operation
0020	96	LDAA $	
0021	30	30	$M_{30} \rightarrow$ ACCA
0022	48	ASLA	Shift left arithmetic
0023	48	ASLA	four times
0024	48	ASLA	
0025	48	ASLA	
0026	9B	ADDA	
0027	40	40	ACCA + $M_{40} \rightarrow$ ACCA
0028	97	STAA	
0029	50	50	ACCA $\rightarrow M_{50}$
002A	3E	WAI	Stop
0030	03	03	unpacked bcd number
0040	07	07	unpacked bcd number
0050	–	–	packed bcd number

Given two bcd numbers such as 0000 0011 (03_{10}) and 0000 0111 (07_{10}) it would require two bytes of memory to store them. Since the first four bits are zero in each case, we can "pack" the two numbers into one byte using the ASLA instruction. This reduces the memory space required by one-half. Program No. 3 accomplishes this task and places the packed bcd result in memory location 50.

Procedure

| ET3400 | | MEK6800D2 |

Step 1
Load Program No. 1.

Step 2
Single step through the program, observing the contents of ACCA at each step. The final result should have been 48_{16} which equals 72_{10}, the product of $8_{10} \times 9_{10}$.

Step 3
Load Program No. 2.

Step 4
Step the program once and observe the contents of ACCA. This should be 09_{16} which was loaded into accumulator A.

Step 5

Step the program again. Now the ASRA instruction shifts the contents of ACCA to the right one place and, in effect, divides the contents by two. The result should be 04_{16} with remainder one. Where do you think the remainder is located?

Check the C flag and you will find it!

Step 6

Single step the program again. The shift right occurs again and now the result is two with a remainder of zero. $(4 \div 2 = 2)$

Step 7

Single step once more and two will be divided by two with a result of one and a remainder of zero.

Step 8

Load and execute Program No. 3. Note that we are shifting the first bcd number four places to the left, then adding the second bcd number to this result.

Step 9

Verify the packed bcd result in memory location 50.

Conclusions

Are there any limitations in multiplying and dividing using shifting techniques?

What is the advantage of packing bcd digits?

EXPERIMENT 4-3

Purpose

To demonstrate a procedure for adding and subtracting multiple-byte numbers. To demonstrate the use of the ADC and SBC instructions.

Equipment
ET3400
MEK6800D2
+5-volt dc power supply

Program

Hex Address	Hex Contents	Mnemonics/ Contents	Operation
0000	96	LDAA$	
0001	A2	A2	$M_{A2} \rightarrow ACCA$
0002	9B	ADDA$	
0003	B2	B2	$ACCA + M_{B2} \rightarrow ACCA$
0004	97	STAA $	
0005	C2	C2	$ACCA \rightarrow M_{C2}$
0006	96	LDAA$	
0007	A1	A1	$M_{A1} \rightarrow ACCA$
0008	99	ADCA$	
0009	B1	B1	$ACCA + M_{B1} + C \rightarrow ACCA$
000A	97	STAA $	
000B	C1	C1	$ACCA \rightarrow M_{C1}$
000C	3E	WAI	STOP
00A1	1A	1A	Most significant byte of first operand
00A2	AF	AF	Least significant byte of first operand
00B1	55	55	Most significant byte of 2nd operand
00B2	9C	9C	Least significant byte of 2nd operand
00C1	–	–	Most significant byte of sum
00C2	–	–	Least significant byte of sum

The preceding program adds two multiple-byte numbers using the ADC (add with carry) instruction. This is called *multiple-precision arithmetic*. Multiple-precision arithmetic is used when two or more bytes are used to represent an operand. The procedure is to add one byte at a time from each operand using the ADC instruction for all *but* the least-significant byte. Therefore, the 6800 can process numbers of any size by simply *stringing* bytes together. The above program adds $1AAF_{16} + 559C_{16} = 704B_{16}$ which is equivalent to adding $6831_{10} + 21,916_{10} = 28,747_{10}$.

Note that the program adds the least significant bytes and stores the result as the least significant byte of the sum at memory location C2. It then adds the most significant bytes *with* the carry flag since a carry was generated from the least significant byte addition. The

$$\begin{array}{r|l}
& \text{Most} & \text{Least} \\
& \text{Significant} & \text{Significant} \\
& \text{Bytes} & \text{Bytes} \\
& C=1 & \\
1AAF_{16} = & 0001\ 1010 & 1010\ 1111_2 \\
+\ 559C_{16} = +& 0101\ 0101 & 1001\ 1100_2 \\ \hline
704B_{16} & 0111\ 0000 & 0100\ 1011_2
\end{array}$$

result of the ADC operation is stored at memory location C1 as the most significant byte of the sum.

Procedure

```
ET3400            MEK6800D2
```

Step 1
Load the program and single step, observing ACCA and the CCR at each step. Note that the carry flag was set after the addition of the least significant bytes. This carry was then used when adding the most significant bytes. Verify the result in memory locations 00C1 and 00C2.

Step 2
Revise the program to subtract the two numbers given in the original program. The result found in memory locations 00C1 and 00C2 should be $C513_{16}$. Note also that the N flag is set indicating a negative result; therefore, using the twos-complement code $C513_{16} = -(3AED_{16}) = -15{,}085_{10}$.

Conclusions

Why didn't we use an ADC instruction to add the least significant bytes? (*Hint:* Suppose that the C flag was set from some previous operation.)

Describe a procedure for adding or subtracting any size number.

EXPERIMENT 4-4

Purpose
To add two multiple-precision bcd numbers.
To demonstrate the use of the DAA instruction.

Equipment
ET3400   MEK6800D2
+5-volt dc power supply

Program

Hex Address	Hex Contents	Mnemonics/ Contents	Operation
0000	96	LDAA$	
0001	A3	A3	$M_{A3} \rightarrow ACCA$
0002	9B	ADDA$	
0003	B3	B3	$ACCA + M_{B3} \rightarrow ACCA$
0004	19	DAA	Convert to bcd Format
0005	97	STAA$	
0006	C3	C3	$ACCA \rightarrow M_{C3}$
0007	96	LDAA$	
0008	A2	A2	$M_{A2} \rightarrow ACCA$
0009	99	ADCA$	$ACCA + M_{B2} + C \rightarrow ACCA$
000A	B2	B2	
000B	19	DAA	Convert to bcd Format
000C	97	STAA$	
000D	C2	C2	$ACCA \rightarrow M_{C2}$
000E	96	LDAA$	
000F	A1	A1	$M_{A1} \rightarrow ACCA$
0010	99	ADCA$	
0011	B1	B1	$ACCA + M_{B1} + C \rightarrow ACCA$
0012	19	DAA	Convert to bcd Format
0013	97	STAA$	
0014	C1	C1	$ACCA \rightarrow M_{C1}$
0015	3E	WAI	STOP
00A1	00	00	
00A2	68	68	bcd operand
00A3	31	31	
00B1	02	02	
00B2	19	19	bcd operand
00B3	16	16	
00C1	—	—	
00C2	—	—	bcd result
00C3	—	—	

The two numbers previously added in Experiment 4-3 were $6831_{10} + 21,916_{10}$ which is equivalent to $(0110\ 1000\ 0011\ 0001_{bcd}) + (0010\ 0001\ 1001\ 0001\ 0110_{bcd})$ in binary coded decimal. This sum would be $0010\ 1000\ 0111\ 0100\ 0111_{bcd}$ $(28,747)_{10}$. Therefore, in the preceding program, we enter 006831 in addresses A1 through A3 and 021916 in addresses B1 through B3. The result is stored at addresses C1 through C3. Note that the DAA instruction is used to provide the proper bcd result for each arithmetic operation.

Procedure

| ET3400 | | MEK6800D2 |

Step 1
Load the program and single step, observing the contents of ACCA and the CCR at each step. Verify to yourself that these register contents are correct.

Step 2
Examine the result of the bcd addition at memory locations C1 through C3. You should find 028747.

Step 3
Change the program to add any two or more bcd numbers. You now have all you need.

Conclusion
Explain the procedure for adding multiple-precision bcd numbers.

CHAPTER 5

6800 Branching, Indexing, and Stacks

INTRODUCTION

There will be many cases when you will want your program to alter its execution path based on the status of the CCR flags. Recall from Chapter 4 that these flags can be set or cleared as a result of the data test and compare instructions. Once a test or comparison has been made, the 6800 must be capable of making a decision based on the results. Instructions that give the 6800 this decision-making capability are called *branch* instructions. If a branch is initiated, it will cause a new address to be loaded into the program counter. This will cause the program to alter its flow so that program execution continues with the new address specified by the branch operation. The 6800 instruction set contains 16 different branch instructions. Each of these instructions utilizes an addressing mode called *relative addressing*. These instructions and relative addressing will be discussed in the first part of this chapter.

Later in this chapter, we will expand the architecture of the 6800 to include two additional 16-bit registers—the index register and stack pointer. The index register will provide you with the most powerful form of addressing available in the 6800, *indexed addressing*. This type of addressing, along with the branch instructions, will allow you to perform data transfer and arithmetic operations on large quantities of data very efficiently without numerous program instructions. Most of the instructions we have already discussed in Chapters 3 and 4 can utilize indexed addressing to significantly increase their capabilities. The stack pointer register will allow you to "create" areas in memory known as *stacks*. The stack can be used to temporarily save register data in the event that the 6800 is required to deviate from, or leave, its main program. Saving the internal register data will allow the 6800 to resume operation of the main program at the point at which it left to perform some other task. Both the index register and stack pointer have instructions associated with them that will be discussed in this chapter.

Finally, you will apply your knowledge of branches and stacks in a discussion of *subroutines* to finish up the 6800 software. Subroutines or subprograms are usually small, frequently used programs that can be *called* by the main program when the task that they perform is required. Since they are frequently used by different programs, they are normally stored in read-only memory (ROM) such that they are not lost when power is removed from the system. The 6800 has four instructions which will allow you to call on a subroutine and to then automatically return to the main program when the subroutine has been completed. These instructions will be discussed in this chapter.

OBJECTIVES

At the end of this chapter you will be able to do the following:

- Define what is meant by the terms relative address, unconditional branch, and conditional branch.
- Determine relative addresses for branching forward and backward.
- Be familiar with all the conditional branch instructions.
- Explain the function of the index register as related to indexed addressing.
- Understand the INX, DEX, LDX, STX, and CPX instructions and how they are used with the index register and the various addressing modes.
- Explain the function of the stack pointer and how it is related to a memory stack.
- Explain the function of a memory stack.
- Be familiar with the INS, DES, LDS, STS, TXS, and TSX instructions and how they are used with the stack pointer and the various addressing modes.
- Understand what is meant by a subroutine and how the 6800 uses subroutines.

- Understand the function of and differences between the JMP, JSR, RTS, and BSR instructions as related to subroutines.

BRANCHING

Branch instructions tell the 6800 to go to an address other than the next one, in sequence for its next instruction. If a branch is to occur, you must tell the program where to branch. The branch *destination* is an address in memory where the next instruction is to be found. This destination address is determined by adding the contents of the program counter to a *relative address*. Therefore, 6800 branch instructions use a mode of addressing called *relative addressing*. The 6800 branch instructions are always two bytes long. The instruction is followed by a one-byte relative address as shown in Fig. 5-1. This address is *relative* to the contents of the program counter. Remember from Chapter 1 that the program counter always contains the address of the *next* instruction to be fetched in a "straight-line" program. Since the branch instruction is always two bytes long, the contents of the program counter will be the location of the branch instruction plus two. The 6800 adds the relative address to the program counter contents to determine the branching destination. In practice, you usually know the branching destination and you can determine the contents of the program counter. Therefore, the problem is to determine the relative address.

Fig. 5-1. Branch instruction format.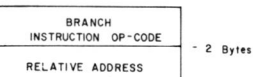

Example 5-1: Relative Address Determination for Forward Branch

Suppose that you have a branch instruction located at address 0010 and you wish to branch to memory location 0020. Determine the *relative address* required.

Since your branch instruction is at location 0010 and branch instructions are only two bytes long, the program counter contains $0010 + 2 = 0012$. You want to branch to location 0020. Therefore, the question is: "What must be added to 0012 to get 0020?" The answer is $0020 - 0012 = 0E$. Therefore, the relative address is 0E.

Example 5-2: Destination Determination

Given a branch instruction located at address 002B with a relative address of 6F. Determine the branch destination.

The program counter contains $002B + 2 = 002D$. The destination equals the program counter contents plus the relative address $= 002D + 6F = 009C$.

In the two preceding examples, the program branched *forward* in both cases. Suppose that you wish to branch backward. The 6800 accomplishes this by using signed twos-complement addition of the relative address. If bit 7 of the relative address is 0, the 6800 will branch forward; if bit 7 is 1, it will branch backward. This brings about a limitation on the branching range. The maximum forward branch is $0111\ 1111_2$, or 127_{10}, memory locations. The maximum backward branch is $1000\ 0000_2$, or 128_{10}, memory locations.

Example 5-3: Relative Address Determination for Backward Branch

Suppose that you wish to insert a branch instruction in your program at location 009F and you desire to branch backward to location 005C. Determine the relative address required. The contents of the program counter are $009F + 2 = 00A1$. Therefore, the relative address required is the destination minus the program counter contents.

$$\frac{005C}{-00A1} = \frac{0101\ 1100_2}{-1010\ 0001_2} = \frac{0101\ 1100_2}{+0101\ 1111_2} = 1011\ 1011_2 = BB$$

Note that the number of memory locations from 00A1 back to 005C is 69_{10} and the twos complement of BB is 69_{10}. Therefore, this is the correct relative address. To make the process simpler, refer to Table 5-1 for determining relative addresses.

BRANCH INSTRUCTIONS

There are two types of branch instructions, unconditional and conditional. The *unconditional* branch is one that causes the program to branch regardless of any conditions. In the 6800, this is the BRA instruction. The *conditional* branch is one which is dependent upon some condition as indicated by the condition code register. If the condition is met, the branch will occur. If not, the program will continue to the next sequential address without branching. Examples of this type of branching are branch if equal zero (BEQ) and branch if minus (BMI). Table 5-2 lists all of the branch instructions along with their respective op codes. In the case of the conditional branches, the test that is made on the condition code register is also indicated.

The instructions involving a direct check on one of the condition code register bits are self-explanatory and are usually used after an arithmetic or logic instruction. The other instructions are less obvious and, thus, justify some explanation. The BGE, BGT, BHI, BLE, BLS, and BLT instructions are all normally used immediately

Table 5-1. M6800 Branch Address Calculator Table

MSH-B LSH-B	F	E	D	C	B	A	9	8	LSH-F
–	–	16	32	48	64	80	96	112	0
F	1	17	33	49	65	81	97	113	1
E	2	18	34	50	66	82	98	114	2
D	3	19	35	51	67	83	99	115	3
C	4	20	36	52	68	84	100	116	4
B	5	21	37	53	69	85	101	117	5
A	6	22	38	54	70	86	102	118	6
9	7	23	39	55	71	87	103	119	7
8	8	24	40	56	72	88	104	120	8
7	9	25	41	57	73	89	105	121	9
6	10	26	42	58	74	90	106	122	A
5	11	27	43	59	75	91	107	123	B
4	12	28	44	60	76	92	108	124	C
3	13	29	45	61	77	93	109	125	D
2	14	30	46	62	78	94	110	126	3E
1	15	31	47	63	79	95	111	127	F
0	16	32	48	64	80	96	112	–	–
	0	1	2	3	4	5	6	7	MSH-F

1. Count the number of bytes (in decimal) from the instruction following the branch to the branch target instruction.
2. Find this number inside the table.
3. Read this hexadecimal equivalent.
   a. Top and left for branching backward.
   b. Bottom and right for branching forward.

Examples: Back 15_{10} bytes $F1_{16}$, Forward 77_{10} bytes = $4D_{16}$, Back 107_{10} bytes = 95_{16}.

4. Key:
   MSH-B = Most significant hex – backward
   LSH-B = Least significant hex – backward
   MSH-F = Most significant hex – forward
   LSH-F = Least significant hex – forward

Courtesy Mr. Ray Boaz, 1516 Jarvis Pl., San Jose, Calif. 95118

after execution of any of the compare or subtract instructions, CBA, CMPA, CMPB, SBA, SUBA, and SUBB. The compare and subtract instructions can be used to test data to determine if it is positive, negative, or zero. Once the instruction is executed, the N and Z flags will be set accordingly. Then, the branch can occur based on the flag status.

The following instructions are used with twos-complement signed binary numbers:

Branch if $\geq$ *Zero (BGE)*—The branch will occur if the signed accumulator contents are greater than or equal to the signed memory contents.

Branch if $>$ *Zero (BGT)*—The branch will occur if the signed accumulator contents are greater than the signed memory contents.

Table 5-2. 6800 Branch Instructions

Operation	Mnemonic	Op Code	Branch Test
Branch Always	BRA	20	None
Branch if Carry Clear	BCC	24	$C = 0$
Branch if Carry Set	BCS	25	$C = 1$
Branch if = Zero	BEQ	27	$Z = 1$
Branch if ⩾ Zero	BGE	2C	$N \oplus V = 0$
Branch if > Zero	BGT	2E	$Z + (N \oplus V) = 0$
Branch if Higher	BHI	22	$C + Z = 0$
Branch if ⩽ Zero	BLE	2F	$Z + (N \oplus V) = 1$
Branch if Lower or Same	BLS	23	$C + Z = 1$
Branch if < Zero	BLT	2D	$N \oplus V = 1$
Branch if Minus	BMI	2B	$N = 1$
Branch if Not Equal Zero	BNE	26	$Z = 0$
Branch if Overflow Clear	BVC	28	$V = 0$
Branch if Overflow Set	BVS	29	$V = 1$
Branch if Plus	BPL	2A	$N = 0$
Branch to Subroutine	BSR	8D	Special (See *Subroutines* in this Chapter)

Branch if ⩽ *Zero (BLE)*—The branch will occur if the signed contents of the accumulator are less than or equal to the signed memory contents.

Branch if < *Zero (BLT)*—The branch will occur if the signed contents of the accumulator are less than the signed memory contents.

The next two instructions are used with unsigned binary numbers:

Branch if Higher (BHI)—The branch will occur if the unsigned contents of the accumulator are greater than the unsigned memory contents.

Branch if Lower or Same (BLS)—The branch will occur if the unsigned contents of the accumulator are less than or equal to unsigned memory contents.

The branch to subroutine (BSR) instruction will be discussed later in this chapter.

Example 5-4: Execution of the BNE Instruction

Suppose that the 6800 encounters the following set of instructions in your program:

```
CMPB #
00
BNE
FB
WAI
```

What will happen?

Here, you are comparing accumulator B immediately with the operand 00. Recall that the compare instruction subtracts this operand from the specified register (ACCB in this case) and sets or clears the CCR flags accordingly. In this example you are concerned with the Z-flag and it will be set *only* when ACCB contents are 00. BNE is the branch if not equal instruction. From Table 5-2, you see that the branch test for this instruction is on the Z flag. When Z=0, the branch will occur. When the Z flag is set, the program will not branch. Therefore, this program will branch until ACCB contents are 00. When ACCB contents are 00, the Z flag will be set. As a result, the branch will not occur and the WAI instruction will be executed causing the program to stop.

In which direction, and how many steps, will the program branch?

The relative address is FB = $1111\ 1011_2$. Bit 7 is one; therefore, the program will branch backward. From Table 5-1 you will see that the program will branch five steps backwards from the WAI struction location.

Example 5-5: Execution of the BGT Instruction

Suppose that the 6800 encounters the following set of instructions in your program:

	CMPA $$
	01
	00
	BGT
What will happen?	05

In this example you are comparing accumulator A with the contents of memory location 0100. If the *signed* accumulator A contents are greater than the signed contents at address 0100, the program will branch forward five steps from the location of the next instruction. If the branch test is not satisfied, the next instruction will be executed.

Example 5-6: Execution of the BHI Instruction

What would happen if BGT were replaced with BHI in Example 5-5?

The only difference is that the 6800 would *not* look at the accumulator and memory contents as twos-complement signed numbers. The branch would occur if the *unsigned* accumulator A contents are greater than the *unsigned* contents of memory location 0100.

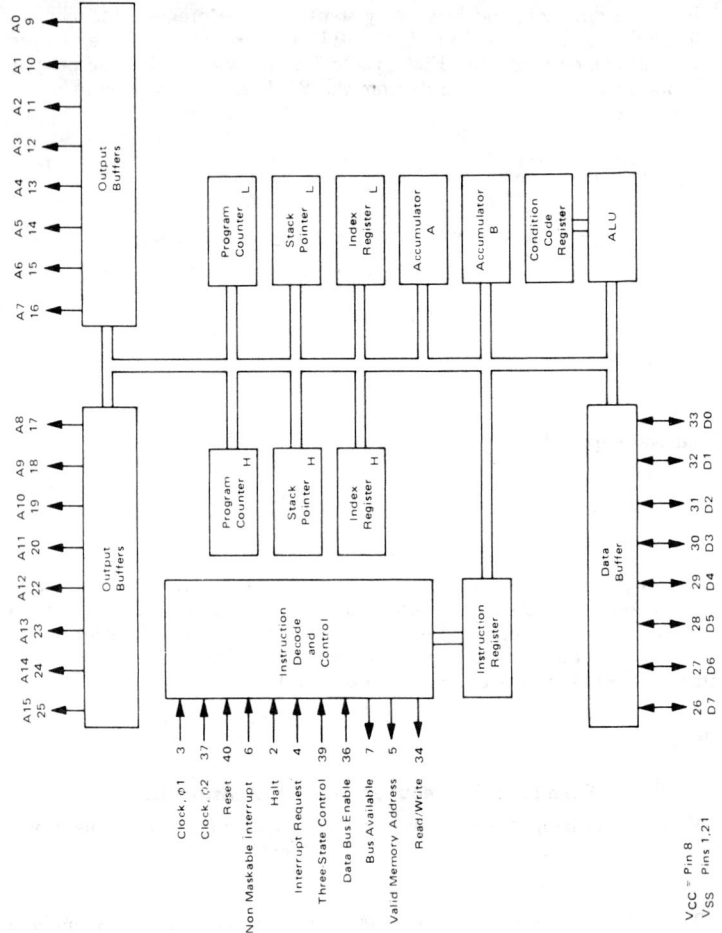

Courtesy Motorola Semiconductor Products Inc.

Fig. 5-2. Expanded block diagram of 6800 microprocessor.

INDEX REGISTER AND ADDRESSING

Now we are ready to make the 6800 a very powerful processing unit. Fig. 5-2 represents an expanded block diagram of the actual 6800 chip structure. In addition to the functional model we discussed in Chapter 3, we note that the chip also contains an index register (IX) and stack pointer (SP). Note in this diagram that all of the registers are connected to a *single* internal bus. Therefore, internally, the address bus and data bus are one and the same. The control section (CON) acts as a "traffic cop" for data and address manipulation on the internal bus. This type of structure is referred to as *single-bus architecture* and is typical of most standard microprocessors, such as the 6800, 8080, and Z-80. The disadvantage of a single-bus system is its slow operation.

The index register (IX) is a two-byte register that can be used to store data or 16-bit addresses in conjunction with the indexed mode of memory addressing.

Indexed Addressing

This mode of addressing is often referred to as the most powerful mode of addressing available to the 6800 since the index register contents may be manipulated with special instructions. An instruction utilizing indexed addressing always consists of two bytes— the instruction byte and an *offset* address as shown in Fig. 5-3. The idea is simple. In order to form the address of the operand, the

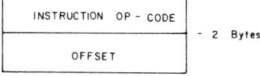

Fig. 5-3. Indexed addressing instruction format.

6800 simply adds the offset address to the contents of the index register. Since the index register is a 16-bit register, we can access any address in memory with this mode of addressing. At first glance, this might seem to be the same as extended addressing. However, as you will see, the index register can be incremented and decremented which allows data to be stored or retrieved from consecutive memory locations. Also, the indexed addressing mode only requires two bytes while extended addressing requires three bytes.

Example 5-7: Indexed Addressing

Suppose that the index register contains the number A5. We will use an "X" after a mnemonic to denote indexed addressing. Now suppose the following instruction is encountered by the 6800:

$$\text{STAA X}$$
$$05$$

What will happen?

The 6800 will add the offset address (05) to the index register contents (A5) and obtain AA. The contents of ACCA will then be stored at memory location AA.

Table 5-3 lists all the 6800 instructions that directly affect the index register.

From Table 5-3 we see that the index register can be incremented and decremented using the inherent instructions INX and DEX. We may load the index register (LDX) using immediate, direct, indexed, or extended addressing. Since the index register is a 16-bit register, the specified memory address contents (M) will be loaded into the high byte of the index register with the next consecutive memory address contents (M+1) being loaded into the low byte of the index register. We may also store the index register contents using direct, indexed, or extended addressing. Here, the

Table 5-3. Index Register Instructions

Operation	Mnemonic	Op Code	Operation Symbol
Increment Index Register	INX	08	$X + 1 \rightarrow X$
Decrement Index Register	DEX	09	$X - 1 \rightarrow X$
Load Index Register	LDX #	CE	
	LDX $	DE	$M \rightarrow X_H$
	LDX X	EE	$(M + 1) \rightarrow X_L$
	LDX $$	FE	
Store Index Register	STX $	DF	$X_H \rightarrow M$
	STX X	EF	$X_L \rightarrow (M + 1)$
	STX $$	FF	
Compare Index Register	CPX #	8C	
	CPX $	9C	$(X_H/X_L) - (M/M + 1)$
	CPX X	AC	
	CPX $$	BC	

Key: Address Mode Symbols
  no symbol = inherent $$ = extended
  # = immediate   X = indexed
  $ = direct

Example 5-8: Loading the Index Register Using Direct Addressing

Suppose that the 6800 encounters the following instruction in your program:

$$\text{LDX \$}$$
$$\text{B7}$$

What will happen?

The LDX $ instruction means to load the index register using direct addressing. Therefore, the contents of memory location B7 (M) will be loaded into the high byte of the index register and the contents of memory location B8 (M+1) will be loaded into the low byte of the index register. Referring to the operation symbol in Table 5-3 for this instruction, note that $M \rightarrow X_H$ and $M+1 \rightarrow X_L$. Here, M=B7 and M+1=B7+1=B8. Remember, however, that these are memory *addresses* and the contents of memory at these addresses are actually what is being loaded into X_H and X_L, respectively.

high byte of the index register is stored in the specified memory location M and the low byte stored in the next memory location M+1. The compare index register instruction (CPX) allows us to compare any two consecutive bytes of memory with the index register contents using the immediate, direct, indexed, or extended addressing modes.

Example 5-9: Storing the Index Register Using Indexed Addressing

Suppose that the 6800 encounters the following instruction in your program:

$$\text{STX X}$$
$$\text{05}$$

Also, suppose the index register presently looks as follows:

Index Register

C7	02
X_H	X_L

What will happen?

The STX X instruction means to store the contents of the index register using indexed addressing. The offset in this example is 05 and the index register contents are C702. Therefore, the high byte of the index register (C7) will be stored at memory location C702+05=C707 and the low byte of the index register (02) will be stored at memory location C707+1=C708. Note that the index register contents will remain unchanged.

Example 5-10: Comparing the Index Register Using Immediate Addressing

Suppose that the 6800 encounters the following instruction in your program:

$$\text{CPX \#}$$
$$00$$
$$50$$

What will happen?

The CPX # instruction means to compare the index register with what follows *immediately*. Therefore, 0050 will be compared with the index register contents. This means that 0050 will be subtracted from X_H/X_L, with the condition code register flags being set accordingly. Remember that no result is generated with any compare operation. If the contents of the index register equal 0050, the Z flag will be set. If the index register contents are less than 0050, the N flag will be set.

Most of the 6800 arithmetic and logic instructions can utilize the indexed addressing mode. Refer to the complete 6800 instruction set in Appendix C for their respective op codes.

Consult the experiment section of this chapter for examples of programs using indexed addressing.

STACKS AND STACK POINTER

Referring to the expanded block diagram of the 6800 in Fig. 5-2, we see that there is one more register that we need to discuss. This is the 16-bit *stack pointer*. The stack pointer is a temporary storage register that will contain the memory address of the *top* of a memory stack.

A memory stack is a series of consecutive memory locations set aside by the programmer in which data or addresses are stored and from which they may be retrieved. Stack instructions can be used to establish one or more stacks anywhere in R/W memory. The stack length is limited only by the amount of memory available. The memory stack is also used by the 6800 to save its internal register contents when it is required to perform other functions aside from the main program, such as those in interrupt routines and subroutines (to be discussed shortly). The *top* of the stack is always the memory address just above the last byte placed on the stack. Therefore, the stack pointer "points" to the *next available* stack location. Fig. 5-4 shows a typical stack structure and corresponding stack pointer contents.

The 6800 has instructions which allow us to push and pull information to and from the stack from or to either accumulator. The *push* instructions, PSHA and PSHB, will deposit accumulator information at the memory location indicated by the stack pointer (SP). Once the information is deposited on the stack, the stack pointer is decremented by one to point to the new available stack location. Fig. 5-5 shows the stack before and after the execution of a typical stack push operation. In this case, we are pushing a byte of information from accumulator A onto the stack (PSHA). Note that the information does not move within the stack. However, the

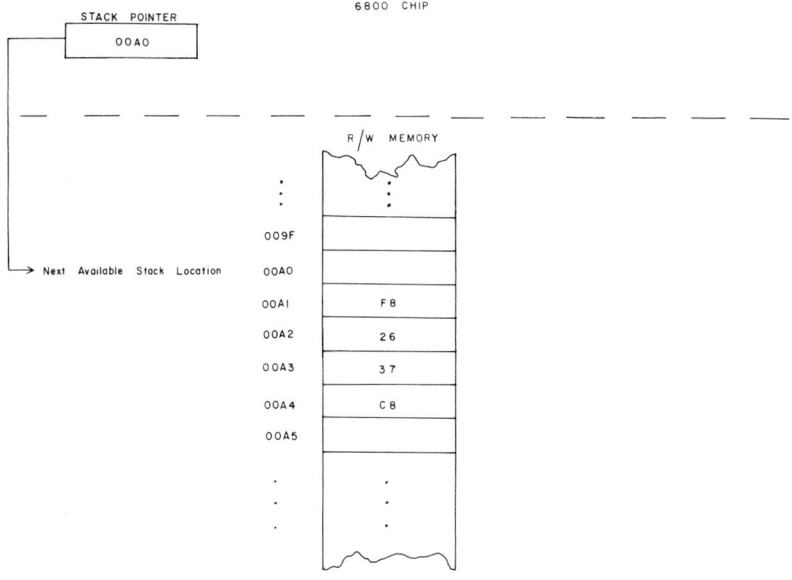

Fig. 5-4. Memory stack structure and stack pointer.

stack pointer moves with relation to the top of the stack. The *pull* instructions, PULA and PULB, will retrieve stack information beginning with the last byte pushed onto the stack.

The term last-in, first-out (LIFO) is used when retrieving stack information. Fig. 5-6 shows the stack before and after the execution of a typical stack pull operation. Here, you are pulling a byte of information from the stack and placing it into accumulator B (PULB). Note that since the "reset" position of the stack pointer is the next lowest address, just below the address of the last stack location used, the 6800 automatically increments the stack pointer by one before retrieving any information from the stack. Table 5-4 shows a complete listing of all the stack and stack-pointer-related instructions.

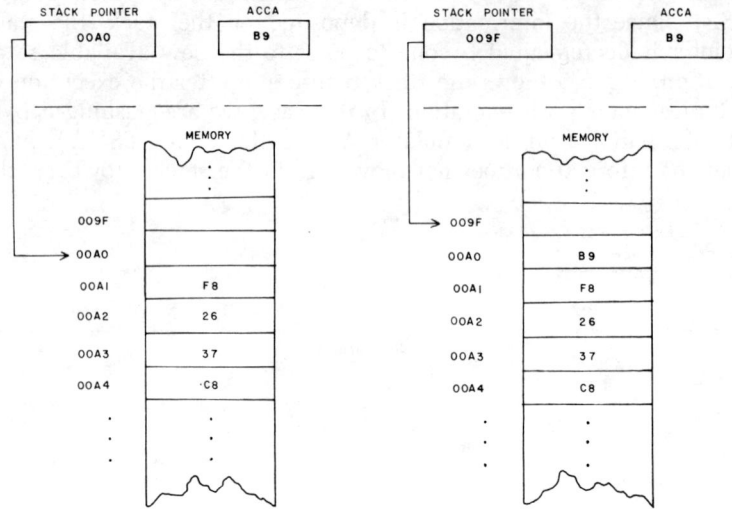

(A) 6800 chip and stack before PSHA.   (B) 6800 chip and stack after PSHA.
Fig. 5-5. Stack push operation.

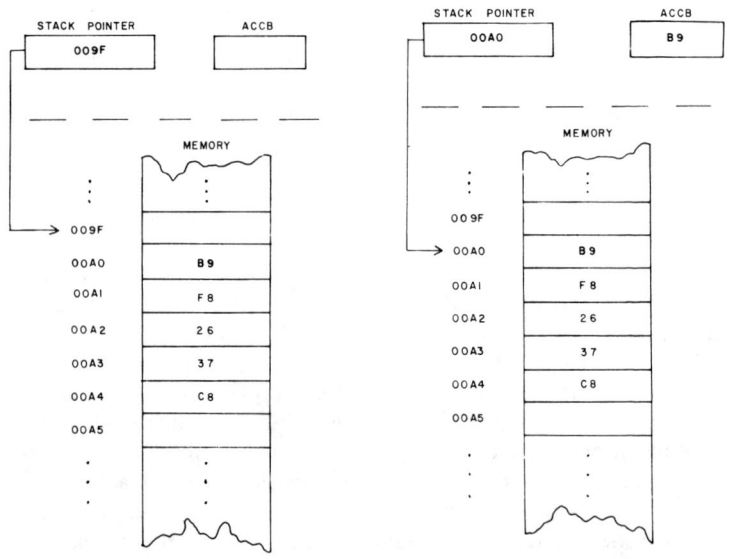

(A) 6800 chip and stack before PULB.   (B) 6800 chip and stack after PULB.
Fig. 5-6. Stack pull operation.

Table 5-4. Stack and Stack Pointer Instructions

Operation	Mnemonic	Op Code	Operation Symbol
Push Data	PSHA	36	A → M$_{SP}$, SP − 1 → SP
	PSHB	37	B → M$_{SP}$, SP − 1 → SP
Pull Data	PULA	32	SP + 1 → SP, M$_{SP}$ → A
	PULB	33	SP + 1 → SP, M$_{SP}$ → B
Increment SP	INS	31	SP + 1 → SP
Decrement SP	DES	34	SP − 1 → SP
Load SP	LDS #	8E	
	LDS $	9E	M → SP$_H$, (M + 1) → SP$_L$
	LDS X	AE	
	LDS $$	BE	
Store SP	STS $	9F	
	STS X	AF	SP$_H$ → M, SP$_L$ → (M + 1)
	STS $$	BF	
IX → SP	TXS	35	X − 1 → SP
SP → IX	TSX	30	SP + 1 → X

Key: Address Mode Symbols
no symbol = inherent $$ = extended
= immediate   X = indexed
$ = direct

Table 5-4 shows that the stack pointer can be incremented and decremented using the inherent instructions INS and DES, respectively. You may also load the stack pointer using immediate, direct, indexed, or extended addressing. Since the stack pointer is a 16-bit register, the specified memory address contents (M) will be loaded into the high byte of the stack pointer with the next consecutive memory address (M+1) being loaded into the low byte of the stack pointer. You may also store the stack pointer contents using direct, indexed, or extended addressing. Here, the high byte of the stack pointer is stored in the specified memory location (M) and the low byte is stored in the next memory location (M+1). Note that you may also transfer the index register contents to the stack pointer and vice versa. The TXS instruction loads the stack pointer with the contents of the index register minus one, leaving the index register contents unchanged and TSX loads the index register with the contents of the stack pointer plus one, leaving the previous stack pointer unchanged.

SUBROUTINES

The final topic that we must discuss to complete our understanding of 6800 software is subroutines. A *subroutine* or subprogram is usually a group of instructions within a main program or a group of instructions residing in a block of memory aside from the main program. The subroutine usually performs a short but frequently required task. The subroutine may be used many times within the execution of the main program. Typical uses of subroutines would be for repetitive addition, time delays, multiplication, division, bcd-to-binary translations, etc. The 6800 has four instructions that may be used in conjunction with subroutines as indicated by Table 5-5.

Jump (JMP)

The jump instruction is similar to the unconditional branch instruction, branch always (BRA). Recall that the BRA instruction is a two-byte instruction utilizing relative addressing. It can be used to branch backward or forward, depending on the relative address. But since the relative address is only one byte, you are limited to branching within the range of -128_{10} bytes to $+127_{10}$ bytes from the address in the program counter. The JMP instruction is more powerful since it allows you to jump to any location in memory, regardless of the range. To do this, the JMP instruction can use either extended or indexed addressing. Fig. 5-7 shows the execution of a JMP instruction using extended addressing. Note that the computer program is jumping forward to address 011A. The program will *go to* this address and then continue its execution from this point. Fig. 5-8 shows the execution of a JMP instruction utilizing indexed addressing. Here, the computer program is jumping backward to address 0109. Note that this destination is computed by adding the offset (09) to the index register contents (0100). Also, once the JMP is encountered by the program (Fig. 5-8), it will repeat (loop) itself endlessly between addresses 0109 and 0111. Fig. 5-9 shows how you might utilize the JMP instruction

Table 5-5. Subroutine Instructions

Operation	Mnemonic	Op Code
Jump	JMP X	6E
	JMP $$	7E
Jump to Subroutine	JSR X	AD
	JSR $$	BD
Return from Subroutine	RTS	39
Branch to Subroutine	BSR (relative)	8D

Key: Address Mode Symbols
no symbol = inherent $$ = extended
= immediate   X = indexed
$ = direct

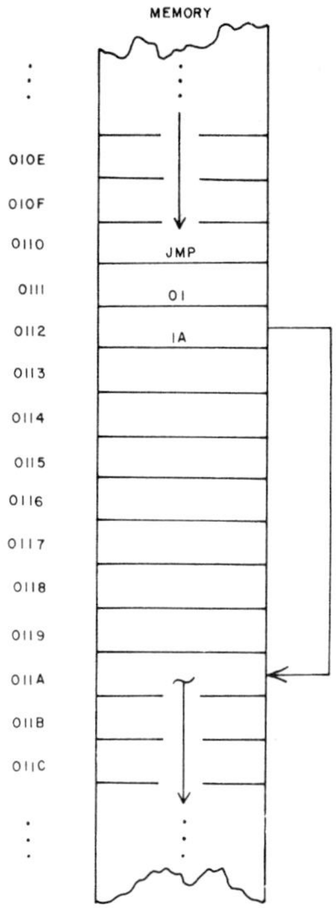

Fig. 5-7. JMP instruction using extended addressing.

Address	Memory
010E	
010F	
0110	JMP
0111	01
0112	1A
0113	
0114	
0115	
0116	
0117	
0118	
0119	
011A	
011B	
011C	

to *call* a subroutine. Note that you must also use a JMP instruction at the end of the subroutine to return to the main program. What would be the disadvantage of using this method to call a subroutine?

The disadvantage would be that you could only call the subroutine once from the main program. Suppose that you wish to call the same subroutine again later in the main program. The problem with using the JMP instruction is getting back to the main program once the subroutine is completed. The first time the subroutine is called there is no problem; however, the second time you call the same subroutine the return jump instruction must be changed to indicate the new return address. Although you could do this through a software routine, there is a much easier way to go about this as you shall now see.

Jump to Subroutine (JSR)/Return from Subroutine (RTS)

The combined use of the instructions JSR and RTS eliminates the return-from-subroutine problem. The JSR instruction is used in the same manner as the JMP instruction when it is used to call a subroutine. It can utilize either extended or indexed addressing. However, the RTS is an inherent instruction that must be used at the end of the subroutine to return to the main program. How does the 6800 know the proper address to which it is to return in the main program?

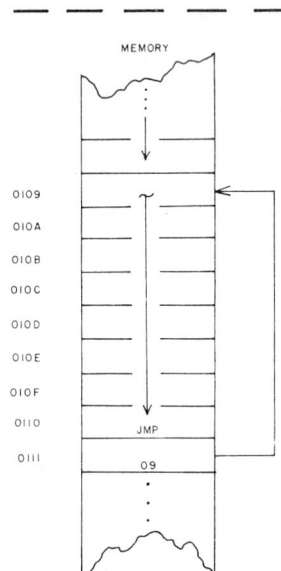

Fig. 5-8. JMP instruction using indexed addressing.

The return-from-subroutine operation uses the contents of the program counter that existed before the jump to subroutine occurred. Recall that when the JSR operation is executed, the contents of the program counter will be the address of the *next* instruction; that is, the location that the computer must return to. The JSR instruction causes the contents of the program counter to be pushed into a memory stack. The low byte goes into the stack first followed by the high byte. When the RTS instruction is encountered in the subroutine, the old program count is automatically pulled from the stack and placed in the program counter. Therefore, the 6800 will return to the main program at the proper location. Now the program can jump to, or call, a subroutine any number of times within the main

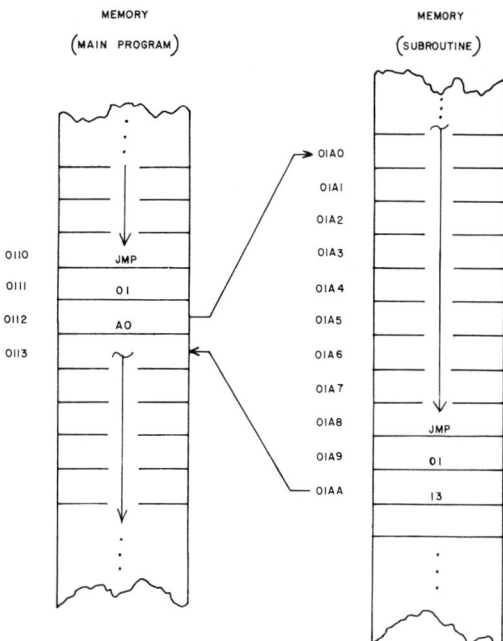

Fig. 5-9. JMP being used to call a subroutine.

program. Fig. 5-10 illustrates the execution of the JSR and RTS instructions. The JSR and RTS instructions now make possible the use of *nested* subroutines. A *nested* subroutine is a subroutine within a subroutine. For example, the main program may call subroutine A, while subroutine A further calls subroutine B, while subroutine B calls subroutine C, and so on. Each time we jump to a new subroutine, the contents of the program counter are saved on the stack.

Since the stack operates on the last-in, first-out principle, it can work its way back to the proper return point in the main program after each successive subroutine has been completed. Fig. 5-11 illustrates the nested subroutine concept.

Branch to Subroutine (BSR)

The last subroutine instruction we have is the branch to subroutine (BSR) instruction. The execution of the BSR instruction is the same as the JSR instruction, except that we only need two bytes to cause the jump. It utilizes relative addressing; therefore, the subroutine must be within the -128_{10} to 127_{10} address range of the program counter. When the BSR instruction is used, the old program count is saved on the stack and the RTS must be used at the end of the subroutine to cause the program return to the main program.

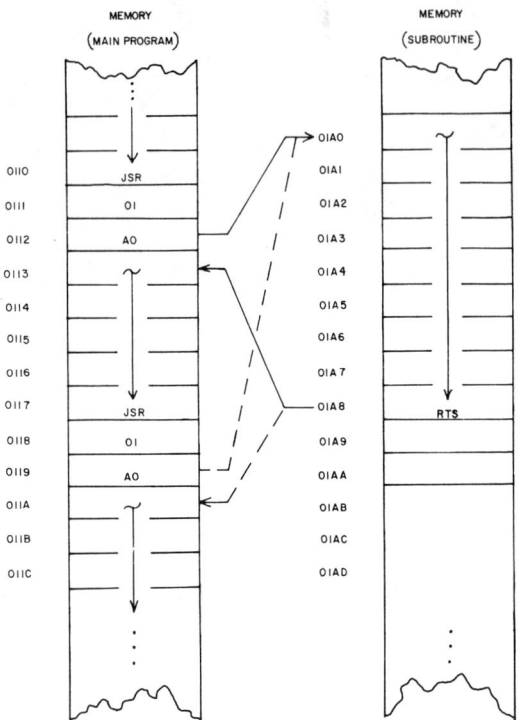

Fig. 5-10. Use of the JSR and RTS instructions.

REVIEW QUESTIONS

1. Branch instructions are always _____ bytes long.
2. The second byte of a branch instruction is called the _____.
3. The two types of branch instructions are the _____ and _____.
4. A branch instruction is located at address 001E and has a relative address of 20. Where will the program branch?

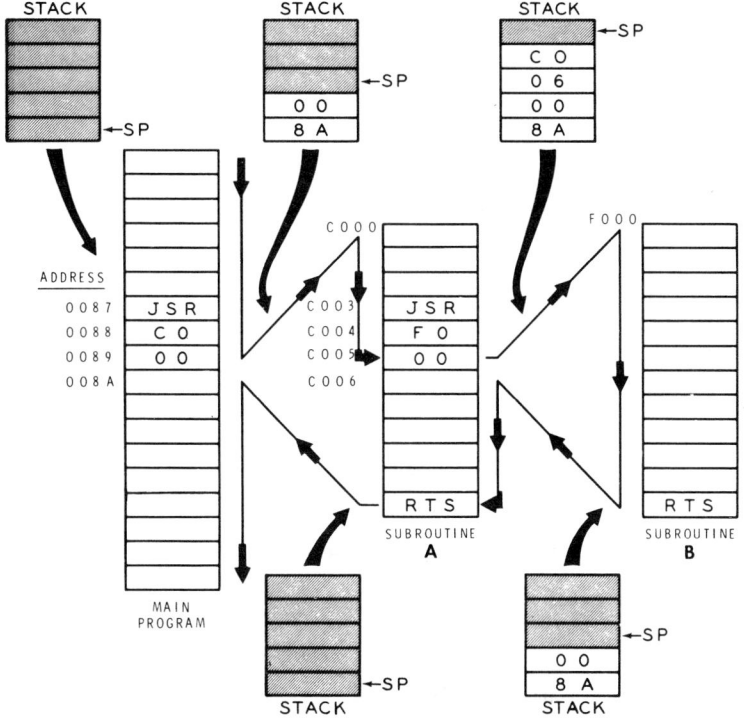

Fig. 5-11. Nested subroutines.

Courtesy Heath Co.

5. A branch instruction is to be located at address 0A18 of your program. At this point you desire to branch back to address 0A00 if a certain condition exists. Determine the relative address required.

6. The maximum branching range using relative addressing is — _____ bytes to + _____ bytes from the program count.

7. What designates a forward branch? A backward branch?

8. Most standard microprocessors, such as the 6800, use _____ architecture for internal data transfers.

9. The index register is a _____-bit register.

10. Instructions using indexed addressing are always _____ bytes long.

11. The second byte of an instruction using indexed addressing is called the _____ .

12. How is the operand address determined using indexed addressing?

13. What is one advantage of indexed over extended addressing?

14. The 6800 encounters the following instruction in your program:
    LDX $$
    0A
    59
    What will happen?

15. The stack pointer is a _____-bit register.
16. Explain what is meant by the term "memory stack."

17. The stack pointer always points to what location?

18. The two instructions used to move information in and out of the stack are the _____ and _____ instructions.
19. The 6800 encounters the following instruction in your program:
    STS X
     00
    What will happen?

20. When are stacks normally used?

21. A jump (JMP) instruction is always _____ bytes long.
22. When would you use a subroutine?

23. What is the advantage of the JSR over the JMP instruction?

24. The 6800 encounters the following instruction:
    JSR X
     05
    What will happen?

25. When would you use a BSR in lieu of a JSR instruction?

26. When using BSR or JSR, the subroutine must always contain a _____ instruction to get back to the main program.

ANSWERS

1. two

2. relative address

3. unconditional and conditional

4. Since the branch instruction is located at address 001E, the program count is $001E + 2 = 0020$. The destination is the program count plus the relative address $= 0020 + 20 = 0040$. It will be a forward branch since bit 7 of the relative address is zero.

5. From Table 5-1, the relative address would be E6.

6. -128_{10} bytes to $+127_{10}$ bytes

7. Bit 7 of the relative address is zero. Bit 7 of the relative address is one.

8. single bus

9. 16

10. two

11. offset

12. By adding the offset to the contents of the index register.

13. Instructions using indexed addressing are only two bytes long where extended addressing requires three bytes.

14. LDX $$ means to load the index register using extended addressing. The high byte of the index register will be loaded with the contents of memory location 0A59 and the low byte of the index register will be loaded with the contents of memory location $0A59+1 = 0A5A$.

15. 16

16. A memory stack is a series of consecutive memory locations set aside by the programmer in which data or addresses are stored and retrieved.

17. The next available location in the stack.

18. PUSH and PULL

19. STS X means to store the stack pointer contents using indexed addressing. Since the offset is 00, the high byte of the stack pointer will be stored at the memory location specified by the index register (M) and the low byte of the stack pointer will be stored at the memory location specified by the index register plus one (M+1).

20. To save internal register information during interrupts and subroutines.

21. two or three

22. When performing a short but frequently used task.

23. With the JSR instruction, a subroutine can be called more than once in a main program without special software being needed to get back to the main program.

24. JSR X means to jump to subroutine using indexed addressing. The 6800 will leave the main program and jump to a subroutine located at address (05 + index register contents). The 6800 will then return to the main program when the RTS instruction is encountered at the end of the subroutine.

25. When calling subroutine which is within a -128_{10} to 127_{10} byte range.

26. RTS

EXPERIMENT 5-1

Purpose

To demonstrate the use of branching and indexed addressing in clearing consecutive memory locations (0000 through 0009).

Equipment

ET3400   MEK6800D2
                     +5-volt dc power supply

Program

Hex Address	Hex Contents	Mnemonics/ Contents	Operation
000A	CE	LDX #	
000B	00	00	00 → X_H
000C	00	00	00 → X_L
000D	6F	CLR X	
000E	00	00	00 → M
000F	08	INX	X + 1 → X
0010	8C	CPX #	
0011	00	00	(X_H/X_L) − (00/0A)
0012	0A	0A	
0013	26	BNE	
0014	F8	F8	Branch if Z flag clear (to address 000D)
0015	3E	WAI	STOP

This program illustrates how branching and indexed addressing are used to clear the first ten R/W memory locations. Note that since you wish to clear memory locations 0000 through 0009, your program must reside in memory above location 0009. Therefore, you start loading the program at address 000A. You start off by clearing the index register. Then the CLR X instruction clears the address indicated by the index register since the offset is 00. The next step is to increment the index register (INX). Then you come to the

CPX # 000A instruction which will compare the contents of the index register to 000A. If they are not equal, the BNE instruction causes the program to return to the CLR X instruction to clear the next memory location. When the index register equals 000A, the program will stop.

Procedure

| ET3400 | | MEK6800D2 |

Step 1
Load the program starting at address 000A.

Step 2
Single step the program once and observe the index register contents. (Remember to start single stepping at address 000A.)

> NOTE: With the Heath ET3400, press the key marked "index" to observe the index register contents. With the Motorola MEK6800D2, sequence the G key once to display the index register.

The index register should contain 0000 since it was cleared with the first instruction.

Step 3
Single step the program again and observe memory location 0000. You should observe 00 since you just cleared that location with the CLR X instruction.

> NOTE: With the MEK6800D2 system, you must exit then display memory location 0000. When you exit from a single step routine using this system, you must reinsert the breakpoint before you can single step the program again since the exit removes the initial breakpoint. In this case you should reinsert the breakpoint at the address where the exit occurred (000F).

Step 4
Single step the program again and examine the contents of the index register. You should observe 0001 since you just incremented it (INX).

Step 5

Single step again and observe the contents of the CCR. You just performed the compare index register instruction (CPX). The Z flag should not be set since the index register does not equal 000A.

Step 6

Single step and examine the program counter contents. You should observe 000D. Why? The branch test was Z=0; therefore, the branch occurred back to address 000D.

Step 7

Continue to single step until the program comes to a halt. Observe the index register contents at each step.

Step 8

Examine the contents of the CCR. Notice that the Z flag is set. This happened when the index register contents equaled 000A. Therefore, the branch did not take place after this point and the program stopped.

Step 9

Examine memory locations 0000 through 0009. They should all contain 00.

Step 10

Revise the program to clear the first 100_{10} memory locations. Remember, your program must be stored in memory above the last location to be cleared.

Step 11

Execute the new program and verify that the locations have been cleared.

Conclusions

How would the program have to be written without the power of indexed addressing?

Recalculate the relative address given in the program and verify to yourself that it is correct.

What did the 6800 look for before *deciding* to branch or not to branch?

Could the program be revised using the DEX instruction rather than the INX instruction? If so, how?

EXPERIMENT 5-2
Purpose

To demonstrate the use of branching and indexed addressing to add a series of consecutive numbers from memory.

Equipment

ET3400

MEK6800D2
+5-volt dc power supply

Program

Hex Address	Hex Contents	Mnemonics/ Contents	Operation
0000	CE	LDX #	
0001	00	00	00 → X_H
0002	C0	C0	C0 → X_L
0003	4F	CLRA	00 → ACCA
0004	AB	ADDA X	
0005	00	00	ACCA + M → ACCA
0006	08	INX	X + 1 → X
0007	8C	CPX #	
0008	00	00	(X_H/X_L) − (00/CA)
0009	CA	CA	
000A	26	BNE	
000B	F8	F8	Branch if Z flag clear (to address 0004)
000C	B7	STAA $$	
000D	00	00	ACCA → 0050
000E	50	50	
000F	3E	WAI	STOP
00C0	01	01	DATA
00C1	02	02	DATA
00C2	03	03	DATA
00C3	04	04	DATA
00C4	05	05	DATA

00C5	06	06	DATA
00C6	07	07	DATA
00C7	08	08	DATA
00C8	09	09	DATA
00C9	0A	0A	DATA
0050	–	–	RESULT

This program illustrates how branching and indexed addressing are used to add data located in ten consecutive memory locations (00C0-00C9). Again, the index register is incremented each time you *loop* through the program. You are adding using indexed addressing; therefore, the operand address is determined by adding the offset (00) to the index register contents. You start by loading the index register with the location of the first operand. Since the offset is 00, the index register specifies the operand address directly. By incrementing the index register each time you loop through the program, you add the contents of each successive memory location to accumulator A. Note that you are comparing the index register with 00CA, which is the location just after the last byte. When you get to this point, you want to stop. At this point, the compare instruction will cause the Z flag to be set, the branch will not occur, and the looping will not continue. You then store the result in location 0050 before stopping the program.

Procedure

| ET3400 | MEK6800D2 |

Step 1
Load the program starting at address 0000. Be sure to remember to load the data in memory locations 00C0 through 00C9.

Step 2
Single step through the program, observing the contents of the index register and accumulator A at each step. Verify to yourself that the contents are correct and that the program is operating properly.

Step 3
Examine the final result in memory location 0050. You should observe 37, which is the hex result of 1+2+3+4+5+6+7+8+9+A.

Step 4
Revise the program to add the same list of numbers using the DEX instruction in place of the INX instruction.

Step 5
Execute the new program and verify its results.

Conclusions
Would the relative address associated with the BNE instruction change if the program were located in a different part of memory? Why?

EXPERIMENT 5-3

Purpose
To demonstrate the use of the subroutine instructions.

Equipment
ET3400   MEK6800D2

Program

Hex Address	Hex Contents	Mnemonics/ Contents	Operation
0000	8E	LDS #	
0001	00	00	00 → SP_H
0002	50	50	50 → SP_L
0003	BD	JSR $$	
0004	00	00	Jump to subroutine
0005	30	30	located at address 0030
0006	3E	WAI	Stop
.	.	.	
	(Subroutine)		
0030	CE	LDX #	
0031	00	00	00 → X_H
0032	05	05	05 → X_L
0033	09	DEX	X − 1 → X
0034	8C	CMPX #	
0035	00	00	Compare index register
0036	00	00	immediate with 0000
0037	26	BNE	
0038	FA	FA	Branch if Z flag cleared (to address 0033)
0039	39	RTS	Return to main program

This program shows how a subroutine can be called using the jump-to-subroutine (JSR) instruction. The first instruction loads the stack pointer with 0050. Recall that when the JSR instruction is executed, the program counter contents are saved on the stack such that the 6800 can return to where it left off in the main program when the subroutine is completed. The next instruction is the JSR which will call the subroutine beginning with address 0030. The subroutine loads the index register with 0005 then decrements it down to zero before returning to the main program at address 0006. A subroutine such as this is sometimes used to create a time delay within a program. Loading the index register with a larger value would create a longer delay. More will be said about this in Chapter 8.

Procedure

| ET3400 | | MEK6800D2 |

Step 1
Enter the given program.

Step 2
Set the program counter to 0000 and single step the program. Examine the stack pointer contents by pressing the SP key on the Heath ET3400 or by sequencing the G key five times on the Motorola MEK6800D2. You should observe 0050 since the first instruction loaded this value into the stack pointer.

Step 3
Single step the program and note that the display indicates the first instruction of the subroutine since you have just executed the JSR instruction.

Step 4
The next executable instruction in the *main* program is the WAI instruction located at address 0006. In order to return to the main program at the WAI instruction, the 6800 must save address 0006 on the stack. The stack pointer was set to 0050 and, therefore, the low address byte (06) should be saved in memory location 0050 and the high address byte (00) should be in memory location 004F. Verify this by examining these two addresses.

Step 5

Now examine the stack pointer contents. You should observe 004E since the stack pointer has been decremented twice during the process of saving the program count.

Step 6

Single step through the subroutine until you return to the main program at address 0006 via the RTS instruction. You should observe the index register contents while single stepping the subroutine. Note that the index register will be decremented down to 0000 before the 6800 will return to the main program. *Do not* execute the WAI instruction.

Step 7

Examine the stack pointer contents. You should observe 0050 since the old program count (0006) was *pulled* from the stack causing the stack pointer to increment twice.

Conclusion

Could a BSR instruction be used in place of the JSR instruction? (Try it!)

How would a JMP instruction be used to call the same subroutine? (Try it!)

What limitations are involved with the BSR and JMP instructions?

CHAPTER 6

6800 Input/Output

INTRODUCTION

Now that you have completed the chapters about the 6800 software, you are ready to learn about the *hardware* aspects of the 6800. In this chapter and subsequent chapters, we will primarily concern ourselves with how to interface this powerful processor to the "outside world" in order to perform real computer-controlled functions. Our discussion will begin with a minimum 6800 system configuration that will enable you to accommodate 80 to 90 percent of all microcomputer applications. Most microcomputer applications are the small *dedicated* ones which do not require the large amounts of memory and higher speeds that minicomputers and larger computers can supply. In most cases, the 6800 will provide more speed and memory capability than is required by the application. When interfacing, keep in mind what the application requires so as not to overdesign the system. One of the big advantages of a microprocessor-based system is that it can be expanded if the *application* so dictates. Therefore, when designing a microcomputer system, *always* use the simplest possible approach that gets the job done.

After configuring the basic system, we will discuss 6800 data input/output (i/o). You will see that no special instructions are needed to accomplish data i/o since each i/o device will be treated as a memory location or group of locations. Therefore, you will simply use the load- and store-accumulator instructions to input and output data. This type of data i/o is referred to as *memory-*

mapped i/o. After discussing simple data i/o, two basic techniques used for scheduling data transfers between the 6800 and its i/o devices will be discussed. They are *programmed i/o (polling)* and *interrupts*. You will see that programmed i/o is the simplest method and is adequate for most applications. However, where an i/o device requires immediate service (fast response), interrupts must be utilized. A complete discussion of all the 6800 interrupts is given later in this chapter. (See *6800 Interrupts*.)

You will then learn the three basics of interfacing: *three-state buffering, latching*, and *decoding*. We will not spend a great deal of time discussing digital-logic design techniques for accomplishing these three functions. This is because these functions can now be performed by using inexpensive *smart* peripheral interface chips, such as the 6821 peripheral interface adapter (PIA). These chips are so inexpensive that it would cost more in hardware to replace their functions with conventional digital-logic chips, let alone the time it would take to design a conventional circuit to achieve the same function. "*Smart*" means that the chips are programmable and, therefore, very flexible. They are very easy to use and they eliminate a lot of aggravation. A complete discussion of the PIA will be given in Chapters 8 and 9.

Finally, in this chapter, you will learn the function of each of the 40 pins on the 6800 chip. These functions can be divided into four main categories: *power, data, address*, and *control*. The first three categories are almost self-explanatory. However, you will want to pay particular attention to the functions of the various control pins since they play a very important part in interfacing.

OBJECTIVES

At the end of this chapter you will be able to do the following:

- Know what is required to make up a minimum 6800 microcomputer system configuration.
- Define what is meant by the term *interfacing* and the various techniques that can be utilized to accomplish interfacing.
- Understand how to use existing instructions to input and output data between the 6800 and its i/o devices.
- Explain what is meant by an *address map* and how it is used in microcomputer system design.
- Understand the power and clocking requirements of the 6800.
- Explain the three basics of interfacing and the function of each.
- Explain the difference between programmed i/o and interrupts.

- Understand how the 6800 handles the NMI, IRQ, SWI, and Reset interrupts.
- Know what is meant by a *vectored interrupt*.
- Explain the total significance of the WAI instruction.
- Explain the difference between full and partial decoding and how to accomplish each.
- Understand how to use the 7442 and 74154 decoder chips.
- Describe the function of each of the 40 pins on the 6800.

GENERAL I/O CONCEPTS

Fig. 6-1 represents a typical 6800 system configuration and, for that matter, a typical configuration used with most standard microprocessors. Note that there are three external buses to all of the external chips: the bidirectional data and control buses and the unidirectional address bus. The data bus is an 8-bit bus which connects to the 8 data pins of the MPU, representing data bits D0 through D7. The address bus is a 16-bit bus which connects to the 16 address pins of the 6800, representing address bits A0 through A15. The control lines are utilized to provide timing, synchronization, and supervision of data exchange between the 6800 and the external chips. Aside from the 6800, a typical system will consist of read/write memory (R/W), read-only memory (ROM), and a peripheral interface adapter (PIA). As mentioned earlier, R/W

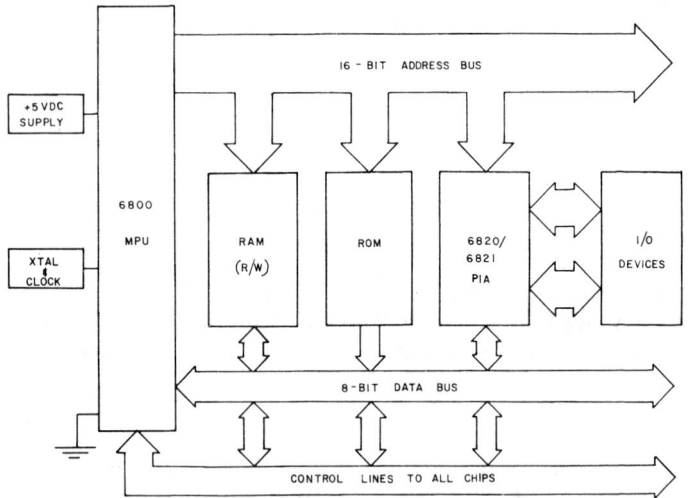

Fig. 6-1. 6800 microcomputer system configuration.

memory is used to temporarily store data and user programs and is *volatile*. This means that if power to the system is lost, any program or data information in R/W memory will also be lost. The ROM is used to store programs that are frequently called upon to perform various tasks. Actually, ROM is usually made up of a series of small frequently used subroutines. The ROM is *nonvolatile,* meaning that you will not lose its contents when power to the system is lost. However, by definition, we can only read information from ROM and it cannot be used for temporary program and data storage. The 6820/6821 PIA is a single chip which makes communication with the outside world much easier. We will see that it is a *smart* chip, meaning it can actually be programmed. The PIA can be thought of as a buffer and supervisor of data communication between the 6800 and i/o devices, such as switches, relays, LEDs, keyboards, etc. Finally, note that the 6800 requires an external clock and a 5-volt power supply. Two nonoverlapping clock signals ($\phi 1$ and $\phi 2$) must be provided. The requirements of these signals are shown in Fig. 6-2. There are three versions of the 6800 available—the 6800, the 68A00, and the 68B00. Each version requires a different clock frequency. This clock frequency is directly related to MPU speed; that is, the higher the clock frequency, the faster the MPU can execute instructions. The Motorola MC6875 two-phase clock generator can be used to supply the required clock signals for the 6800 series chips. All of the newer Motorola chips, such as the 6802, 6809, and 6801, have on-board clocks and only require an external crystal to determine the clock frequency. The power supply should be capable of supplying +5 volts dc at 1 watt maximum. In addition, the dc voltage should be relatively ripple free.

Fig. 6-1 represents the *minimum* requirements for an effective *microcomputer* system. These requirements include the 6800, power supply, clock, R/W memory, ROM, and PIA. Now that we have developed a microcomputer, we must *interface* it with the outside world in order for it to be useful. We can consider the outside world as being made up of i/o devices, such as switches, relays, keyboards, displays, etc. The microcomputer system must be capable of accepting data from some i/o device, processing the data, and then passing the results to the same or another i/o device. Therefore, the whole idea of interfacing translates to data communication between the microcomputer and its i/o devices. Data communication involves the microcomputer receiving data from an i/o device and the microcomputer sending data to the outside device. Data communication can be achieved in two ways. Some microprocessors, such as the Intel 8080 and 8085, have special input and output in-

ELECTRICAL CHARACTERISTICS (V_{CC} = 5.0 V ± 5%, V_{SS} = 0, T_A = 0 to 70°C unless otherwise noted.)

Characteristic		Symbol	Min	Typ	Max	Unit
Input High Voltage	Logic	V_{IH}	V_{SS} + 2.0	—	V_{CC}	Vdc
	$\phi 1, \phi 2$	V_{IHC}	V_{CC} − 0.3	—	V_{CC} + 0.1	
Input Low Voltage	Logic	V_{IL}	V_{SS} − 0.3	—	V_{SS} + 0.8	Vdc
	$\phi 1, \phi 2$	V_{ILC}	V_{SS} − 0.1	—	V_{SS} + 0.3	
Clock Overshoot/Undershoot — Input High Level		V_{OS}	V_{CC} − 0.5	—	V_{CC} + 0.5	Vdc
— Input Low Level			V_{SS} − 0.5	—	V_{SS} + 0.5	
Input Leakage Current		I_{in}				µAdc
(V_{in} = 0 to 5.25 V, V_{CC} = max)	Logic*		—	1.0	2.5	
(V_{in} = 0 to 5.25 V, V_{CC} = 0.0 V)	$\phi 1, \phi 2$		—	—	100	
Frequency of Operation		f	0.1	—	1.0	MHz
Clock Timing (Figure 1)						
Cycle Time		t_{cyc}	1.0	—	10	µs
Clock Pulse Width		$PW_{\phi H}$				ns
(Measured at V_{CC} − 0.3 V)	$\phi 1$		430	—	4500	
	$\phi 2$		450	—	4500	
Total $\phi 1$ and $\phi 2$ Up Time		t_{ut}	940	—	—	ns
Rise and Fall Times	$\phi 1, \phi 2$	$t_{\phi r}, t_{\phi f}$	5.0	—	50	ns
(Measured between V_{SS} + 0.3 V and V_{CC} − 0.3 V)						
Delay Time or Clock Separation		t_d	0	—	9100	ns
(Measured at V_{OV} = V_{SS} + 0.5 V)						
Overshoot Duration		t_{OS}	0	—	40	ns

*Except $\overline{IRQ}$ and $\overline{NMI}$, which require 3 kΩ pullup load resistors for wire-OR capability at optimum operation.
#Capacitances are periodically sampled rather than 100% tested.

CLOCK TIMING WAVEFORM

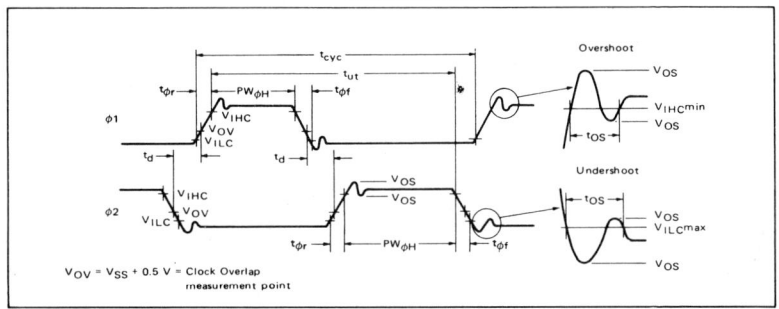

Courtesy Motorola Semiconductor Products Inc.

Fig. 6-2. 6800 clock specifications.

structions that cause data to be transmitted and received via some internal register, usually the accumulator. When these instructions are executed, an i/o device addressing byte must be put onto the address bus to select a particular i/o device.

Another way to communicate with i/o devices is to treat each device as a separate "memory" location or a series of memory locations. This is referred to as *memory-mapped i/o* and it is the way that the 6800 operates. With memory-mapped i/o, no special i/o instructions are needed. To send data out to an i/o device, you simply execute a store-accumulator (STA) instruction and to receive data from some i/o device you execute a load-accumulator (LDA) instruction. This reduces program complexity and makes for a much more efficient operation. Since each device is treated as a memory location, each device must be assigned an address. Therefore, referring back to the typical 6800 system in Fig. 6-1, you must assign addresses to R/W memory, ROM, and the i/o devices (PIA). The available addresses must be *mapped* or assigned according to the external system requirements. In 6800-based systems, you have 65,536 (64K) valid addresses that can be assigned or divided between R/W memory, ROM, and the i/o devices. Fig. 6-3 shows an

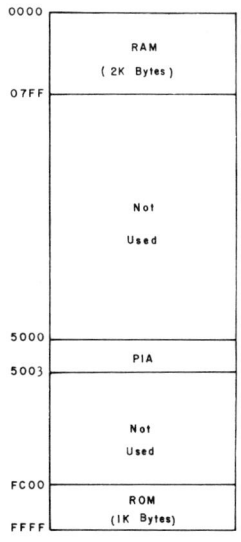

Fig. 6-3. Memory address map for a typical 6800 system.

address map for a typical 6800 system. Notice that R/W memory is assigned to the lower memory addresses (0000–07FF) and ROM to the higher memory addresses (FC00–FFFF), given 2K of R/W memory and 1K of ROM. The i/o devices, represented by the PIA, are assigned addresses 5000 through 5003. If more R/W memory, ROM, or i/o is required, you would need to use more of the available addresses. However, for most small applications, very few of the 64K available addresses are utilized. When a device address is put on the address bus, the particular device must recognize its address. To do this, each i/o device or group of devices will have an associated address-decoder circuit.

Fig. 6-4 represents the simplest type of input device, the switch. Here, four switches are being used to feed four bits of binary data into the 6800 system. The switches are connected to the +5-volt dc supply through *pull-up* resistors. An open switch will cause a logic one to be present while a depressed switch will cause a logic zero to be present. Note that the switches are driving *three-state buffers*. These buffers will pass information from their input to output only when they are enabled. This type of buffering is required to effectively isolate the switches from the data bus when they are not being addressed. When the buffers are not enabled, they repre-

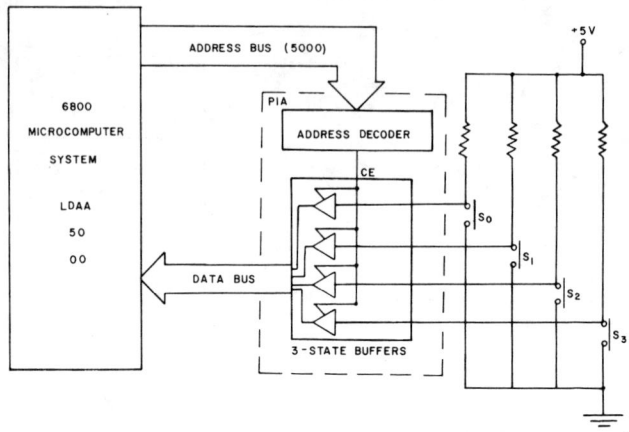

Fig. 6-4. Switches used as data input devices.

sent an infinite impedance (off state) between the data bus and switches. Three-state buffering is a *must* when working with bus systems. The *address decoder* is connected directly to the enabling line of the buffers. When the decoder recognizes the proper address on the address bus, it will enable the three-state buffers such that the switch data is passed to the 6800 via the data bus. In Fig. 6-4 the switches are assigned address 5000. When the LDAA 5000 instruction is executed, the switch data will be loaded into accumulator A.

Fig. 6-5 shows the simplest type of output device, the light. In this case the lights are light-emitting diodes (LEDs). The LEDs are connected in a common-anode configuration. A "0" output from the latch will forward bias the diode and cause an LED to illuminate, while a "1" will reverse-bias the diode and provide *no* illumination. In Fig. 6-5 the LEDs are assigned address 5002. When this address appears on the address bus, the decoder will enable the 4-bit latch. Simultaneously, the 6800 places the accumulator data on the data bus and the latch will then store the data bus information. The latch is required since the data is only present on the data bus for a very short period of time (less than one microsecond). However, once we store the data in the latch, it appears at the latch output and, hence, at the LEDs until it is desired to output new information. In this example, when the STAA 5002 instruction is executed, accumulator A information will be passed to the LEDs. In both of these examples, we were only utilizing four bits of the 8-bit data bus.

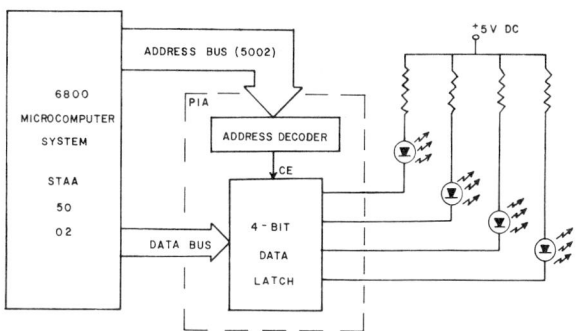

Fig. 6-5. LEDs used for data output.

We will see shortly that the PIA can perform all of the address decoding, three-state buffering, and latching for most i/o applications.

DECODING

In Figs. 6-4 and 6-5 you saw the use of an address decoder. Recall that the address decoder was necessary to recognize the proper address from the address bus and then to enable the i/o circuitry for data transfer. The i/o devices must be assigned an address or, in the case of memory, a group of addresses. An address decoder can be a series of logic gates configured to recognize a particular address or it can be a decoding chip that makes the logic design less complicated.

Suppose, as in Fig. 6-4, our i/o device is assigned address 5000. Our decoder circuit must be capable of detecting this address and then enabling the three-state buffers. A typical logic circuit that could perform this function is shown in Fig. 6-6. The decoding chart at the bottom of Fig. 6-6 indicates the necessary address bit status for address 5000. Note that we are decoding *all* of the address lines such that the *only* address that will cause a chip enable is the address 5000. When all of the address lines are decoded, we say the address is *fully decoded.*

Another way to decode the same address is shown in Fig. 6-7. Here we are only decoding part of the address bus. This type of decoding is referred to as *partial decoding.* In this example we are

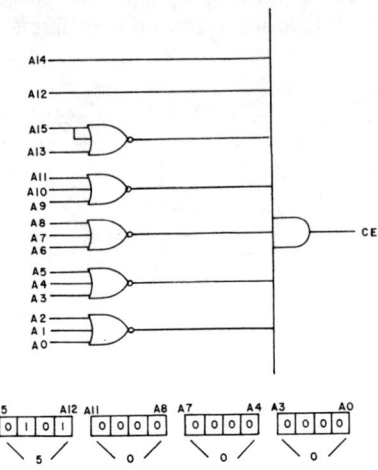

Fig. 6-6. Full decoding circuit for address 5000.

only decoding the upper eight bits of the address bus. The advantage of this decoding method is that fewer logic gates are required. However, the disadvantage is that any address from 5000 through 50FF will cause an enable condition. This is the price we must pay to reduce the hardware required. Since we usually have many addresses available to use (2^{16}=64K), it probably will not pose a problem to allocate addresses 5000 through 50FF to one i/o

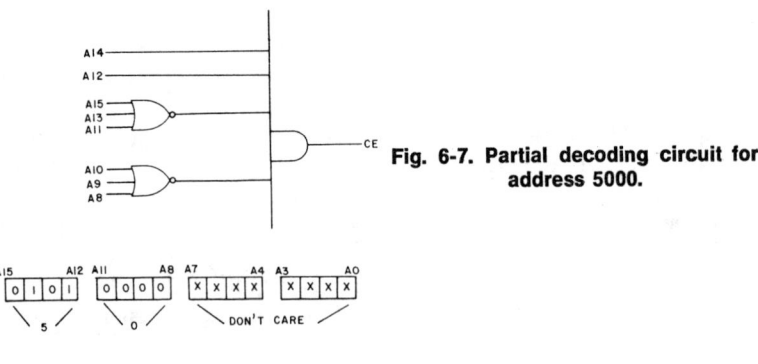

Fig. 6-7. Partial decoding circuit for address 5000.

device. In Fig. 6-7, we show the lower half of the decoding chart filled with Xs, indicating a *don't-care* state, either logic 1 or logic 0.

Another way to provide decoding is through decoding chips. We will discuss two decoders that are commonly used in microcomputer interfacing. A 7442 decoder is shown in Fig. 6-8, along with its input/output truth table. This is a 16-pin chip of which 10 pins are output. The outputs are lines 0 through 9 shown inside the block while the input lines are A, B, C, and D. The numbers on each line represent the respective chip pin number. This type of decoder is referred to as a 1-of-10 *decoder* since only one of the output lines is at a logic 0 state for any binary representation of decimals

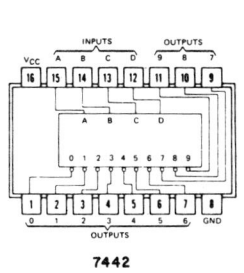 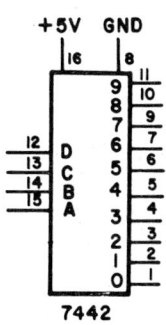

The truth table for the chip is as follows:

Inputs				Outputs									
D	C	B	A	0	1	2	3	4	5	6	7	8	9
0	0	0	0	0	1	1	1	1	1	1	1	1	1
0	0	0	1	1	0	1	1	1	1	1	1	1	1
0	0	1	0	1	1	0	1	1	1	1	1	1	1
0	0	1	1	1	1	1	0	1	1	1	1	1	1
0	1	0	0	1	1	1	1	0	1	1	1	1	1
0	1	0	1	1	1	1	1	1	0	1	1	1	1
0	1	1	0	1	1	1	1	1	1	0	1	1	1
0	1	1	1	1	1	1	1	1	1	1	0	1	1
1	0	0	0	1	1	1	1	1	1	1	1	0	1
1	0	0	1	1	1	1	1	1	1	1	1	1	0
1	0	1	0	1	1	1	1	1	1	1	1	1	1
1	0	1	1	1	1	1	1	1	1	1	1	1	1
1	1	0	0	1	1	1	1	1	1	1	1	1	1
1	1	0	1	1	1	1	1	1	1	1	1	1	1
1	1	1	0	1	1	1	1	1	1	1	1	1	1
1	1	1	1	1	1	1	1	1	1	1	1	1	1

Courtesy E&L Instruments, Inc.

Fig. 6-8. 7442 decoder with truth table.

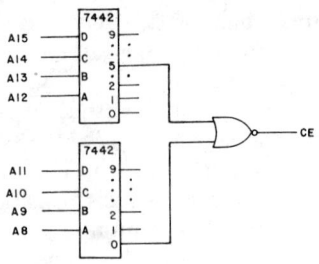

Fig. 6-9. Using the 7442 to partially decode address 5000.

```
 A15      A12 A11      A8 A7        A4 A3        A0
[0|1|0|1] [0|0|0|0]  [x|x|x|x]   [x|x|x|x]
```

0 through 9 on the input. We may also refer to the 7442 as a *bcd-to-decimal decoder* since, with a bcd combination at the input, you get a logic 0 state on the corresponding decimal output line. Fig. 6-9 shows how we might use the 7442 to partially decode the address 5000. Note that we only need to use one output line from each 7442. In this case, we use lines 5 and 0 which correspond to the high byte of the address being decoded. We could use these same two chips to decode another address and utilize different output lines to provide decoding for another i/o device.

A 74154 decoder with its truth table is shown in Fig. 6-10. This is a *1-of-16 decoder* which will convert a 4-bit binary input word to a logic 0 state at *one* of the output lines among 16 possible lines. Note that the 74154 is a 24-pin chip with 4 input lines (A, B, C, D), 16 output lines (0–15), and 2 enable lines (G1, G2). Both G1 and G2 must be at a logic 0 state for the chip to be enabled. Fig. 6-11 shows how we might use the 74154 to partially decode address 5000. Here we are using the enabling lines (G1, G2) to provide more complete decoding. With this circuit, addresses 5000 through 500F will cause a chip enable where in the 7442 circuit (Fig. 6-9) addresses 5000 through 50FF would enable the i/o device. Thus, the 74154 circuit provides more complete decoding.

I/O TECHNIQUES

There are two main i/o techniques that can be utilized with a 6800 system. They are *polling* and *interrupts*.

Polling

Polling is also referred to as *programmed i/o*. It is the simplest type of i/o and is normally used for small, dedicated applications.

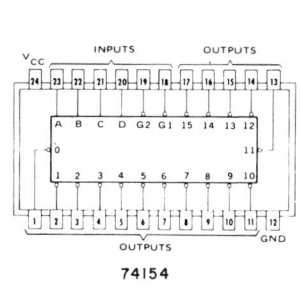
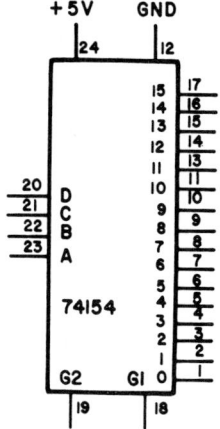

	Inputs					Outputs															
G1	G2	D	C	B	A	0	1	2	3	4	5	6	7	8	9	10	11	12	13	14	15
0	0	0	0	0	0	0	1	1	1	1	1	1	1	1	1	1	1	1	1	1	1
0	0	0	0	0	1	1	0	1	1	1	1	1	1	1	1	1	1	1	1	1	1
0	0	0	0	1	0	1	1	0	1	1	1	1	1	1	1	1	1	1	1	1	1
0	0	0	0	1	1	1	1	1	0	1	1	1	1	1	1	1	1	1	1	1	1
0	0	0	1	0	0	1	1	1	1	0	1	1	1	1	1	1	1	1	1	1	1
0	0	0	1	0	1	1	1	1	1	1	0	1	1	1	1	1	1	1	1	1	1
0	0	0	1	1	0	1	1	1	1	1	1	0	1	1	1	1	1	1	1	1	1
0	0	0	1	1	1	1	1	1	1	1	1	1	0	1	1	1	1	1	1	1	1
0	0	1	0	0	0	1	1	1	1	1	1	1	1	0	1	1	1	1	1	1	1
0	0	1	0	0	1	1	1	1	1	1	1	1	1	1	0	1	1	1	1	1	1
0	0	1	0	1	0	1	1	1	1	1	1	1	1	1	1	0	1	1	1	1	1
0	0	1	0	1	1	1	1	1	1	1	1	1	1	1	1	1	0	1	1	1	1
0	0	1	1	0	0	1	1	1	1	1	1	1	1	1	1	1	1	0	1	1	1
0	0	1	1	0	1	1	1	1	1	1	1	1	1	1	1	1	1	1	0	1	1
0	0	1	1	1	0	1	1	1	1	1	1	1	1	1	1	1	1	1	1	0	1
0	0	1	1	1	1	1	1	1	1	1	1	1	1	1	1	1	1	1	1	1	0
0	1	X	X	X	X	1	1	1	1	1	1	1	1	1	1	1	1	1	1	1	1
1	0	X	X	X	X	1	1	1	1	1	1	1	1	1	1	1	1	1	1	1	1
1	1	X	X	X	X	1	1	1	1	1	1	1	1	1	1	1	1	1	1	1	1

Courtesy E&L Instruments, Inc.

Fig. 6-10. 74154 decoder with truth table.

The idea here is that the 6800 will periodically ask each i/o device if it needs to be serviced. If a need for service is indicated, the 6800 will enter into a service routine for that device. If no service is needed, the 6800 will *poll* the next device, and so on. With this scheme, each device must be *polled* for any input or output transfer of data several times a second. This requires a program called a *polling loop*. The method of asking an i/o device if it needs to be serviced and then responding accordingly is also referred to as *handshaking*. Usually, when a device is polled, a *flag* is tested on the device. If the flag test is positive, a service routine will be initiated.

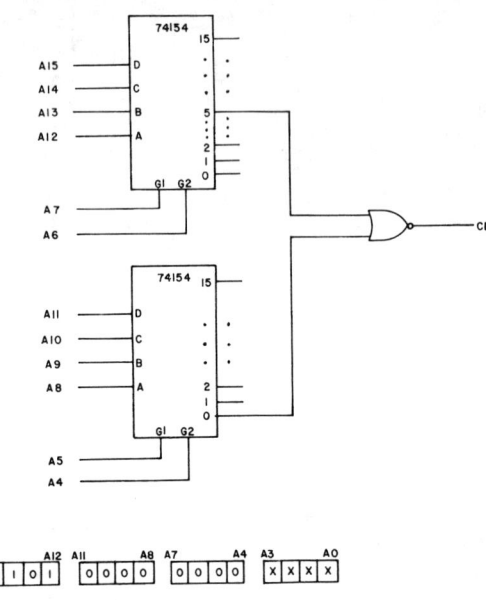

Fig. 6-11. Using the 74154 to partially decode address 5000.

An even simpler method of programmed i/o would be to repeatedly read data in from input devices and write data out to output devices, regardless of whether or not service is needed. In Figs. 6-4 and 6-5, this would require a program loop that continually inputs data from the switches and outputs it to the LEDs.

The advantages of programmed i/o are that it requires minimal interfacing hardware and only a few control lines. Also, you know exactly when each i/o device is being serviced and how long each service routine will take. You can schedule your i/o operations and nothing will interfere with that schedule. Therefore, we say that programmed i/o is *synchronous* or synchronized with program execution.

The greatest disadvantages of programmed i/o are that it requires extensive software in the form of polling loops and it wastes time since the 6800 cannot perform other tasks if it is to check the various devices on a regular basis. Also, as the number of i/o devices increases, the loop gets larger and the time period between polling increases. In this case, the 6800 could miss an event such as a momentary switch closure.

Interrupts

Interrupts are used when the system becomes more sophisticated and the microprocessor's time is critical. They are also used when fast response times are required by the i/o devices. When the interrupt technique is used, the i/o device has the responsibility of notifying the 6800 of its desire to be serviced. When the 6800 is interrupted, it must break away from its current operation and service the interrupt. After the interrupt has been serviced, the 6800 will return to the original operation at the point that it was interrupted and it will continue with this task until it is interrupted again. Interrupts fall into two main categories: the *maskable* and the *nonmaskable* interrupt. The 6800 has the option of accepting or ignoring the maskable interrupt, while it has no choice but to accept a nonmaskable interrupt. Once an interrupt has been accepted, the 6800 must determine which i/o device generated the interrupt. If several i/o devices generate interrupts simultaneously, they must be assigned a priority since only one device can be serviced at a time. The assignment of the priorities may be difficult and it usually requires extra hardware and software.

Interrupts are analogous to a situation you have probably experienced—your supervisor talking with you in his office. While talking, his phone rings, representing an interruption. He answers the phone (servicing the interrupter), then continues his discussion with you—hopefully where he left off. If more than one call comes in at once, he must decide on which one to service first, second, and so on before getting back to you—if he ever does. However, before your talk begins, he could tell his sceretary to "hold all calls" (maskable interrupt) until he completes his discussion with you.

If we are to apply this analogy to programmed i/o, your supervisor would not have a bell on his telephone and he would periodically have to pick up the phone to see if anyone is on the other end requesting service.

The advantage of interrupts is that they provide fast response times for i/o devices. The disadvantages are that extra hardware and software are needed, especially if interrrupts are to be assigned priorities. Also, interrupts are *asynchronous* when compared to the execution of a program, meaning that they are not scheduled. You do not know exactly when they will take place or how much time the servicing might require.

In most small dedicated applications it is advantageous to stay away from interrupts. Instead, polled i/o should be used as frequently as possible to solve interfacing tasks.

6800 INTERRUPTS

There are four different types of interrupts utilized by the 6800. They are:

Reset
Nonmaskable Interrupt (NMI)
Interrupt Request (IRQ)
Software Interrupt (SWI)

Each one of these interrupts is a *vectored interrupt*. Recall from the previous section that when an interrupt occurs, the 6800 must break away from its main program routine and branch to a service routine. Therefore, a service-routine address must be supplied for each interrupt. This address is called an *interrupt vector* since it points to the address of the service routine for the interrupt. Each of the 6800 interrupts has a specific location in memory where the 6800 looks for these vectors. The 6800 interrupt vector address map is shown in Fig. 6-12. As shown in Fig. 6-12, the last eight memory addresses in the 64K memory space are assigned to these vectors.

In a typical 6800 system we will usually assign ROM to these high memory addresses. Therefore, the vectors will occupy the last eight bytes of ROM. When an interrupt occurs, the 6800 will automatically look to these memory addresses for the proper service routine vector. The reset, NMI, and IRQ interrupts are referred to as *hardware interrupts* since there are actual pins on the 6800 chip whereby an external device can initiate the interrupt. The SWI is a

MEMORY ADDRESS	MEMORY CONTENTS
FFF8	IRQ - HI ADDR
FFF9	IRQ - LO ADDR
FFFA	SWI - HI ADDR
FFFB	SWI - LO ADDR
FFFC	NMI - HI ADDR
FFFD	NMI - LO ADDR
FFFE	RESET - HI ADDR
FFFF	RESET - LO ADDR

Fig. 6-12. 6800 interrupt vector address map.

software interrupt since it is caused by a program instruction. Now, we will discuss each of the different types of 6800 interrupts in detail.

Reset

The *reset* interrupt is a nonmaskable interrupt and is normally used to initialize or restart the system. It provides a starting point for program execution by placing the address of the first instruction to be executed in the program counter. A reset subroutine, located in ROM, will normally be required to initialize the system. Therefore, the reset vector which is located in ROM addresses FFFE and

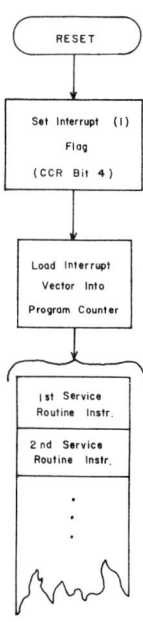

Fig. 6-13. Program flow for reset interrupt.

FFFF will direct the 6800 to the beginning of the reset subroutine. Fig. 6-13 shows the sequence of events that takes place when the reset interrupt is encountered. Note that the first thing to happen is that the interrupt (I) flag is set in the condition code register. This will prevent any maskable interrupts from taking place during the reset operation. The 6800 then goes to addresses FFFE and FFFF to obtain the reset interrupt vector. This vector is loaded into the program counter and the service routine for the reset interrupt is then executed. After this subroutine or subprogram has been executed, it branches to the main program that is started to control the operation of the computer/interface system.

Nonmaskable Interrupt (NMI)

As the name implies, this is a nonmaskable interrupt and it will take place regardless of any other 6800 operation except reset. Fig. 6-14 shows the sequence of events for this interrupt. Note that there are two main differences between this and the reset interrupt. The first difference is that the present instruction that the 6800 is executing is completed before the interrupt actually takes effect. The second, and most important, difference is that the contents of the internal registers are saved in a memory stack. Prior to the start of the interrupt service routine, the program counter, index register, accumulator A, accumulator B, and the condition code register are pushed onto the stack in that specific order. The stack will be located at whatever memory location the stack pointer specifies at the time the interrupt occurs. Of course, the stack pointer must have been set to point to a stack area in R/W memory prior to the use of any interrupts.

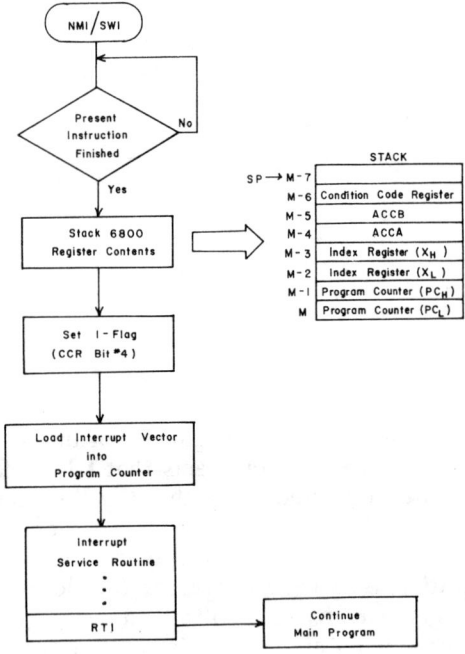

Fig. 6-14. Sequence of events for nonmaskable interrupt (NMI).

Note that after this operation occurs, the sequence of events is the same as for the reset interrupt. That is, the I flag is set, the NMI interrupt vector located at locations FFFC and FFFD is loaded into the program counter, and the nonmaskable interrupt service routine is executed. Once the interrupt service routine has been completed, execution must be directed back to the main program. This is done by using a return-from-interrupt instruction (RTI, op code 3B) as the last instruction in the interrupt service routine. The RTI returns the 6800 to its previous status by pulling the old register contents from the stack. It is very similar to the RTS instruction. Pushing and pulling this information to and from the stack tables takes place automatically when a nonmaskable interrupt occurs and when the RTI instruction is executed.

When a reset interrupt took place, the internal register contents did not need to be saved in a stack since the reset input is used to restart or initialize the system. Since the system is being restarted, we also have no need for the RTI instruction at the end of the service routine for the reset interrupt.

Nonmaskable interrupts can be used for emergency situations. For example, nonmaskable interrupts might be used for limit switches on machine tools, fire alarms, security alarms, or any situation where the main program *must* be interrupted.

Interrupt Request (IRQ)

The IRQ is a maskable interrupt. Refer to Fig. 6-15 for the IRQ sequence of events. You may *mask out* the IRQ with the I flag in the condition code register (CCR). If the I flag is set (logic 1) when the request is made, the interrupt will be ignored. If the I flag is cleared (logic 0), the interrupt will be accepted. Except for this condition, the IRQ sequence of events is the same as for nonmaskable interrupt. Once the interrupt has been accepted, the internal register contents are saved on the stack, the I flag is set, the IRQ interrupt vector located at locations FFF8 and FFF9 is loaded into the program counter, and the interrupt service routine is executed. Again, you must use the RTI instruction at the end of your interrupt service routine to get back to the main program. Why should a maskable interrupt set the I flag status to a logic 1 condition? Because this action prevents other maskable interrupts from interrupting while the first interrupt is being serviced. However, you could clear the I flag at the beginning of your service routine to allow other maskable interrupts to interrupt. If not, the I flag will be cleared when the return from interrupt is executed. When the maskable interrupt is used, you can protect critical parts

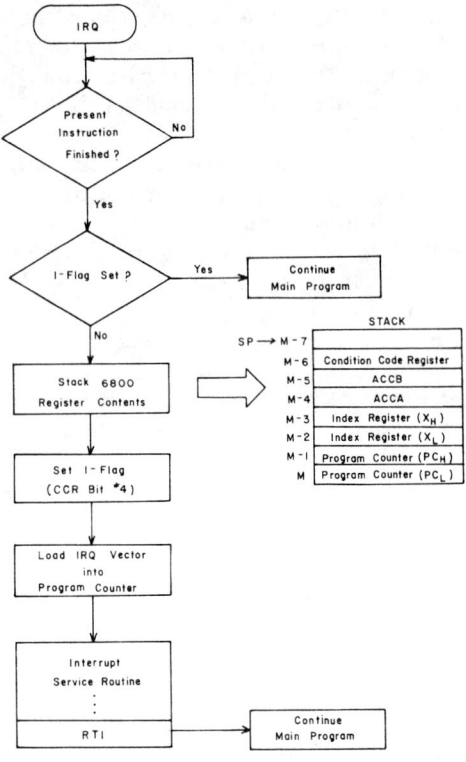

Fig. 6-15. Sequence of events for interrupt request (IRQ).

of the main program from being interrupted except for emergency situations.

At the beginning of a critical main program section, you can set the I flag with the SEI (0F) instruction, and at the end of this section you can clear the I flag with the CLI (0E) instruction. Then, during this portion of the program the 6800 will ignore all maskable interrupt requests (IRQs). However, the 6800 could be interrupted if an emergency condition exists in the form of a nonmaskable interrupt (NMI).

Software Interrupt (SWI)

A software interrupt is one which is caused by the execution of a special instruction. In the 6800 a software interrupt is caused by the SWI instruction (op code 3F). It is an inherent instruction, and when encountered in the program, it causes a nonmaskable interrupt to occur. The sequence of events for the SWI are identical to the NMI (refer to Fig. 6-14). The software interrupt vector is located at memory locations FFFA and FFFB. Once the service routine is finished, the RTI instruction must be utilized to get back to the main program. Software interrupts are normally used to simulate a hardware interrupt during system design and can also be used to insert pauses into a program. The Heath ET3400 trainer uses this interrupt to perform the single-step function.

Wait for Interrupt (WAI)

Up to this point, the WAI (3E) instruction has been used at the end of programs to cause the 6800 to stop or halt its execution. Although it does cause the 6800 to halt, it takes on much more significance. The WAI instruction also puts the 6800 in a *wait-for-interrupt* state. The sequence of events associated with the wait instruction is shown in Fig. 6-16. When the 6800 encounters the

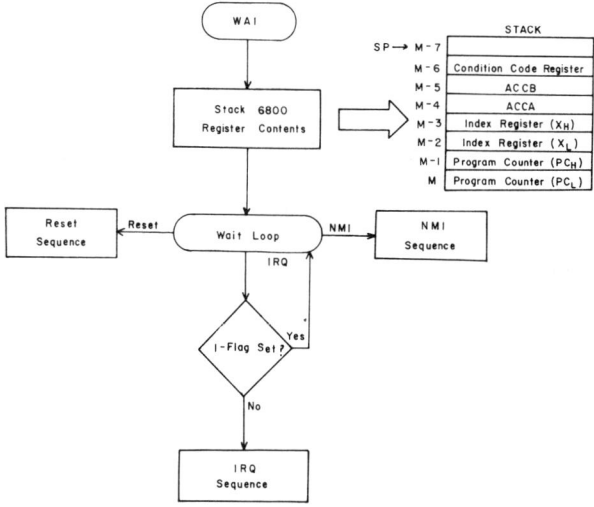

Fig. 6-16. Wait for interrupt (WAI) sequence of events.

WAI instruction, it immediately pushes the internal register contents onto the stack and then enters a *wait loop*. The wait loop may be broken only by any of three interrupts—reset, NMI, or IRQ. Note that the I flag in the condition code register must be cleared to allow the IRQ to break the wait loop. Once the loop is broken by one of the three preceding interrupts, the respective interrupt sequence is initiated.

6800 PIN ASSIGNMENTS

The 6800 pin assignments, sometimes referred to as "pinouts," are shown in Fig. 6-17, with the direction of signal flow for each pin shown by the arrows. Note that the 6800 is a 40-pin dual in-line package (DIP) integrated circuit. The following is a brief description of each pin function. A more complete description of the pin functions will follow as more interfacing is discussed.

Ground (Pins 1 and 21)

These pins must be connected to the power supply ground.

$\overline{\text{HALT}}$ (Pin 2)

This pin provides for a hardware halt of the 6800 operation. When you supply a logic zero (0) state to this pin, all activity in the 6800 will be halted. When this happens, the three-state buffers of the data and address lines will go into their high-impedance state and effectively disconnect the 6800 from the external data and address buses. This function is normally used for hardware troubleshooting and program debugging since it allows an external device to control program execution one step at a time. You will normally have this pin connected to the +5-volt dc supply for uninterrupted system operation.

Clocks (ϕ1, ϕ2: Pins 3 and 37)

These two pins are used to provide the 6800 with a two-phase nonoverlapping clock as discussed in the first part of this chapter. The ϕ1 clock is used for internal 6800 timing while the ϕ2 clock is used to synchronize data communication between the 6800 and its external chips.

Interrupt Request ($\overline{\text{IRQ}}$: pin 4)

Interrupt request (IRQ), as discussed earlier, is a hardware interrupt controlled by an external device. The sequence of events shown in Fig. 6-15 will be initiated when pin 4 goes from a high (1) to low (0) state.

Valid Memory Address (VMA: Pin 5)

The Valid Memory Address (VMA) pin is an output control line. It will go to a logical 1 state when the 6800 places a valid address on the address bus. This is necessary because an improper address can occasionally appear on the bus. The VMA line should be part of any address-decoding scheme such that all i/o devices

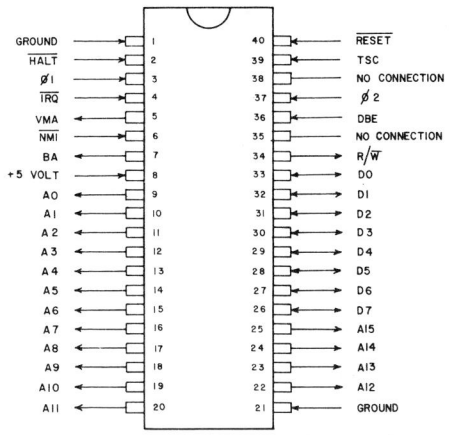

Fig. 6-17. 6800 pin assignments.

will be disabled if it is at a logic 0 state, indicating an address which is not valid. One standard TTL load may be directly driven by this pin.

Nonmaskable Interrupt (NMI: Pin 6)

Nonmaskable interrupt (NMI), as discussed earlier, is a hardware interrupt controlled by an external device. The sequence of events shown in Fig. 6-14 will be initiated when pin 6 goes from a high (1) to low (0) state.

Bus Available (BA: Pin 7)

BA stands for *Bus Available*. It is an output control pin used to tell external devices that the 6800 has stopped executing instructions for one of two reasons. Either a WAI instruction has been encountered or the HALT input has changed to a logic 0 state. When either of the above take place, the BA pin will go to a logic 1 state. At the same time, the 6800 disables the three-state buffers for the data and address buses, thereby effectively isolating itself from these buses. When this happens, an external device may take command of the address and data bus and gain access to R/W memory or ROM to provide *direct memory access* (DMA) to the external device.

+5-Volt Power (Pin 8)

Pin 8 is connected to the +5-volt dc power supply.

Address (A0–A15: Pins 9–20 and 22–25)

These pins provide the external-address-bus address lines A0 through A15. Recall that the address bus is unidirectional (one way) from the 6800 to external devices. Therefore, these pins are output only from the 6800 to external chips. They are three-state buffered and each is capable of driving one TTL load.

Data (D0–D7: Pins 26–33)

Pins 26 through 33 provide the external data bus lines D7 to D0. They are bidirectional and have three-state output buffers capable of driving one TTL load.

Read/Write (R/$\overline{\text{W}}$: Pin 34)

This is an output control line which tells i/o devices that the MPU is in either a *read* or *write* mode. A logic 1 on this line indicates that the 6800 is performing a read operation while a logic 0 indicates a write operation. It is three-state buffered and it is capable of driving one standard TTL load. This line will be disabled when the processor is halted due to a WAI or $\overline{\text{HALT}}$ function. It may also be enabled or disabled by the TSC line (pin 39) to be discussed shortly.

Data Bus Enable (DBE: Pin 36)

This is an input signal that will enable and disable the three-state data bus buffers. A logic 1 will enable the data lines while a logic 0 will effectively disconnect the data lines from the external data bus. All data transfers between the 6800 and external i/o devices must take place when the $\phi 2$ clock is high; therefore, the DBE line is often directly connected to the $\phi 2$ clock line.

Three-State Control (TSC: Pin 39)

The TSC line is an input control line that can be used by an external device to gain control of the address bus to provide direct memory access (DMA). This will allow an external device to gain direct access to memory without going through the 6800. When the TSC line goes high, all the address lines and the R/$\overline{\text{W}}$ line will go into their off or high-impedance state. The data lines are not affected since they have their own three-state control line (DBE). The TSC line should be brought to a logic 1 state when $\phi 1$ clock is high. It then requires the $\phi 1$ clock to be *held* at a high state and clock $\phi 2$ to be held at a low state for this function to operate properly. The address bus will then be available for other devices to access memory directly. The 6800 can only be held in this state for 4.5 microseconds or internal register data will be lost. Since DMA is seldom required for small applications, you may connect the TSC line to ground permanently.

RESET (Pin 40)

The reset function, as discussed earlier, is a hardware interrupt. The system will restart or be reinitiated when pin 40 goes from a high (1) to a low (0) state (refer to Fig. 6-13).

Finally, note that pins 35 and 38 are not used and that no connection should be made to these pins.

REVIEW QUESTIONS

1. A minimum workable 6800 system would consist of what major functional parts?

2. The three external buses required for a 6800 system are the _____, _____, and _____.

3. What three functions are necessary for i/o device interfacing?

4. PIA stands for _____.
5. ϕ_2 clock is normally used where?

6. What is meant by the term "memory-mapped i/o"?

7. A _____ instruction would be used to send data to an i/o device.
8. What is a "memory address map"?

9. Explain the difference between programmed i/o and interrupts.

10. When would the use of interrupts be justified?

11. "Handshaking" is synonymous with _____.
12. State an advantage and a disadvantage of programmed i/o.

13. The two main categories of interrupts are _____ and _____.

14. Interrupts are _____ with program execution.
15. The four interrupts utilized by the 6800 are the _____, _____, _____, and _____.
16. What is an interrupt vector?

17. In what order are the internal 6800 registers pushed onto the stack during an interrupt?

18. The RTI instruction must be used with which interrupts?

19. The _____ instruction will set the interrupt mask bit.
20. What does the WAI instruction do?

21. State the differences between partial and full decoding.

22. What is the disadvantage of partial decoding.

23. Two chips that are utilized in microcomputer systems for decoding are the _____ and _____.
24. What does the VMA pin do and how should it be utilized?

25. Explain the function of the R/$\overline{W}$ pin.

ANSWERS

1. +5-volt dc power supply (Vcc)
   1–2-MHz two-phase nonoverlapping clock ($\phi 1$ & $\phi 2$)
   6800 Microprocessor Chip
   RAM
   ROM
   PIA

2. address, data, and control

3. Decoding, latching, and three-state buffering.

4. peripheral interface adapter

5. To synchronize data communication between the 6800 and its external chips.
6. Each i/o device or group of devices is treated as a memory location or group of memory locations.
7. store accumulator
8. A chart showing address assignments to RAM, ROM, and i/o devices.
9. With programmed i/o, the 6800 polls or contacts the i/o devices to provide them service. With interrupts, the i/o devices independently request service from the 6800 when needed.
10. When fast i/o response times are required.
11. polling, but can also be provided by using interrupts.
12. Advantages:
    Minimum interfacing hardware.
    Minimum control lines.
    Synchronous with program execution.
    Disadvantages:
    Wastes computer time.
    Momentary events could be missed.
13. maskable and nonmaskable
14. asynchronous
15. reset, NMI, IRQ, and SWI
16. An address which points to the beginning of an interrupt service routine.
17. Program counter, index register, ACCA, ACCB, condition code register.
18. NMI, IRQ, and SWI.
19. set interrupt mask (SEI: op code 0F)
20. The WAI instruction halts program execution, places the internal 6800 register contents in a memory stack, and then remains in a wait loop until broken with a reset, NMI, or IRQ interrupt.
21. Full decoding decodes all 16 address lines while partial decoding only decodes part of the address lines.
22. More than one address may enable an i/o device.
23. 7442 and 74154
24. VMA stands for *valid memory address* and goes high when the 6800 places a valid address on the address bus. It should be used in all decoding schemes so that the i/o devices will not be enabled for invalid addresses.
25. R/W stands for read/write. This pin goes high (1) when the 6800 is in the read mode and goes low (0) when it is in the write mode. It is used to tell the external chips what the 6800 is doing and should be part of i/o decoding schemes.

EXPERIMENT 6-1

Purpose
To verify the 74154 truth table and demonstrate its operation.

Equipment
ET3400   74154 decoder

Schematic Diagram (Fig. 6-18)

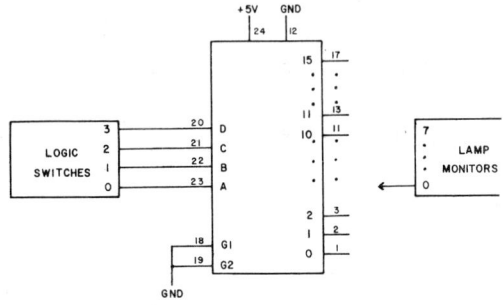

Fig. 6-18. Schematic diagram for Experiment 6-1.

Procedure

```
ET3400
```

Step 1
Construct the circuit in Fig. 6-18 on the breadboard block using 4 logic switches and 1 lamp monitor. The 4 logic switches will be used as inputs and the lamp monitor will be used to test each of the 16 output lines.

Step 2
Set the 4 logic switches to 0000 and then test output line zero (pin 1) with the lamp monitor. The lamp should not light, indicating a logic zero (0) state. Test each of the other 15 lines and observe that they all cause the lamp to light, indicating a logic one (1) state.

Step 3
Set the 4 logic switches such that DCBA (pins 20, 21, 22, 23) equals 0001. Which output line is at logic zero?

We conclude that output line No. 1 is at logic zero and all the remaining lines are at a logic 1 state.

Step 4

Complete the following truth table.

Inputs DCBA	Outputs 0 1 2 3 4 5 6 7 8 9 10 11 12 13 14 15
0 0 0 0	0 1 1 1 1 1 1 1 1 1 1 1 1 1 1 1
0 0 0 1	1 0 1 1 1 1 1 1 1 1 1 1 1 1 1 1
0 0 1 0	
0 0 1 1	
0 1 0 0	
0 1 0 1	
0 1 1 0	
0 1 1 1	
1 0 0 0	
1 0 0 1	
1 0 1 0	
1 0 1 1	
1 1 0 0	
1 1 0 1	
1 1 1 0	
1 1 1 1	

Conclusions

Where could the 74154 be used in a microcomputer system?

How many 74154 decoders would be required to decode at least half of the 6800 address lines?

EXPERIMENT 6-2

Purpose

To provide partial decoding of the 6800 address bus using 74154 decoders. To demonstrate data latching using a 7475 latch.

Equipment

ET3400
Two 74154 decoders
7427 NOR Gate
7475 latch

171

Schematic Diagram (Fig. 6-19)

The decoder circuit in Fig. 6-19 is designed to partially decode address 5000. When address 5000 is on the address bus, the decoder circuit will enable the 7475 latch such that the logic switch data will be transferred to the lamp monitor(s).

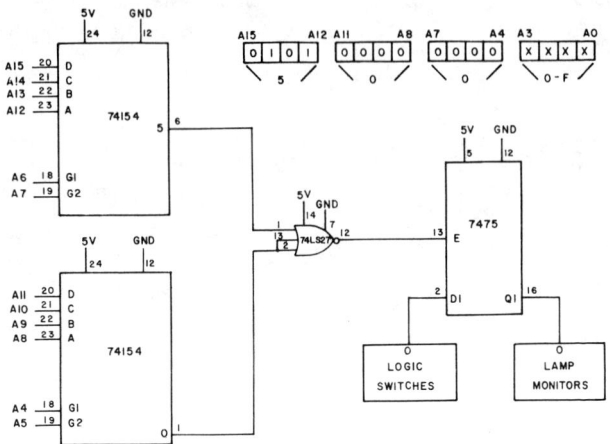

Fig. 6-19. Schematic diagram for Experiment 6-2.

Program

Hex Address	Hex Contents	Mnemonics/ Contents	Operation
0000	B7	STAA $$	
0001	50	50	ACCA → M_{5000}
0002	00	00	
0003	3E	WAI	Stop

This program will allow the 6800 to place address 5000 on the address bus for decoding.

Procedure
Step 1

Construct the decoding circuit as shown in Fig. 6-19.

Step 2

Enter the program beginning at address 0000.

Step 3

Set the logic switch 0 to a logic-one position (up).

Step 4

Execute the program. The lamp monitor should illuminate.

Step 5

Set logic switch 0 to a logic-zero position (down).

Step 6

Execute the program. The lamp monitor should now go out. Why?

Step 7

Change address 0002 to 0F and repeat Steps 3 through 6. Verify your results.

Step 8

Change address 0002 to 10 and repeat Steps 3 through 6. Verify your results.

Conclusions

Why did the lamp respond to the program change of Step 7 and not Step 8?

What is the function of the 7475 latch?

How could you use this circuit in a microcomputer system?

EXPERIMENT 6-3

Purpose

To simulate a nonmaskable interrupt using the software interrupt (SWI) instruction.

Equipment

ET3400
512 bytes of R/W memory

MEK6800D2

NOTE: You must have at least 512 bytes of R/W memory (RAM) with your trainer to do this experiment. With the Heath ET3400 trainer, *all* four RAM chip sockets must contain a 2112 RAM chip.

Program

Hex Address	Hex Contents	Mnemonics/ Contents	Operation
0000	4F	CLRA	00 → ACCA
0001	5F	CLRB	00 → ACCB
0002	53	COMB	$\overline{ACCB}$ → ACCB
0003	CE	LDX #	
0004	33	33	33 → X_H
0005	55	55	55 → X_L
0006	8E	LDS #	
0007	00	00	00 → SP_H
0008	50	50	50 → SP_L
0009	06	TAP	ACCA → CCR
000A	3F	SWI	Software interrupt
000B	3E	WAI	(vector = 00FA)
.	.	.	
.	.	.	
.	.	(Interrupt Service Routine)	
00FA	CE	LDX #	
00FB	00	00	00 → X_H
00FC	05	05	05 → X_L
00FD	09	DEX	X − 1 → X
00FE	8C	CMPX #	Compare index register
00FF	00	00	immediate with 0000
0100	00	00	
0101	26	BNE	Branch if Z flag cleared
0102	FA	FA	(to address 00FD)
0103	3B	RTI	Return to main program

You will analyze each program instruction while single stepping the program.

Procedure

Step 1
Enter the given program.

Step 2
Set the program counter to 0000.

Step 3
Single step the program and examine ACCA. You should observe 00 since the first instruction cleared ACCA.

Step 4

Single step the program *twice* and examine ACCB. You should observe FF since the two instructions you just executed cleared and then complemented ACCB.

Step 5

Single step the program and examine the index register. You should observe 3355 as a result of the LDX instruction.

Step 6

Single step the program and examine the stack pointer. You should observe 0050 as a result of the LDS instruction.

Step 7

Single step the program and examine the condition code register (CCR). You should observe 000000 as a result of the TAP instruction.

Step 8

To summarize, the 6800 internal registers should now contain the following:

Stack Pointer—0050
Condition Code—000000
Accumulator B—FF
Accumulator A—00
Index Register—3355

After the SWI instruction, the next executable instruction is the WAI instruction at address 000B. When the SWI instruction is executed, the 6800 will save the register contents just given along with 000B as the program count on the stack. Address 000B is saved so that the 6800 can return to the main program after the interrupt service routine is executed.

Now, execute the SWI instruction by single stepping the program. The display should now indicate the address of the first instruction of the interrupt service routine. You have entered a short interrupt service routine beginning at address 00FA that will load and decrement the index register to provide a software delay before returning to the main program. Note, address 00FA is obtained indirectly by the ET3400 monitor program. The actual SWI vector located at addresses FFFA: FFFB is 00F4.

Examine the stack pointer. You should now observe 0049. Why? Now examine the seven memory locations above the stack pointer (004A–0050). You should observe the following:

Address	Contents	
004A	C0	CCR contents
004B	FF	ACCB contents
004C	00	ACCA contents
004D	33	X_H
004E	55	X_L
004F	00	PC_H
0050	0B	PC_L

NOTE: The CCR contents saved are C0 rather than 00 since bits 6 and 7 of the CCR are always set.

Step 9

Examine the condition code register and note that the SWI instruction has also set the I flag such that all maskable interrupts will be masked out.

Step 10

Single step through the service routine until you return to the main program at address 000B via the RTI instruction. You might want to observe the index register contents while single stepping the service routine. *Do not* execute the WAI instruction.

Step 11

Now that you have returned to the main program, examine the stack pointer. You should observe 0050 since the register information has now been pulled from the stack causing the stack pointer to be incremented back to its original value.

Step 12

Verify that the original information has been returned to the internal registers.

Conclusion

Why was the SWI service routine located at address 00FA?

Why is the SWI instruction useful in developing system programs?

CHAPTER 7

Interfacing With Memory

INTRODUCTION

Now you are ready to begin constructing a complete, workable microcomputer system using the 6800. The system you will study in the remaining chapters will be the minimum 6800 system configuration developed in Chapter 6. Recall that this system consisted of read/write memory or R/W, read-only memory (ROM), and a peripheral interface adapter (PIA). Before looking at specific memory chips, it would be beneficial at this point to discuss the technology that has made the microcomputer possible. This chapter will provide a brief history of electronic *integrated-circuit* technology and then discuss such present-day technologies as *bipolar, integrated-injection logic* (I^2L), *metal oxide semiconductor* (*MOS*), *charge coupled devices* (*CCDs*), and *magnetic bubbles*. In choosing a particular technology to fit an application there are four main considerations: *speed, cost, size,* and *power consumption.* Comparisons between the different technologies will be provided so that *you* can decide what is best for *your* application.

In this chapter you will become familiar with two different read/write memory chips—the Motorola MCM6810 and the Intel 2112. There are many different memory chips on the market and these two were chosen as typical for small system applications. Another reason for choosing these two chips is that the Heath ET3400 microcomputer trainer uses the 2112 chip and the Motorola MEK6800D2 trainer kit uses the 6810. The pin assignments of each chip will be discussed as well as how each would be connected to the 6800 to provide read/write memory for your system. A discussion of read-only memory (ROM) will then be provided. You will become familiar with the terms *mask-programmed* read-only memory (ROM), programmable read-only memory (PROM), *erasable-programmable* read-only memory (EPROM), and *electrically alterable* read-only memory (EAROM). Each of these read-only memories has a particular advantage over the other, depending on the application. Each type will be discussed briefly in this chapter. The two read-only memory chips that will be discussed are the Motorola 6830 and 68708 (Intel 2708). The 6830 is a 1K-byte mask-programmed ROM and the 68708 is a 1K-byte EPROM. Both are completely compatible with your 6800 system. This chapter will discuss the pin assignments of each chip and show how each would be connected to the 6800 to provide read-only memory for your system.

OBJECTIVES

At the end of this chapter you will be able to do the following:

- State what is meant by the terms SSI, MSI, LSI, VLSI, SLSI.
- Be familiar with the various integrated-circuit technologies, such as bipolar, I^{2}L, PMOS, NMOS, CMOS, CCD, and bubbles.
- State the three main categories of memory.
- Define what is meant by the term "K" as related to chips versus systems.
- Explain the differences between static and dynamic R/W memory.
- Understand the 6810 and 2112 RAM pin assignments.
- Explain how to connect the 6810 and 2112 RAM chips to provide read/write memory for a 6800 system.
- Explain the differences between mask-programmed ROM, PROM, EPROM, and EAROM.
- Understand the 6830 ROM and 68708 EPROM pin assignments.
- Explain how to connect the 6830 ROM chip and 68708 EPROM chip to provide read-only memory for a 6800 system.

MEMORY TECHNOLOGY

Since the invention of the transistor in 1947 the major thrust of the industry has been to *integrate* as many transistors as possible on a small silicon substrate, typically 25mm^2, called a *chip*. Tran-

Table 7-1. Integrated-Circuit Development

Technology	Transistors per Chip	Period
SSI	1 to 50	early 1960s
MSI	50 to 500	mid-1960s
LSI	500 to 20,000	late 1960s to mid-1970s
VLSI	20,000 to 100,000	late 1970s to 1980s
SLSI	Over 100,000	1980s

sistor devices along with their associated components are formed within the chip using a *photolithographic* process or, more recently, an *electron-beam-lithography* process. After the transistors have been integrated into the chip, leads are attached and a plastic or ceramic package is formed around the chip and lead assembly. Once the process has been completed, the package is referred to as an *integrated circuit* (IC). Integrated-circuit technology developed through the 1960s from small scale integration (SSI) to large scale integration (LSI). Computer and memory technology naturally paralleled these developments since the ICs were being incorporated into computers and memories. The early and mid-1960s saw the development of small scale integration and medium scale integration which resulted in the digital and linear integrated-circuit markets. Large scale integration, developed in the late 1960s, led to the first microprocessors. The 1970s have taken us into very-large scale integration (VLSI) and provided the new generation microcomputers, such as the 6801 and 6809. The 1980s will lead us into super-large scale integration (SLSI) and, hopefully, provide a one-million-bit memory chip. A rough breakdown of the different IC developments is shown in Table 7-1. Note that with each development, more and more transistors were being *packed* into the same chip area. This has resulted in ICs with increased capabilities at lower cost. *Packing density* is a term used to indicate the number of transistor devices per chip.

Four basic design considerations must be kept in mind when designing a microcomputer system. They are:

- cost
- speed
- packing density (size)
- power consumption

These considerations must be applied to each part of the system independently, as well as to the overall system. The priority placed on each might not be in the order shown here since the *application* will dictate the priority. For example, if a system were being designed to be used in a satellite, size and power consumption would probably take on a high priority with speed and cost assuming lower priorities. These design considerations should be kept in mind as we look at some different LSI technologies. Each of the following technologies has advantages and/or disadvantages as related to the aforementioned design considerations.

Bipolar

Bipolar technology is the oldest transistor technology. It is the basis for all of the transistor-transistor logic (TTL) series of digital electronic chips, SN7400, SN74L00, SN74LS00, and others. Bipolar devices have a characteristic high speed; however, they also have low packing density and relatively high power consumption. A CPU chip utilizing bipolar technology could have an instruction cycle time of between 50 to 100 nanoseconds versus one microsecond for the 6800 microprocessor. A lower power version of bipolar is low-power Schottky TTL (LPSTTL). Another form of bipolar is *integrated injection logic* (I^2L) technology. I^2L has been developed for the small-calculator and digital-watch markets. It promises to have the characteristic high speed of bipolar technology along with lower power consumption and high packing density. However, more development needs to be done until all of the predictions for I^2L are fulfilled. If these predictions become reality, I^2L could become a major technology to be utilized in the microcomputer industry. Usually, but not always, cost is an inverse function of packing density. A technology such as bipolar, which has a relatively low packing density, will have a relatively high cost as compared to high density technologies. Presently, bipolar technology does not allow the implementation of a complete microprocessor on a chip due to its characteristic low packing density. Therefore, the most common use of bipolar technology has been in the *bit-slice* microprocessor industry, where the main consideration is speed.

MOS

Along with developments in packing density, new transistor technologies were developed. One technology that has allowed greater packing densities and has had a great impact on the microcomputer industry is MOS technology. The acronym MOS stands for *metal-oxide semiconductor*. In general, MOS technology offers higher density and lower power consumption at a lower cost than bipolar technology. There are several varieties of MOS technology that can presently be identified. They are:

- PMOS
- NMOS
- CMOS
- VMOS
- DMOS

Each MOS technology has its own particular advantage over the others and each of them will now be discussed.

PMOS

PMOS stands for *p-channel* MOS. It is an older MOS technology and its manufacturing processes are well developed, resulting in a relatively low cost. PMOS provides excellent densities (11,000 to 15,000 transistors per chip) but is relatively slow as compared to the other MOS technologies. It was used for the first microprocessors and is still utilized quite extensively for memory chips where speed is less important than cost, such as in calculators.

NMOS

NMOS stands for *n-channel* MOS. Most of the present-day microprocessors and microcomputers, such as the 6800, 6809, and 6801, utilize this technology. NMOS offers higher speed but less density than PMOS. A microprocessor utilizing NMOS technology will be at least two times as fast as an equivalent processor that uses PMOS technology. More devices are utilizing this technology as its manufacturing processes become better developed, resulting in costs comparable to PMOS-implemented circuits.

CMOS

CMOS is an acronym for *complementary metal-oxide semiconductor*. It is a combination of PMOS and NMOS and, therefore, has speed and packing density characteristics somewhere between those of NMOS and PMOS. The main advantage to CMOS is its very low power consumption. It is typically used in military or space applications, or any application where power consumption is an important consideration. For example, most read/write memory is volatile and in many applications it is desirable to maintain memory if a loss of system power occurs. This can be done with a battery backup unit. However, CMOS RAM must be utilized since PMOS or NMOS would cause too much of a battery drain to maintain the information in the memory for extended periods. Another advantage of CMOS is its excellent noise immunity as compared to the other technologies. A typical application of CMOS is in electronic watches which must operate for long periods of time on a small battery.

VMOS

Vertical MOS (VMOS) is a MOS technology that uses a V-shaped groove in the silicon chip to achieve greater packing densities. Its characteristics are similar to those of PMOS or NMOS. However, it's not as widely used since the manufacturing processes are not as well developed.

DMOS

Double-diffused MOS (DMOS) is another MOS technology that provides very high packing densities. It is presently used in high-density memories and, again, the manufacturing processes need more development before DMOS becomes economical.

Fig. 7-1 shows a speed and power consumption comparison between the major bipolar and MOS technologies.

Charge-Coupled Devices

Charge-coupled devices (CCDs) are probably the most promising technology of the future, especially as related to memories. The

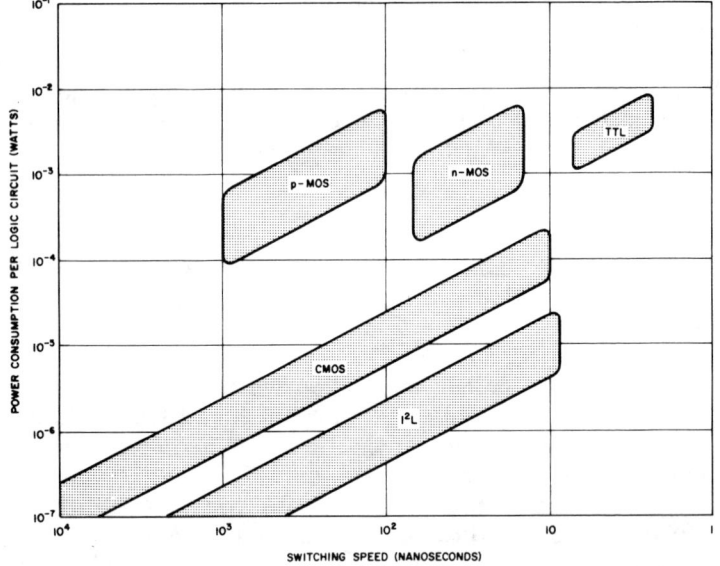

From *Microelectronic Circuit Elements*, by James D. Meindl.
Copyright 1977 by Scientific American, Inc. All rights reserved.

Fig. 7-1. Comparison of bipolar and MOS technologies.

greatest advantage here is in packing density. A 64K-bit memory on a chip has already been produced and CCD technology will probably lead to a one-megabit chip. The big disadvantage of CCD is speed. CCD memories have a very slow *access time*. Access time is the time required to fetch a word from memory. An R/W memory using NMOS technology will have a typical access time of 50–250 nanoseconds, whereas the same R/W memory using CCD technology would have an access time of more than 100 microseconds. CCD memories might someday replace mass-memory units, such as floppy disks, but will probably not replace the main working memory of the computer due to their slow access time.

Magnetic Bubbles

Magnetic-bubble memories have recently begun to appear on the commercial market. They are different from the preceding technologies in that they are magnetic devices. An inherent advantage of magnetic devices is that they are nonvolatile, meaning they retain their contents when power is removed. The *biggest* advantage of "bubbles" is their extremely high densities. One-megabit magnetic-bubble memory units have been successfully produced (Intel). Magnetic bubbles also offer low power consumption and are lightweight. The disadvantages of magnetic bubbles are speed and cost. Bubble memories are presently slower than CCDs and the cost of using bubbles in place of a MOS R/W memory would be intolerable. However, the cost per bit for bubble memories goes down as the amount of memory goes up. Therefore, magnetic bubble memories are another likely candidate to replace disk memories in the future.

Microcomputer Memory Devices

CPU memories may be divided into three main categories—*internal memory, main working memory,* and *mass memory.* Internal memory would include the internal registers on the CPU chip along with any read/write memory that might be included as part of the CPU chip. This type of memory is the fastest and is normally configured using bipolar or MOS technology. The main working memory is that memory that is separate from the CPU chip but is connected directly to the address lines of the CPU chip. In 6800-based systems, the main working memory can be up to 64K bytes and it is usually fast. Presently, MOS devices are used to provide the read/write and ROM parts of this memory. The mass memory in a microcomputer system will usually be a magnetic cassette recorder or floppy-disk unit. Mass memory is nonvolatile and is used to save programs and large amounts of data. The cost per bit of mass memory is relatively low when compared to the other memory categories; however, it is very slow. Fig. 7-2 shows cost and speed comparisons for the different categories of memory technology. Note that bipolar memory is the fastest but most expensive and magnetic tape is the slowest and cheapest. Also note where CCD and magnetic bubbles fit into the picture. They both seem to represent a compromise that fills the gap between MOS R/W memory and magnetic mass memory.

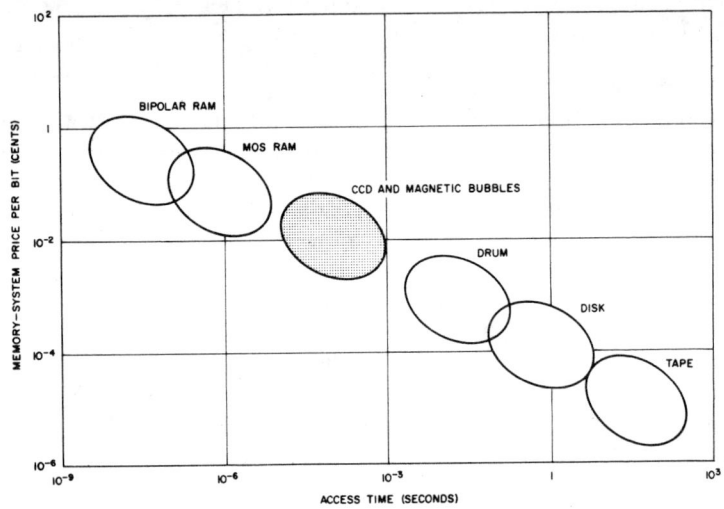

From *Microelectronic Memories*, by David A. Hodges. Copyright 1977 by Scientific American, Inc. All rights reserved.

Fig. 7-2. Memory cost and speed comparisons.

INTERFACING WITH READ/WRITE MEMORY

The development of R/W memory has naturally followed the integrated-circuit developments. The first 1K R/W memory chip was marketed by the Intel Corporation in 1971. In 1973 4K chips were introduced and in 1978, 16K chips became available. By 1980 you can expect to have a 64K chip commercially available. As IC technology gets better and starts moving into VLSI and SLSI in the 1980s, you will see memory chips with very high densities.

Now some of the terms associated with memories need to be discussed. As mentioned earlier in this book, "K" stands for the number 1024. However, you must define the units that "K" is being applied to. The accepted convention is that when you apply the term K to a *system* memory, you mean K *bytes* of memory. When K is applied to a memory chip, you mean K *bits* of individual memory locations. For example, the 6800 is capable of addressing 64K *bytes* of memory, but the Motorola MCM4116 is a 16K-*bit* R/W memory chip. Various terms and abbreviations are used to describe memory chips in the manufacturer's specifications. The following are some of the more common terms that are used to describe memory chips.

Access Time (t_A, t_{acc})

Access time is probably the *most* standardized term used to indicate memory speed. It is the time from when the address and chip select inputs are applied to, when memory data is available on the data output pins.

Read-Cycle Time (t_{RC}, $t_{cyc(R)}$)

Read-cycle time is the time from when the memory is addressed to when the memory is ready for the next read operation.

NOTE: t_A will usually be less than t_{RC}.

Write-Cycle Time (t_{WC}, $t_{cyc(W)}$)

Write-cycle time is the time required to write data into an addressed memory location.

Setup Time (t_S)

Setup time is the minimum time interval, immediately *preceding* the chip enabling pulse or pulses, that the address information and/or data must be maintained at the chip to ensure its recognition. Examples are address time (t_{AS}) and data setup time (t_{DS}).

Hold Time (t_H)

Hold time is the minimum time interval, immediately *following* the chip enabling pulse or pulses, that the address information and/or data must be maintained at the chip to ensure its continued recognition. Examples would be address hold time (t_{AH}) and data hold time (t_{DH}).

Unfortunately, there has not been much standardization of specifications between the memory chip manufacturers. It might very well happen that two manufacturers will specify the same memory chip characteristics in different terms. You might also see the terms R/W and RAM used synonymously. Technically, this is incorrect since ROM is also random-access memory. However, the term RAM has been accepted over the years to mean read/write memory.

R/W memory is internally organized in matrices of words × bits. For example, the Motorola MCM4116 R/W memory previously mentioned is a 16K × 1 chip. This means the chip contains 16,384 1-bit words; therefore, eight of them would be needed to configure a 16K-byte memory. The Motorola MCM2114 is a 1K × 4 R/W memory chip, meaning it contains 1024 4-bit words. Two of these chips would be required to configure a 1K-byte memory and 32 would be needed to configure a 16K-byte memory. Finally, the MCM6810 is a 128 × 8 R/W memory meaning that it contains 128 8-bit words. Here, only one chip would be needed to provide 128 bytes of memory for a system; however, it would require 128 of these chips to provide a 16K-byte memory system.

The Motorola MCM2114 and MCM2147 are both 4K R/W memory chips. However, the 2114 is a 1K × 4 chip and the 2147 is a 4K × 1 chip. Note that they both contain the same number of bits but they have different internal structures. A memory system might be configured differently depending upon which types of chips are to be used. The main point here is that, even though the 2114 and 2147 are both 4K R/W memory chips, they are not interchangeable.

There are two general categories of R/W memory—*static* and *dynamic*. Static R/W memory utilizes the flip-flop (refer to Appendix A) as its basic storage element. Recall that one of the properties of a flip-flop is that it will stay latched in one of two states as long as power is supplied. A *dynamic* memory stores binary information as a charge. For example, a charge being present might indicate a binary one and no charge present would indicate a binary zero. The dynamic R/W memory actually uses the capacitance between the gate and substrate of a MOS transistor to store the charge. However, you know that a capacitor does not hold a charge indefinitely and that it must be recharged. This is the main disadvantage of dynamic RAM. Within a few milliseconds, most of the charge is lost and you must refresh the charge. This is normally accomplished by reading the stored information out of the memory and then writing it back into the same memory locations once every one to two milliseconds. You would not want to tie up the CPU to perform this function; therefore, extra *refresh circuitry* must be provided. We can achieve about four times greater density with dynamic RAM than with static RAM, reducing the cost per bit significantly. In fact, it costs about the same to produce a 16K dynamic RAM as it does to produce a 4K static RAM. However, the addition of the refresh circuitry required for dynamic RAM makes this type of memory less economical for small systems. Most microcomputer systems use static RAM since it is cheaper when relatively small amounts of memory are required and makes the system design process less complicated. Dynamic RAM is normally used in minicomputer and large computer applications where larger amounts of memory are required.

Now we will consider some real memory products. Again, large amounts of memory are not required for most microcomputer applications. In many cases 512 bytes of memory are more than enough to do the job. In this section the Motorola 6810, which is a 128 × 8 static R/W memory, and the Intel 2112, a 256 × 4 static R/W memory, will be discussed.

MCM 6810 R/W MEMORY

The 6810 is a 24-pin NMOS static R/W memory. It is organized as 128 bytes of 8 bits, operates from a single 5-volt power supply, and has a maximum access time of 450 nanoseconds. The following is an explanation of the 6810 pin assignments as shown in Fig. 7-3.

Ground (V_{ss}: Pin 1)

Pin 1 should be connected to the system ground.

Data (D0–D7: Pins 2–9)

These pins are connected to the eight data bus lines D0 through D7 of the 6800. They are bidirectional and have three-state output buffers capable of driving one TTL load.

Chip-Select Inputs (CS0–CS5: Pins 10–15)

These pins are used to select or enable the chip. The chip will be enabled when CS0 and CS3 are high and $\overline{CS1}$, $\overline{CS2}$, $\overline{CS4}$, and $\overline{CS5}$ are low. You can connect these chip-select lines to the address bus in such a way that only one 6810 R/W memory is enabled at a

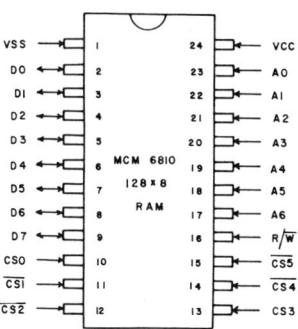

Fig. 7-3. Pin assignment for 6810 R/W memory.

time. These lines will provide you with the chip decoding scheme. The availability of six chip-select lines allows you to use this R/W memory with little or no external address decoding. The use of these pins will be discussed in more detail shortly.

Read/Write (R/$\overline{W}$: Pin 16)

This pin is connected directly to the R/W pin of the 6800. It tells the memory chip that the 6800 is in the read or write mode as described in Chapter 6.

Address Inputs (A0–A6: Pins 23–17)

There are seven address pins which can address 2^7, or 128, different locations within the chip. These pins will always be connected to address lines A0–A6, respectively, on the 6800. They are used to select a particular word in the chip once that chip has been enabled. Even if there is more than one 6810 in the system, the address pins on each chip will always be connected to the address bus lines (A0–A6) of the 6800. The different memory chips will be selected independently through the chip-select configuration of each chip.

V_{cc} (Pin 24)

Connect this pin to the system +5-volt dc power supply. Each 6810 in the system will draw approximately 80 mA from the supply.

Fig. 7-4 shows a functional block diagram of the 6810 chip. Note that the three basic interfacing requirements, decoding, three-state buffering, and latching, are all provided for in this single-chip package. Decoding is accomplished by using the chip-select pins, and the internal A0–A6 address decoder. Three-state buffering is included as an internal part of the data lines. When R/W memory is not enabled, the data lines will go on their off (high-impedance) state. Latching is inherent since this is a memory chip.

Fig. 7-5 shows how you would interface two 6810 chips to the 6800 microprocessor to provide 256 bytes of RAM. First, note how the 6800 control pins are connected. Reset is connected to the 5-volt

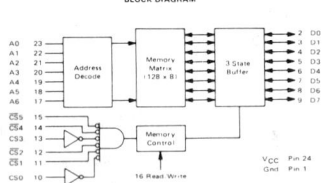

Fig. 7-4. Functional block diagram of 6810 R/W memory.

Courtesy Motorola
Semiconductor Products Inc.

source through a pull-up resistor and to ground through a switch. With the switch open, $\overline{\text{Reset}}$ will be held high. When the switch is closed, Reset will go low causing a reset interrupt sequence to occur. The $\overline{\text{IRQ}}$, $\overline{\text{HALT}}$, and $\overline{\text{NMI}}$ inputs are all held high with the 5-volt source since their functions are not required for this application. The $\phi1$ and $\phi2$ clock signals are applied to their respective pins on the 6800. However, note that the $\phi2$ clock signal to the DBE pin is also being applied. Read/write operations will take place only

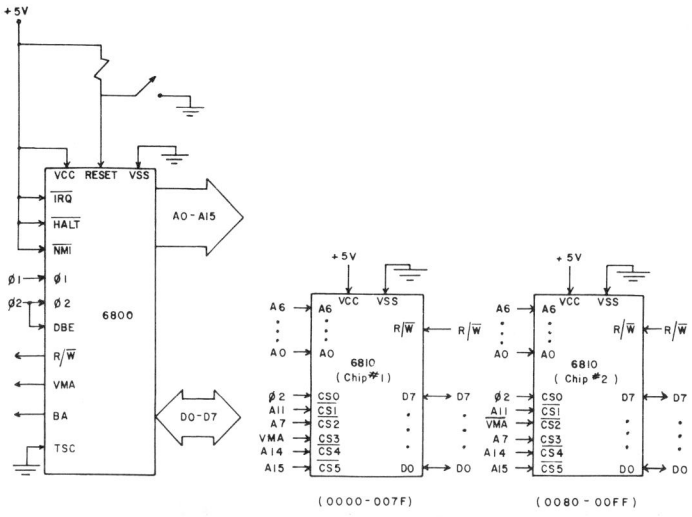

Fig. 75. Interfacing 256 bytes of RAM using two 6810 R/W memories.

when $\phi2$ is high. Therefore, by tying $\phi2$ to DBE, you will only enable the data bus during the read/write operations. This is normally done to isolate the 6800 data lines from the data bus when the bus is not being utilized by the 6800. The $R/\overline{W}$ signal is connected directly to the $R/\overline{W}$ pin on each 6810 chip. The VMA line is used in the 6810 decoding scheme. The BA pin is a 6800 output line that is not being used and, therefore, no connection is made to this pin. Finally, the TSC pin is held low since its function is not required.

Now consider the 6810 connections. Address lines A0 through A6 of the 6800 microprocessor are connected to the A0–A6 pins of both of the 6810 chips. This will allow the computer to select one of the 128 bytes within either chip using the lowest seven address lines (A0–A6). In this scheme, the chip-select lines are connected such that chip No. 1 will use addresses 0000 through 007F and chip

No. 2 will use addresses 0080 through 00FF. An address decoding chart for each chip is shown in Fig. 7-6. Note that in each case the address bus is being only partially decoded. Full decoding would require more logic external to each 6810 chip. Chip-select inputs $\overline{CS1}$, $\overline{CS4}$, and $\overline{CS5}$ provide partial decoding for the upper eight address lines. Address lines A11, A14, and A15 are connected to these chip selects. Address line A7 is "decoded" to select either chip No. 1 or chip No. 2. On chip No. 1, A7 is connected to $\overline{CS2}$ to

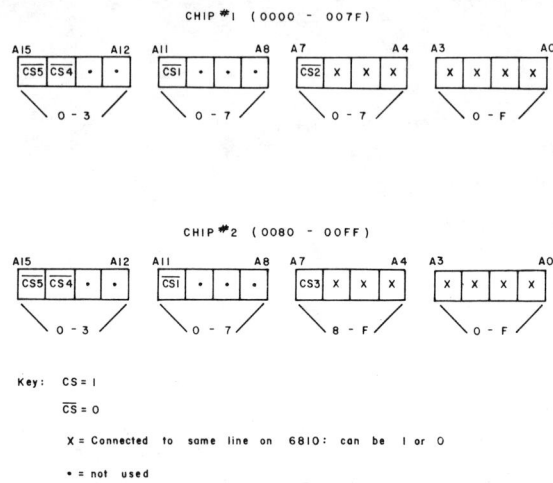

Fig. 7-6. 6810 chip decoding charts.

enable that chip when A7 is low, while on chip No. 2, A7 is connected to CS3 such that chip No. 2 is enabled when A7 is high. This will allow chip No. 1 to provide the lower 128 bytes of R/W memory and chip No. 2 to provide the upper 128 bytes of the 256 bytes implemented. On each chip, the $\phi 2$ and VMA signals are connected to the remaining chip selects such that the chip will only be enabled when $\phi 2$ and VMA are high.

The data i/o pins, D0 through D7, on each 6810 chip are connected to lines D0 through D7 on the 6800 data bus. The 6810 R/W line is tied directly to the 6800 R/W line.

2112 R/W MEMORY

The 2112 is a 16-pin 256 × 4-bit static R/W memory. It operates on a single 5-volt power supply and has an access time similar to that of the 6810. To obtain 256 bytes of R/W memory would require two 2112s since each is only four bits. Recall that the 6810 is a 128 × 8 R/W memory. Both of these chips contain the same number of storage cells (1024), but internally they have been structured differently. The following is an explanation of the pin assignments for the 2112 as shown in Fig. 7-7.

Address (A0–A7: Pins 1–7, 15)

These eight address pins can address $2^8 = 256$ different 4-bit locations in the chip. They will always be connected to address lines A0 through A7, respectively, on the 6800. As with the 6810 chip, the address lines are used to select a particular word within the chip, once that chip has been selected.

Ground (V_{ss}: Pin 8)

Pin 8 should be connected to the system ground.

Data (I/O1–I/O4: Pins 9–12)

I/O1 through I/O4 provide the four data lines to and from the chip. Since each 2112 memory has only four data lines and since the 6800 has an 8-bit data bus, you will be interfacing blocks of 8-bit bytes by using pairs of 2112 chips. Each pair of 2112 chips will provide 256 bytes of R/W memory. Therefore, within any one pair, I/O1 through I/O4 of one 2112 must be connected to D0 through D3 of the data bus and I/O1 through I/O4 of the other 2112 must be tied to D4 through D7 of the data bus.

Chip Enable ($\overline{CE}$: Pin 13)

When pin 13 goes low (0), the chip will be enabled. Since this is the only chip-select pin available on this chip, you will have to provide external address decoding as discussed in Chapter 6. The $\overline{CE}$ pin will connect to the output of your address decoder.

Read/Write (R/W: Pin 14)

You will connect this pin directly to the $R/\overline{W}$ pin of the 6800. It tells an enabled memory chip that data is to be read from or written into its storage cells.

V_{cc} (Pin 16)

Connect this pin to the +5-volt dc power supply of the system. Fig. 7-8 shows how two 2112 chips would have to be connected to the 6800 to provide 256 bytes of RAM. The connections to the 6800 are the same as were required for the 6810 interfacing. Note that the two 2112 chips are enabled simultaneously by the address

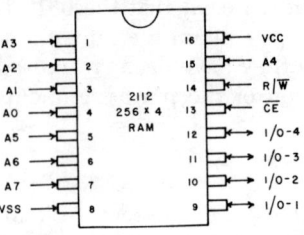

Fig. 7-7. Pin assignments for the 2112 R/W memory.

decoder that decodes the upper eight address lines. External decoding must be provided for the 2112 chips, since only one chip-enable pin is provided. The lower eight address lines are used to select the particular byte required in the memory. To obtain the full byte of data, chip No. 1 is connected to data lines D0 through D3 and chip No. 2 is connected to data lines D4 through D7.

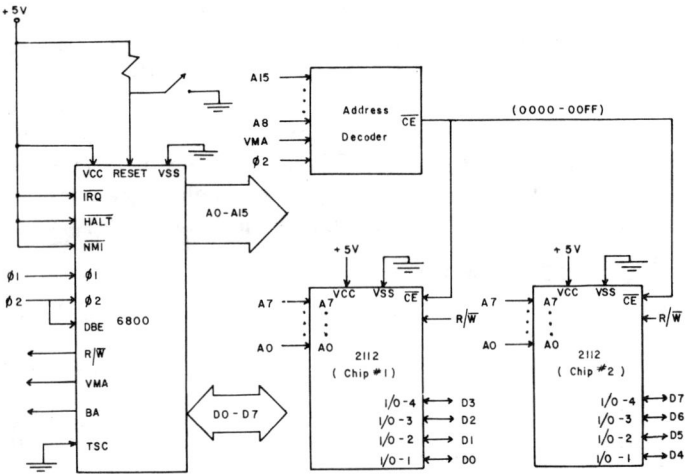

Fig. 7-8. Interfacing 256 bytes of RAM using two 2112 R/W memories.

INTERFACING WITH READ-ONLY MEMORY (ROM)

Your system will require some type of read-only memory to provide such functions as restarting (reset), program loading, single stepping, address examination, and any frequently used program required for your application. Several types of read-only memory are available. A brief discussion of each follows.

Mask-Programmable ROM

This type of read-only memory can only be programmed by the manufacturer. When purchasing a mask-programmed ROM, you must supply the manufacturer with the program you desire to have implemented into ROM. Your program may be forwarded to the manufacturer in several different formats. Refer to the specifications for the Motorola 6830 ROM in Appendix D for an example of custom programming requirements. The 1s and 0s that make up the op codes and those in your program will be *masked* into the ROM chip during the last manufacturing step. This step is referred to as the metallization step. The manufacturer will actually produce a mask from your program to be used in the *metallization* process. Since production of this mask is quite costly, the manufacturer will usually require you to place a minimum order. The minimum order required depends on the manufacturer and the stage of process development.

An obvious disadvantage of a mask-programmed ROM is the delivery time. Once you place an order, it will typically take three to six weeks for the manufacturer to fill that order. Also, the program cannot be modified once the ROM is produced. If modification is required, the existing ROM must be discarded and a new order placed. The advantages of this type of ROM are its high packing density and lower cost in large quantities once a program has been debugged.

PROM (Programmable ROM)

This type of read-only memory is *user-programmed,* meaning that you can program your own PROMs using a device called a PROM programmer. Most of the PROMs used today are erasable PROMs, sometimes called EPROMs. The erasable devices can be easily identified since they have a transparent quartz window above the chip. When these chips are exposed to ultraviolet light for several minutes, all of the internal storage cells are returned to either a zero or one state, depending upon the particular device. After erasing, the PROM may be reprogrammed using the PROM programmer. The nonerasable PROMs, or one-shot ROMs, are a smaller part of the market since they may only be programmed once and then discarded if the program requirements change.

The PROM devices will generally meet the microcomputer manufacturer's speed or access-time specification, but they are generally much slower and larger than mask-programmed ROMs. While 16K-bit PROMs are readily available, 64K-bit ROMs are common.

Normally, you will develop your system using the PROM devices. Once the system is debugged, you can then order mask-programmed ROMs for large-volume production runs of systems initially using the PROMs. For applications which do not involve large production runs, the PROMs may be used as the permanent read-only memory.

EAROM (Electrically Alterable ROM)

This type of ROM could actually be classified as a read/write memory since you can electrically write information into it as well as read from it. However, the write operation is very slow (typically one millisecond) and, therefore, it is not used as a general read/write memory. A better classification for EAROM would be *read-mostly* memory. One advantage of EAROM is that a special *burner* is not required for programming. Usually all that is required is a 26-volt dc level which can be supplied by a simple power-supply circuit. Once this voltage is supplied, you can write information into the EAROM by transferring data located in RAM to the EAROM memory locations. This data transfer can be accomplished very easily with the 6800 by using indexed addressing. The data-transfer cycle should be repeated (looped) several times to assure proper EAROM programming. If the program is to be changed, the change is made in RAM and then the procedure repeated. EAROMs are nonvolatile and should be considered for applications which require small amounts of read-only memory since they are relatively expensive. Now two typical read-only memory chips, the Motorola MCM 6830 ROM and the MCM 68708 (Intel 2708) EPROM will be discussed.

MCM 6830 ROM

The 6830 is a 24-pin mask-programmable ROM containing 1K bytes (1024 × 8) of memory. It uses NMOS technology and has an access time of 250–350 nanoseconds. The 6830 pin assignments are shown in Fig. 7-9. The following is a brief functional description of each pin.

Ground (V_{ss}: Pin 1)

Pin 1 should be connected to the system ground.

Data (D0–D7: Pins 2–9)

These pins are connected to the eight data bus lines, D0 through D7, on the 6800 microprocessor. They are only used for output, since data is only *read* from a ROM. These lines are three-state buffered and capable of driving one TTL load. When the ROM is not enabled, its data lines will go into their off (high-impedance) state.

Chip-Select Inputs (CS0–CS3: Pins 10, 11, 13, 14)

These pins are used to partially decode the address bus to enable the chip. They are *user defined*, meaning that the user will specify to the manufacturer which pins are to be high and which are to be

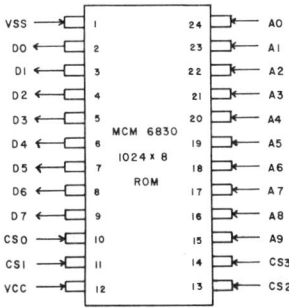

Fig. 7-9. Pin assignments for the MCM 6830 ROM.

low. The chip selects will then be manufactured into the chip, as specified, during the mask-program step of the manufacturing process. As with the 6810, the chip-select pins will be tied to the address bus so that only one ROM will be enabled at a time.

V_{cc} (Pin 12)

Connect this pin to the system +5-volt dc power supply. Each 6830 will draw approximately 130 mA maximum from the power supply.

Address (A0–A9: Pins 24–15)

There are ten address pins which can address 2^{10}, or 1024, different 8-bit locations within the chip. These pins will always be connected to address lines A0 through A9, respectively, on the 6800 microprocessor. They are used to select a particular word in the chip once that chip has been enabled. If there is more than one 6830 in the system, the ten address pins on each chip will still be connected to address bus lines A0 through A9 in each case. The different chips will be selected independently through the chip-select configuration of each chip.

Fig. 7-10 shows how the 6830 chip might be connected to your 6800 system. It is desirable to locate the 1K of ROM at addresses

FC00 through FFFF. The decoding chart at the top of Fig. 7-10 will provide partial decoding for this group of addresses if it is assumed that the ROM has been mask-programmed to make CS1, CS2, and CS3 high. It is also assumed that CS0 has been mask-programmed low. Note that $\overline{\text{CS0}}$ is being driven by a NAND gate whose

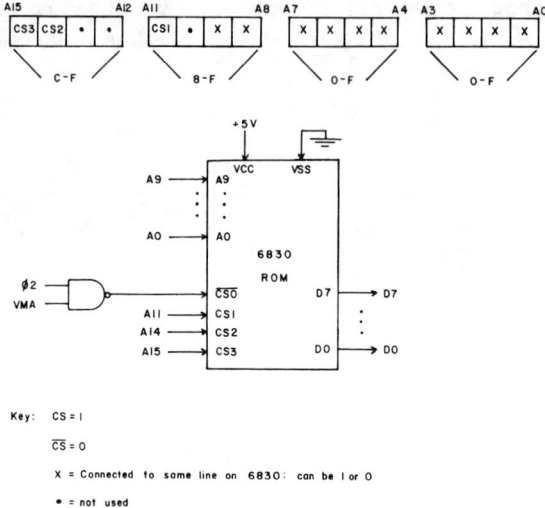

Fig. 7-10. Interfacing 1K bytes of ROM using the 6830.

inputs are $\phi 2$ and VMA. This allows the ROM to be enabled only when $\phi 2$ and VMA are high. Once the chip is enabled, address lines A0 through A9 will select the one of 1024 bytes required. The chip data lines (D0–D7) are connected to the 6800 data bus.

MCM 68708 (INTEL 2708) EPROM

The 68708 is a 24-pin erasable PROM containing 1K bytes (1024 × 8) of read-only memory. It has an access time of 300–450 nanoseconds and is equivalent to the Intel 2708 EPROM. A system that has been developed and debugged using this device may then be produced in large volume runs using the Motorola MCM 65308 or MCM 68308 or the Intel 2308 mask-programmed ROMs. These ROMs are pin-for-pin compatible with the 68708. The following is a brief functional description of the 68708 pin assignments shown in Fig. 7-11.

Address (A0–A9: Pins 8–1, 23, 22)

These are the ten address pins which access the 1024 different 8-bit word locations within the chip. These pins will always connect lines A0–A9 on the 6800 respectively.

Data (D0–D7: Pins 9–11, 13–17)

These pins are connected to the eight data bus lines, D0 through D7, on the 6800. They are used as output for the read mode and as

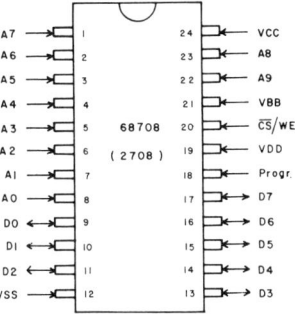

Fig. 7-11. Pin assignments for the Motorola 68708 or Intel 2708 EPROM.

input during the chip programming mode. The data lines are three-state buffered and capable of driving one TTL load.

Ground (V_{ss}: Pin 12)

Pin 12 should be connected to the system ground.

Program (Progr: Pin 18)

This pin is used during the chip programming mode. When programming the chip, a 26-volt pulse with a pulse width of approximately 0.5 ms must be supplied for each address being programmed to allow data storage at that address. During the chip-read mode, this pin must be at the V_{ss} (ground) level.

V_{DD} (Pin 19)

This pin must be connected to a +12-volt dc supply.

Chip Select/Write Enable ($\overline{CS}$/WE: Pin 20)

This pin performs two functions. In the read mode, it functions as a chip-select input. A low level (logic 0) at pin 20 will enable the chip. In the programming mode, this pin must be raised to a +12-volt dc level to allow data to be entered through the data pins.

V$_{BB}$ (Pin 21)

This pin must be connected to a −5-volt dc supply.

V$_{cc}$ (Pin 24)

This pin must be connected to the +5-volt dc supply.

As you can see from the discussion of the pin assignments, there are two modes in which the chip can function—a *programming mode* and *read mode*.

Program Mode

After completion of an erase operation, every bit in the device is in the 1 state. Data is then entered by programming 0s into the required bits. The words within the chips are addressed the same as in the read mode. To set the chip up for the programming mode, the $\overline{CS}$/WE input (Pin 20) must be raised to +12 volts. The logic levels for the data lines and address lines and the supply voltages (V$_{cc}$, V$_{BB}$, V$_{DD}$) are the same as for the read mode. After address and data setup, one program pulse per address is applied to the Progr. input (pin 18). A program loop is a full pass through all addresses. The number of program loops required for complete programming is a function of the Progr. input pulse width. If the pulse width is 0.5 ms, 200 program loops will be required. See the 68708 specification in Appendix D for the programming pulse timing requirements and a more detailed explanation of the programming mode.

Read Mode

In the read mode, the 68708 is treated just like any memory. A group of addresses is assigned to the chip and data is read from the PROM using the 6800 LDA instructions. Fig. 7-12 shows how the 68708 chip might be connected to your 6800 system. Note that the Progr. input is tied to ground. A logic 0 at $\overline{CS}$ will enable the chip and provide data output from the location specified by address lines A0 through A9. Since the 68708 is "bus compatible" with your 6800 system, no special logic is needed between the 6800 system and the 68708.

The 68708 can be erased by exposing the chip to a high-intensity ultraviolet light source with a wavelength of 2537 angstroms. The ultraviolet source should be placed about one inch away from the 68708 chip window for approximately 30 minutes. After erasing, every bit is in the 1 state and data is entered by programming 0s

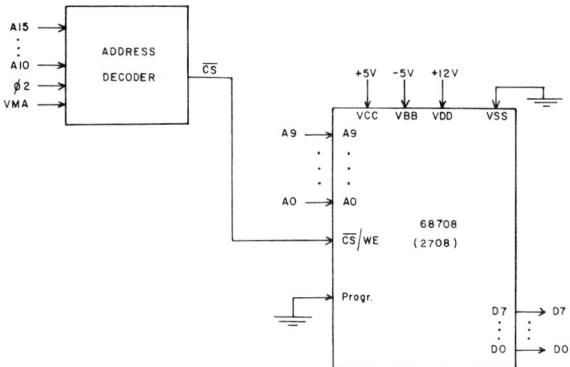

Fig. 7-12. Interfacing 1K bytes of EPROM using the Motorola 68708 or the Intel 2708.

into the bits. A programmed 0 can only be changed to a 1 by the erasing process.

The 6830 or 68708 can now be connected directly to either the 6810 system or the 2112 system developed in Figs. 7-5 and 7-8, respectively, to provide a system containing both R/W memory and ROM. The PIA is the only other device that must be added to complete the basic microcomputer system.

REVIEW QUESTIONS

1. VLSI is an acronym for: _____.
2. The four basic design considerations for configuring a microcomputer system are _____, _____, _____, and _____.
3. The fastest integrated-circuit technology available is _____.
4. I²L stands for _____.
5. The 6800 is manufactured using _____ integrated-circuit technology.
6. An integrated-circuit technology which has very low power consumption is _____.
7. Memories can be divided into three main categories. They are _____, _____, and _____.
8. A 16K memory chip contains 16K _____ of memory.

9. A 4K × 4 memory chip is organized as _____ words, each word consisting of _____ bits.
10. The two general categories of R/W memory are _____ and _____.
11. _____ R/W memory requires refresh circuitry.
12. The 6810 is a _____ × _____ static R/W memory chip.
13. The chip-select pins of the 6810 are connected to the _____ to provide _____.
14. Pins A0 through A6 of the 6810 are always connected to _____.
15. Pins D0 through D7 of the 6810 are always connected to _____.
16. The 2112 is a _____ × _____ static R/W memory chip.
17. Recall, the three basics of interfacing are three-state buffering, decoding and latching. Which of these are not provided internal to the 2112 chip? _____
18. Name three types of read-only memory. _____, _____, _____.
19. What type of read-only memory is the 6830? _____ the 68708? _____
20. A type of read-only memory which can be erased with ultraviolet light and then reprogrammed is _____.
21. The 6830 has _____ chip selects to provide partial decoding.
22. Pins A0 through A9 of the 6830 and 68708 are always connected to _____.
23. With the 6830, the active states of the chip selects are defined by _____.
24. When assigning addresses to various parts of a microcomputer system, you would normally assign ROM to what group of addresses? _____
25. A ROM chip having 11 address pins and 8 data pins would be a _____ × _____ ROM.
26. A +26-volt level is required on the _____ pin to program the 68708.
27. When the 68708 is erased, all the storage bits are returned to _____.

28. The 68708 requires three supply voltages of _____, _____, and _____ volts.

ANSWERS

1. very-large scale integration
2. cost, speed, size, and power consumption
3. bipolar
4. integrated-injection logic
5. NMOS
6. CMOS
7. internal, main-working, and mass
8. bits
9. 4K, four
10. static and dynamic
11. Dynamic
12. 128 × 8
13. address bus to provide partial decoding for the chip
14. A0 through A6 of the address bus
15. D0 through D7 of the data bus
16. 256 × 4
17. Decoding.
18. Mask-programmed, PROM, EAROM, EPROM.
19. Mask-programmed.
    Erasable-programmable.
20. EPROM
21. four
22. A0 through A9 of the address bus
23. the user in the mask program
24. High addresses FFFF on down, depenidng on the size of ROM.
25. $2^{11} \times 8$ or 2048×8 or $2K \times 8$ or 16K bits
26. Progr

27. a logic 1 state

28. +5 volts, −5 volts, and +12 volts

EXPERIMENT 7-1

Purpose

To interface 128 bytes of R/W memory to the 6800 system using the 6810 memory chip.

Equipment

ET3400
6810 R/W memory chip
7400 digital IC (2-bit NAND)
74LS27 digital IC (3-bit NOR)
74LS30 digital IC (8-bit NAND)

Schematic Diagram (Fig. 7-13)

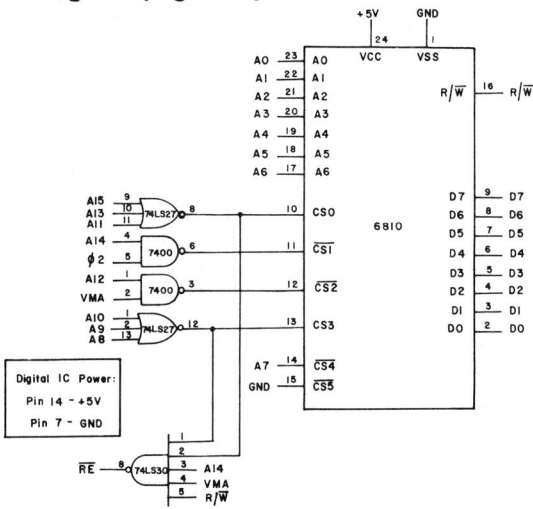

Fig. 7-13. Schematic diagram for Experiment 7-1.

Program

Hex Address	Hex Contents	Mnemonics/ Contents	Operation
0000	CE	LDX #	Load the index register
0001	50	50	immediate with 5000
0002	00	00	
0003	6F	CLR X	Clear using indexed
0004	00	00	addressing
0005	08	INX	Increment the index register

0006	8C	CPX #	
0007	50	50	Compare the index register
0008	80	80	immediate to 5080
0009	26	BNE	Branch if Z flag clear
000A	F8	F8	(to address 0003)
000B	3E	3E	Stop

This program uses a routine similar to the one used in Experiment 5-1 to clear a series of memory locations. However, here you will clear memory locations 5000 through 507F. These are the 128 addresses that have been assigned to the 6810 R/W memory chip in your circuit.

Procedure

Step 1

Construct the circuit shown in the schematic diagram.
CAUTION: Be extremely careful when handling the 6810 memory chip since it is a MOS device and is very sensitive to static electricity. Make sure you are grounded with a ground strap. Also, when not using the 6810, be sure to place it in conductive foam or a protective device.

The extra logic circuitry is used to completely decode the address bus for addresses 5000 through 507F. Also, the 74LS30 NAND gate is used to enable the data input lines of the Heath ET3400 trainer through $\overline{RE}$. The ET3400 trainer uses three-state buffering between the 6800 data bus and the data i/o connector blocks provided on the trainer. These buffers are normally enabled to allow data transfer from the bus to the connector blocks. However, a logic zero must be applied to $\overline{RE}$ to allow data to be transferred from the data blocks onto the data bus. The 74LS30 supplies the logic zero state when a read operation is performed.

Step 2

Examine memory location 5000 and change its contents.

Step 3

Re-examine 5000. The contents should be the changed value, indicating that you have accessed a 6810 memory location. This is the first byte of memory in the 6810.

Step 4

Repeat Steps 2 and 3 for memory location 507F. This is the last byte of memory in the 6810.

Step 5

Repeat Steps 2 and 3 for memory locations 4FFF and 5080. You should observe that the contents of these locations cannot be changed since you have wired the 6810 to respond *only* to addresses 5000 through 507F (128 bytes).

Step 6

Execute the given program.

Step 7

Examine memory locations 5000 through 507F. You should observe that all these locations have been cleared by the program execution.

Conclusions

Verify from the schematic diagram that the 6810 has been assigned to addresses 5000 through 507F.

How many 2112 R/W memory chips would be required to provide the same 128 bytes of memory?

What must you do to provide 256 bytes of R/W memory using the 6810?

EXPERIMENT 7-2

Purpose

To interface 256 bytes of R/W memory to the 6800 system using the 2112 memory chip.

Program

Hex Address	Hex Contents	Mnemonics/ Contents	Operation
0000	CE	LDX #	Load the index register
0001	50	50	immediate with 5000
0002	00	00	
0003	6F	CLR X	Clear using indexed
0004	00	00	addressing
0005	08	INX	Increment the index register
0006	8C	CPX #	Compare the index register
0007	51	51	immediate to 5100
0008	00	00	
0009	26	BNE	Branch if Z flag clear
000A	F8	F8	(to address 0003)
000B	3E	WAI	Stop

This program uses a routine similar to the ones used in Experiments 5-1 and 7-1 to clear a series of memory locations. However, here you will clear memory locations 5000 through 50FF. These are the 256 addresses that have been assigned to the 2112 memory chips in the circuit.

Equipment

ET304
Two 2112 R/W memory chips
7400 digital IC (2-bit NAND)
74LS27 digital IC (3-bit NOR)
Two 74154 decoders

Schematic Diagram (Fig. 7-14)

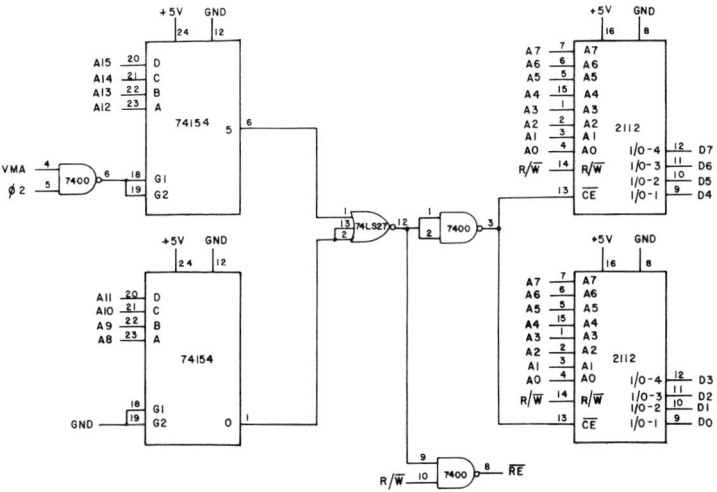

Fig. 7-14. Schematic diagram for Experiment 7-2.

Procedure

Step 1

Construct the circuit shown in the schematic diagram.

CAUTION: Be extremely careful when handling the 2112 memory chips. These are MOS devices which are very sensitive to static electricity. Make sure you are grounded with a ground strap. Also, when not using the 2112s, be sure to place them in conductive foam or a protective device.

The two 74154 decoders are used to completely decode the address bus for addresses 5000 through 50FF. This decoding circuit is similar to the one you constructed in Experiment 6-2. When any of these addresses appear on the address bus, the 2112 chips will be enabled via $\overline{CE}$. One 2112 is connected to data lines D0 through D3 and the other to data lines D4 through D7. The ET3400 trainer uses three-state buffering between the 6800 data bus and the data I/O connector blocks provided on the trainer. These buffers are normally enabled to allow data transfer from the bus to the connector blocks. However, a logic zero must be applied to $\overline{RE}$ to allow data to be transferred from the data connector blocks onto the 6800 data bus. A 7400 NAND gate supplies this signal.

Step 2
Examine memory location 5000 and change its contents.

Step 3
Re-examine location 5000. The contents should be the changed value, indicating that you have accessed a read/write memory location supplied by the 2112s.

Step 4
Repeat Steps 2 and 3 for memory location 50FF.

Step 5
Repeat Steps 2 and 3 for memory locations 4FFF and 5100. You should observe that the contents of these locations cannot be changed since you have wired the 2112s to respond *only* to addresses 5000 through 50FF (256 bytes).

Step 6
Execute the given program.

Step 7
Examine memory locations 5000 through 50FF. You should observe that all of these locations have been cleared by the program execution.

Conclusion

Verify the decoding scheme used on the schematic diagram.

Why are $\phi 2$ clock and VMA used in the decoding scheme?

What is the reason for R/W on the 2112 chips?

How many 2112 chips would be required to provide 128 bytes of memory? 512 bytes? 1024 bytes?

CHAPTER 8

The 6820/6821 Peripheral Interface Adapter

INTRODUCTION

You will now complete your 6800 microcomputer system with the Motorola 6820/6821 peripheral interface adapter (PIA). For all functional purposes, the 6820 and 6821 are interchangeable and either chip can be used in your system. Motorola was the first major chip manufacturer to provide a programmable (smart) chip for interfacing the microprocessor to the "outside world." Since Motorola introduced the PIA, other manufacturers have introduced similar chips, such as the Intel 8255 programmable peripheral interface (PPI) and the Zilog programmable input-output (PIO) chip. Each chip has its advantages and disadvantages. However, the function is the same: to provide the basic interfacing requirements of address decoding, three-state buffering, and latching. The PIA has two 8-bit *channels* or *ports* that may be connected to peripheral devices. These ports can be programmed as either input or output ports. In fact, each bit within the port can be *separately* programmed for either input or output transfers, a feature that is only available on one of the three ports on the 8080-family 8255 i/o chip. Once the port lines have been designated as input or output lines, you will simply treat each port as if it were a separate memory location and then transfer data between the 6800 and the PIA using the 6800 load and store instructions.

The PIA also has the capability of generating interrupt requests that are sent to the 6800 after having been initiated by a peripheral device. A problem with the 6800 interrupt request (IRQ) is that, without the PIA chip (or an external flag circuit), the request will be lost if the I flag of the 6800 is set. However, when a peripheral device generates an interrupt request through the PIA, an interrupt flag bit is set within the PIA that causes the interrupt request signal to be generated until the interrupt has been serviced. Therefore, the request is not lost even if the I flag is set when the request is initially made.

Another common use of the PIA is to provide *complete* and *partial handshaking* between the 6800 and a peripheral device. That is, the PIA can be used as a communicator between the 6800 and a peripheral device to tell the 6800 when service is requested and then to tell the peripheral device when that service has been rendered.

Because of its flexibility and low cost, the PIA can easily be part of any 6800 microcomputer system. It makes the job of interfacing much easier. In this chapter you will become familiar with the internal structure and pin assignments of the PIA. You will also learn how to initialize and program the PIA to perform its various functions. Then, in Chapter 9, you will learn how to connect the PIA to the 6800 and i/o devices such as switches, relays, keyboards, and displays.

OBJECTIVES

At the end of this chapter you will be able to do the following:

- Describe the internal registers of the PIA.
- Program the PIA port lines for input and output operations.
- Explain the *initialization* procedure for the PIA and write an initialization program.
- Describe the 6820/6821 pin assignments.
- Explain how to connect the PIA to the 6800 system.
- Write a program to provide data i/o using the PIA.
- Describe the procedure for addressing the PIA and for internal register selection.
- Describe the function of each control bit in the PIA control registers.
- Understand how interrupts are processed through the PIA.
- Understand how the PIA may be used to provide complete and partial *handshaking* with peripheral devices.

6821 FUNCTIONAL DESCRIPTION

Before entering into a detailed discussion of the PIA pin assignments and interfacing requirements, let us take a look at the PIA from a functional viewpoint. A functional diagram of the 6821 is shown in Fig. 8-1. First, note that the PIA can be looked at functionally as having two sides—a 6800 side and a peripheral side. The 6800 side includes the data, address, and control lines which interface to the 6800 data, address, and control buses. The peripheral side

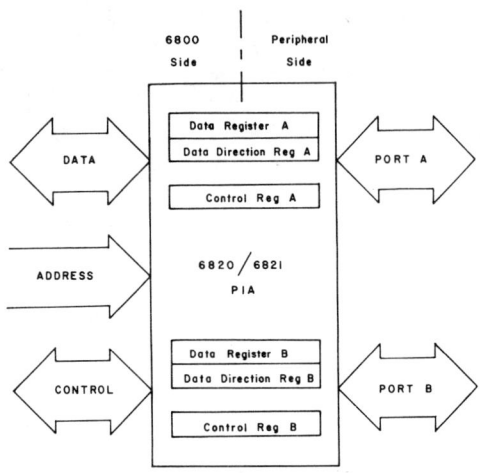

Fig. 8-1. Functional diagrams of the 6820/6821 PIA.

contains two *i/o ports* (A and B) which will interface to peripheral devices. Each port contains eight data lines which may be configured independently as input or output. This allows for a high degree of interfacing flexibility. Shortly the procedure for port configuration will be discussed. Internally, the PIA contains six 8-bit registers. Three registers apply to port A and three apply to port B. Each group of three registers has the same function with respect to its respective port. Each group of three registers contains a data register (DRA or DRB, data direction register (DDRA or DDRB), and control register (CRA or CRB). A discussion of each follows.

Data Registers (DRA and DRB)

Each data register acts as a temporary 8-bit storage register for data being transferred between the 6800 and the i/o device connected to the PIA chip. Each of the eight bits in the data registers is connected to one of the i/o port data lines. Recall that each port contains eight i/o data lines. For example, port A contains eight data lines, PA0 through PA7. Therefore, bit 0 of DRA is tied to PA0, bit 1 of DRA is tied to PA1, and so on. The same arrangement is used for the DRB bits and lines PB0 through PB7. The register bits are latched when used for output operations and they are unlatched (simple gates) when they are used for input.

Data Direction Registers (DDRA and DDRB)

The data direction registers are 8-bit registers which define the port lines as being used for either input or output operations. Each bit within the DDR configures its corresponding port data line. A 1 in a DDR bit will cause its corresponding port line to be configured as an output line, while a zero will cause it to be configured as an input line. For example, if DDRA bit 3 contains a 1, the PA3 line will be configured as an output data line. If DDRA bit 4 contained a 0, the PA4 line would be configured as an input data line. The ports are configured by storing a data byte into each data direction register. To configure port A as an input port and port B as an output port, you would store 00 in DDRA and FF in DDRB. Remember that since the data direction register and the data register are considered to be memory locations, they are loaded with memory-reference instructions.

Control Registers (CRA and CRB)

The control registers are 8-bit registers which are used for a variety of control functions. Each bit within the register controls a particular function. The control register will allow four of the peripheral control lines of the PIA to be used for interrupt servicing and polling routines. The control register is also used to select either the DR or DDR for use in a data transfer operation. A more detailed discussion of the control register is included later in this chapter.

6820/6821 PIN ASSIGNMENTS

The PIA is a 40-pin integrated circuit. The various pin assignments are shown in Fig. 8-2. A functional description of each pin follows.

V_{ss} (Ground: Pin 1)

Pin 1 should be connected to the system ground.

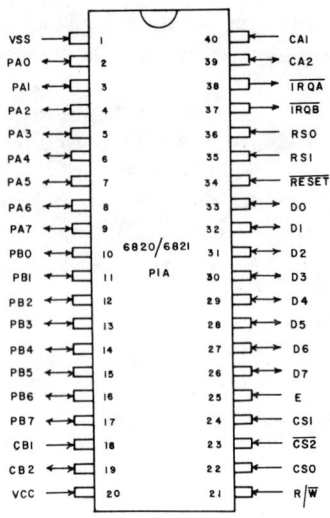

Fig. 8-2. Pin assignments for the 6820/6821 PIA.

Port A Data Lines (PA0–PA7: Pins 2–9)

As stated earlier, each of these lines may be used as an input or an output line. The use of a particular line is determined through proper selection of individual bits in the data direction register (DDRA).

Data will be transferred into the 6800 through the lines that have been configured as input. This will be accomplished when a load instruction is executed, transferring the information from the PIA port input lines to the 6800 internal register that is being loaded. In the input mode, each input data line represents a maximum of one TTL load.

Data will be output to the i/o devices through the data lines that have been configured as output lines. This output transfer will be accomplished with a store instruction which, when executed, will transfer data from the desired 6800 register to data register A (DRA). The data that has been stored in DRA will then appear on the port A data lines which have been configured as output lines. With the 6820, the port A lines only have CMOS drive capabilities and must be buffered to provide drive for TTL devices. With the 6821, they are directly TTL compatible.

Port B Data Lines (PB0–PB7: Pins 10–17)

These lines are used very similar to the port A data lines. You may configure each of the lines as being either an input or an output line through the use of data direction register B (DDRB). With the 6820, one major difference between ports A and B is that when the port B lines have been configured as output, they are TTL compatible and each may be used as a source of up to 1 milliampere at 1.5 volts to directly drive the base of a transistor switch. With the 6821 *both* ports have TTL drive capabilities.

Interrupt Input—Port B (CB1: Pin 18)

This is an input-only line used to set bit 7 of control register B which is used as a flag to indicate that a peripheral wishes to interrupt the 6800. This will be discussed in more detail later in this chapter (see *PIA Control Registers*).

Peripheral Control—Port B (CB2: Pin 19)

This line can be programmed through the use of control register B to act as an interrupt input or as a peripheral control output to provide handshaking. When in the output mode, it is TTL compatible and when configured as an interrupt input, it represents one TTL load. This pin will be discussed in more detail later in this chapter (see *PIA Control Registers*).

V_{cc} (Pin 20)

This pin is connected to the system +5-volt dc power supply.

Read/Write (R/$\overline{W}$: Pin 21)

This pin is connected directly to the R/$\overline{W}$ line on the 6800. A low state on this line allows data to be transferred from the 6800 to the PIA. A high state allows for data transfer from the PIA to the 6800. Data will only be transferred when the proper address and enabling pulse are present at the PIA. PIA addressing and enabling will be discussed shortly.

Chip Selects (CS0, CS2, CS1: Pins 22–24)

These pins are used in the same way that the chip-select signals were used on the 6810 R/W memory and 6830 ROM chips. They will partially decode the address bus to select the PIA. To select the PIA, CS0 and CS1 must be high and $\overline{CS2}$ must be low.

Enable (E: Pin 25)

This pin is used to supply a timing signal to the PIA and, therefore, is normally connected directly to the $\phi 2$ clock. To completely enable the PIA, the chip selects must be held in their active state for the duration of the E($\phi 2$) pulse.

Data (D0–D7: Pins 33–26)

These pins are connected directly to the eight data bus lines D0 through D7. The data bus lines are bidirectional and allow data transfer between the 6800 and PIA. The output drivers are three-state buffered and remain in their high-impedance state except when a PIA read operation is being performed.

Reset ($\overline{\text{Reset}}$: Pin 34)

A high-to-low transition at this pin will cause all register bits in the PIA to be reset to a logical 0 state. It can be used with a power-on reset signal or tied to the 6800 reset interrupt pin to reset the PIA when the entire system is reset.

Register Selects (RS0, RS1: Pins 36, 35)

These two lines are used to select the various registers within the PIA. They are normally tied to address lines A0 and A1, respectively, and are used in conjunction with the control registers to select the specific register that is desired. This selection process is discussed in the next section of this chapter.

Interrupt Requests ($\overline{\text{IRQA}}$, $\overline{\text{IRQB}}$: Pins 38, 37)

These are output lines that are normally *wire*-ORed together to be connected directly to the 6800 $\overline{\text{IRQ}}$ line. When an i/o device generates an interrupt, an interrupt flag bit of the respective PIA control register will be set which, in turn, causes the respective $\overline{\text{IRQ}}$ line to go low. This generates an interrupt request that is sent to the 6800. Each of these lines has two interrupt flag bits in its respective control register that can cause the $\overline{\text{IRQ}}$ line to go low. Each of these internal flags corresponds to a particular peripheral interrupt line; CA1 and CA2 correspond to port A and CB1 and CB2 correspond to port B. Once an internal interrupt flag has been set, the $\overline{\text{IRQ}}$ line will remain low until the flag is cleared by servicing the interrupt with a PIA read or write operation. Therefore, an interrupt request is not lost if the I flag in the 6800 condition code register is set, which disables it from recognizing interrupts.

Peripheral Control (CA2: Pin 39)

This line is used in essentially the same way as the CB2 line (pin 19). It can be programmed through the use of control register A to act as an interrupt input line or it may be used as a peripheral control output line. When in the output mode, it is TTL compatible and when configured as an interrupt input, it represents one TTL load. A more detailed discussion of this pin function will follow in this chapter (see *PIA Control Registers*).

Interrupt Input (CA1: Pin 40)

This line is similar to the CB1 line (pin 18). It is an input-only line used to set bit 7 of control register A which is used as a flag to indicate a peripheral interrupt. This, in turn, can cause the $\overline{\text{IRQA}}$ line to go low, generating an interrupt request.

PIA INTERFACING AND ADDRESSING

Fig. 8-3 shows how the various pins would be utilized to interface the PIA to the 6800. The PIA data lines would be connected directly to the 6800 data lines D0 through D7. For control, the following PIA lines would be connected directly to the corresponding signals on the 6800 control bus: R/$\overline{\text{W}}$, $\overline{\text{RESET}}$, $\overline{\text{IRQA}}$, $\overline{\text{IRQB}}$, +5V, and GND.

Chip Selection

To access the PIA, you will use the PIA register-select, chip-select, and enable lines. Recall that the chip-select pins along with the enable pin will select or access the PIA. In Fig. 8-3, we are connecting the 6800 VMA line to the CS1 line on the PIA. This is done so

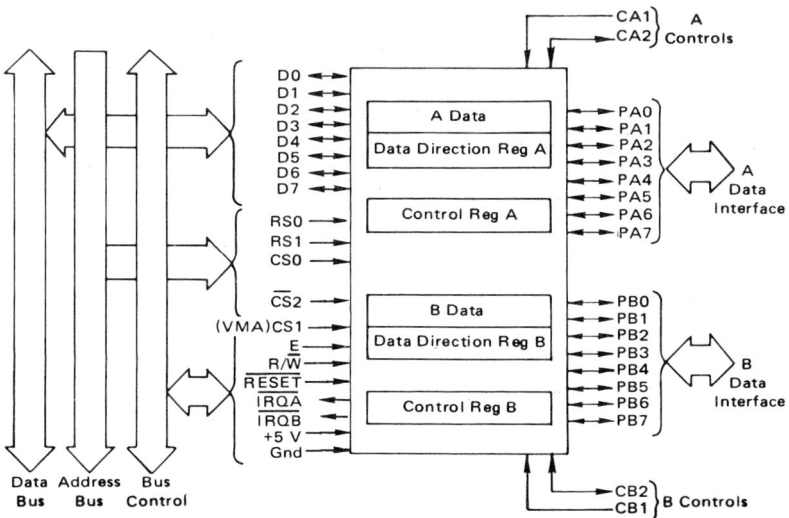

Courtesy Motorola Semiconductor Products Inc.

Fig. 8-3. PIA interfacing.

215

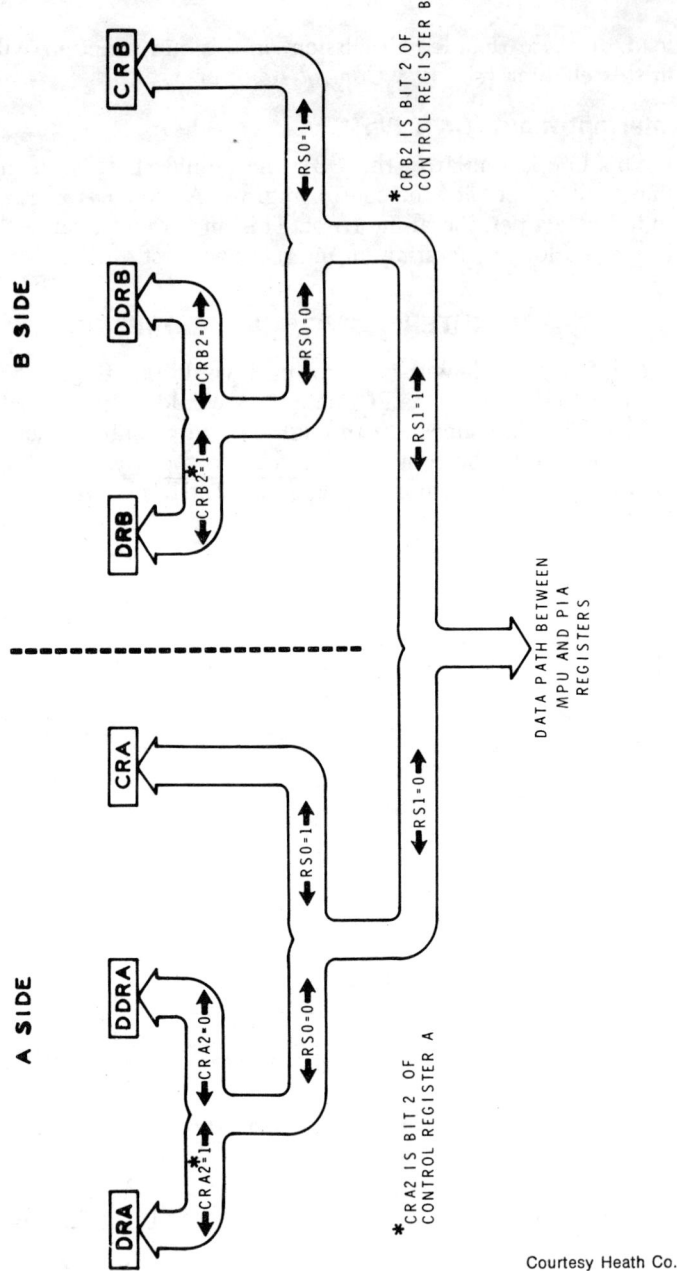

Fig. 8-4. PIA register selection.

that the PIA will be selected only when a valid memory address appears on the address bus. In practice, the VMA may be ANDed with an address line to provide more complete decoding. To provide timing between the 6800 and the PIA, you will connect the $\phi 2$ clock to the PIA enable pin (E). The remaining chip selects (CS0 and $\overline{CS2}$) are tied to the 6800 address bus to provide partial decoding for the chip.

Register Selection

The register select pins, RS0 and RS1, are always connected to address lines A0 and A1, respectively. Recall that these pins are used to select one of six registers within the PIA. This creates a problem since there are only four possible logic combinations for these two pins. However, we wish to select one of *six* registers. The solution to the problem is the PIA control register. The register selection process is shown in Fig. 8-4. The RS1 bit is used to access either port A or port B. If RS1 is low, port A will be selected, but if RS1 is high, port B will be selected. The RS0 bit narrows the selection

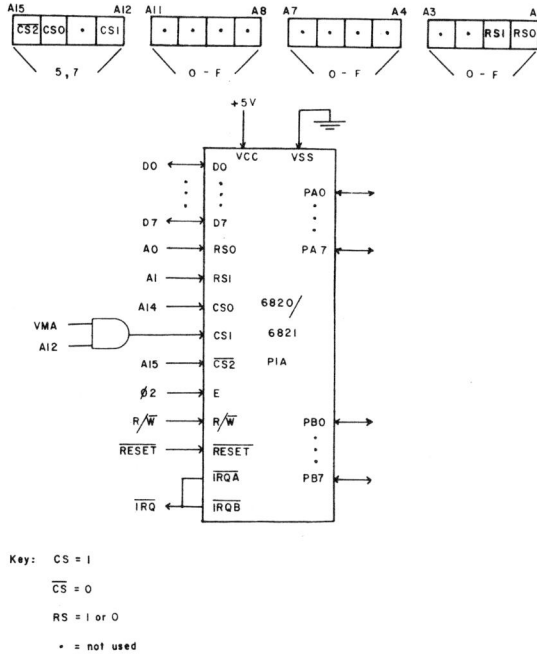

Fig. 8-5. PIA pin connections and decoding chart.

still further by selecting either the control register or the data register/data direction register of the selected port. If RS0 is high, the control register will be selected, but if RS0 is low, either the data register *or* the data direction register will be selected, depending upon the status of *bit 2* of the respective control register. If bit 2 of the control register is low and RS0 is low, the data direction register will be selected. However, if bit 2 of the control register is high, the data register is selected. For example, suppose RS1 = 1, RS0 = 0, and bit 2 of control register B is low. With these conditions, the data direction register of port B (DDRB) will be selected.

Fig. 8-5 shows how a PIA might be connected to the 6800 system. It is necessary only to allocate four addresses to select any register in the PIA. In this example, we have used addresses 5000 through 5003. Naturally, we are only partially decoding the address bus since from the decoding chart you can see that the PIA will be enabled for addresses 5000-5FFF and 7000-7FFF. This does not create a problem as long as no other chips are assigned to any of these addresses. Using this decoding scheme, the information in Fig. 8-6 shows how the PIA would respond to addresses 5000 through 5003 and which register would be selected for each address. Note that with addresses 5000 and 5002, the data direction *or* data register can be selected. The specific register that is selected will depend on the status of bit 2 in the respective control register. The control registers are selected with addresses 5001 and 5003.

ADDRESS	CS0	CS1	$\overline{CS2}$	RS1	RS0	PIA Register Selected
5000	1	1	0	0	0	DDRA or DRA *
5001	1	1	0	0	1	CRA
5002	1	1	0	1	0	DDRB or DRB *
5003	1	1	0	1	1	CRB

* Depends on Bit 2 of the Control Register

Fig. 8-6. Example of PIA register selection.

PIA INITIALIZATION AND SERVICING

Prior to using the PIA for data transfer, you must initialize it by defining the port lines as either input or output lines. As you saw in the first part of this chapter, this is accomplished by the 1s and 0s placed in the bits in each data direction register (DDR). Recall that if a 1 existed in a DDR bit, its corresponding port line would be configured as an output data line while if a 0 existed, its port line would be an input data line. To initialize the PIA, you will have to execute an initialization program that will store a binary number in each data direction register and, thus, configure each port. The initialization procedure will be as follows:

1. Clear bit 2 of both control registers.
2. Store a number in DDRA to configure port A.
3. Set bit 2 of control register A (CRA).
4. Store a number in DDRB to configure port B.
5. Set bit 2 of control register B (CRB).

In the above procedure, Step 1 clears bit 2 of both control registers so that the data *direction* register will be selected rather than the data register. The ports will then be configured by storing a binary number in each data direction register (Steps 2 and 4). After each port has been configured, bit 2 of the control register is set such that the data register will be selected for subsequent data transfer.

Example 8-1: PIA Initialization

The following program will configure port A as an 8-bit input port and port B as an output port. We will assume that the PIA has been assigned addresses 5000 through 5003 and that the system has been reset prior to executing the initialization program.

Hex Address	Mnemonics/ Contents	Operation
0000	LDAA #	
0001	00	00 → ACCA
0002	STAA $$	
0003	50	ACCA → DDRA
0004	00	
0005	LDAA #	
0006	04	04 → ACCA
0007	STAA $$	
0008	50	ACCA → CRA
0009	01	
000A	LDAA #	
000B	FF	FF → ACCA
000C	STAA $$	
000D	50	ACCA → DDRB
000E	02	
000F	LDAA #	
0010	04	04 → ACCA
0011	STAA $$	
0012	50	ACCA → CRB
0013	03	

First, resetting the system will reset the PIA if the $\overline{\text{RESET}}$ pin on the PIA is connected to the system reset, as is usually the case. This will cause all of the registers in the PIA to be cleared, and therefore, the first step of the initialization procedure is accomplished. Port A is configured as an input port by loading 00 into accumulator A and then storing this in data direction register A. This register will be selected since bit 2 of control register A is zero. Bit 2 of control register A is then set by loading 04 (0000 0100) into accumulator A and then storing this in the control register. This allows you to access the data register for subsequent i/o. The instructions for configuring port B as an output port are very similar except that the data direction register is being loaded with all ones (FF).

Example 8-2: PIA Data I/O

Assuming that the PIA has been configured as in Example 8-1, the following program will input data from port A and output the same data to port B.

Hex Address	Mnemonics/ Contents	Operation
0000	LDAA $$	
0001	50	Port A → ACCA
0002	00	(read port A data)
0003	STAA $$	
0004	50	ACCA → Port B
0005	02	(store data to port B)
0006	WAI	STOP

To input data from port A, you simply use a load instruction that addresses the port A data register. The data register will be selected rather than the data direction register since you have already set bit 2 of the control register in your initialization program. To output the data to port B, you will use a store instruction that addresses the port B data register. This is a very simple program since data is just being transferred from an input port to an output port. However, once the data is in the 6800, you have the full power of the 6800 instruction set available to analyze that data to determine the output conditions.

PIA Control Registers

Now we will discuss the control registers of the PIA in more detail. Besides the bit-2 function of the control register which has already been discussed, the control register is used mainly for control of interrupts. The bit format of each control register is shown in Fig. 8-7. Actually, each control register is identical in format and

	7	6	5	4	3	2	1	0
CRA	IRQA1	IRQA2	CA2 Control			DDRA Access	CA1 Control	

	7	6	5	4	3	2	1	0
CRB	IRQB1	IRQB2	CB2 Control			DDRB Access	CB1 Control	

Courtesy Motorola Semiconductor Products Inc.

Fig. 8-7. Control register format.

function. Therefore, we will confine our discussion to control register A, keeping in mind that the function of control register B is the same. Our discussion will begin with bit 0 (CRA-0) and bit 1 (CRA-1).

Bits 0 and 1 (CRA-0 and CRA-1) of the control register are labeled CA1 Control since they are used to define the effect and active state of the CA1 pin on the PIA. Recall that CA1 is an input-only pin that can be used by an i/o device to generate interrupt requests. When the pin is activated, the interrupt flag bit (CRA-7) of the control register will be set, indicating an interrupt request has been generated. Bit 0 (CRA-0) of the control register will determine the effect of setting this flag. If CRA-0 is set (1), the flag

CRA-1 (CRB-1)	CRA-0 (CRB-0)	Interrupt Input CA1 (CB1)	Interrupt Flag CRA-7 (CRB-7)	MPU Interrupt Request $\overline{IRQA}$ ($\overline{IRQB}$)
0	0	↓ Active	Set high on ↓ of CA1 (CB1)	Disabled — $\overline{IRQ}$ remains high
0	1	↓ Active	Set high on ↓ of CA1 (CB1)	Goes low when the interrupt flag bit CRA-7 (CRB-7) goes high
1	0	↑ Active	Set high on ↑ of CA1 (CB1)	Disabled — $\overline{IRQ}$ remains high
1	1	↑ Active	Set high on ↑ of CA1 (CB1)	Goes low when the interrupt flag bit CRA-7 (CRB-7) goes high

Notes: 1. ↑ indicates positive transition (low to high)
2. ↓ indicates negative transition (high to low)
3. The Interrupt flag bit CRA-7 is cleared by an MPU Read of the A Data Register, and CRB-7 is cleared by an MPU Read of the B Data Register.
4. If CRA-0 (CRB-0) is low when an interrupt occurs (Interrupt disabled) and is later brought high, $\overline{IRQA}$ ($\overline{IRQB}$) occurs after CRA-0 (CRB-0) is written to a "one".

Courtesy Motorola Semiconductor Products Inc.

Fig. 8-8. Function of control register bits 0 and 1.

will cause the $\overline{IRQA}$ output pin to go low, thus generating an interrupt request to the 6800. If CRA-0 is cleared (0), the $\overline{IRQA}$ pin will remain high, *masking* out any interrupt request. Thus, CRA-0 determines whether the interrupt mode for the port is active or inactive. Bit 1 of control register A (CRA-1) defines the *active state* of pin CA1. If CRA-1 is set (1), a low-to-high transition on the CA1 pin will cause the interrupt flag bit (CRA-7) of the control register to be set. If CRA-1 is cleared (0), a high-to-low transition will cause the interrupt flag bit to be set. Thus, either a positive pulse or a negative pulse may be used to generate an interrupt signal. Fig. 8-8 summarizes the function of these two control register bits.

Bit 2 of the control register (CRA-2) has already been discussed and is used entirely for register selection. Bits 3, 4, and 5 of the control register (CRA-3, CRA-4, and CRA-5) are labeled CA2 Control since they are used to define the function, effect, and active states of the CA2 pin on the PIA. Recall that the CA2 pin can be designated as either input or output. This designation is accomplished by CRA-5 of the control register. When CRA-5 is cleared, the CA2 pin is configured as an input line. When CRA-5 is set, CA2 is designated as an output line.

CA2 Input

When configured as an input line, the CA2 pin is used as an interrupt line similar to CA1. In this mode, an active level on CA2 will cause bit 6 (CRA-6) of the control register to be set. CRA-6 is the interrupt flag used in conjunction with the CA2 pin in the same way that CRA-7 is used in conjunction with CA1. When being used as an interrupt input, the CA2 active state and effect are defined by bits 3 and 4 of the control register (CRA-3 and CRA-4). CRA-3 is used to determine the effect of setting the CRA-6 flag similar to the way CRA-0 was used in conjunction with the CRA-7 flag. If CRA-3 is set, the CRA-6 flag will cause the $\overline{IRQA}$ pin to go low, thus generating an interrupt request to the 6800. If CRA-3 is cleared, the $\overline{IRQA}$ pin will remain high, thus masking out the interrupt request. Bit 4 of control register A (CRA-4) will define the active state

CONTROL OF CA2 AND CB2 AS INTERRUPT INPUTS
CRA5 (CRB5) is low

CRA-5 (CRB-5)	CRA-4 (CRB-4)	CRA-3 (CRB-3)	Interrupt Input CA2 (CB2)	Interrupt Flag CRA-6 (CRB-6)	MPU Interrupt Request $\overline{IRQA}$ ($\overline{IRQB}$)
0	0	0	↓ Active	Set high on ↓ of CA2 (CB2)	Disabled — $\overline{IRQ}$ remains high
0	0	1	↓ Active	Set high on ↓ of CA2 (CB2)	Goes low when the interrupt flag bit CRA-6 (CRB-6) goes high
0	1	0	↑ Active	Set high on ↑ of CA2 (CB2)	Disabled — $\overline{IRQ}$ remains high
0	1	1	↑ Active	Set high on ↑ of CA2 (CB2)	Goes low when the interrupt flag bit CRA-6 (CRB-6) goes high

Notes:
1. ↑ indicates positive transition (low to high)
2. ↓ indicates negative transition (high to low)
3. The Interrupt flag bit CRA-6 is cleared by an MPU Read of the A Data Register and CRB-6 is cleared by an MPU Read of the B Data Register.
4. If CRA-3 (CRB-3) is low when an interrupt occurs (Interrupt disabled) and is later brought high, $\overline{IRQA}$ ($\overline{IRQB}$) occurs after CRA-3 (CRB-3) is written to a "one".

Courtesy Motorola Semiconductor Products Inc.

Fig. 8-9. Function of control register bits when CA2 is used as an input line.

of pin CA2 similar to the way CRA-1 defines the active state of CA1. If CRA-4 is set (1), a low-to-high transition on the CA2 pin will cause the interrupt flag bit (CRA-6) to be set. If CRA-4 is cleared (0), a high-to-low transition will cause the interrupt flag bit to be set. Fig. 8-9 summarizes the function of these control register bits when CA2 is used as an *input line.*

CA2 Output

Recall that CA2 will be configured as an output line when bit 5 of the control register is set. When CA2 is designated as an output line, the interrupt flag (CRA-6) will be cleared and remain in that state as long as bit 5 is set.

You will use CA2 as an output for polling and handshaking routines. Recall the discussion of handshaking in Chapter 5. Handshaking or polling required the use of status bits that would indicate when a peripheral device has requested service and when the 6800 has completed the service. The use of CA1 as an input and CA2 as an output as shown in Fig. 8-10 will provide the proper status levels to permit handshaking between the 6800 and a peripheral device. The procedure will be as follows.

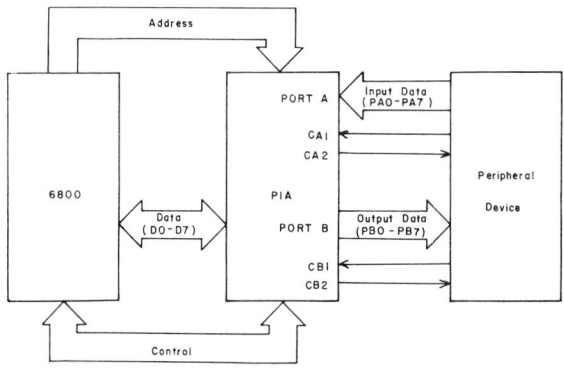

Fig. 8-10. Complete input and output handshaking using the PIA.

1. The peripheral device will generate an interrupt by activating the CA1 line on the PIA, signaling that it has data to give the 6800.
2. The CA1 interrupt causes the interrupt flag bit CRA-7 to set.
3. The interrupt flag causes an interrupt request to be generated to the 6800 and *also* causes CA2 to go high.
4. When the interrupt request is acknowledged, the 6800 will read the data from the port A data register (DRA).

5. After the read operation takes place, the CA2 line will go low and CRA-7 signaling is cleared, the peripheral that the interrupt has been serviced and the 6800 is ready for more data. Thus, the handshake is complete.

To achieve this complete handshake, CRA-5 must be set with CRA-3 and CRA-4 cleared. Therefore, bits 5, 4, and 3 of control register A would be 100.

If you do not desire to use interrupts and decide to use programmed i/o, CA1 would be eliminated from Fig. 8-10 and CA2 would be used as an output to signal the peripheral device. Here, the peripheral device would make data available on a continuing basis to the PIA port, but it needs to know when the 6800 has read the data from the data register so that new data can be supplied. This is a partial handshake. In this mode, CA2 will normally be high, then go low after a read-port A operation is executed. It will remain low for one enable signal ($\phi 2$) cycle. To achieve this mode, CRA-5 and CRA-3 must be set with CRA-4 cleared. Therefore, bits 5, 4, and 3 of control register A would be 101.

CRA-5 is high

CRA-5	CRA-4	CRA-3	CA2 Cleared	CA2 Set
1	0	0	Low on negative transition of E after an MPU Read "A" Data operation.	High when the interrupt flag bit CRA-7 is set by an active transition of the CA1 signal.
1	0	1	Low on negative transition of E after an MPU Read "A" Data operation.	High on the negative edge of the first "E" pulse which occurs during a deselect.
1	1	0	Low when CRA-3 goes low as a result of an MPU Write to Control Register "A".	Always low as long as CRA-3 is low. Will go high on an MPU Write to Control Register "A" that changes CRA-3 to "one".
1	1	1	Always high as long as CRA-3 is high. Will be cleared on an MPU Write to Control Register "A" that clears CRA-3 to a "zero".	High when CRA-3 goes high as a result of an MPU Write to Control Register "A".

Courtesy Motorola Semiconductor Products Inc.

Fig. 8-11. Control of CA-2 as an output.

There are two other possibilities for the output condition of CA2. They are:

1. CRA-5, CRA-4, CRA-3 = 110
2. CRA-5, CRA-4, CRA-3 = 111

In the first case, the CA2 output line will be held in a low state and in the second case CA2 will be held high.

CONTROL OF CB2 AS AN OUTPUT
CRB-5 is high

CRB-5	CRB-4	CRB-3	CB2 Cleared	CB2 Set
1	0	0	Low on the positive transition of the first E pulse following an MPU Write "B" Data Register operation.	High when the interrupt flag bit CRB-7 is set by an active transition of the CB1 signal.
1	0	1	Low on the positive transition of the first E pulse after an MPU Write "B" Data Register operation.	High on the positive edge of the first "E" pulse following an "E" pulse which occurred while the part was deselected.
1	1	0	Low when CRB-3 goes low as a result of an MPU Write in Control Register "B".	Always low as long as CRB-3 is low. Will go high on an MPU Write in Control Register "B" that changes CRB-3 to "one".
1	1	1	Always high as long as CRB-3 is high. Will be cleared when an MPU Write Control Register "B" results in clearing CRB-3 to "zero".	High when CRB-3 goes high as a result of an MPU Write into Control Register "B".

Courtesy Motorola Semiconductor Products Inc.

Fig. 8-12. Control of CB-2 as an output.

When CA2 and CB2 are used as output lines, they have slightly different functions. When handshaking, port A will be used completely as an input port and port B will be used as an output port. Therefore, CA2 will indicate when the 6800 has read (loaded) data from the port A data register (DRA) and CB2 will indicate when the 6800 has written (stored) data into the port B data register (DRB). Figs. 8-11 and 8-12 summarize the functions of CA2 and CB2, respectively, when used as an output line. The following examples should help to clarify the above discussion.

Example 8-3

Suppose you store the hex number 27 into control register B. How will this control port B? The control register would be configured as shown below:

CRB-7	CRB-6	CRB-5	CRB-4	CRB-3	CRB-2	CRB-1	CRB-0
0	0	1	0	0	1	1	1

This configuration will provide complete *data output* handshaking through port B. The following is a description of each bit function:

CRB-0 set will cause an interrupt to be generated when the interrupt flag (CRB-7) is set.
CRB-1 set will cause the CRB-7 interrupt flag to set on a low-to-high transition of the CB1 pin.
CRB-2 set selects the data register of port B.
CRB-3 and CRB-4 cleared permits CB2 to go high when the interrupt flag bit is set by an active transition of CB1 and to go low after the 6800 *stores* data to the port B data register.

CRB-5 set designates CB2 as an output line.
CRB-6 cleared as a result of CRB-5 being set.
CRB-7 cleared to be used as an interrupt flag for CA1.

Example 8-4:

Suppose you store the hex number 27 into control register A. How will this control port A? The control register bit structure would be the same as control register B was in Example 8-4. However, here CA2 would go high after an interrupt is generated on CA1 and go low after a *read* (load) operation has been performed on the port A data register. Therefore, this would provide for complete *data input* handshaking through port A.

Example 8-5:

Suppose you store the hex number 0F into control register A. How will this control the port? The control register bit structure would be as shown below:

CRA-7	CRA-6	CRA-5	CRA-4	CRA-3	CRA-2	CRA-1	CRA-0
0	0	0	0	1	1	1	1

CRA-0 set will cause an interrupt to be generated when the interrupt flag bit (CRA-7) is set.
CRA-1 set will cause the CRA-7 interrupt flag to set on a low-to-high transition of the CA1 pin.
CRA-2 set selects the data register of port A.
CRA-3 set will cause an interrupt to be generated when the interrupt flag bit (CRA-6) is set.
CRA-4 cleared will cause the CRA-6 interrupt flag bit to set on a high-to-low transition of CA2.
CRA-5 cleared designates CA2 as an input pin.
CRA-6 cleared to be used as an interrupt flag for CA2.
CRA-7 cleared to be used as an interrupt flag for CA1.

Fig. 8-13 summarizes the control register bit functions.

REVIEW QUESTIONS

1. List the six internal registers of the PIA.

   ————, ————, ————

   ————, ————, ————.

2. The PIA has ———— programmable data lines. (How many?)
3. Draw the flowchart of the register selection process.

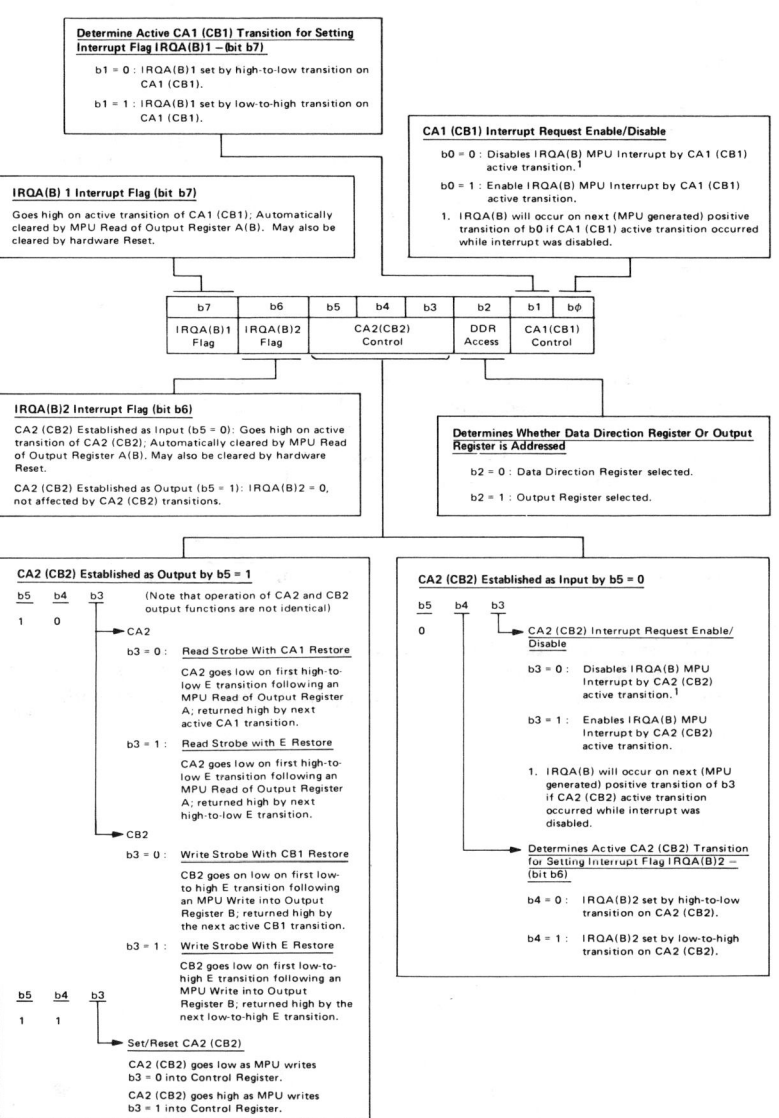

Courtesy Motorola Semiconductor Products Inc.

Fig. 8-13. Control register bit functions.

4. What type of integrated-circuit technology is used to manufacture the PIA? _____

5. To configure PA0 through PA3 as input and PA4 through PA7 as output, DDRA must contain _____ $_{(16)}$.

6. Port _____ of the PIA can always be used to drive the base of a transistor directly.

7. Two pins on the PIA that *are always* used as interrupt inputs are _____ and _____.

8. Bit _____ of the control register designates CA2 (CB2) as input or output.

9. When CA2 (CB2) is used as an interrupt input, bit _____ of the control register is used as the CA2 (CB2) interrupt flag bit.

10. The E (Enable) pin of the PIA is usually connected to the _____.

11. A high-to-low transition on the $\overline{\text{Reset}}$ pin of the PIA will cause what to happen?

12. How are the interrupt request pins ($\overline{\text{IRQA}}$ and $\overline{\text{IRQB}}$) usually connected?

13. Write an initialization program to configure port A as an output port and and port B as an input port. Assume the PIA is assigned to addresses 8000 through 8003 and a reset has occurred prior to the program execution.

14. Assuming the PIA has been initialized as in problem 12, write a program to input data from port B, and output the *complement* of that data to port A.

15. When would CA2 (CB2) be used as an output pin?

16. Describe what is meant by *complete handshaking*.

17. How would the PIA ports be configured to provide *complete* input and output handshaking?

18. Bit 7 of control register A is labeled _____ and what is its function?

19. When CA1 (CB1) and CA2 (CB2) are used as interrupt inputs, bits _____ and _____ of the control register are used to define the active levels of these pins.

20. To provide complete input handshaking, bits 5, 4, and 3 of CRA must be _____ _____ _____ .

ANSWERS

1. Data Register A (DRA)
   Data Direction Register A (DDRA)
   Control Register A (CRA)
   Data Register B (DRB)
   Data Direction Register B (DDRB)
   Control Register B (CRB)

2. 16

3.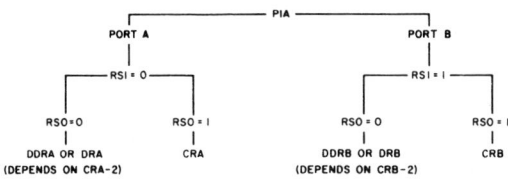

4. NMOS.

5. F0₁₆

6. B

7. CA1 and CB1

8. five
9. six
10. φ2 clock
11. All internal PIA registers will be cleared.
12. Wire-oRed together then connected to the 6800 $\overline{\text{IRQ}}$ line.
13.
LDAA #	
FF	Stores all 1s in
STAA $$	DDRA to configure
80	Port A as output
00	
LDAA #	
04	Sets bit #2 of
STAA $$	control register A
80	
01	
CLRA	Stores all 0s in
STAA $$	DDRB to configure
80	port B as input
02	
LDAA	
04	Sets bit #2 of control
STAA $$	register B
80	
03	

14.
LDAA $$	
80	Reads data from port B
02	
COMA	Complements data
STAA $$	
80	Writes data to port A
00	

15. To provide complete or partial handshaking between the 6800 and a peripheral device.
16. A peripheral device requests service from the 6800; the 6800 acknowledges the request and signals the peripheral device when the service is completed.
17. Port A as an input port with CA1 as an interrupt input line and CA2 as an output peripheral control line. Port B as an output port with CB1 as an interrupt input line and CB2 as an output peripheral control line.
18. Bit 7 of control register A is the CA1 interrupt request flag for port **A** (IRQA1). It is used as an interrupt flag for interrupts generated on pin CA1.

19. one and four
20. 100

EXPERIMENT 8-1

Purpose

To interface the PIA to the 6800 and demonstrate the PIA data output procedure.

Equipment

ET3400   6820/6821 PIA

Schematic Diagram (Fig. 8-14)

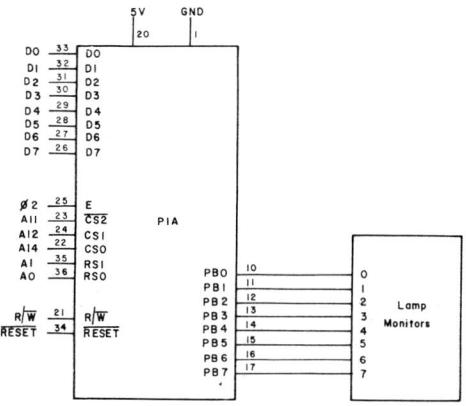

Fig. 8-14. Schematic diagram for Experiments 8-1 and 8-2.

Program

Hex Address	Hex Contents	Mnemonics/ Contents	Operation
0000	4F	CLRA	
0001	43	COMA	
0002	B7	STAA $$	
0003	50	50	PIA Initialized
0004	02	02	Port B = Output
0005	86	LDAA #	CRB bit 2 set
0006	04	04	
0007	B7	STAA $$	
0008	50	50	
0009	03	03	

231

000A	86	LDAA #	Load ACCA with
000B	FF	FF	output data
000C	B7	STAA $$	ACCA → DRB
000D	50	50	(store output data
000E	02	02	to port B)
000F	3E	WAI	Stop

Using the schematic diagram, the PIA is wired to the address bus such that it is assigned addresses 5000 through 5003. The first part of the program initializes the PIA by configuring port B as an output port. Bit 2 of control register B is set such that subsequent port B PIA operations will address the data register rather than the data direction register. The remainder of the program loads accumulator A with an 8-bit number (FF), then stores it to port B of the PIA. Since the lamp monitors are connected to port B, they should illuminate to indicate the stored value when the program is executed.

Procedure

Step 1
Construct the circuit shown in the schematic diagram on the ET3400 breadboard block using a PIA and the eight lamp monitors. The lamp monitors are being used as data output indicators. CAUTION: Be extremely careful when handling the PIA since it is a MOS device and very sensitive to static electricity. Make sure you are grounded with a ground strap. Also, when not using the PIA, be sure to place it in conductive foam or protective device.

Step 2
Load and execute the given program. All the lamp monitors should immediately illuminate upon program execution since you have stored all 1s (FF) to port B. If this doesn't happen, recheck your program and circuit construction.

Step 3
Change address 000B to 55 and re-execute the program. Lamp monitors #0, 2, 4, and 6 should now illuminate indicating a binary 0101 0101.

Step 4
Change address 000B to any value and note the lamp monitor pattern upon program execution.

Step 5
Save the wired circuit for the next experiment.

Conclusions

Briefly explain the PIA initialization procedure that you executed in the program.

What group of addresses will the PIA respond to using this decoding scheme? (Remember, you are only partially decoding the address bus.)

EXPERIMENT 8-2

Purpose
To demonstrate the use of a software time delay for data output.

Equipment
ET3400   6820/6821 PIA

Program

Hex Address	Hex Contents	Mnemonics/ Contents	Operation
0000	4F	CLRA	
0001	43	COMA	
0002	B7	STAA $$	
0003	50	50	PIA Initialized
0004	02	02	Port B = Output
0005	86	LDAA #	CRB bit 2 set
0006	04	04	
0007	B7	STAA $$	
0008	50	50	
0009	03	03	
000A	4F	CLRA	Clear ACCA
000B	4C	INCA	Increment ACCA
000C	01	NOP	No Operation
000D	01	NOP	No Operation
000E	01	NOP	No Operation
000F	B7	STAA $$	
0010	50	50	ACCA → DRB
0011	02	02	(store output data to port B)
0012	7E	JMP $$	Jump to address 000B
0013	00	00	
0014	0B	0B	

This program will initialize the PIA and configure port B as an output port. Accumulator A is then cleared and incremented. The result is stored to port B and displayed on the lamp monitors. The program will then jump back to the increment instruction. The accumulator will again increment with the results being displayed on the lamp monitors. You are actually creating a binary counter. The NOP instructions are added so that you may insert additional instructions required in a later step without re-entering the entire program. The 6800 will ignore the NOP instructions.

Schematic Diagram

Same as for Experiment 8-1.

Procedure

Step 1

Construct the circuit used in Experiment 8-1.

Step 2

Load and execute the program. According to the program explanation, you are creating a binary counter and the display should indicate the count each time the accumulator is incremented. However, all the lamp monitors are illuminated. Why?

Because the count takes place so fast, it looks like a constant output with all lamp monitors illuminated.

Step 3

In order to see the count, you must slow the process down. To do this, enter the following delay subroutine beginning at address 0030:

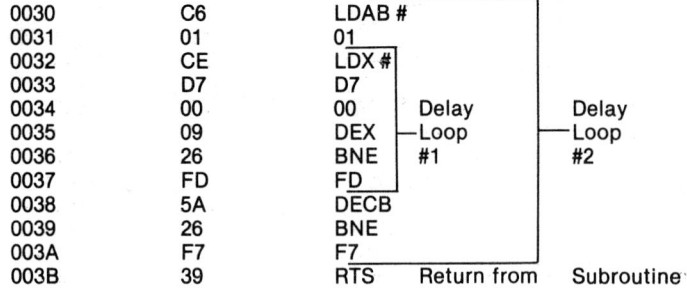

0030	C6	LDAB #		
0031	01	01		
0032	CE	LDX #		
0033	D7	D7		
0034	00	00	Delay	Delay
0035	09	DEX	Loop	Loop
0036	26	BNE	#1	#2
0037	FD	FD		
0038	5A	DECB		
0039	26	BNE		
003A	F7	F7		
003B	39	RTS	Return from	Subroutine

To call the subroutine, you must insert a jump to subroutine (JSR) in your main program. Therefore, insert:

BD-JSR
00-00
30-30

in place of the NOP instructions in the main program. The subroutine you just entered will provide approximately a 1-second delay between counts.

Step 4

Execute your program. The lamp monitors should now count in binary with a 1-second delay between each count. Let us take a closer look at the delay subroutine. Note that we have indicated two delay loops (#1 and #2). Delay loop #1 loads the index register with D700, then decrements it down to zero before coming out of the loop. Once out of loop #1, accumulator B is decremented. If the accumulator is not zero after the decrement, the index register loop (loop #1) will be executed again. If the accumulator is zero, the 6800 will return to the main program. In this case, you only executed loop #1 once, since you loaded a 01 in accumulator B at the beginning of the subroutine. To provide a longer delay, a larger value would be loaded into *accumulator B*. If you were to load 02 into accumulator B, loop #1 would be executed twice for approximately a 2-second delay. To provide a shorter delay time, a smaller value would be loaded into the *index register* for loop #1. The precise software delay time can be calculated based on the number of MPU cycles required for the delay routine. You can determine the number of MPU cycles required for each instruction from the instruction listings in Appendix C. Multiplying the total number of cycles in the delay by the 6800 cycle time of one microsecond will give you the software delay time. However, to get the *total* delay time, you must consider the propagation delay within the PIA. We have found that loading the index register with D700 and executing loop #1 once will provide about a 1-second delay.

Step 5

Change memory location 0031 to 0A and execute the program. This should provide about a 10-second delay between counts.

Step 6

Change the value being loaded into the index register to 0055 and execute the program. The count should now be very rapid.

Step 7

Save the circuit for the next experiment.

Conclusions

What is the longest delay obtainable with this subroutine (approximate)?

What is the shortest delay obtainable with this subroutine (approximate)?

How could the subroutine be modified to provide delays longer than 256 seconds?

How could the subroutine be modified if only short delays were required (less than one second)?

EXPERIMENT 8-3

Purpose

To demonstrate data input and output using the PIA.

Equipment

ET3400	7400 digital IC (2-bit NAND)
6820/6821 PIA	74LS27 digital IC (3-bit NOR)
	74LS30 digital IC (8-bit NAND)

Program

This program initializes the PIA by configuring port A as input and port B as output. The PIA decoding scheme partially decodes the address bus to recognize addresses 5000 through 5003. Once the PIA is initialized, the binary switch data is read from port A, then stored to port B to illuminate the lamp monitors.

Hex Address	Hex Contents	Mnemonics/ Contents	Operation
0000	4F	CLRA	
0001	B7	STAA $$	
0002	50	50	
0003	00	00	
0004	43	COMA	
0005	B7	STAA $$	
0006	50	50	PIA Initialized
0007	02	02	Port A = Input
0008	86	LDAA #	Port B = Output
0009	04	04	CRA bit 2 set
000A	B7	STAA $$	CRB bit 2 set
000B	50	50	
000C	01	01	
000D	B7	STAA $$	
000E	50	50	
000F	03	03	
0010	B6	LDAA $$	DRA → ACCA
0011	50	50	(Read port A data)
0012	00	00	
0013	B7	STAA $$	ACCA → DRB
0014	50	50	(Store data to port B)
0015	02	02	
0016	3E	WAI	

Schematic Diagram (Fig. 8-15)

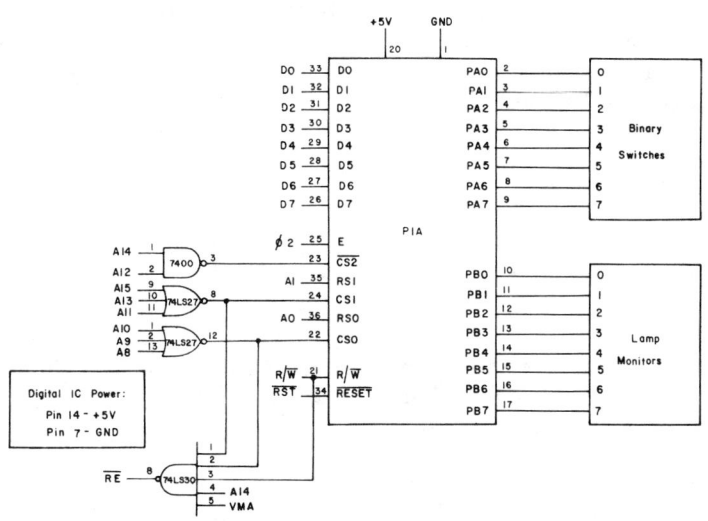

Fig. 8-15. Schematic diagram for Experiment 8-3.

Procedure

Step 1

Construct the circuit shown in the schematic diagram (Fig. 8-15). Use caution when handling the PIA.

The extra logic circuitry is used to more completely decode the address bus and to enable the data input lines through $\overline{RE}$ of the Heath trainer. The ET3400 trainer uses three-state buffering between the 6800 data bus and the data i/o connector blocks. These buffers are normally enabled to allow data transfer from the bus to the connector blocks. However, a logic zero must be applied to $\overline{RE}$ to allow data to be transferred from the data blocks to the data bus. Therefore, the 74LS30 NAND gate is wired to supply a logic zero state to $\overline{RE}$ during the data input operation.

Step 2

Load the given program.

Step 3

Set the binary switches to any arbitrary configuration and execute the program. The lamp monitors should show the previously set binary switch pattern. Note that the lamp monitors stay illuminated even though the program has stopped. This is because the port B data register acts as a storage register. The output data will not change until the port B data register contents are changed.

Step 4

Change the binary switch configuration and note that it has no effect on the output until the program is re-executed.

Step 5

Add a delay to the data transfer by inserting the delay subroutine given in Experiment 8-2. Remember to add the jump-to-subroutine instruction in the main program.

Step 6

Change the program to complement the binary switch data before it is stored to the lamp monitors.

Conclusions

Why do the lamps go out when you RESET the system?

What group of addresses will the PIA respond to using this decoding scheme? (Remember, you are still only partially decoding the address bus.)

CHAPTER 9

6800 System Interfacing

INTRODUCTION

Now that you are familiar with the PIA, you will see how this powerful i/o chip can be used to interface your system to the outside world. This discussion of 6800 system interfacing begins with switch interfacing. Many microcomputer input devices are simply a group of switches. Even a complicated keyboard can be broken down to a set of single switches. Therefore, it is important that you understand the basics of interfacing to a single switch. Once this is accomplished, you will see how a group of switches arranged in both a switch column and switch matrix can be interfaced to your system. This will lead you to a discussion of un-encoded and fully encoded keyboard interfacing.

A major output device in the microcomputer industry is the 7-segment LED display. In this chapter 7-segment LEDs will be discussed and you will see how they can be interfaced to your 6800 system via the PIA. A single display will be interfaced first, then you will see how a group of displays can be interfaced to display intelligible messages. You will be given programs throughout the discussion to show you how the PIA is initialized and the display characters are generated.

Finally, many electrical and mechanical input and output devices produce or require a continuous range of voltage or current values rather than two-state binary logic. For example, a thermocouple will produce continuous voltage values as a function of temperature. These continuous values are referred to as *analog* signals. In order for the 6800 to recognize these signals and to operate on them, they must be *converted* to *digital* information. Other devices, such as motors, might require that the digital information produced by a microcomputer system be converted to analog signals for control purposes. Fortunately, there are single chips that will perform these conversions. They are referred to as digital-to-analog (D/A) and analog-to-digital (A/D) converters. In this chapter, you will see how the following converters can be interfaced to your 6800 system via the PIA:

Signetics NE5018 D/A Converter
Motorola MC1408-8/MC1508-8 D/A Converter
Intersil ICL7109 A/D Converter
Teledyne 8703 A/D Converter

OBJECTIVES

At the end of this chapter you will be able to do the following:

- Interface your 6800 system to a single push-button switch.
- Interface your 6800 system to a switch column.
- Interface your 6800 system to a switch matrix.
- Interface your 6800 system to an un-encoded or fully encoded keyboard.
- Interface your 6800 system to a single seven-segment LED.
- Multiplex several seven-segment LEDs to provide the display of messages.
- Interface your 6800 system to the Signetics NE5018 and Motorola MC1408-8/MC1508-8 D/A converters.
- Interface your 6800 system to the Intersil ICL7109 and Teledyne 8703 A/D converters.

INTERFACING WITH SWITCHES

You will begin this section by interfacing your 6800 system to a single push-button switch. Then, you will interface the system to a switch column and switch matrix. When interfacing to a switch or switches, there are four basic interfacing requirements. They are *switch addressing, detecting switch closure, switch debouncing,* and *switch decoding.*

The first requirement, switch addressing, will be fulfilled by addressing the PIA. You can connect a single push-button switch to one of the PIA port lines as shown in Fig. 9-1. Then, you can address the switch by simply addressing the PIA.

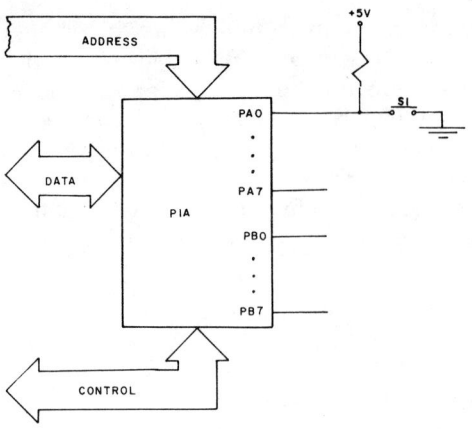

Fig. 9-1. Interfacing a single push-button switch.

Once you have addressed the switch or switches, you must detect a switch closure, if any. Note in Fig. 9-1 that switch S1 is connected to PA0 of the PIA through a pull-up resistor. This will cause a logical one (1) to appear at PA0 until the switch is closed. Recall from Chapter 3 that a logical AND operation was used to determine a device condition. The procedure involved ANDing a *status* byte with a *mask* byte to determine if a device is on or off. In this case, the device is a switch. A logic one indicates that the switch is off while a logic zero indicates the switch is closed. The status byte will be the port A input data byte. The mask byte will be 00000001 since, in this case, the switch is connected to PA0. For example, if the switch were connected to PA5, the mask byte would be 00100000. Now, if the switch at PA0 is open, the status byte would be 0000 0001. If you AND this with a mask byte of 0000 0001 the result is 0000 0001. However, if the switch is closed, the status byte would be 00000000. ANDing this with the mask byte would provide a result of 00000000. If this operation were performed by the 6800, the Z flag of the condition code register would be set upon switch closure. Therefore, the Z flag would act as a flag to indicate switch closure. Once the closure is detected, you can store the binary input information in a memory location. In this example (Fig. 9-1) we will simply store 01 in memory location 0060 to indicate that switch closure has been detected. If memory location 0060 is cleared, no closure has been detected. The program in Example 9-1 will detect switch closure by addressing the switch through the PIA.

The next requirement for switch closure is debouncing. Each single closure of a mechanical switch does not produce a single volt-

Example 9-1: Detecting Switch Closure

The following program is used to detect switch closure.

Hex Address	Hex Contents	Mnemonics/ Contents	Operation
0000	7F	CLR $$	
0001	50	50	
0002	01	01	
0003	7F	CLR $$	PIA Initialized
0004	50	50	
0005	00	00	Port A = Input
0006	86	LDAA #	Set CRA bit 2
0007	04	04	
0008	B7	STAA $$	
0009	50	50	
000A	01	01	
000B	7F	CLR $$	Clear M_{60}
000C	00	00	
000D	60	60	
000E	B6	LDAA $$	
000F	50	50	DRA → ACCA
0010	00	00	(read Port A)
0011	84	ANDA #	ACCA·01 → ACCA
			(AND status and
0012	01	01	mask bytes)
0013	26	BNE	Branch if Z flag clear
0014	F9	F9	(to address 000E)
0015	7C	INC $$	
0016	00	00	Increment M_{60}
0017	60	60	
0018	3E	WAI	Stop

The program assumes that the PIA is located at addresses 5000 through 5003. Note that the PIA is first initialized by configuring port A as an input port. Then, the mask byte is ANDed with the port A data until contact closure is detected.

age transition because the mechanical contacts "bounce." That is, the switch contacts are open-closed, open-closed, etc., for a few milliseconds before settling to a firm closure. This bounce can look like a series of 1s and 0s to a microprocessor. Therefore, you must wait until the bounce period ends before you read the data from the switch. This can be accomplished two ways. You can use a cross-coupled NAND gate circuit that will immediately latch in one state and ignore all switch bouncing, or you can provide a software delay in your program during the bounce period. In the latter case, the 6800 is performing the debouncing action. A typical delay period is 10 milliseconds; however, this will vary from switch to switch. To provide software debouncing, you will provide a 10-millisecond delay after you detect contact closure. Then, after the delay, your program will read the data from the switch (switches) again. If closure is still detected, you can be certain the switch is closed. The program in Example 9-2 will address the switch, detect closure, and provide software debouncing.

Example 9-2: Detecting Switch Closure and Providing Software Debouncing

The following program is used to detect switch closure and provide software debouncing.

Hex Address	Hex Contents	Mnemonics/ Contents	Operation
0000	7F	CLR $$	
0001	50	50	
0002	01	01	
0003	7F	CLR $$	PIA Initialized
0004	50	50	
0005	00	00	Port A = Input
0006	86	LDAA #	Set CRA bit 2
0007	04	04	
0008	B7	STAA $$	
0009	50	50	
000A	01	01	
000B	7F	CLR $$	
000C	00	00	Clear M_{60}
000D	60	60	
000E	B6	LDAA $$	
000F	50	50	DRA → ACCA
0010	00	00	(read Port A)
0011	84	ANDA #	ACCA·01 → ACCA
0012	01	01	(AND status and mask bytes)
0013	26	BNE	Branch if Z flag clear
0014	F9	F9	(to address 000E)
0015	BD	JSR $$	Jump to subroutine at
0016	00	00	address 0030
0017	30	30	(debouncing delay)
0018	B6	LDAA $$	
0019	50	50	DRA → ACCA
001A	00	00	(read port A)
001B	84	ANDA #	ACCA·01 → ACCA
001C	01	01	(AND status and mask bytes)
001D	26	BNE	Branch if Z flag cleared
001E	EF	EF	(to address 000E)
001F	7C	INC $$	
0020	00	00	Increment M_{60}
0021	60	60	
0022	3E	WAI	Stop
.	.	.	.
.	.	.	.

		(Debouncing Delay: 10 ms)	
0030	CE	LDX #	05 → X$_H$
0031	05	05	00 → X$_L$
0032	00	00	
0033	09	DEX	Decrement the index
0034	8C	CPX #	register
0035	00	00	Compare 0000 to the
0036	00	00	index register
0037	26	BNE	Branch if Z flag clear
0038	FA	FA	(to address 0033)
0039	39	RTS	Return to main program
			(address 0018)

The first 11 instructions (0000–000A) initialize the PIA and configure port A as an input port. Memory location 0060 is then cleared since this location will be incremented when sure switch closure is detected. Now the data at port A is read and a logic AND operation is performed to determine switch closure. If no closure is detected (Z flag cleared), the program will branch back to read the port until closure is detected (Z flag set). When closure is detected, the 6800 will jump to the subroutine located at address 0030. This subroutine will provide a 10-millisecond delay for switch debouncing using the index register. Once the delay has been provided, the 6800 returns to the main program to read port A and again verify contact closure. If closure is detected again, memory location 0060 is incremented. If no closure is detected, the program will branch back to the first port A read operation and the cycle will repeat itself until a firm closure is detected.

The last requirement for switch interfacing is switch decoding. After the 6800 detects a switch closure, it must decide which switch

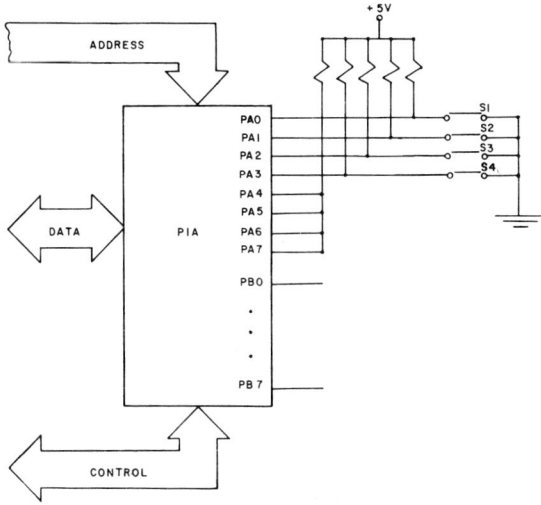

Fig. 9-2. Interfacing to a switch column.

is closed. Naturally, this is not a problem with a single switch. However, with multiple switches, a decoding procedure must be provided. Fig. 9-2 shows how four switches might be connected to your system. Note that switches S1 through S4 are connected to PA0 through PA3, respectively, and port A lines PA4 through PA7 are held high. When one of the switches is closed, its corresponding port line goes low. Therefore, when you load port A data into the accumulator, the corresponding bit is also 0. All the other accumulator bits will be 1 and the zero bit can be *decoded* by rotating the accumulator contents into the carry flag of the condition code register until that flag is cleared. The 6800 can then determine which switch is closed by counting the number of rotations that it takes to detect the cleared, or logic zero bit, position. Assuming switch closure has been detected and debounced, the program in Example 9-3 will *decode* the switches.

Example 9-3: Decoding a Switch Column

The following program is used to decode a switch column.

Hex Address	Hex Contents	Mnemonics/ Contents	Operation
0000	B6	LDAA $$	DRA → ACCA
0001	50	50	(read port A)
0002	00	00	
0003	CE	LDX #	
0004	00	00	Clear the index register
0005	00	00	
0006	46	RORA	Rotate Right — ACCA
0007	08	INX	Increment the index register
0008	25	BCS	Branch if Carry Set
0009	FC	FC	(to address 0006)
000A	DF	STX $	
000B	5F	5F	X_H → M_{5F}, X_L → M_{60}
000C	3E	WAI	Stop

The program will load port A data into the accumulator then rotate that data until the carry flag is cleared. After each rotation, the index register is incremented to count the number of rotations necessary to clear the C flag. The proper switch number is then stored in memory location 0060.

This program assumes that switch closure has been detected. When more than one switch is connected in a *column* to the PIA as in Fig. 9-2, you will use a compare instruction rather than a logic AND to detect closure. In this case, comparing the input data immediately to FF would detect closure. If none of the switches were closed, the Z flag would set as a result of the compare instruction. However, if a switch is closed the Z flag would clear as a result of the compare instruction and the debouncing routine would then be initiated, followed by the decoding scheme.

The same general procedure can be used to interface up to 16 switches in a column using one PIA. Naturally, with this many switches, you would have to utilize both PIA ports and two data bytes.

INTERFACING WITH KEYBOARDS

Keyboards are simply a collection of switches and, therefore, they can be connected to the PIA in a switch column as discussed in the first part of this chapter. In this case, the keyboard becomes a set of switches in which each key is connected to a separate input port line. When interfacing a keyboard in this manner, the procedure for detecting key closure, debouncing, and decoding are the same as discussed earlier. This is fine for a small number of keys, but when more than eight keys are involved, you must use mutibyte operations since more than one input port will be required. The number of port lines required may be reduced by connecting the keys in a switch *matrix*. The matrix will be an n-by-m, or n × m, matrix where n is the number of rows and m is the number of columns in the matrix. Each key will represent the intersection of a row and column.

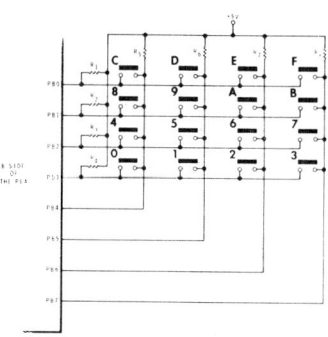

Fig. 9-3. Interfacing to a keyboard matrix.

Courtesy Heath Co.

A typical keyboard matrix is shown in Fig. 9-3. This is a 4 × 4 matrix which only requires eight port lines. In this scheme, an m × n keyboard matrix will always require m + n port lines while if you were to connect the keys in a switch column configuration, you would need m × n port lines. Here, we are connecting the matrix rows to PB0 through PB3 and the columns to PB4 through PB7. The keys are labeled to correspond to a hexadecimal keyboard. Each matrix row contains four keys as does each column. You will configure PB0 through PB3 as input lines and PB4 through PB7 as output lines.

The procedure for detecting key closure will be to *scan* each column by successively applying a logic zero to each output line PB4 through PB7. For example, suppose a logic zero is applied to column one (PB4). This can be done by storing EF in the B data register of the PIA. If none of the switches along the PB4 line (0, 4, 8, or C) are closed, the input lines (PB0 through PB3) will all be held at a logic one by pull-up resistors R1 through R4. However, if one of the keys is depressed, its corresponding input line will go low since the low state of PB4 will be applied directly to the input line through the switch. If no closure is detected in the first column, the logic zero will be removed from PB4 and applied to PB5 by storing DF in the data register B. The program can then check to see if any of the keys connected to the PB5 line (1, 5, 9, or D) are closed. You would continue to scan the keyboard matrix in this manner, one line at a time, until closure is detected. Once detected, you must provide debouncing and decoding program steps as discussed in the first part of the chapter. A rotate right procedure will be used to detect key closure within a column.

This procedure could be used to interface a keyboard containing as many as 64 keys using only one PIA. The keys would have to be configured in an 8 × 8 matrix and both PIA ports utilized. The technique just described was for an *un-encoded keyboard*. Another type of keyboard which makes the job of interfacing much easier is the *encoded keyboard*. This keyboard contains the key switches along with internal logic that will perform all the scanning and decoding which *you* had to provide for the un-encoded keyboard. The encoded keyboard will provide a unique code for each key. This code is usually an ASCII (American Standard Code for Information Interchange) value, but can be any code that would identify each key uniquely or separately. Most encoded keyboards will also provide circuitry for switch debouncing, thus further simplifying the interfacing task. The trade-off between the two types is the simpler software required by the encoded keyboard versus the lower cost of the un-encoded keyboard.

Fig. 9-4 shows how you would interface an encoded keyboard to your 6800 system. Here, the keyboard data is supplied to port A. The encoded keyboard will also supply a keyboard *strobe* pulse for each data transfer. The keyboard strobe will indicate a new key closure and will be connected to the CA1 pin on the PIA. Recall that the CA1 pin is an input-only line used to set an interrupt flag (bit 7) of control register A. If bit 0 of CRA is set, this flag will

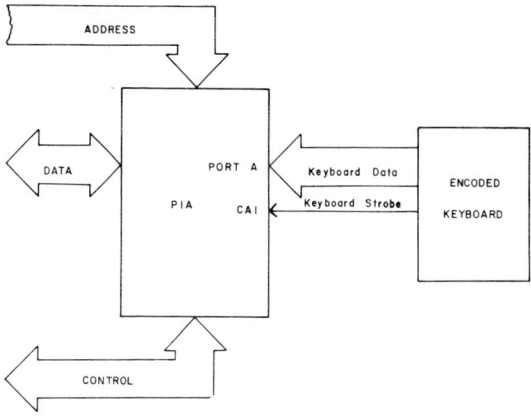

Fig. 9-4. Interfacing to an encoded keyboard.

cause an interrupt request to be generated to the 6800. The flag will be cleared when keyboard data is read from port A. After the flag has been cleared, the 6800 will be ready to accept another key closure through port A by a strobe pulse on the CA1 pin. Recall that the active state of CA1 can also be controlled with bit 1 of control register A. If bit 1 of CRA is set, the system will recognize a low-to-high strobe and if bit 1 of CRA is cleared, a high-to-low strobe will be recognized. You can make use of the interrupt capabilities of the 6800 and PIA as just discussed or you might want to use a polling routine to enter keyboard data. The program in Example 9-4 uses a polling routine.

Example 9-4: Polling Routine for Encoded Keyboards

The following program is a polling routine for encoded keyboards.

Hex Address	Hex Contents	Mnemonics/ Contents	Operation
0000	7F	CLR $$	
0001	50	50	
0002	01	01	
0003	7F	CLR $$	PIA Initialized
0004	50	50	Port A = Input
0005	00	00	Set CRA bits 1, 2
0006	86	LDAA #	
0007	06	06	
0008	B7	STAA $$	
0009	50	50	
000A	01	01	
000B	B6	LDAA $$	CRA → ACCA
000C	50	50	(read CRA)
000D	01	01	

000E	2A	BPL	Branch if plus
000F	FB	FB	(to address 000B)
0010	B6	LDAA $$	
0011	50	50	DRA → ACCA
0012	00	00	(read port A)
0013	3E	WAI	Stop

Note that only CRA bits 1 and 2 are set during initialization. Setting bit 2 will naturally cause the port A data register to be selected for subsequent read operations. Setting bit 1 will cause the interrupt flag bit to set on a low-to-high transition at pin CA1. Bit 0 of CRA is cleared, thereby preventing the interrupt flag from generating an interrupt request to the 6800. Instead, the contents of the control register will be polled. If no strobe has occurred, bit 7 of the control register will remain cleared. The 6800 will therefore recognize the control register data as "positive" and branch until a "negative" (bit 7=1) condition is recognized. When a keyboard strobe has caused bit 7 of the control register to set, the 6800 will recognize the control register data as "negative" and will read the keyboard data from the port A data register. When the read operation occurs, bit 7 will be cleared to allow for another keyboard strobe. The data values are not "signed," but we have used the sign flag for the keyboard detecting function.

INTERFACING WITH DISPLAYS

In Chapter 7 you saw how the PIA could be used to interface your system to a group of single-lamp monitor displays. Recall that you simply connected the lamp monitors to port B of the PIA and configured this port as an output port. To cause a particular light pattern to be displayed, you would store the respective bit pattern in the port B data register. This type of display is fine for indicating status, conditions, and codes. However, it is not very meaningful unless specifically defined for the user. A more meaningful display would be one that could give you an alphanumeric display such that decimal and hex numbers could be represented as well as a limited alphabet so that messages could be displayed. Such a display is the 7-segment LED display.

A typical 7-segment display is shown in Fig. 9-5. The display consists of seven separate LED "bar" displays labeled "a" through "g" and a decimal point display labeled DP. There are two general

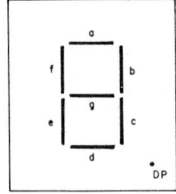

Fig. 9-5. A typical 7-segment display.

Fig. 9-6. LED segment assignments for 7-segment display.

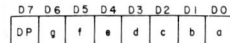

categories of 7-segment LED displays. They are: *common cathode* and *common anode*. The common-cathode display has the LED cathodes tied together and connected to ground. Therefore, a logic 1 must be applied to supply the current to illuminate a particular LED segment. This is referred to as *positive logic*. The common-anode variety has the LED anodes tied together and connected to the +5-volt dc supply. This type of display uses *negative logic*, meaning that a logic 0 must be applied in order to *sink* the current necessary to illuminate a particular LED segment.

Regardless of whether the display is common anode or common cathode, each LED segment will be assigned to a specific data line on the data bus as shown in Fig. 9-6. In this manner, you can control the LED illumination by the data that appears on the bus. Since there are eight total LED segments including the decimal point utilizing the 8-bit data bus, there are 256 possible unique displays available. However, many of these displays are meaningless and you will actually use less than 50 different combinations to form the numbers, letters, and characters shown in Table 9-1.

You will connect the common-cathode 7-segment display to port B of the PIA as shown in Fig. 9-7. Port B will provide the neces-

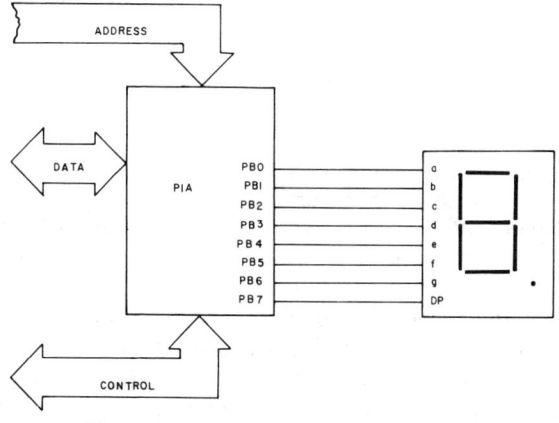

Fig. 9-7. Interfacing to a 7-segment LED.

Table 9-1. Hexadecimal Display Representations

Display	Hexadecimal Representation	
	Common Cathode	Common Anode
0	3F	C0
1	06	F9
1	5B	A4
3	4F	B0
4	66	99
5	6D	92
6	7D	82
7	07	F8
8	7F	80
9	67	98
A	77	88
C	39	C6
E	79	86
F	71	8E
H	76	89
I	06	F9
J	1E	E1
L	38	C7
O	3F	C0
P	73	8C
U	3E	C1
Y	66	99
b	7C	83
c	58	A7
d	5E	A1
h	74	8B
n	54	AB
o	5C	A3
r	50	AF
u	1C	E3
-	40	BF
?	53	AC
.	80	7F

sary drive to properly illuminate the LED segments. You will configure port B as an output port and then to display a particular character you will store the character representation in the port B data register. The program in Example 9-5 will accomplish this task.

If you desire to display a hexadecimal number directly from its binary equivalent, you must provide a conversion since the character designations are different from the actual hex numbers. Such a conversion can be provided by means of a *look-up table*. A look-up table is simply a set of consecutive memory locations that contain the proper character designations. You can access the table and

Example 9-5: Output of 7-Segment LED Character Designations

The following program is used to output 7-segment LED character designations via the PIA.

Hex Address	Hex Contents	Mnemonics/ Contents	Operation
0000	86	LDAA #	
0001	FF	FF	
0002	B7	STAA $$	
0003	50	50	
0004	02	02	PIA Initialized
0005	86	LDAA #	Port B = Output
0006	04	04	Set CRB bit 2
0007	B7	STAA $$	
0008	50	50	
0009	03	03	
000A	86	LDAA #	Load accumulator A with
000B	–	–	character designation
000C	B7	STAA $$	ACCA → DRB
000D	50	50	(Output character
000E	02	02	designation to port B)
000F	3E	WAI	Stop

This program assumes that the PIA has been assigned to address 5000 through 5003. The character designation will be inserted at address 000B.

provide the proper conversion with the use of indexed addressing as shown in Example 9-6.

In order to display intelligible words and messages, several 7-segment displays must be *multiplexed* together from one common display bus. Fig. 9-8 shows how the PIA can be utilized to multiplex eight separate 7-segment LED displays. Note that port A of the PIA is supplying the character representation code to a common display bus. Therefore, port A must be configured as an output port. The port A data lines are buffered to provide the drive potential needed by the displays. The displays are of the common-cathode variety requiring positive logic. However, the port A data lines are also inverted which requires the 6800 to supply negative logic to the PIA. The displays are sequentially enabled by port B. Therefore, port B provides for the display multiplexing and will also be configured as an output port.

Recall that port B can be used to directly drive the base of a transistor. A logic 1 state on a particular port B output line will forward bias the corresponding transistor base-emitter junction enabling the LED display that is connected to it. Once the display is enabled, you will load the proper character representation code in the port A data register such that the correct display is achieved. To display a message, you will simply enable each display sequen-

Example 9-6: 7-Segment LED Character Designation Look-Up Table

The following program is used to provide hexadecimal 7-segment LED character designations.

Hex Address	Hex Contents	Mnemonics/ Contents	Operation
0000	97	STAA $	Store accumulator A
0001	06	06	at address 0006
0002	CE	LDX #	Load the index register
0003	00	00	with the first address
0004	30	30	of the table
0005	A6	LDAA X	Load accumulator A
0006	—	—	with the proper character designation
0007	B7	STAA $$	ACCA → DRB
0008	50	50	(Output character
0009	02	02	designation to port B)

(Look-Up Table)

Hex Address	Hex Contents	7-Segment Representation
0030	C0	hex designation for 0
0031	F9	hex designation for 1
0032	A4	hex designation for 2
0033	B0	hex designation for 3
0034	99	hex designation for 4
0035	92	hex designation for 5
0036	82	hex designation for 6
0037	F8	hex designation for 7
0038	80	hex designation for 8
0039	98	hex designation for 9
003A	88	hex designation for A
003B	83	hex designation for B
003C	C6	hex designation for C
003D	A1	hex designation for D
003E	86	hex designation for E
003F	8E	hex designation for F

The program again assumes that the PIA is located at addresses 5000 through 5003. It also assumes that the 7-segment *common-anode* LED display is connected to port B and this port has been configured as an output port. Once the binary number is in accumulator A, the program will convert it to its proper character designation then output that designation to port B such that the proper display is achieved. Note that the key to the whole procedure is in using the accumulator contents as the indexed offset to access the look-up table.

tially by rotating a logic 1 through port B. As you do this, the proper character representation codes must also be sequentially stored to port A. Usually, you will want to display a particular message as

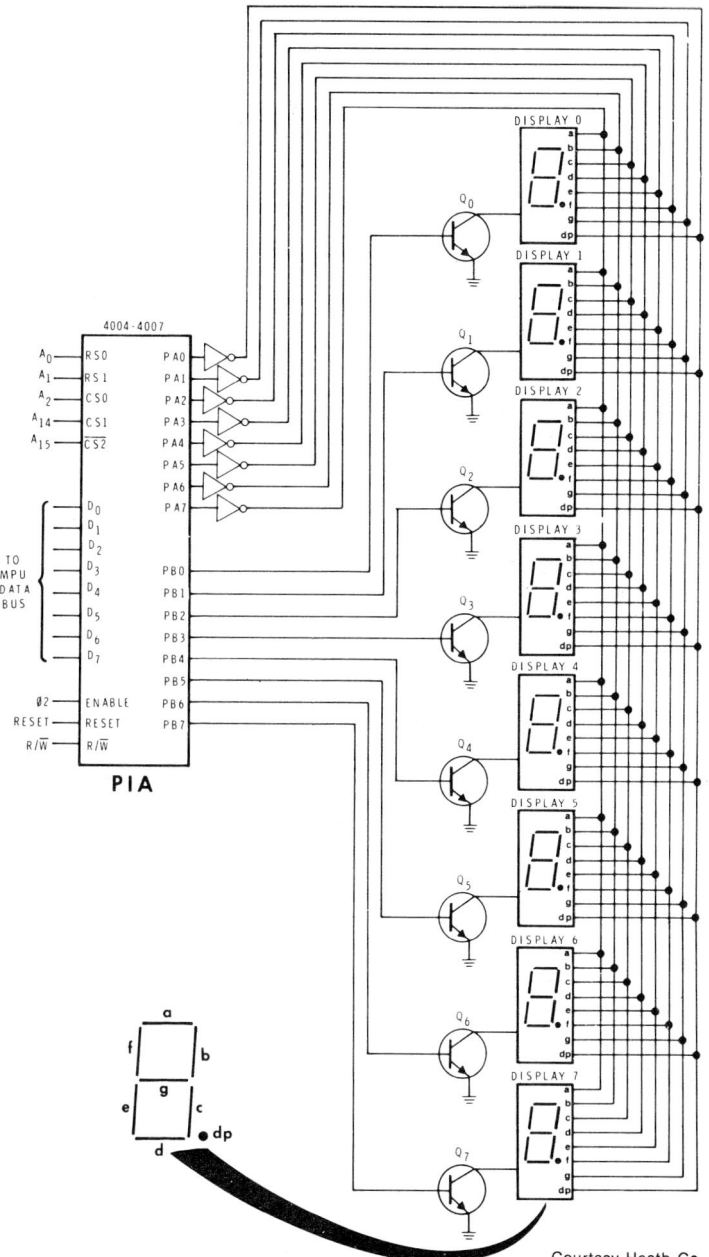

Fig. 9-8. Using the PIA to multiplexing 7-segment LED displays.

the result of some condition. The program in Example 9-7 is a subroutine that could be used to display a given message:

Example 9-7: 7-segment LED Multiplexing Subroutine

The following program is used to multiplex 7-segment LED displays in order to display a given message.

Hex Address	Hex Contents	Mnemonics/ Contents	Operation
0000	7F	CLR $$	
0001	40	40	
0002	01	01	
0003	4F	CLRA	
0004	43	COMA	
0005	B7	STAA $$	
0006	40	40	PIA Initialized
0007	00	00	Port A = Output
0008	7F	CLR $$	Port B = Output
0009	40	40	CRA bit 2 set
000A	03	03	CRB bit 2 set
000B	B7	STAA $$	
000C	40	40	
000D	02	02	
000E	86	LDA #	
000F	04	04	
0010	B7	STAA $$	
0011	40	40	
0012	01	01	
0013	B7	STAA $$	
0014	40	40	
0015	03	03	
0016	FE	LDX $$	Load index register
0017	00	00	with (beginning address
0018	4F	4F	of code table) −1
0019	5F	CLRB	Clear ACCB
001A	0D	SEC	Set C flag
001B	4F	CLRA	Clear ACCA
001C	43	COMA	FF → ACCA
001D	B7	STAA $$	Store FF to port A
001E	40	40	to blank all displays
001F	00	00	
0020	59	ROLB	Point to next display
0021	F7	STAB	
0022	40	40	Enable next display
0023	02	02	
0024	24	BCC	Branch if carry clear
0025	01	01	(to address 0027)
0026	39	RTS	Return if message complete
0027	08	INX	Point to next character code
0028	A6	LDAA X	Load next character
0029	00	00	code in ACCA
002A	B7	STAA $$	

002B	40	40		Display next
002C	00	00		character code
002D	4F	CLRA		
002E	4C	INCA		Delay approximately 15 ms
002F	26	BNE		
0030	FD	FD		
0031	20	BRA		Branch Always
0032	E8	E8		(to address 001B)

The main program would call this subroutine using a jump-to-subroutine (JSR) instruction. The first part of the subroutine initializes the PIA by configuring both ports as output ports. The PIA is located at addresses 4000 through 4003. The subroutine will then load the index register with the address immediately before the beginning address of the eight consecutive memory locations that contain the character codes. In this example, addresses 0050 through 0057 contain the eight character codes for the message; therefore, the index register is loaded with 004F. The subroutine will then clear accumulator B, set the carry flag, and set accumulator A to FF by clearing and complementing. The accumulator A contents (FF) are then stored to port A so that all displays will be blanked. While the displays are blanked, the carry flag will be rotated into bit 0 of accumulator B, then the accumulator B contents will be stored to port B. This will enable display No. 0. A branch if carry clear (BCC) instruction is inserted so that the program will return to the main program (RTS) if the carry is set, meaning the C flag has been completely rotated through accumulator B and the entire message has been displayed. However, at this point, the C flag is cleared since it was just rotated into bit 0 of accumulator B. Therefore, the index register is incremented and accumulator A is loaded with the first character code. The code is then stored to port A, causing display No. 0 to display the proper character. You will then clear and increment accumulator A through FF to 00 to provide a delay which will allow the display to illuminate for approximately 15 milliseconds.

The procedure is then repeated by blanking the displays, and rotating accumulator B to enable display No. 1. The character code for display No. 1 is then stored to port A to provide its proper display. The cycle is repeated until all eight displays have been illuminated and the entire message has been displayed. In practice, you would want to call this subroutine many times a second to give the impression of a constant display. Since these types of displays require constant refreshing, an interrupt is sometimes used to interrupt the main program to refresh the display. Refresh rates of 50 to 60 Hz are quite common, with lower rates resulting in display flicker.

INTERFACING WITH DIGITAL-TO-ANALOG CONVERTERS (DACs)

Digital-to-analog converters (DACs) are needed in many practical systems to translate the system digital code to a continuous voltage level (analog signal) required by motors, ovens, relays, and other electromechanical devices. These converters can be made from standard resistors and op-amp circuitry or can be purchased as a single-chip device. Since the cost of these single-chip devices is very reasonable (and decreasing), you will find it more economical and less time consuming to use a manufactured DAC rather than designing your own circuit. In this section we will discuss two D/A converter chips: the Signetics NE5018 and the Motorola MC1408-8/MC1508-8.

The Signetics NE5018 will convert an 8-bit digital signal to a continuous output voltage level. Interfacing this chip to your system is relatively simple. You will configure port B of the PIA as an output port and use CB2 as an output strobe to enable the DAC. The interfacing scheme is shown in Fig. 9-9. The NE5018 contains an input latch that will store the digital input data when a high-to-low transition is seen on $\overline{LE}$. This transition is supplied by CB2. Recall from Chapter 8 that CB2 can be configured as an output strobe. In this mode, CB2 will normally be high then go low after a *write* port B operation is executed. It will remain low for one enable signal ($\phi 2$) cycle. This is long enough to allow the NE5018 converter to latch the digital input data. To achieve the output strobe mode, CRB-5 and CRB-3 must be set with CRB-4 cleared. Therefore, bits 5, 4, and 3 of control register B would be 101 respectively. The program in Example 9-8 could be used to configure the PIA and supply the digital information to the NE5018.

The Motorola MC1408-8/MC1508-8 DAC interfacing is even more straightforward. This DAC does not contain a latch and, therefore, does not require a strobe or enabling pulse as did the NE5018. You will use the latching capabilities of the PIA to provide data latching to the MC1408-8/MC1508-8. The interfacing scheme is shown in

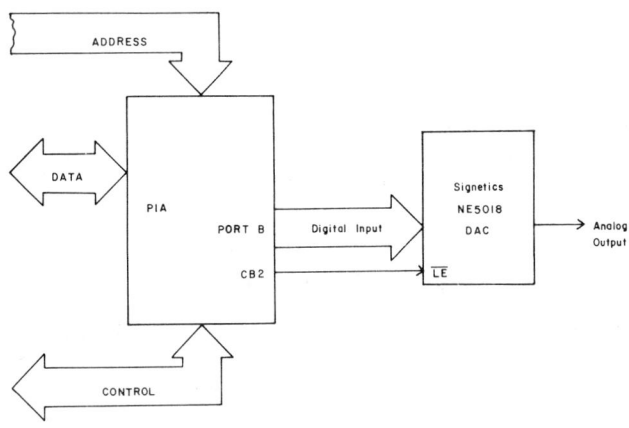

Fig. 9-9. Interfacing to the Signetics NE5018 D/A converter.

Example 9-8: NE5018 Data Transfer Program

The following program is used to transfer data from the PIA to the NE5018 DAC.

Hex Address	Hex Contents	Mnemonics/ Contents	Operation
0000	7F	CLR $$	
0001	50	50	
0002	03	03	
0003	86	LDAA #	
0004	FF	FF	PIA Initialized
0005	B7	STAA $$	Port B = Output
0006	50	50	CRB bits 5, 3, 2
0007	02	02	
0008	86	LDAA #	
0009	2C	2C	
000A	B7	STAA $$	
000B	50	50	
000C	03	03	
000D	96	LDAA $	$M_{30} \rightarrow$ ACCA
000E	30	30	(get digital data)
000F	B7	STAA $$	
0010	50	50	Store digital
0011	02	02	data to port B

The program assumes the PIA is located at addresses 5000 through 5003. To configure CB2 as an output strobe, bits 5, 3, and 2 of control register B must be set. This requires you to store $00101100_2 = 2C_{16}$ in CRB. Once the PIA is initialized, the program assumes the digital data is located at memory location 0030. The data is obtained from that location and then written to port B. Immediately after the write operation occurs, CB2 will automatically go low for one clock pulse, allowing the data to be transferred to the NE5018. The converter will then produce a corresponding analog output within a few microseconds.

Fig. 9-10. You will configure port B as an output port. Then, to provide a conversion, you will simply store an 8-bit data word to port B. The MC1408/MC1508 will then provide a continuous analog output voltage level which corresponds to the digital input. This DAC will yield 256 different output voltage levels from 0 to −4.980 volts corresponding to the digital input data. Consult Appendix D for more information on both the Signetics NE5018 and Motorola MC1408/MC1508 DACs.

INTERFACING WITH ANALOG-TO-DIGITAL CONVERTERS

Many input devices such as various types of sensors and transducers generate analog signals. Before the 6800 microprocessor can process the signal, it must be converted to a digital data word. This

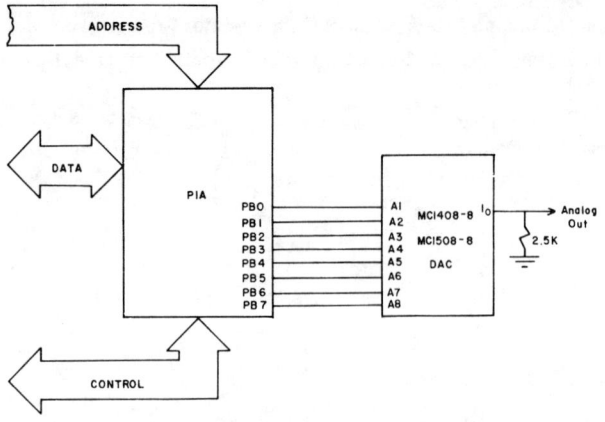

Fig. 9-10. Interfacing to the Motorola MC1408-8/MC1508-8 D/A converter.

conversion process is not a simple task if you must provide the external analog and digital circuitry as well as the software required for an accurate conversion. Fortunately, complete A/D converter chips are becoming increasingly available at low cost. Such a chip is the Intersil ICL7109. This device is a complete A/D converter that will convert an analog signal to a 12-bit binary word plus a 2-bit indication for signal polarity and overrange. It will provide up to 30 conversions per second and can be operated in a partial or complete handshaking mode. Fig. 9-11 shows one way in which the ICL7109 can be interfaced to your 6800 system.

Given an analog input signal, the ICL7109 will provide 14 bits of output data to the PIA—12 data bits (B1–B12) plus a polarity (POL) bit and an overrange (OR) bit. The 12 data bits are di-

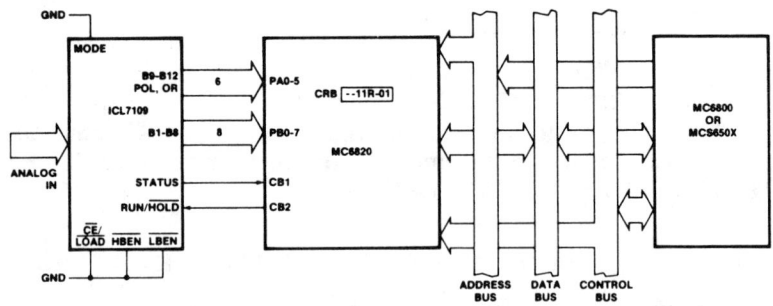

Courtesy Intersil, Inc.

Fig. 9-11. Interfacing to the Intersil ICL7109 A/D converter.

vided into a low-order data byte (B1–B8) and a high-order data byte (B9–B12). The low-order byte is connected to PIA lines PB0 through PB7 and the high order byte connected to PA0 through PA3. Therefore, both PIA ports must be configured as input ports. The control register for port B can be set up so that CB1 will be activated and generate an interrupt request on a high-to-low transition of the ICL7109 STATUS pin. Also, CB2 will be designated as an output line to the ICL7109 via its RUN/$\overline{\text{HOLD}}$ pin. This configuration would require that $00111101_2 = 3D_{16}$ be stored in CRB during the initialization process. Using this scheme, CB2 will always be held high (refer to Fig. 8-12). With CB2 held high, the ICL7109 will be allowed to *RUN* and provide continuous conversions by interrupting the 6800 via the CB1 line when each conversion becomes available. The ICL7109 also contains an output latch so that the data will not be lost before the 6800 acknowledges the interrupt.

Now, if you were to clear bit 3 of the control register, CB2 will go low and thus *HALT* the conversion process in the ICL7109. Then a conversion may be initiated when desired by again setting bit 3 with a write to-CRB-instruction. This process allows for conversions to be initiated under software control. Consult the ICL7109 specifications in Appendix D for other methods of interfacing and more chip detail.

Another common A/D converter is the Teledyne 8703. This is an 8-bit converter which also has an output latch. The interfacing scheme is essentially the same as for the ICL7109 previously discussed. Fig. 9-12 shows how the 8703 might be connected to your

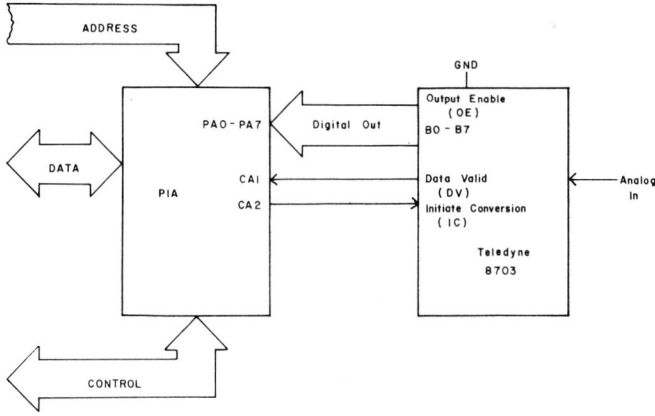

Fig. 9-12. Interfacing to the Teledyne 8703 A/D converter.

system. The eight digital data bits (B0–B7) are connected to port A lines PA0 through PA7. Control line CA2 is used to initiate a conversion. You will do this by changing bit 3 of control register A from low to high then back to low again. This provides the initiate-conversion pulse needed to start the conversion process. Once the conversion is complete, the 8703 data-valid line will go from low to high indicating data is available. This will cause an interrupt to be generated via CA1. A read operation can then be performed on port A to enter the converted data into the system. This A/D converter is also available in a 10-bit version (8704) and 12-bit version (8705). Naturally, with more than eight bits, multibyte data operations will be involved. However, a better digital resolution of the analog signal can be achieved with more data bits.

You have now had a brief introduction to show you how some D/A and A/D devices can be connected to the 6800. For more information on these devices and interfacing techniques, consult the following:

1. Titus, Jonathan A.; Titus, Christopher A.; Rony, Peter R.; and Larsen, David G., *Microcomputer—Analog Converter Software and Hardware Interfacing.* Indianapolis: Howard W. Sams and Co., Inc., 1978.
2. Jung, Walter G., *IC Converter Cookbook.* Indianapolis: Howard W. Sams and Co., Inc., 1978.
3. *Analog-Digital Conversion Notes,* Analog Devices, Inc., Norwood, MA 02062, 1977.

REVIEW QUESTIONS

1. What are the four basic interfacing requirements when interfacing to switches? _____, _____, _____, _____.
2. Which one of the above requirements is fulfilled by the PIA? _____
3. How is switch closure detected when interfacing to a single switch?

4. A typical software delay that would provide switch debouncing is _____ seconds.

5. The debouncing delay is usually provided by decrementing the _____.
6. How is switch closure detected in a switch column?

7. How is a switch column decoded?

8. A 2 × 2 switch matrix would require that _____ PIA port lines be used.
9. How is a switch closure detected and decoded in a keyboard matrix?

10. Two types of keyboards available are the _____ and _____.
11. A common-anode LED display would use _____ logic.
12. The LED character designations are generated from a _____ located in memory.
13. To display words and messages, several displays must be _____ together.
14. A message should be refreshed at a _____ rate to prevent flickering.
15. What is the difference between the Signetics NE5018 DAC and Motorola MC1408-8 DACs?

16. The Intersil ICL7109 is a _____ bit A/D converter.
17. The Teledyne 8703 is a _____ bit A/D converter.
18. What is the advantage of more data bits in an A/D converter?

19. An analog signal can be defined as _____.
20. The Intersil ICL7109 A/D converter provides 12 data bits plus a 2-bit indication of _____ and _____.

ANSWERS

1. Switch addressing, detecting switch closure, switch debouncing, switch decoding.

2. Switch addressing.

3. By ANDing a mask byte to the switch status byte, then checking the Z-flag status with a branch-if-not-zero (BNE) instruction.

4. 10 milliseconds

5. index register

6. By *comparing* the switch status byte to FF.

7. By rotating the switch status byte through the C flag, checking the C-flag status after each rotation, and counting the number of notations required to clear the flag.

8. four

9. With the matrix connected as in Fig. 9-3, switch closure is detected by scanning each column with port B of the PIA and simultaneously reading port A. A compare operation is then used to detect the closure and a rotate-right operation is used to decode the closure within a particular column.

10. un-encoded and fully encoded.

11. negative

12. look-up table

13. multiplexed

14. 50–60 Hz

15. The NE5018 has an internal 8-bit latch, requiring an output strobe or enabling pulse from the PIA.

16. 12

17. 8

18. Greater precision.

19. continuous voltage or current values

20. signal polarity and overrange

EXPERIMENT 9-1

Purpose

To demonstrate switch closure detection and debouncing.

Equipment

ET3400
6820/6821 PIA

7400 digital IC (2-bit NAND)
74LS27 digital IC (3-bit NOR)

74LS30 digital IC (8-bit NAND)
Push-button switch
 (Heath #64-724)
1K-ohm ¼-watt resistor
Extra connector block
 (Heath #432-875)

Program

Hex Address	Hex Contents	Mnemonics/ Contents	Operation
0000	86	LDAA #	
0001	04	04	PIA Initialized
0002	B7	STAA $$	Port A = Input
0003	50	50	CRA bit 2 set
0004	01	01	
0005	7F	CLR $$	

0006	00	00	Clear M₆₀
0007	60	60	
0008	B6	LDAA $$	
0009	50	50	DRA → ACCA
000A	00	00	(read port A)
000B	84	ANDA #	ACCA·01 → ACCA
000C	01	01	(AND status and mask bytes)
000D	26	BNE	Branch if Z flag clear
000E	F9	F9	(to address 0008)
000F	BD	JSR $$	Jump to subroutine
0010	00	00	at address 0030
0011	30	30	(debouncing delay)
0012	B6	LDAA $$	DRA → ACCA
0013	50	50	(read port A)
0014	00	00	
0015	84	ANDA #	ACCA·01 → ACCA
0016	01	01	(AND status and mask bytes)
0017	26	BNE	Branch if Z flag cleared
0018	EF	EF	(to address 0008)
0019	7C	INC $$	
001A	00	00	Increment M₆₀
001B	60	60	
001C	3E	WAI	Stop
.	.	.	.
.	.	.	.
.		(Debouncing Delay: 10 ms)	.
0030	CE	LDX #	05 → X_H
0031	05	05	00 → X_L
0032	00	00	
0033	09	DEX	Decrement index register
0034	8C	CPX #	
0035	00	00	Compare 0000 to the
0036	00	00	index register
0037	26	BNE	Branch if Z flag clear
0038	FA	FA	(to address 0033)
0039	39	RTS	Return to main program
			(address 0012)

This program is essentially the same as the one we discussed earlier in this chapter to provide switch closure detection and debouncing. The only difference is in the PIA initialization procedure. Here, you are able to eliminate the first two clear instructions since you have wired the PIA $\overline{\text{RESET}}$ to the system reset. This will clear all the PIA registers automatically when you reset the system.

Procedure

Step 1

Construct the circuit shown in the schematic diagram.

NOTE: An extra breadboard block will be needed to mount the push-button switch.

Schematic Diagram (Fig. 9-13)

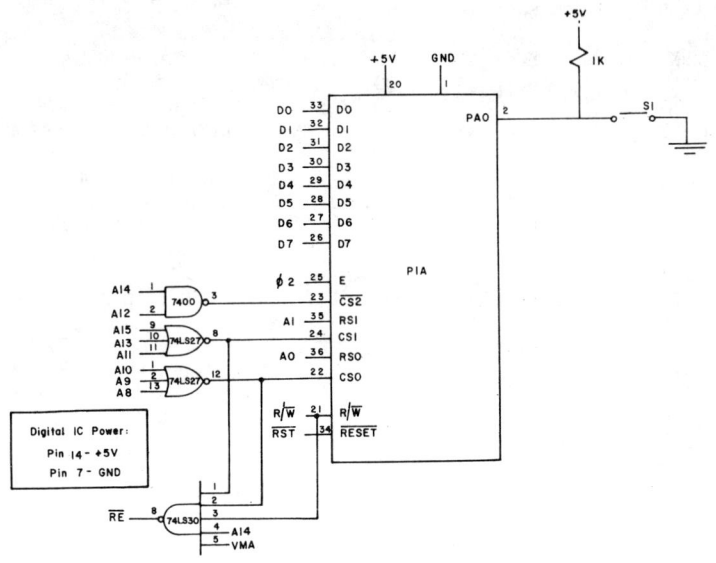

Fig. 9-13. Schematic diagram for Experiment 9-1.

Step 2
Enter the given program.

Step 3
Execute the program without depressing the switch and examine memory location 0060.

You should find memory location 0060 cleared.

Step 4
Execute the program and depress the switch.

Step 5
Examine memory location 0060.

The contents should be 01, indicating that switch closure detection and debouncing has been achieved.

Step 6
Save your circuit for the next experiment.

Conclusion

Why is the external digital logic required when reading data into the Heath trainer?

Summarize the switch closure detection and debouncing procedure.

How would you modify the circuit and program to provide a lamp monitor indication of switch closure?

EXPERIMENT 9-2

Purpose
To provide a lamp monitor indication of switch closure.

Equipment
ET3400
6820/6821 PIA
7400 digital IC (2-bit NAND)
74LS27 digital IC (3-bit NOR)
74LS30 digital IC (8-bit NAND)

Push-button switch
  (Heath #64-724)
1K-ohm ¼-watt resistor
Extra connector block
  (Heath #432-875)

Schematic Diagram
The circuit will be the same as the one you constructed in Experiment 9-1 except that you must connect a wire from PB0 (pin 10) of the PIA to lamp monitor No. 0.

Program

Hex Address	Hex Contents	Mnemonics/ Contents	Operation
0000	4F	CLRA	
0001	43	COMA	
0002	B7	STAA $$	
0003	50	50	

0004	02	02	PIA Initialized
0005	86	LDAA #	Port A = Input
0006	04	04	Port B = Output
0007	B7	STAA $$	CRA bit 2 set
0008	50	50	CRB bit 2 set
0009	01	01	
000A	B7	STAA $$	
000B	50	50	
000C	03	03	
000D	7F	CLR $$	
000E	00	00	Clear M_{60}
000F	60	60	
0010	B6	LDAA $$	DRA → ACCA
0011	50	50	(read port A)
0012	00	00	
0013	84	ANDA	ACCA·01 → ACCA
0014	01	01	(AND status and mask bytes)
0015	26	BNE	Branch if Z flag clear
0016	F9	F9	(to address 0010)
0017	BD	JSR $$	Jump to Subroutine
0018	00	00	at address 0030
0019	30	30	(debouncing delay)
001A	B6	LDAA $$	DRA → ACCA
001B	50	50	(read port A)
001C	00	00	
001D	84	ANDA #	ACCA·01 → ACCA
001E	01	01	(AND status and mask bytes)
001F	26	BNE	Branch if Z flag clear
0020	EF	EF	(to address 0010)
0021	7C	INC	
0022	00	00	Increment M_{60}
0023	60	60	
0024	D6	LDAB $	M_{60} → ACCA
0025	60	60	
0026	F7	STAB $$	Illuminate lamp
0027	50	50	monitor No. 0
0028	02	02	
0029	3E	WAI	Stop
.	.	.	
.	.	.	
		(Debouncing Delay: 10 ms)	
0030	CE	LDX #	05 → X_H
0031	05	05	00 → X_L
0032	00	00	
0033	09	DEX	Decrement index register
0034	8C	CPX #	Compare 0000 to the
0035	00	00	index register
0036	00	00	
0037	26	BNE	Branch if Z flag clear
0038	FA	FA	(to address 0033)
0039	39	RTS	Return to main program

This program is similar to the one in Experiment 9-1. However, here you have configured port B as an output port and will store the contents of memory location 0060 to port B. This will provide a lamp monitor indication after switch closure has been detected and debounced.

Procedure
Step 1
Using the circuit in Experiment 9-1, connect a wire from PB0 (pin 10) of the PIA to lamp monitor No. 0.

Step 2
Enter the given program.

Step 3
Execute the program.

Step 4
Depress the switch and the lamp monitor should illuminate indicating switch closure has been detected and debounced.

Step 5
Save this circuit for the next experiment.

Conclusions
What additional instructions were required to provide the lamp monitor indication of switch closure?

How would the program have to be modified to detect switch closure for any one of four switches connected to the PIA in a switch column configuration?

EXPERIMENT 9-3
Purpose
To interface a four-switch column to the 6800 system and to demonstrate switch closure detection, debouncing, and decoding.

Equipment

ET3400
6820/6821 PIA
7400 digital IC (2-bit NAND)
74LS27 digital IC (3-bit NOR)
74LS30 digital IC (8-bit NAND)

Four push-button switches
(Heath #64-724, 64-725, 64-726, and 64-727)
Five 1K-ohm ¼-watt resistors
Extra connector block
(Heath #432-875)

Schematic Diagram

The circuit will be the same as the one you used in Experiment 9-1 except you must wire the push-button switches to the system as shown in Fig. 9-2.

Program

Hex Address	Hex Contents	Mnemonics/ Contents	Operation
0000	4F	CLRA	
0001	43	COMA	
0002	B7	STAA $$	
0003	50	50	
0004	02	02	PIA Initialized
0005	86	LDAA #	Port A = Input
0006	04	04	Port B = Output
0007	B7	STAA $$	CRA bit 2 set
0008	50	50	CRB bit 2 set
0009	01	01	
000A	B7	STAA $$	
000B	50	50	
000C	03	03	
000D	B6	LDAA $$	
000E	50	50	DRA → ACCA
000F	00	00	(read port A)
0010	81	CMPA #	Compare port A data to FF
0011	FF	FF	(Is a switch closed?)
0012	27	BEQ	Branch if Z flag set
0013	F9	F9	(to address 000D)
0014	BD	JSR $$	Jump to Subroutine
0015	00	00	at address 0030
0016	30	30	(debouncing delay)
0017	B6	LDAA $$	DRA → ACCA
0018	50	50	(read port A)
0019	00	00	
001A	81	CMPA #	Compare port A data to FF
001B	FF	FF	(Is switch still closed?)
001C	27	BEQ	Branch if Z flag set
001D	EF	EF	(to address 000D)
001E	CE	LDX #	
001F	00	00	Clear index register
0020	00	00	

0021	46	RORA	Rotate ACCA Right
0022	08	INX	Increment index register
0023	25	BCS	Branch if C flag set
0024	FC	FC	(to address 0021)
0025	DF	STX $	Store index register count
0026	5F	5F	($X_H \rightarrow$ 5F, $X_L \rightarrow$ 60)
0027	D6	LDAB $	$M_{60} \rightarrow$ ACCB
0028	60	60	(Load ACCB with count)
0029	F7	STAB $$	ACCB $\rightarrow$ DRB
002A	50	50	(store count to port B)
002B	02	02	
002C	7E	JMP $$	Jump to address 000D
002D	00	00	(look for another
002E	0D	0D	switch closure)
.	.	.	
.	.	.	
		(Debouncing Delay: 10 ms)	
0030	CE	LDX #	05 $\rightarrow X_H$
0031	05	05	00 $\rightarrow X_L$
0032	00	00	
0033	09	DEX	Decrement index register
0034	8C	CPX #	Compare 0000 to the
0035	00	00	index register
0036	00	00	
0037	26	BNE	Branch if Z flag clear
0038	FA	FA	(to address 0033)
0039	39	RTS	Return to main program

This program first initializes the PIA by configuring port A as an input port and port B as an output port. Then, switch closure is detected by reading and comparing the port A data to FF. If no switches are depressed, the port A data will be FF, the Z flag will set, the program will branch, and it will continue to read and compare port A until a closure is detected. Once a switch closure is detected, the debouncing subroutine is called. After debouncing, the port A data is read and compared again to be sure of switch closure. Once switch closure is assured, the switch column must be decoded. Since the switches are connected to the system via pull-up resistors, a switch closure will represent a zero on its respective port A data line. The 6800 decodes the zero by reading the port A data into accumulator A then rotating the data until the C flag is cleared. Each time a rotate is executed the index register is incremented to count the number of rotations. The final index register count is the switch number that is closed. This count is then stored to port B such that the lamp monitors will illuminate to indicate which particular switch has been depressed.

Procedure
Step 1
Make the following additional connections to the circuit you constructed in Experiment 9-2:

1. Connect push-button switches S2, S3, and S4 to the PIA as shown in Fig. 9-2. Each switch will be connected via a 1K-ohm pull-up resistor. Switch S2 will be connected to PA1 (pin 3), switch S3 to PA2 (pin 4), and switch S4 to PA3 (pin 5).
2. Connect PA4, PA5, PA6, and PA7 (pins 6, 7, 8, and 9) together and through a 1K-ohm pull-up resistor to the +5-volt supply as shown in Fig. 9-2.
3. Connect PB1, PB2, and PB3 (pins 11, 12, and 13) to lamp monitor No. 1, No. 2, and No. 3.

Step 2
Enter the given program.

Step 3
Execute the program.

Step 4
Depress the switches at random. The lamp monitors should indicate the binary representation of the particular switch number being depressed. If not, check the circuit and examine your program.

Step 5
Save the circuit for the next experiment.

Conclusion
Why did PA4, PA5, PA6, and PA7 have to be connected to the +5-volt supply?

Explain the procedure for detection, debouncing, and decoding a switch closure in a switch column.

How would you have to modify the circuit and program if the switches were connected in a 2 × 2 matrix configuration?

EXPERIMENT 9-4

Purpose

To interface a 7-segment LED to the 6800 system.

Equipment

ET3400
7400 digital IC (2-bit NAND)
74LS27 digtial IC (3-bit NOR)
74LS30 digital IC (8-bit NAND)

TIL-312 common-anode 7-segment LED (Heath #411-831)
Extra connector block (Heath #432-875)

Schematic Diagram (Fig. 9-14)

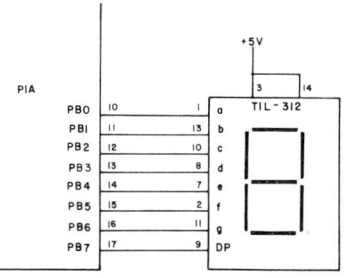

Fig. 9-14. Schematic diagram for Experiment 9-4.

Program

Hex Address	Hex Contents	Mnemonics/ Contents	Operation
0000	4F	CLRA	
0001	43	COMA	
0002	B7	STAA $$	
0003	50	50	PIA Initialized
0004	02	02	Port B = Output
0005	86	LDAA #	CRB bit 2 set
0006	04	04	
0007	B7	STAA $$	
0008	50	50	
0009	03	03	
000A	4F	CLRA	Clear ACCA
000B	97	STAA $	ACCA → M_{11}
000C	11	11	(Store index offset)
000D	CE	LDX #	Load the index
000E	00	00	register with the first
000F	50	50	address of the table
0010	A6	LDAA X	Load ACCA with the proper
0011	No Entry	No Entry	character designation
0012	08	INX	Increment index register
0013	B7	STAA $$	ACCA → DRB
0014	50	50	(Output character
0015	02	02	designation to port B)

0016	86	LDAA #		
0017	FF	FF		
0018	C6	LDAB #		
0019	FF	FF		
001A	5A	DECB	Delay Loop #1	Delay Loop #2
001B	26	BNE		
001C	FD	FD		
001D	4A	DECA		
001E	26	BNE		
001F	F8	F6		
0020	8C	CPX #	Compare immediate	
0021	00	00	to 0060	
0022	60	60		
0023	27	BEQ	Branch if Z flag set	
0024	E8	E8	(to address 000D)	
0025	20	BRA	Branch to address 0010	
0026	E9	E9		

(Look-up Table)

0050	C0	hex designation for 0
0051	F9	hex designation for 1
0052	A4	hex designation for 2
0053	B0	hex designation for 3
0054	99	hex designation for 4
0055	92	hex designation for 5
0056	82	hex designation for 6
0057	F8	hex designation for 7
0058	80	hex designation for 8
0059	98	hex designation for 9
005A	88	hex designation for A
005B	83	hex designation for B
005C	C6	hex designation for C
005D	A1	hex designation for D
005E	86	hex designation for E
005F	8E	hex designation for F

This program initializes the PIA by configuring port B as an output port. The character designation look-up table begins at address 0050. The program will start with the first character designation and, using indexed addressing, sequentially store each character designation to the 7-segment LED via PIA port B. After each character is displayed, a delay of approximately one second is provided before the next character is displayed. This delay is provided by delay loops No. 1 and No. 2, using the two accumulators similar to the way you used accumulator A and the index register in Experiment 8-2. You cannot use the index register for the delay routine in this program because you are using it to sequence through the look-up table.

Procedure
Step 1
Connect the 7-segment LED to port B as shown in the schematic diagram (Fig. 9-14). Use the circuit from Experiment 9-3 for the remaining connections.

NOTE: Do not destroy the switch connections to port A.

Step 2
Enter the given program.

Step 3
Execute the program. The LED should sequentially display the hexadecimal characters and then repeat the cycle until the system is reset.

Step 4
Save the circuit for the next experiment.

Conclusion
How would you modify the circuit and program to have the 7-segment LED indicate which switch in a switch column has been depressed?

How would you decrease the delay time between character displays in the above program? (Try it!)

Explain how indexed addressing is used in conjunction with the LED character designation look-up table.

EXPERIMENT 9-5
Purpose
To provide a switch column input and 7-segment output for the 6800 system.

Equipment

ET3400
7400 digital IC (2-bit NAND)
74LS27 digital IC (3-bit NOR)
74LS30 digital IC (8-bit NAND)
TIL-312 common-anode 7-segment LED (Heath #411-831)
Four push-button switches (Heath #64-724, 64-725, 64-726, and 64-727)
Five 1K-ohm ¼-watt resistors
Extra connector block (Heath #432-875)

Schematic Diagram

The circuit will be the same as the one you used in the previous experiment.

Program

Hex Address	Hex Contents	Mnemonics/ Contents	Operation
0000	4F	CLRA	
0001	43	COMA	
0002	B7	STAA $$	
0003	50	50	
0004	02	02	
0005	86	LDAA #	PIA Initialized
0006	04	04	Port A · Input
0007	B7	STAA $$	Port B · Output
0008	50	50	CRA bit 2 set
0009	01	01	CRB bit 2 set
000A	B7	STAA $$	
000B	50	50	
000C	03	03	
000D	B6	LDAA $$	
000E	50	50	
000F	00	00	
0010	81	CMPA #	Detect switch closure
0011	FF	FF	
0012	27	BEQ	
0013	F9	F9	
0014	BD	JSR	Jump to debounce
0015	00	00	Subroutine at address 0040
0016	40	40	
0017	B6	LDAA $$	
0018	50	50	
0019	00	00	Verify switch closure
001A	81	CMPA #	after debounce
001B	FF	FF	
001C	27	BEQ	
001D	EF	EF	

001E	CE	LDX #	
001F	00	00	
0020	00	00	
0021	46	RORA	
0022	08	INX	Decode switch
0023	25	BCS	column and store
0024	FC	FC	switch number in ACCB
0025	DF	STX $	
0026	5F	5F	
0027	D6	LDAB $	
0028	60	60	
0029	D7	STAB $	
002A	2F	2F	
002B	CE	LDX #	
002C	00	00	Look up switch number
002D	50	50	designation and
002E	A6	LDAA X	store to port B (LED)
002F	No Entry	No Entry	
0030	B7	STAA $$	
0031	50	50	
0032	02	02	
0033	7E	JMP	
0034	00	00	Repeat the cycle
0035	0D	0D	

(Debouncing Delay)

0040	CE	LDX #
0041	05	05
0042	00	00
0043	09	DEX
0044	8C	CPX #
0045	00	00
0046	00	00
0047	26	BNE
0048	FA	FA
0049	39	RTS

(Look-Up Table)

0050	C0	hex designation for 0
0051	F9	hex designation for 1
0052	A4	hex designation for 2
0053	B0	hex designation for 3
0054	99	hex designation for 4

This program combines the ideas of Experiments 9-3 and 9-4. You should now be able to verify all the functional aspects of the program and see how the different parts (PIA initialization, switch closure detection, switch debouncing, switch decoding, and 7-segment character output via a look-up table) interrelate.

Procedure

Step 1
Using the circuit from Experiment 9-4, enter the given program.

Step 2
Execute the program.

Step 3
Depress the push-button switches at random. The 7-segment LED should indicate the switch number being depressed.

Conclusion

Explain the major ideas for interfacing to a switch column and providing a 7-segment LED indication of switch closure.

APPENDIX A

Digital Review

BASIC LOGIC GATES

Recall the basic logic gates used in digital electronics. The following summary includes the gate symbol, the Boolean expression for the gate, and the truth table for the gate.

Inverter

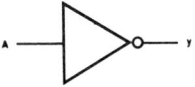

A	y
0	1
1	0

$y = \text{NOT } A = \overline{A}$

OR Gate

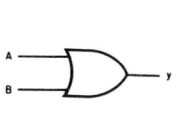

AB	y
00	0
01	1
10	1
11	1

$y = A \text{ OR } B = A + B$

AND Gate

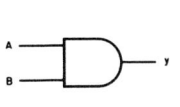

AB	y
00	0
01	0
10	0
11	1

$y = A \text{ AND } B = A \cdot B$

Exclusive OR Gate

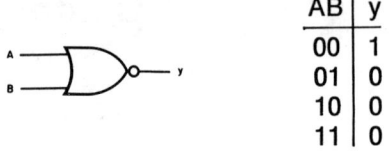

AB	y
00	0
01	1
10	1
11	0

$y = A$ Exclusive-or $B = A \oplus B$

NOR Gate

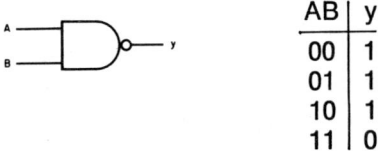

AB	y
00	1
01	0
10	0
11	0

$y = \text{NOT}(A \text{ or } B) = \overline{A + B}$

NAND Gate

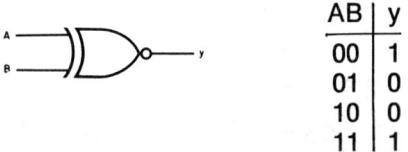

AB	y
00	1
01	1
10	1
11	0

$y = \text{NOT}(A \text{ and } B) = \overline{A \cdot B}$

Exclusive NOR Gate

AB	y
00	1
01	0
10	0
11	1

$y = \text{NOT}(A \text{ Exclusive-or } B) = \overline{A \oplus B}$

Gate Conversions

If we want to express one gate in terms of others the following conversion chart diagrams might be handy:

GATE CONVERSIONS

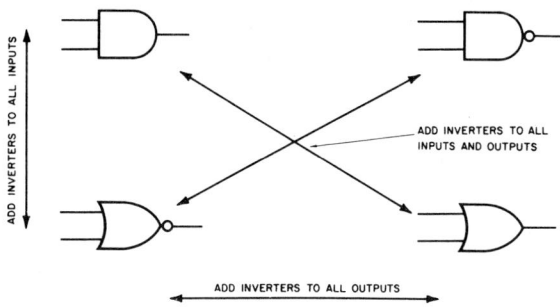

Convert the Following to NAND *Logic:*

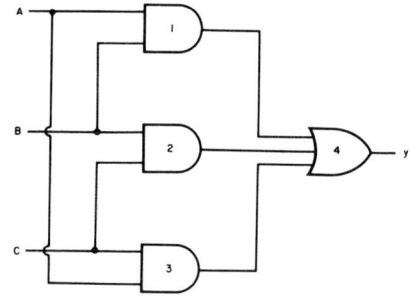

By using the above conversion diagram, we get:

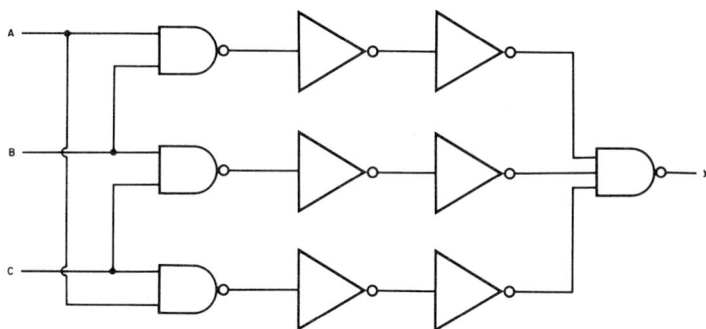

NOTE: The double inversions will cancel each other.

FLIP-FLOPS

A flip-flop is simply an electronic device that is used to store a binary digit. It will "latch" (hold) in one of two states (0 or 1) depending on what it sees at its input *when clocked*. There are two basic types we will be concerned with—the D flip-flop and the JK flip-flop.

D Flip-Flop

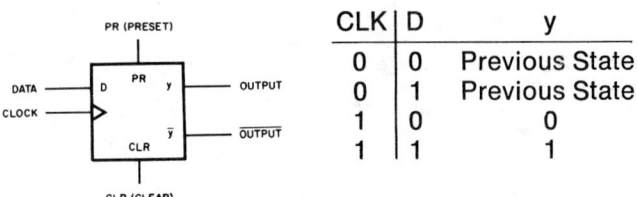

CLK	D	y
0	0	Previous State
0	1	Previous State
1	0	0
1	1	1

Note that the inputs are D (data line) and CLK (clock). The outputs are y and $\bar{y}$, where $\bar{y}$ is simply NOT y. By observing the truth table, you can see that binary data on the data line is transferred to the output when a clock pulse is provided. The outputs at y and $\bar{y}$ will remain latched until another clock pulse is provided. PR (preset) and CLR (clear) functions are also provided. A high at PR implies y=1 while a high at CLR implies y=0. No clocking is needed to preset or clear the latch. D flip-flops are used most commonly as storage registers.

4-Bit Storage Register

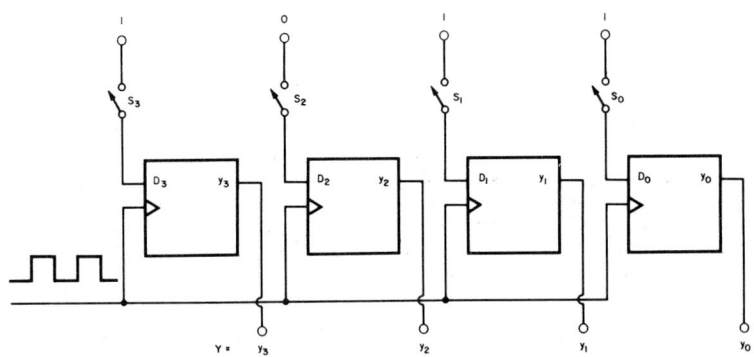

If in the beginning the four switches are open, the output is left floating and will be a random 4-bit number. After the switches are closed and a clock pulse provided, the output word will be Y= $y_3y_2y_1y_0$=1011. If you now would open the four switches, the output would remain at 1011 regardless of the amount of clocking. You can change the output by changing the input data, closing the switches, and clocking the circuit.

JK Flip-Flop

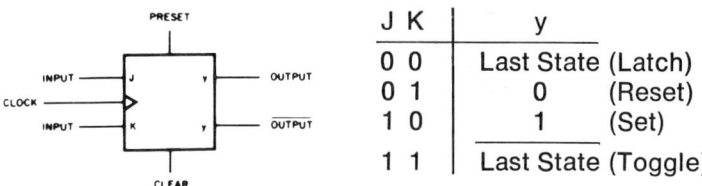

J K	y
0 0	Last State (Latch)
0 1	0 (Reset)
1 0	1 (Set)
1 1	Last State (Toggle)

Here, the J *and* K inputs determine what the latch does when it is clocked. When J and K are both low, the clock pulse has no effect. When J and K are both high, the output will "toggle" (change) with each clock pulse. This idea of toggling is demonstrated in the following example.

4-Bit Counter

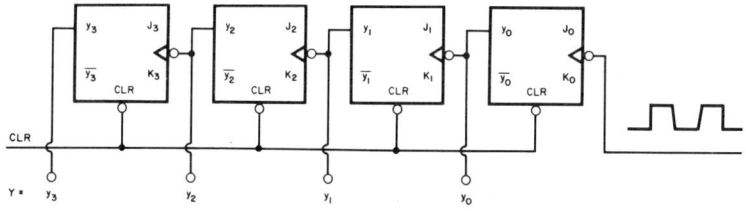

First note that the J K inputs are not connected (floating). In this floating mode, the flip-flop toggles the same as if $J = 1$ and $K = 1$. The "bubble" at the clock input indicates that the flip-flop will actuate when the clock goes in a negative direction, i.e., from 1 to 0. The CLR is also "bubbled"; therefore, you will begin by making CLR low → $Y = y_3y_2y_1y_0 = 0000$.

1st negative clock → $y_0 = 1$ → $Y = y_3y_2y_1y_0 = 0001$
2nd negative clock → $y_0 = 0$ → $y_1 = 1$ → $Y = 0010$

Note in the above case, y_0 went from a high to a low condition. Therefore, $y_1 = 1$ since y_0 provides the clock signal for the second gate.

3rd negative clock → $y_0 = 1$ → $y_1 = 1$ → $Y = 0011$

Note here that y_0 toggled but y_1 remained the same since its clock (y_0) went high. Again, the flip-flop will only toggle when its clock goes low.

4th negative clock → $y_0 = 0$ → $y_1 = 0$ → $y_2 = 1$ → $Y = 0010$

Here ①y_0 toggled

②y_1 toggled since its clock (y_0) went low.
③y_2 toggles since its clock (y_1) went low.

Following this procedure,

5th negative clock → $Y = 0101$
6th negative clock → $Y = 0110$
7th negative clock → $Y = 0111$
8th negative clock → $Y = 1000$
9th negative clock → $Y = 1001$
10th negative clock → $Y = 1010$
11th negative clock → $Y = 1011$
12th negative clock → $Y = 1100$
13th negative clock → $Y = 1101$
14th negative clock → $Y = 1110$
15th negative clock → $Y = 1111$
16th negative clock → $Y = 0000$ (Reset)

The circuit in this example is a binary counter. J K flip-flops are commonly used in this type of counter.

APPENDIX B

Number Systems and Computer Arithemetic

NUMBER SYSTEMS

Digital computers are made up of a series of logic gates integrated onto "chips." These gates are composed of standard electronic devices such as resistors, capacitors, diodes, and transistors. Each of these devices can be made to function like a switch; that is, to represent an "on" or "off" state. A resistor is either conducting or not conducting. A capacitor is charged or not charged. The diode or transistor is either conducting or not conducting. Thus, all of these devices can be used to represent one of two states—on or off. Digital computers, therefore, ultimately use a two-state system to represent numbers. Binary is a number system ideally suited for digital computers since it comprises only two digits, one and zero which can be used to represent on and off states. Even though a computer operates on binary information, it is very cumbersome to you and me. Therefore, it is easier for us to use a higher-order number system or computer language when communicating with the computer. Two such number systems commonly used with microcomputers are octal (base 8) and hexidecimal (base 16).

Decimal (Base 10)

This is the system familiar to all of us. It utilizes the digits 0 through 9. Remember how you learned to read decimal numbers. You started with the decimal point. To the left of that point, each position represented a positive power of 10 from 10^0 on up. To the right of that point, each position represented a negative power of 10 from 10^{-1} on down. Positional weights in the decimal system are arranged as follows:

Positional Weights > $\cdots$ $[10^2]$ $[10^1]$ $[10^0]$ • $[10^{-1}]$ $[10^{-2}]$ $\cdots$

To interpret a number you simply:

1. Determine the positional weight of each digit.
2. Multiply the digit times its positional weight.
3. Add all of the above products.

Decimal Interpretation

Interpret the number $(537)_{10}$.

$$\begin{aligned}(537)_{10} &= 5 \quad 3 \quad 7 \quad \cdot \\ &= (5 \times 10^2) + (3 \times 10^1) + (7 \times 10^0) \\ &= \quad 500 \quad + \quad 30 \quad + \quad 7\end{aligned}$$

Think about it. Isn't this what you do mentally to determine the "weight" of a number?

Binary (Base 2)

This is the number system used by the electronics of all digital computers. It uses the digits 0 and 1. The idea here is the same as with decimal numbers except that powers of 2 are used rather than 10 for the digit weights. Positional weights in the binary number system are arranged as follows:

Positional Weights > $\cdots$ $[2^2]$ $[2^1]$ $[2^0]$ • $[2^{-1}]$ $[2^{-2}]$ $\cdots$

To interpret a binary number the procedure is the same:

1. Determine the positional weight of each digit.
2. Multiply the digit by its positional weight.
3. Add the above products.

Binary → Decimal

Convert 1101_2 to decimal.

$$\begin{aligned}(1101)_2 &= 1 \quad 1 \quad 0 \quad 1 \quad \cdot \\ &= (1 \times 2^3) + (1 \times 2^2) + (0 \times 2^1) + (1 \times 2^0) \\ &= \quad 8 \quad + \quad 4 \quad + \quad 0 \quad + \quad 1 \\ &= \quad (13)_{10}\end{aligned}$$

You now have a feeling for the weight of the binary number 1101 since you have expressed it as a decimal number—something you are familiar with. Now suppose you wish to express the decimal 13 as a binary number. The procedure is as follows:

$13/2 = 6$ with remainder 1
$6/2 = 3$ with remainder 0
$3/2 = 1$ with remainder 1
$1/2 = 0$ with remainder 1

Read Up

Therefore, $(13)_{10} = (1101)_2$

To summarize the process, you see that the binary number is obtained by repetitive division by the base number, 2 in this case. If you need some brushing-up on binary numbers, study the preceding examples and work the related problems at the end of the appendix until you feel comfortable with the process.

Octal (Base 8)

Now that you know the decimal and binary systems, octal will be easy. Octal uses eight digits, 0 through 7. The idea of positional weights is the same as in decimal and binary except that now you use powers of 8 as follows.

Positional Weights > · · · $[8^2]$ $[8^1]$ $[8^0]$ • $[8^{-1}]$ $[8^{-2}]$ · · ·

The interpretation procedures are the same as you used for the binary system.

Octal → Decimal

Interpret the number $(257)_8$.

$$(257)_8 = 2\ 5\ 7\ \cdot$$
$$= (2 \times 8^2) + (5 \times 8^1) + (7 \times 8^0)$$
$$= 128 + 40 + 7$$
$$= (175)_{10}$$

Decimal → Octal

Express $(175)_{10}$ as an octal number.

$175/8 = 21$ with remainder 7
$21/8 = 2$ with remainder 5
$2/8 = 0$ with remainder 2

Read Up

Therefore, $(175)_{10} = (257)_8$ which checks with the above example. As before, work the problems at the end of the appendix if you need practice.

Hexadecimal (Base 16)

The hexadecimal numbering system, or "hex," uses the 10 digits 0 through 9, and the alphabetical characters A, B, C, D, E, and F. It might seem awkward to let the letters A through F represent numbers, but keep in mind that numbers are just symbols for quantities. In this case:

A = (10), B = (11), C = (12), D = (13), E = (14), and F = (15).

Keeping this in mind, the interpretation processes are the same. The positional weights for hex (base 16) are as follows.

Positional Weights > $\cdots$ $[16^2]$ $[16^1]$ $[16^0]$ • $[16^{-1}]$ $[16^{-2}]$ $\cdots$

Hex → Decimal

Interpret the number $(9CF)_{16}$.

$$\begin{aligned}(9CF)_{16} &= \quad 9 \quad C \quad F \quad \cdot \\ &= (9 \times 16^2) + (C \times 16) + (F \times 1) \\ &= (9 \times 256) + (12 \times 16) + (15 \times 1) \\ &= (2511)_{10}\end{aligned}$$

Note the quantity you can represent with just 3 digits using hex.

Decimal → Hex

Express $(2511)_{10}$ as a hex quantity.

2511/16 = 156 with remainder 15 = F
156/16 = 9 with remainder 12 = C   Read Up
9/16 = 0 with remainder 9

Thus, $(2511)_{10} = (9CF)_{16}$

As we said before, you might "talk" to the computer using octal or hex; however, the computer must translate this to binary. Therefore, it might be beneficial if you also could make this translation to better understand the operation of the digital computer.

Octal → Binary

Translate $(257)_8$ to binary.

```
  2       5       7
 / \     / \     / \
010     101     111
```
$(257)_8 = (010101111)_2$

NOTE: You simply expressed each octal digit as a 3-bit number.

Binary → Octal

Translate $(010101111)_2$ to octal.

```
010     101     111
 \ /     \ /     \ /
  2       5       7
```
$(010101111)_2 = (257)_8$

The process is reversed; i.e., divide the binary number into groups of three digits and translate to the octal digit.

Hex → Binary

Translate $(9CF)_{16}$ to binary.

```
  9       C       F
 / \     / \     / \
1001    1100    1111
```
$(9CF)_{16} = (100111001111)_2$

Binary → Hex

Translate $(100111001111)_2$ to hex

```
1001    1100    1111
 \ /     \ /     \ /
  9       C       F
```
$(100111001111)_2 = (9CF)_{16}$

The process is similar to the octal translation except that you break the binary number into groups of four digits.

Bits, Bytes, and Nibbles

A binary digit (1 or 0) is referred to as a "bit." Information in microprocessors and all digital computers is typically represented by a series of bits. A string of 4 bits is referred to as a "nibble" and an 8-bit string is called a "byte." You will see that memory *addresses* used by the 6800 are 16 bits = 4 nibbles = 2 bytes. *Data* within the 6800 are represented using 8 bits = 2 nibbles = 1 byte.

Bits, Bytes, and Nibbles

	4 bits:	1011 = 1 nibble
6800 Data —	8 bits:	1001 1011 = 1 byte
6800 Addresses —	16 bits:	1101 0100 1001 1011 = 2 bytes

A "word" is not as easily defined. Its definition is largely a function of the way we use it. For example, an *address word* for the 6800 is 16 bits while a *data word* is 8 bits in length. The PDP-11 minicomputer has a word length of 16 bits, which means that it represents information as 2 bytes. Some larger computers have word lengths of 24 bits, 32 bits, 64 bits, etc. Note that all of the above words are multiples of 8 bits (1 byte). The lesson here is to be very careful of how you use this "word."

Binary Coded Decimal (BCD)

Binary coded decimal (bcd) is another way in which numbers can be represented in digital computers and digital systems, particularly digital instrumentation. This number system was developed because it is easy to convert between bcd and decimal. When converting from decimal to bcd, *each* decimal digit is represented by its own 4-bit binary equivalent.

Decimal → BCD

To convert 256_{10} to bcd you simply express each decimal digit as a 4-bit binary number.

$$2 = 0010$$
$$5 = 0101$$
$$6 = 0110$$

Therefore, $256_{10} = 0010\ 0101\ 0110_{bcd}$
The reverse procedure is used for converting from bcd to decimal.

BCD → Decimal

To convert $1001\ 0101_{bcd}$ to decimal, you simply divide the bcd number into groups of four bits starting at the right, then convert each group of four bits to decimal.

1st group of four bits: $0101 = 5_{10}$
2nd group of four bits: $1001 = 9_{10}$

Therefore, $1001\ 0101_{bcd} = 95_{10}$
Convert 110111_{bcd} to decimal

1st group of four bits: $0111 = 7_{10}$
2nd group of four bits: $0011 = 3_{10}$

Therefore $110111_{bcd} = 37_{10}$

NOTE, you had to add the leading zeros in the 2nd group of four bits.

CAUTION: bcd and binary are not the same. With bcd, any group of four bits which represent a decimal number larger than nine are considered *invalid*. For example, $1101 = 13_{10}$ is an invalid bcd number. However, in the binary system this bit configuration *is* valid.

As mentioned earlier, many digital instruments use the bcd format for data being transmitted and received. The 6800 has an instruction that will allow you to perform arithmetic operations with bcd numbers. This instruction is the decimal adjust accumulator (DAA) instruction. With this instruction, the 6800 can work with bcd data directly without using special bcd-to-binary conversion routines.

DIGITAL COMPUTER ARITHMETIC

Digital computers utilize the binary number system and, therefore, must add, subtract, multiply, and divide using this system.

Addition

Suppose that you wish to add two binary numbers. Just as you did in decimal, starting with the rightmost column, you simply add each column generating and using the carries as you go. To determine the sum of a column, count the number of 1s in the column.

Binary Addition

Add 10_2 to 11_2.

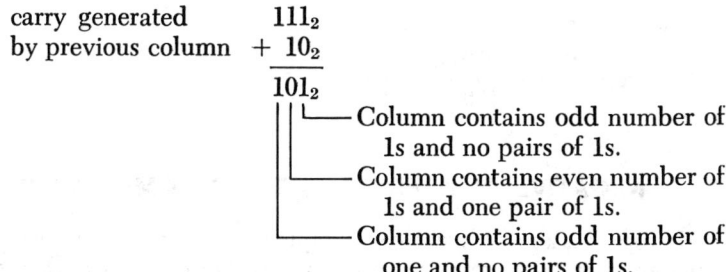

If the number of 1s is odd, the sum will be 1 with a carry generated for each *pair* of 1s. If the number of 1s is even, the sum will be 0 with a carry generated for each *pair* of 1s in the column that was added. Study the above examples.

Check your results by converting to decimal.

$$\begin{array}{r} 11_2 = 3_{10} \\ 10_2 = 2_{10} \\ \hline 101_2 = 5_{10} \end{array}$$

Add 1010_2 to 1110_2

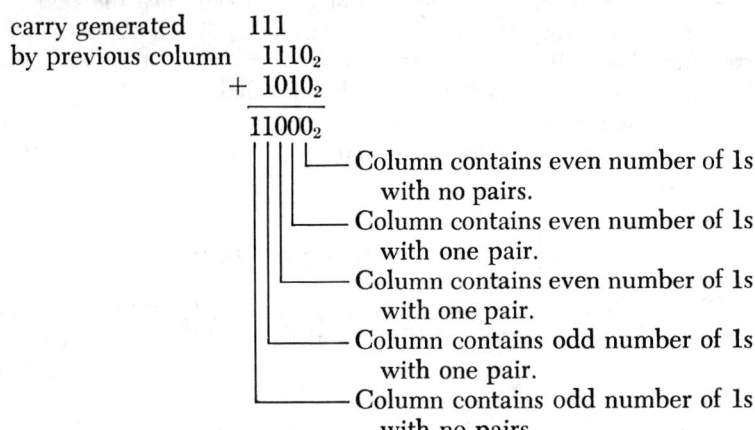

Check: $$\begin{array}{r} 1110_2 = 14_{10} \\ +\ 1010_2 = 10_{10} \\ \hline 11000_2 = 24_{10} \end{array}$$

Add $0010\ 1100_2$ to $0100\ 1010_2$

Check: $$\begin{array}{r} 0010\ 1100_2 = 44_{10} \\ +0100\ 1010_2 = 74_{10} \\ \hline 0111\ 0110_2 = 118_{10} \end{array}$$

NEGATIVE NUMBERS AND TWOS COMPLEMENT

Microprocessors utilize twos complement to represent negative numbers. Let us examine some definitions before we use this idea.

Definition: The *ones complement* of a binary word is obtained by inverting all of the bits within the word. (The ones complement of a word, A, is symbolized by $\overline{A}$.)

Ones Complement

The ones complement of $1101\ 1011_2$ is $0010\ 0100_2$
The ones complement of $0000\ 0111_2$ is $1111\ 1000_2$
The ones complement of $1010\ 0000_2$ is $0101\ 1111_2$

Definition: The *twos complement* of a binary word is obtained by taking the ones complement and adding 1 to it.

Twos Complement

Find the twos complement of each binary word above.
The twos complement of $1101\ 1011_2 =$

$$\begin{array}{r} \text{ones complement} + 1 = 0010\ 0100_2 \\ +\ 1_2 \\ \hline 0010\ 0101_2 \end{array}$$

The twos complement of $0000\ 0111_2 =$

$$\begin{array}{r} \text{ones complement} + 1 = 1111\ 1000_2 \\ +\ 1_2 \\ \hline 1111\ 1001_2 \end{array}$$

The twos complement of $1010\ 0000_2 =$

$$\begin{array}{r} \text{ones complement} + 1 = 0101\ 1111_2 \\ +\ 1_2 \\ \hline 0110\ 0000_2 \end{array}$$

The 6800 uses twos complements to represent negative numbers. Given any positive number, the twos complement of that number will be its negative, within the range of bits allowed.

Given any 8-bit data word $D_7D_6D_5D_4D_3D_2D_1D_0$, we will designate the seventh bit (D_7) to be the sign bit. When this bit is 1, the 6800 will consider the word to be negative. When $D_7 = 0$, the 6800 will recognize the word as positive. Using this scheme and the twos-complement negative number system, it can be shown that the largest possible positive number using an 8-bit data word is $0111\ 1111_2 = +127_{10}$. The maximum negative quantity would be $1000\ 0000_2 = -128_{10}$.

Negative Numbers

What is the 8-bit binary representation for -5_{10}? The 8-bit word for $+5_{10}$ is 0000 0101; therefore, the 8-bit word for -5_{10} is the twos complement of this. Hence, $-5_{10} = 1111\ 1011_2$.

What is the 8-bit binary representation for -127_{10}? It is $+127_{10}$ = $0111\ 1111_2$. The twos complement of $0111\ 1111_2 = 1000\ 0001_2 = -127_{10}$.

What decimal number does $1111\ 0011_2$ represent if it is defined as an 8-bit, twos-complement value? Since $D_7 = 1$, the number is negative. To find its value, take the twos complement and convert to decimal, i.e., $1111\ 0011_2 = -(\text{twos complement})_{10}$. Twos complement of $1111\ 0011_2 = 0000\ 1101_2 = 13_{10}$. Therefore, $1111\ 0011_2 = -13_{10}$.

Subtraction

To subtract, you will simply take the negative (twos complement) of the number to be subtracted and add, *disregarding* any last carry.

Subtraction

Subtract 3_{10} from 7_{10}.
In decimal,

$$\begin{array}{r} 7_{10} \\ -3_{10} \\ \hline 4 \end{array} = \begin{array}{r} 7_{10} \\ +(-3_{10}) \\ \hline 4 \end{array}$$

In binary:

$$\begin{array}{r} 7_{10} = \\ -3_{10} = \\ \hline 4_{10} = \end{array} \begin{array}{r} 0000\ 0111_2 \\ -0000\ 0011_2 \\ \hline \end{array} = \begin{array}{r} 0000\ 0111_2 \\ +(-0000\ 0011_2) \\ \hline \end{array} = \begin{array}{r} 0000\ 0111_2 \\ +1111\ 1101_2 \\ \hline 10000\ 0100_2 \end{array}$$

Disregard last carry

Subtract -25_{10} from -8_{10}

The twos complement of $-25_{10} = 0001\ 1001_2$

$$\begin{array}{r} -8_{10} = \ \ 1111\ 1000_2 \\ +(-25_{10}) = +0001\ 1001_2 \\ \hline 10001\ 0001 = 17_{10}\ (\text{check}) \end{array}$$

disregard ⬆

AND/OR/XOR Logic

The 6800 is capable of ANDing, ORing, and exclusive-OR (XORing) any 8-bit data words. The process is simple; given two 8-bit words, the 6800 just ANDs, ORs, or XORs the word bit by bit.

Logic Operations

$$\begin{array}{rr} & 0101\ 1100_2 \\ \text{AND} & 1110\ 1011_2 \\ \hline & 0100\ 1000_2 \end{array} \qquad \begin{array}{rr} & 0101\ 1100_2 \\ \text{OR} & 1110\ 1011_2 \\ \hline & 1111\ 1111_2 \end{array} \qquad \begin{array}{rr} & 0101\ 1100_2 \\ \text{XOR} & 1110\ 1011_2 \\ \hline & 1011\ 0111_2 \end{array}$$

Multiplication and Division

To multiply or divide with the 6800, you must successively add or subtract, respectively. This is one of the drawbacks of the first generation processors such as the 6800. This process consumes time and memory space. The second and third generation chips such as the 6801, 6803, and 6809 all contain internal hardware multiply functions.

REVIEW QUESTIONS

1. To what decimal numbers do the following binary numbers correspond?

    a. 1101 _____

    b. 1111 1111 _____

    c. 1101 0011 _____

    d. 1111 1111 1111 1111 _____

2. To what hexadecimal numbers do the binary numbers in Question 1 correspond?

    a. _____

    b. _____

    c. _____

    d. _____

3. To what binary numbers do the following hexadecimal numbers correspond?

    a. 00FC _____

    b. 0100 _____

    c. 01CA _____

    d. ED5B _____

    e. ABCD _____

4. To what decimal numbers do the hexadecimal numbers in Question 3 correspond?

    a. _____

    b. _____

    c. _____

d. _____

5. $(0011\ 0101_2) + (0100\ 1110_2) = $ _____ $_{16}$.

6. The ones complement of 0100 1010 is _____.

7. The twos complement of the number in question 6 is _____.

8. Using twos-complement code, what is the 8-bit binary representation for -16_{10}? _____

9. Using twos-complement code, what decimal number does 1011 0110 represent? _____

10. $(0000\ 0101_2) - (0000\ 0011_2) = $ _____ $_2$.
11. $(1010\ 1100_2) \times \text{OR} (0111\ 0010_2) = $ _____ $_2$.
12. Convert the following decimal numbers to binary and bcd: (a) 7 (b) 15 (c) 25 (d) 109

ANSWERS

1. a. 13_{10}
   b. 255_{10}
   c. 211_{10}
   d. $65,535_{10}$

2. a. D_{16}
   b. FF_{16}
   c. $D3_{16}$
   d. $FFFF_{16}$

3. a. 0000 0000 1111 1100$_2$
   b. 0000 0001 0000 0000$_2$
   c. 0000 0001 1100 1010$_2$
   d. 1110 1101 0101 1011$_2$
   e. 1010 1011 1100 1101$_2$

4. a. 252_{10}
   b. 256_{10}
   c. 458_{10}
   d. $60,763_{10}$
   e. $43,981_{10}$

5. 83_{16}

6. 1011 0101$_2$

7. 1011 0110$_2$

8. 1111 0000$_2$

9. -74_{10}

10. 0000 0010$_2$

11. 1101 1110$_2$

12. (a) 0111$_2$
       0111$_{bcd}$
    (b) 1111$_2$
       0001 0101$_{bcd}$
    (c) 11001$_2$
       0010 0101$_{bcd}$
    (d) 1101101$_2$
       0001 0000 1001$_{bcd}$

APPENDIX C

6800 Instruction Set

The following pages contain detailed definitions of the 72 executable instructions. These pages are provided through the courtesy of Motorola Semiconductor Products, Inc.

.1 Nomenclature

The following nomenclature is used in the subsequent definitions.

(a) *Operators*

```
( )     =  contents of
←       =  is transferred to
↑       =  "is pulled from stack"
↓       =  "is pushed into stack"
·       =  Boolean AND
⊙       =  Boolean (Inclusive) OR
⊕       =  Exclusive OR
≈       =  Boolean NOT
```

(b) *Registers in the MPU*

```
ACCA    =  Accumulator A
ACCB    =  Accumulator B
ACCX    =  Accumulator ACCA or ACCB
CC      =  Condition codes register
IX      =  Index register, 16 bits
IXH     =  Index register, higher order 8 bits
IXL     =  Index register, lower order 8 bits
PC      =  Program counter, 16 bits
PCH     =  Program counter, higher order 8 bits
PCL     =  Program counter, lower order 8 bits
SP      =  Stack pointer
SPH     =  Stack pointer high
SPL     =  Stack pointer low
```

297

(c) *Memory and Addressing*
    M   = A memory location (one byte)
    M +1   = The byte of memory at 0001 plus the address of the memory location indicated by "M."
    Rel   = Relative address (i.e. the two's complement number stored in the second byte of machine code corresponding to a branch instruction).
(d) *Bits 0 thru 5 of the Condition Codes Register*
    C = Carry — borrow   bit — 0
    V = Two's complement overflow indicator   bit — 1
    Z = Zero indicator   bit — 2
    N = Negative indicator   bit — 3
    I = Interrupt mask   bit — 4
    H = Half carry   bit — 5
(e) *Status of Individual Bits BEFORE Execution of an Instruction*
    An   = Bit n of ACCA (n=7,6,5,...,0)
    Bn   = Bit n of ACCB (n=7,6,5,...,0)
    IXHn = Bit n of IXH (n=7,6,5,...,0)
    IXLn = Bit n of IXL (n=7,6,5,...,0)
    Mn   = Bit n of M (n=7,6,5,...,0)
    SPHn = Bit n of SPH (n=7,6,5,...,0)
    SPLn = Bit n of SPL (n=7,6,5,...,0)
    Xn   = Bit n of ACCX (n=7,6,5,...,0)
(f) *Status of Individual Bits of the RESULT of Execution of an Instruction*
    (i) For 8-bit Results
        Rn = Bit n of the result (n =7,6,5,...,0)

        This applies to instructions which provide a result contained in a single byte of memory or in an 8-bit register.
    (ii) For 16-bit Results
        RHn = Bit n of the more significant byte of the result
              (n =7,6,5,...,0)
        RLn = Bit n of the less significant byte of the result
              (n =7,6,5,...,0)

        This applies to instructions which provide a result contained in two consecutive bytes of memory or in a 16-bit register.

.2 Executable Instructions (definition of)

Detailed definitions of the 72 executable instructions of the source language are provided on the following pages.

Add Accumulator B to Accumulator A **ABA**

Operation: ACCA ← (ACCA) + (ACCB)

Description: Adds the contents of ACCB to the contents of ACCA and places the result in ACCA.

Condition Codes:
- H: Set if there was a carry from bit 3; cleared otherwise.
- I: Not affected.
- N: Set if most significant bit of the result is set; cleared otherwise.
- Z: Set if all bits of the result are cleared; cleared otherwise.
- V: Set if there was two's complement overflow as a result of the operation; cleared otherwise.
- C: Set if there was a carry from the most significant bit of the result; cleared otherwise.

Boolean Formulae for Condition Codes:
$H = A_3 \cdot B_3 + B_3 \cdot \overline{R}_3 + \overline{R}_3 \cdot A_3$
$N = R_7$
$Z = \overline{R}_7 \cdot \overline{R}_6 \cdot \overline{R}_5 \cdot \overline{R}_4 \cdot \overline{R}_3 \cdot \overline{R}_2 \cdot \overline{R}_1 \cdot \overline{R}_0$
$V = A_7 \cdot B_7 \cdot \overline{R}_7 + \overline{A}_7 \cdot \overline{B}_7 \cdot R_7$
$C = A_7 \cdot B_7 + B_7 \cdot \overline{R}_7 + \overline{R}_7 \cdot A_7$

Addressing Modes, Execution Time, and Machine Code (hexadecimal/octal/decimal):

Addressing Modes	Execution Time (No. of cycles)	Number of bytes of machine code	Coding of First (or only) byte of machine code		
			HEX.	OCT.	DEC.
Inherent	2	1	1B	033	027

Add with Carry ADC

Operation: ACCX ← (ACCX) + (M) + (C)

Description: Adds the contents of the C bit to the sum of the contents of ACCX and M, and places the result in ACCX.

Condition Codes:
H: Set if there was a carry from bit 3; cleared otherwise.
I: Not affected.
N: Set if most significant bit of the result is set; cleared otherwise.
Z: Set if all bits of the result are cleared; cleared otherwise.
V: Set if there was two's complement overflow as a result of the operation; cleared otherwise.
C: Set if there was a carry from the most significant bit of the result; cleared otherwise.

Boolean Formulae for Condition Codes:
$H = X_3 \cdot M_3 + M_3 \cdot \overline{R}_3 + \overline{R}_3 \cdot X_3$
$N = R_7$
$Z = \overline{R}_7 \cdot \overline{R}_6 \cdot \overline{R}_5 \cdot \overline{R}_4 \cdot \overline{R}_3 \cdot \overline{R}_2 \cdot \overline{R}_1 \cdot \overline{R}_0$
$V = X_7 \cdot M_7 \cdot \overline{R}_7 + \overline{X}_7 \cdot \overline{M}_7 \cdot R_7$
$C = X_7 \cdot M_7 + M_7 \cdot \overline{R}_7 + \overline{R}_7 \cdot X_7$

Addressing Formats:

Addressing Modes, Execution Time, and Machine Code (hexadecimal/octal/decimal):

(DUAL OPERAND)

Addressing Modes		Execution Time (No. of cycles)	Number of bytes of machine code	Coding of First (or only) byte of machine code		
				HEX.	OCT.	DEC.
A	IMM	2	2	89	211	137
A	DIR	3	2	99	231	153
A	EXT	4	3	B9	271	185
A	IND	5	2	A9	251	169
B	IMM	2	2	C9	311	201
B	DIR	3	2	D9	331	217
B	EXT	4	3	F9	371	249
B	IND	5	2	E9	351	233

ADD
Add Without Carry

Operation: ACCX ← (ACCX) + (M)

Description: Adds the contents of ACCX and the contents of M and places the result in ACCX.

Condition Codes:
- H: Set if there was a carry from bit 3; cleared otherwise.
- I: Not affected.
- N: Set if most significant bit of the result is set; cleared otherwise.
- Z: Set if all bits of the result are cleared; cleared otherwise.
- V: Set if there was two's complement overflow as a result of the operation; cleared otherwise.
- C: Set if there was a carry from the most significant bit of the result; cleared otherwise.

Boolean Formulae for Condition Codes:

$H = X_3 \cdot M_3 + M_3 \cdot \overline{R}_3 + \overline{R}_3 \cdot X_3$

$N = R_7$

$Z = \overline{R}_7 \cdot \overline{R}_6 \cdot \overline{R}_5 \cdot \overline{R}_4 \cdot \overline{R}_3 \cdot \overline{R}_2 \cdot \overline{R}_1 \cdot \overline{R}_0$

$V = X_7 \cdot M_7 \cdot \overline{R}_7 + \overline{X}_7 \cdot \overline{M}_7 \cdot R_7$

$C = X_7 \cdot M_7 + M_7 \cdot \overline{R}_7 + \overline{R}_7 \cdot X_7$

Addressing Formats:

Addressing Modes, Execution Time, and Machine Code (hexadecimal/octal/decimal):

(DUAL OPERAND)

Addressing Modes	Execution Time (No. of cycles)	Number of bytes of machine code	Coding of First (or only) byte of machine code		
			HEX.	OCT.	DEC.
A IMM	2	2	8B	213	139
A DIR	3	2	9B	233	155
A EXT	4	3	BB	273	187
A IND	5	2	AB	253	171
B IMM	2	2	CB	313	203
B DIR	3	2	DB	333	219
B EXT	4	3	FB	373	251
B IND	5	2	EB	353	235

AND
Logical AND

Operation: ACCX ← (ACCX) · (M)

Description: Performs logical "AND" between the contents of ACCX and the contents of M and places the result in ACCX. (Each bit of ACCX after the operation will be the logical "AND" of the corresponding bits of M and of ACCX before the operation.)

Condition Codes:
- H: Not affected.
- I: Not affected.
- N: Set if most significant bit of the result is set; cleared otherwise.
- Z: Set if all bits of the result are cleared; cleared otherwise.
- V: Cleared.
- C: Not affected.

Boolean Formulae for Condition Codes:

$N = R_7$

$Z = \overline{R}_7 \cdot \overline{R}_6 \cdot \overline{R}_5 \cdot \overline{R}_4 \cdot \overline{R}_3 \cdot \overline{R}_2 \cdot \overline{R}_1 \cdot \overline{R}_0$

$V = 0$

Addressing Formats:

Addressing Modes, Execution Time, and Machine Code (hexadecimal/octal/decimal):

Addressing Modes	Execution Time (No. of cycles)	Number of bytes of machine code	Coding of First (or only) byte of machine code		
			HEX.	OCT.	DEC.
A IMM	2	2	84	204	132
A DIR	3	2	94	224	148
A EXT	4	3	B4	264	180
A IND	5	2	A4	244	164
B IMM	2	2	C4	304	196
B DIR	3	2	D4	324	212
B EXT	4	3	F4	364	244
B IND	5	2	E4	344	228

ASL

Arithmetic Shift Left

Operation:

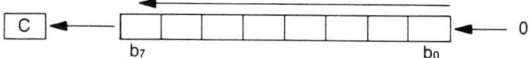

Description: Shifts all bits of the ACCX or M one place to the left. Bit 0 is loaded with a zero. The C bit is loaded from the most significant bit of ACCX or M.

Condition Codes:
- H: Not affected.
- I: Not affected.
- N: Set if most significant bit of the result is set; cleared otherwise.
- Z: Set if all bits of the result are cleared; cleared otherwise.
- V: Set if, after the completion of the shift operation, EITHER (N is set and C is cleared) OR (N is cleared and C is set); cleared otherwise.
- C: Set if, before the operation, the most significant bit of the ACCX or M was set; cleared otherwise.

Boolean Formulae for Condition Codes:

$N = R_7$
$Z = \overline{R_7} \cdot \overline{R_6} \cdot \overline{R_5} \cdot \overline{R_4} \cdot \overline{R_3} \cdot \overline{R_2} \cdot \overline{R_1} \cdot \overline{R_0}$
$V = N \oplus C = [N \cdot \overline{C}] \odot [\overline{N} \cdot C]$
(the foregoing formula assumes values of N and C after the shift operation)
$C = M_7$

Addressing Formats

Addressing Modes, Execution Time, and Machine Code (hexadecimal/octal/decimal):

Addressing Modes	Execution Time (No. of cycles)	Number of bytes of machine code	Coding of First (or only) byte of machine code		
			HEX.	OCT.	DEC.
A	2	1	48	110	072
B	2	1	58	130	088
EXT	6	3	78	170	120
IND	7	2	68	150	104

ASR

Arithmetic Shift Right

Operation: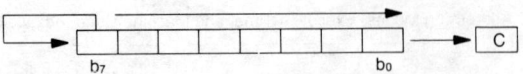

Description: Shifts all bits of ACCX or M one place to the right. Bit 7 is held constant. Bit 0 is loaded into the C bit.

Condition Codes:
- H: Not affected.
- I: Not affected.
- N: Set if the most significant bit of the result is set; cleared otherwise.
- Z: Set if all bits of the result are cleared; cleared otherwise.
- V: Set if, after the completion of the shift operation, EITHER (N is set and C is cleared) OR (N is cleared and C is set); cleared otherwise.
- C: Set if, before the operation, the least significant bit of the ACCX or M was set; cleared otherwise.

Boolean Formulae for Condition Codes:

$N = R_7$

$Z = \bar{R}_7 \cdot \bar{R}_6 \cdot \bar{R}_5 \cdot \bar{R}_4 \cdot \bar{R}_3 \cdot \bar{R}_2 \cdot \bar{R}_1 \cdot \bar{R}_0$

$V = N \oplus C = [N \cdot \bar{C}] \odot [\bar{N} \cdot C]$

(the foregoing formula assumes values of N and C after the shift operation)

$C = M_0$

Addressing Formats:

Addressing Modes, Execution Time, and Machine Code (hexadecimal / octal / decimal):

Addressing Modes	Execution Time (No. of cycles)	Number of bytes of machine code	Coding of First (or only) byte of machine code		
			HEX.	OCT.	DEC.
A	2	1	47	107	071
B	2	1	57	127	087
EXT	6	3	77	167	119
IND	7	2	67	147	103

BCC

Branch if Carry Clear

Operation: PC ← (PC) + 0002 + Rel if (C)=0

Description: Tests the state of the C bit and causes a branch if C is clear.

See BRA instruction for further details of the execution of the branch.

Condition Codes: Not affected.

Addressing Formats:

Addressing Modes, Execution Time, and Machine Code (hexadecimal / octal / decimal):

Addressing Modes	Execution Time (No. of cycles)	Number of bytes of machine code	Coding of First (or only) byte of machine code		
			HEX.	OCT.	DEC.
REL	4	2	24	044	036

BCS
Branch if Carry Set

Operation: PC ← (PC) + 0002 + Rel if (C)=1

Description: Tests the state of the C bit and causes a branch if C is set.

See BRA instruction for further details of the execution of the branch.

Condition Codes: Not affected.

Addressing Formats:

Addressing Modes, Execution Time, and Machine Code (hexadecimal/ octal/ decimal):

Addressing Modes	Execution Time (No. of cycles)	Number of bytes of machine code	Coding of First (or only) byte of machine code		
			HEX.	OCT.	DEC.
REL	4	2	25	045	037

Branch if Equal BEQ

Operation: PC ← (PC) + 0002 + Rel if (Z)=1

Description: Tests the state of the Z bit and causes a branch if the Z bit is set.

See BRA instruction for further details of the execution of the branch.

Condition Codes: Not affected.

Addressing Formats:

Addressing Modes, Execution Time, and Machine Code (hexadecimal/ octal/ decimal):

Addressing Modes	Execution Time (No. of cycles)	Number of bytes of machine code	Coding of First (or only) byte of machine code		
			HEX.	OCT.	DEC.
REL	4	2	27	047	039

BGE
Branch if Greater than or Equal to Zero

Operation: PC ← (PC) + 0002 + Rel if (N) ⊕ (V) = 0

i.e. if (ACCX) ≥ (M)

(Two's complement numbers)

Description: Causes a branch if (N is set and V is set) OR (N is clear and V is clear).

If the BGE instruction is executed immediately after execution of any of the instructions CBA, CMP, SBA, or SUB, the branch will occur if and only if the two's complement number represented by the minuend (i.e. ACCX) was greater than or equal to the two's complement number represented by the subtrahend (i.e. M).

See BRA instruction for details of the branch.

Condition Codes: Not affected.

Addressing Formats:

Addressing Modes, Execution Time, and Machine Code (hexadecimal/ octal/ decimal):

Addressing Modes	Execution Time (No. of cycles)	Number of bytes of machine code	Coding of First (or only) byte of machine code		
			HEX.	OCT.	DEC.
REL	4	2	2C	054	044

BGT
Branch if Greater than Zero

Operation: PC ← (PC) + 0002 + Rel if (Z) $\odot$ [(N) $\oplus$ (V)] = 0
                           i.e. if (ACCX) > (M)
                         (two's complement numbers)

Description: Causes a branch if [Z is clear] AND [(N is set and V is set) OR (N is clear and V is clear)].

If the BGT instruction is executed immediately after execution of any of the instructions CBA, CMP, SBA, or SUB, the branch will occur if and only if the two's complement number represented by the minuend (i.e. ACCX) was greater than the two's complement number represented by the subtrahend (i.e. M).

See BRA instruction for details of the branch.

Condition Codes: Not affected.

Addressing Formats:

Addressing Modes, Execution Time, and Machine Code (hexadecimal / octal / decimal):

Addressing Modes	Execution Time (No. of cycles)	Number of bytes of machine code	Coding of First (or only) byte of machine code		
			HEX.	OCT.	DEC.
REL	4	2	2E	056	046

BHI
Branch if Higher

Operation: PC ← (PC) + 0002 + Rel if (C) $\cdot$ (Z)=0
                           i.e. if (ACCX) > (M)
                         (unsigned binary numbers)

Description: Causes a branch if (C is clear) AND (Z is clear).

If the BHI instruction is executed immediately after execution of any of the instructions CBA, CMP, SBA, or SUB, the branch will occur if and only if the unsigned binary number represented by the minuend (i.e. ACCX) was greater than the unsigned binary number represented by the subtrahend (i.e. M).

See BRA instruction for details of the execution of the branch.

Condition Codes: Not affected.

Addressing Formats:

Addressing Modes, Execution Time, and Machine Code (hexadecimal / octal / decimal):

Addressing Modes	Execution Time (No. of cycles)	Number of bytes of machine code	Coding of First (or only) byte of machine code		
			HEX.	OCT.	DEC.
REL	4	2	22	042	034

BIT
Bit Test

Operation: (ACCX) $\cdot$ (M)

Description: Performs the logical "AND" comparison of the contents of ACCX and the contents of M and modifies condition codes accordingly. Neither the contents of ACCX or M operands are affected. (Each bit of the result of the "AND" would be the logical "AND" of the corresponding bits of M and ACCX.)

Condition Codes: H: Not affected.
I: Not affected.
N: Set if the most significant bit of the result of the "AND" would be set; cleared otherwise.
Z: Set if all bits of the result of the "AND" would be cleared; cleared otherwise.
V: Cleared.
C: Not affected.

Boolean Formulae for Condition Codes:
$N = R_7$
$Z = \bar{R}_7 \cdot \bar{R}_6 \cdot \bar{R}_5 \cdot \bar{R}_4 \cdot \bar{R}_3 \cdot \bar{R}_2 \cdot \bar{R}_1 \cdot \bar{R}_0$
$V = 0$

Addressing Formats:

Addressing Modes, Execution Time, and Machine Code (hexadecimal/octal/decimal):

Addressing Modes	Execution Time (No. of cycles)	Number of bytes of machine code	Coding of First (or only) byte of machine code		
			HEX.	OCT.	DEC.
A IMM	2	2	85	205	133
A DIR	3	2	95	225	149
A EXT	4	3	B5	265	181
A IND	5	2	A5	245	165
B IMM	2	2	C5	305	197
B DIR	3	2	D5	325	213
B EXT	4	3	F5	365	245
B IND	5	2	E5	345	229

Branch if Less than or Equal to Zero   **BLE**

Operation: PC ← (PC) + 0002 + Rel if $(Z) \odot [(N) \oplus (V)] = 1$
                     i.e. if (ACCX) ≤ (M)
                        (two's complement numbers)

Description: Causes a branch if [Z is set] OR [(N is set and V is clear) OR (N is clear and V is set)].

If the BLE instruction is executed immediately after execution of any of the instructions CBA, CMP, SBA, or SUB, the branch will occur if and only if the two's complement number represented by the minuend (i.e. ACCX) was less then or equal to the two's complement number represented by the subtrahend (i.e. M).

See BRA instruction for details of the branch.

Condition Codes: Not affected.

Addressing Formats:

Addressing Modes, Execution Time, and Machine Code (hexadecimal/octal/decimal):

Addressing Modes	Execution Time (No. of cycles)	Number of bytes of machine code	Coding of First (or only) byte of machine code		
			HEX.	OCT.	DEC.
REL	4	2	2F	057	047

BLS
Branch if Lower or Same

Operation: PC ← (PC) + 0002 + Rel if (C)⊙(Z) = 1
                                i.e. if (ACCX) ≤ (M)
                               (unsigned binary numbers)

Description: Causes a branch if (C is set) OR (Z is set).

If the BLS instruction is executed immediately after execution of any of the instructions CBA, CMP, SBA, or SUB, the branch will occur if and only if the unsigned binary number represented by the minuend (i.e. ACCX) was less than or equal to the unsigned binary number represented by the subtrahend (i.e. M).

See BRA instruction for details of the execution of the branch.

Condition Codes: Not affected.
Addressing Formats:
Addressing Modes, Execution Time, and Machine Code (hexadecimal/octal/decimal):

Addressing Modes	Execution Time (No. of cycles)	Number of bytes of machine code	Coding of First (or only) byte of machine code		
			HEX.	OCT.	DEC.
REL	4	2	23	043	035

BLT
Branch if Less than Zero

Operation: PC ← (PC) + 0002 + Rel if (N) ⊕ (V) = 1
                                i.e. if (ACCX) < (M)
                               (two's complement numbers)

Description: Causes a branch if (N is set and V is clear) OR (N is clear and V is set).

If the BLT instruction is executed immediately after execution of any of the instructions CBA, CMP, SBA, or SUB, the branch will occur if and only if the two's complement number represented by the minuend (i.e. ACCX) was less than the two's complement number represented by the subtrahend (i.e. M).

See BRA instruction for details of the branch.

Condition Codes: Not affected.
Addressing Formats:
Addressing Modes, Execution Time, and Machine Code (hexadecimal/octal/decimal):

Addressing Modes	Execution Time (No. of cycles)	Number of bytes of machine code	Coding of First (or only) byte of machine code		
			HEX.	OCT.	DEC.
REL	4	2	2D	055	045

Branch if Minus — BMI

Operation: PC ← (PC) + 0002 + Rel if (N) = 1
Description: Tests the state of the N bit and causes a branch if N is set.
See BRA instruction for details of the execution of the branch.
Condition Codes: Not affected.
Addressing Formats:
Addressing Modes, Execution Time, and Machine Code (hexadecimal/octal/decimal):

Addressing Modes	Execution Time (No. of cycles)	Number of bytes of machine code	Coding of First (or only) byte of machine code		
			HEX.	OCT.	DEC.
REL	4	2	2B	053	043

Branch if Not Equal — BNE

Operation: PC ← (PC) + 0002 + Rel if (Z) = 0
Description: Tests the state of the Z bit and causes a branch if the Z bit is clear.
See BRA instruction for details of the execution of the branch.
Condition Codes: Not affected.
Addressing Formats:
Addressing Modes, Execution Time, and Machine Code (hexadecimal/octal/decimal):

Addressing Modes	Execution Time (No. of cycles)	Number of bytes of machine code	Coding of First (or only) byte of machine code		
			HEX.	OCT.	DEC.
REL	4	2	26	046	038

Branch if Plus — BPL

Operation: PC ← (PC) + 0002 + Rel if (N) = 0
Description: Tests the state of the N bit and causes a branch if N is clear.
See BRA instruction for details of the execution of the branch.
Condition Codes: Not affected.
Addressing Formats:
Addressing Modes, Execution Time, and Machine Code (hexadecimal/octal/decimal):

Addressing Modes	Execution Time (No. of cycles)	Number of bytes of machine code	Coding of First (or only) byte of machine code		
			HEX.	OCT.	DEC.
REL	4	2	2A	052	042

BRA

Branch Always

Operation: PC ← (PC) + 0002 + Rel

Description: Unconditional branch to the address given by the foregoing formula, in which R is the relative address stored as a two's complement number in the second byte of machine code corresponding to the branch instruction.

> Note: The source program specifies the destination of any branch instruction by its absolute address, either as a numerical value or as a symbol or expression which can be numerically evaluated by the assembler. The assembler obtains the relative address R from the absolute address and the current value of the program counter PC.

Condition Codes: Not affected.

Addressing Formats:

Addressing Modes, Execution Time, and Machine Code (hexadecimal/ octal/ decimal):

Addressing Modes	Execution Time (No. of cycles)	Number of bytes of machine code	Coding of First (or only) byte of machine code		
			HEX.	OCT.	DEC.
REL	4	2	20	040	032

BSR

Branch to Subroutine

Operation: PC ← (PC) + 0002
                     ↓ (PCL)
                     SP ← (SP) − 0001
                     ↓ (PCH)
                     SP ← (SP) − 0001
                     PC ← (PC) + Rel

Description: The program counter is incremented by 2. The less significant byte of the contents of the program counter is pushed into the stack. The stack pointer is then decremented (by 1). The more significant byte of the contents of the program counter is then pushed into the stack. The stack pointer is again decremented (by 1). A branch then occurs to the location specified by the program.

> See BRA instruction for details of the execution of the branch.

Condition Codes: Not affected.

Addressing Formats:

Addressing Modes, Execution Time, and Machine Code (hexadecimal/ octal/ decimal):

Addressing Modes	Execution Time (No. of cycles)	Number of bytes of machine code	Coding of First (or only) byte of machine code		
			HEX.	OCT.	DEC.
REL	8	2	8D	215	141

BRANCH TO SUBROUTINE EXAMPLE

		Memory Location		Machine Code (Hex)	Label	Assembler Language Operator	Operand
A.	Before						
	PC	←	$1000	8D		BSR	CHARLI
			$1001	50			
	SP	←	$EFFF				
B.	After						
	PC	←	$1052	**	CHARLI	***	*****
	SP	←	$EFFD				
			$EFFE	10			
			$EFFF	02			

Branch if Overflow Clear   BVC

Operation: PC ← (PC) + 0002 + Rel if (V) = 0

Description: Tests the state of the V bit and causes a branch if the V bit is clear.

See BRA instruction for details of the execution of the branch.

Condition Codes: Not affected.

Addressing Formats:

Addressing Modes, Execution Time, and Machine Code (hexadecimal/ octal/ decimal):

Addressing Modes	Execution Time (No. of cycles)	Number of bytes of machine code	Coding of First (or only) byte of machine code		
			HEX.	OCT.	DEC.
REL	4	2	28	050	040

Branch if Overflow Set   BVS

Operation: PC ← (PC) + 0002 + Rel if (V) = 1

Description: Tests the state of the V bit and causes a branch if the V bit is set.

See BRA instruction for details of the execution of the branch.

Condition Codes: Not affected.

Addressing Formats:

Addressing Modes, Execution Time, and Machine Code (hexadecimal/ octal/ decimal):

Addressing Modes	Execution Time (No. of cycles)	Number of bytes of machine code	Coding of First (or only) byte of machine code		
			HEX.	OCT.	DEC.
REL	4	2	29	051	041

CBA
Compare Accumulators

Operation: (ACCA) − (ACCB)

Description: Compares the contents of ACCA and the contents of ACCB and sets the condition codes, which may be used for arithmetic and logical conditional branches. Both operands are unaffected.

Condition Codes:
- H: Not affected.
- I: Not affected.
- N: Set if the most significant bit of the result of the subtraction would be set; cleared otherwise.
- Z: Set if all bits of the result of the subtraction would be cleared; cleared otherwise.
- V: Set if the subtraction would cause two's complement overflow; cleared otherwise.
- C: Set if the subtraction would require a borrow into the most significant bit of the result; clear otherwise.

Boolean Formulae for Condition Codes:

$N = R_7$
$Z = \overline{R_7} \cdot \overline{R_6} \cdot \overline{R_5} \cdot \overline{R_4} \cdot \overline{R_3} \cdot \overline{R_2} \cdot \overline{R_1} \cdot \overline{R_0}$
$V = A_7 \cdot \overline{B_7} \cdot \overline{R_7} + \overline{A_7} \cdot B_7 \cdot R_7$
$C = \overline{A_7} \cdot B_7 + B_7 \cdot R_7 + R_7 \cdot \overline{A_7}$

Addressing Modes, Execution Time, and Machine Code (hexadecimal/octal/decimal):

Addressing Modes	Execution Time (No. of cycles)	Number of bytes of machine code	Coding of First (or only) byte of machine code		
			HEX.	OCT.	DEC.
INHERENT	2	1	11	021	017

CLC
Clear Carry

Operation: C bit ← 0

Description: Clears the carry bit in the processor condition codes register.

Condition Codes:
- H: Not affected.
- I: Not affected.
- N: Not affected.
- Z: Not affected.
- V: Not affected.
- C: Cleared

Boolean Formulae for Condition Codes:

$C = 0$

Addressing Modes, Execution Time, and Machine Code (hexadecimal/octal/decimal):

Addressing Modes	Execution Time (No. of cycles)	Number of bytes of machine code	Coding of First (or only) byte of machine code		
			HEX.	OCT.	DEC.
INHERENT	2	1	0C	014	012

CLI

Clear Interrupt Mask

Operation: I bit ← 0

Description: Clears the interrupt mask bit in the processor condition codes register. This enables the microprocessor to service an interrupt from a peripheral device if signalled by a high state of the "Interrupt Request" control input.

Condition Codes:
- H: Not affected.
- I: Cleared.
- N: Not affected.
- Z: Not affected.
- V: Not affected.
- C: Not affected.

Boolean Formulae for Condition Codes:

I = 0

Addressing Modes, Execution Time, and Machine Code (hexadecimal/octal/decimal):

Addressing Modes	Execution Time (No. of cycles)	Number of bytes of machine code	Coding of First (or only) byte of machine code		
			HEX.	OCT.	DEC.
INHERENT	2	1	0E	016	014

Clear

CLR

Operation: ACCX ← 00
or: M ← 00

Description: The contents of ACCX or M are replaced with zeros.

Condition Codes:
- H: Not affected.
- I: Not affected.
- N: Cleared
- Z: Set
- V: Cleared
- C: Cleared

Boolean Formulae for Condition Codes:

N = 0
Z = 1
V = 0
C = 0

Addressing Formats:

Addressing Modes, Execution Time, and Machine Code (hexadecimal/octal/decimal):

Addressing Modes	Execution Time (No. of cycles)	Number of bytes of machine code	Coding of First (or only) byte of machine code		
			HEX.	OCT.	DEC.
A	2	1	4F	117	079
B	2	1	5F	137	095
EXT	6	3	7F	177	127
IND	7	2	6F	157	111

CLV

Clear Two's Complement Overflow Bit

Operation: V bit ← 0

Description: Clears the two's complement overflow bit in the processor condition codes register.

Condition Codes:
- H: Not affected.
- I: Not affected.
- N: Not affected.
- Z: Not affected.
- V: Cleared.
- C: Not affected.

Boolean Formulae for Condition Codes:
$V = 0$

Addressing Modes, Execution Time, and Machine Code (hexadecimal/octal/decimal):

Addressing Modes	Execution Time (No. of cycles)	Number of bytes of machine code	Coding of First (or only) byte of machine code		
			HEX.	OCT.	DEC.
INHERENT	2	1	0A	012	010

CMP

Compare

Operation: (ACCX) − (M)

Description: Compares the contents of ACCX and the contents of M and determines the condition codes, which may be used subsequently for controlling conditional branching. Both operands are unaffected.

Condition Codes:
- H: Not affected.
- I: Not affected.
- N: Set if the most significant bit of the result of the subtraction would be set; cleared otherwise.
- Z: Set if all bits of the result of the subtraction would be cleared; cleared otherwise.
- V: Set if the subtraction would cause two's complement overflow, cleared otherwise.
- C: Carry is set if the absolute value of the contents of memory is larger than the absolute value of the accumulator; reset otherwise.

Boolean Formulae for Condition Codes:

$N = R_7$

$Z = \overline{R}_7 \cdot \overline{R}_6 \cdot \overline{R}_5 \cdot \overline{R}_4 \cdot \overline{R}_3 \cdot \overline{R}_2 \cdot \overline{R}_1 \cdot \overline{R}_0$

$V = X_7 \cdot \overline{M}_7 \cdot \overline{R}_7 + \overline{X}_7 \cdot M_7 \cdot R_7$

$C = \overline{X}_7 \cdot M_7 + M_7 \cdot R_7 + R_7 \cdot \overline{X}_7$

Addressing Formats:

Addressing Modes, Execution Time, and Machine Code (hexadecimal/octal/decimal):
(DUAL OPERAND)

Addressing Modes	Execution Time (No. of cycles)	Number of bytes of machine code	Coding of First (or only) byte of machine code		
			HEX.	OCT.	DEC.
A IMM	2	2	81	201	129
A DIR	3	2	91	221	145
A EXT	4	3	B1	261	177
A IND	5	2	A1	241	161
B IMM	2	2	C1	301	193
B DIR	3	2	D1	321	209
B EXT	4	3	F1	361	241
B IND	5	2	E1	341	225

Complement   COM

Operation: ACCX ← ≈ (ACCX) = FF − (ACCX)
or: M ← ≈ (M) = FF − (M)

Description: Replaces the contents of ACCX or M with its one's complement. (Each bit of the contents of ACCX or M is replaced with the complement of that bit.)

Condition Codes:
- H: Not affected.
- I: Not affected.
- N: Set if most significant bit of the result is set; cleared otherwise.
- Z: Set if all bits of the result are cleared; cleared otherwise.
- V: Cleared.
- C: Set.

Boolean Formulae for Condition Codes:

$N = R_7$
$Z = \overline{R_7} \cdot \overline{R_6} \cdot \overline{R_5} \cdot \overline{R_4} \cdot \overline{R_3} \cdot \overline{R_2} \cdot \overline{R_1} \cdot \overline{R_0}$
$V = 0$
$C = 1$

Addressing Formats:

Addressing Modes, Execution Time, and Machine Code (hexadecimal/octal/decimal):

Addressing Modes	Execution Time (No. of cycles)	Number of bytes of machine code	Coding of First (or only) byte of machine code		
			HEX.	OCT.	DEC.
A	2	1	43	103	067
B	2	1	53	123	083
EXT	6	3	73	163	115
IND	7	2	63	143	099

Compare Index Register   **CPX**

Operation: (IXL) − (M+1)
                     (IXH) − (M)

Description: The more significant byte of the contents of the index register is compared with the contents of the byte of memory at the address specified by the program. The less significant byte of the contents of the index register is compared with the contents of the next byte of memory, at one plus the address specified by the program. The Z bit is set or reset according to the results of these comparisons, and may be used subsequently for conditional branching.

The N and V bits, though determined by this operation, are not intended for conditional branching.

The C bit is not affected by this operation.

Condition Codes:
- H: Not affected.
- I: Not affected.
- N: Set if the most significant bit of the result of the subtraction from the more significant byte of the index register would be set; cleared otherwise.
- Z: Set if all bits of the results of both subtractions would be cleared; cleared otherwise.
- V: Set if the subtraction from the more significant byte of the index register would cause two's complement overflow; cleared otherwise.
- C: Not affected.

Boolean Formulae for Condition Codes:

$N = RH_7$

$Z = (\overline{RH_7} \cdot \overline{RH_6} \cdot \overline{RH_5} \cdot \overline{RH_4} \cdot \overline{RH_3} \cdot \overline{RH_2} \cdot \overline{RH_1} \cdot \overline{RH_0}) \cdot$
$\phantom{Z = {}}(\overline{RL_7} \cdot \overline{RL_6} \cdot \overline{RL_5} \cdot \overline{RL_4} \cdot \overline{RL_3} \cdot \overline{RL_2} \cdot \overline{RL_1} \cdot \overline{RL_0})$

$V = IXH_7 \cdot \overline{M_7} \cdot \overline{RH_7} + \overline{IXH_7} \cdot M_7 \cdot RH_7$

Addressing Formats:

Addressing Modes, Execution Time, and Machine Code (hexadecimal/octal/decimal):

Addressing Modes	Execution Time (No. of cycles)	Number of bytes of machine code	Coding of First (or only) byte of machine code		
			HEX.	OCT.	DEC.
IMM	3	3	8C	214	140
DIR	4	2	9C	234	156
EXT	5	3	BC	274	188
IND	6	2	AC	254	172

Decimal Adjust ACCA   **DAA**

Operation: Adds hexadecimal numbers 00, 06, 60, or 66 to ACCA, and may also set the carry bit, as indicated in the following table:

State of C-bit before DAA (Col. 1)	Upper Half-byte (bits 4-7) (Col. 2)	Initial Half-carry H-bit (Col.3)	Lower to ACCA (bits 0-3) (Col. 4)	Number Added after by DAA (Col. 5)	State of C-bit after DAA (Col. 6)
0	0-9	0	0-9	00	0
0	0-8	0	A-F	06	0
0	0-9	1	0-3	06	0
0	A-F	0	0-9	60	1
0	9-F	0	A-F	66	1
0	A-F	1	0-3	66	1
1	0-2	0	0-9	60	1
1	0-2	0	A-F	66	1
1	0-3	1	0-3	66	1

Note: Columns (1) through (4) of the above table represent all possible cases which can result from any of the operations ABA, ADD, or ADC, with initial carry either set or clear, applied to two binary-coded-decimal operands. The table shows hexadecimal values.

Description: If the contents of ACCA and the state of the carry-borrow bit C and the half-carry bit H are all the result of applying any of the operations ABA, ADD, or ADC to binary-coded-decimal operands, with or without an initial carry, the DAA operation will function as follows.

Subject to the above condition, the DAA operation will adjust the contents of ACCA and the C bit to represent the correct binary-coded-decimal sum and the correct state of the carry.

Condition Codes: H: Not affected.
 I: Not affected.
 N: Set if most significant bit of the result is set; cleared otherwise.
 Z: Set if all bits of the result are cleared; cleared otherwise.
 V: Not defined.
 C: Set or reset according to the same rule as if the DAA and an immediately preceding ABA, ADD, or ADC were replaced by a hypothetical binary-coded-decimal addition.

Boolean Formulae for Condition Codes:

$N = R_7$

$Z = \overline{R_7} \cdot \overline{R_6} \cdot \overline{R_5} \cdot \overline{R_4} \cdot \overline{R_3} \cdot \overline{R_2} \cdot \overline{R_1} \cdot \overline{R_0}$

C = See table above.

Addressing Modes, Execution Time, and Machine Code (hexadecimal/ octal/ decimal):

Addressing Modes	Execution Time (No. of cycles)	Number of bytes of machine code	Coding of First (or only) byte of machine code		
			HEX.	OCT.	DEC.
INHERENT	2	1	19	031	025

DEC

Decrement

Operation:	ACCX ← (ACCX) − 01
or:	M ← (M) − 01
Description:	Subtract one from the contents of ACCX or M.
	The N, Z, and V condition codes are set or reset according to the results of this operation.
	The C bit is not affected by the operation.
Condition Codes:	H: Not affected.
	I: Not affected.
	N: Set if most significant bit of the result is set; cleared otherwise.
	Z: Set if all bits of the result are cleared; cleared otherwise.
	V: Set if there was two's complement overflow as a result of the operation; cleared otherwise. Two's complement overflow occurs if and only if (ACCX) or (M) was 80 before the operation.
	C: Not affected.

Boolean Formulae for Condition Codes:

$N = R_7$

$Z = \overline{R}_7 \cdot \overline{R}_6 \cdot \overline{R}_5 \cdot \overline{R}_5 \cdot \overline{R}_4 \cdot \overline{R}_3 \cdot \overline{R}_2 \cdot \overline{R}_1 \cdot \overline{R}_0$

$V = X_7 \cdot \overline{X}_6 \cdot \overline{X}_5 \cdot \overline{X}_4 \cdot \overline{X}_3 \cdot \overline{X}_2 \cdot \overline{X}_0 = \overline{R}_7 \cdot R_6 \cdot R_5 \cdot R_4 \cdot R_3 \cdot R_2 \cdot R_1 \cdot R_0$

Addressing Formats:

Addressing Modes, Execution Time, and Machine Code (hexadecimal/octal/decimal):

Addressing Modes	Execution Time (No. of cycles)	Number of bytes of machine code	Coding of First (or only) byte of machine code		
			HEX.	OCT.	DEC.
A	2	1	4A	112	074
B	2	1	5A	132	090
EXT	6	3	7A	172	122
IND	7	2	6A	152	106

DES

Decrement Stack Pointer

Operation:	SP ← (SP) − 0001
Description:	Subtract one from the stack pointer.
Condition Codes:	Not affected.

Addressing Modes, Execution Time, and Machine Code (hexadecimal/octal/decimal):

Addressing Modes	Execution Time (No. of cycles)	Number of bytes of machine code	Coding of First (or only) byte of machine code		
			HEX.	OCT.	DEC.
INHERENT	4	1	34	064	052

Decrement Index Register DEX

Operation: IX ← (IX) − 0001

Description: Subtract one from the index register.
Only the Z bit is set or reset according to the result of this operation.

Condition Codes:
- H: Not affected.
- I: Not affected.
- N: Not affected.
- Z: Set if all bits of the result are cleared; cleared otherwise.
- V: Not affected.
- C: Not affected.

Boolean Formulae for Condition Codes:

$$Z = (\overline{RH_7} \cdot \overline{RH_6} \cdot \overline{RH_5} \cdot \overline{RH_4} \cdot \overline{RH_3} \cdot \overline{RH_2} \cdot \overline{RH_1} \cdot \overline{RH_0}) \cdot$$
$$(\overline{RL_7} \cdot \overline{RL_6} \cdot \overline{RL_5} \cdot \overline{RL_4} \cdot \overline{RL_3} \cdot \overline{RL_2} \cdot \overline{RL_1} \cdot \overline{RL_0})$$

Addressing Modes, Execution Time, and Machine Code (hexadecimal/octal/decimal):

Addressing Modes	Execution Time (No. of cycles)	Number of bytes of machine code	Coding of First (or only) byte of machine code		
			HEX.	OCT.	DEC.
INHERENT	4	1	09	011	009

Exclusive OR EOR

Operation: ACCX ← (ACCX) ⊕ (M)

Description: Perform logical "EXCLUSIVE OR" between the contents of ACCX and the contents of M, and place the result in ACCX. (Each bit of ACCX after the operation will be the logical "EXCLUSIVE OR" of the corresponding bit of M and ACCX before the operation.)

Condition Codes:
- H: Not affected.
- I: Not affected.
- N: Set if most significant bit of the result is set; cleared otherwise.
- Z: Set if all bits of the result are cleared; cleared otherwise.
- V: Cleared
- C: Not affected.

Boolean Formulae for Condition Codes:

$N = R_7$
$Z = \overline{R_7} \cdot \overline{R_6} \cdot \overline{R_5} \cdot \overline{R_4} \cdot \overline{R_3} \cdot \overline{R_2} \cdot \overline{R_1} \cdot \overline{R_0}$
$V = 0$

Addressing Formats:

Addressing Modes, Execution Time, and Machine Code (hexadecimal/octal/decimal):

Addressing Modes	Execution Time (No. of cycles)	Number of bytes of machine code	Coding of First (or only) byte of machine code		
			HEX.	OCT.	DEC.
A IMM	2	2	88	210	136
A DIR	3	2	98	230	152
A EXT	4	3	B8	270	184
A IND	5	2	A8	250	168
B IMM	2	2	C8	310	200
B DIR	3	2	D8	330	216
B EXT	4	3	F8	370	248
B IND	5	2	E8	350	232

INC
Increment

Operation: $ACCX \leftarrow (ACCX) + 01$
or: $M \leftarrow (M) + 01$

Description: Add one to the contents of ACCX or M.

The N, Z, and V condition codes are set or reset according to the results of this operation.

The C bit is not affected by the operation.

Condition Codes:
H: Not affected.
I: Not affected.
N: Set if most significant bit of the result is set; cleared otherwise.
Z: Set if all bits of the result are cleared; cleared otherwise.
V: Set if there was two's complement overflow as a result of the operation; cleared otherwise. Two's complement overflow will occur if and only if (ACCX) or (M) was 7F before the operation.
C: Not affected.

Boolean Formulae for Condition Codes:

$N = R_7$
$Z = \overline{R}_7 \cdot \overline{R}_6 \cdot \overline{R}_5 \cdot \overline{R}_4 \cdot \overline{R}_3 \cdot \overline{R}_2 \cdot \overline{R}_1 \cdot \overline{R}_0$
$V = \overline{X}_7 \cdot X_6 \cdot X_5 \cdot X_4 \cdot X_3 \cdot X_2 \cdot X_1 \cdot X_0$
$C = \overline{R}_7 \cdot \overline{R}_6 \cdot \overline{R}_5 \cdot \overline{R}_4 \cdot \overline{R}_3 \cdot \overline{R}_2 \cdot \overline{R}_1 \cdot \overline{R}_0$

Addressing Formats:

Addressing Modes, Execution Time, and Machine Code (hexadecimal/octal/decimal):

Addressing Modes	Execution Time (No. of cycles)	Number of bytes of machine code	Coding of First (or only) byte of machine code		
			HEX.	OCT.	DEC.
A	2	1	4C	114	076
B	2	1	5C	134	092
EXT	6	3	7C	174	124
IND	7	2	6C	154	108

INS

Increment Stack Pointer

Operation: SP ← (SP) + 0001

Description: Add one to the stack pointer.

Condition Codes: Not affected.

Addressing Modes, Execution Time, and Machine Code (hexadecimal/octal/decimal):

Addressing Modes	Execution Time (No. of cycles)	Number of bytes of machine code	Coding of First (or only) byte of machine code		
			HEX.	OCT.	DEC.
INHERENT	4	1	31	061	049

INX

Increment Index Register

Operation: IX ← (IX) + 0001

Description: Add one to the index register.

Only the Z bit is set or reset according to the result of this operation.

Condition Codes:
- H: Not affected.
- I: Not affected.
- N: Not affected.
- Z: Set if all 16 bits of the result are cleared; cleared otherwise.
- V: Not affected.
- C: Not affected.

Boolean Formulae for Condition Codes:

$Z = (\overline{RH_7} \cdot \overline{RH_6} \cdot \overline{RH_5} \cdot \overline{RH_4} \cdot \overline{RH_3} \cdot \overline{RH_2} \cdot \overline{RH_1} \cdot \overline{RH_0}) \cdot$
$(\overline{RL_7} \cdot \overline{RL_6} \cdot \overline{RL_5} \cdot \overline{RL_4} \cdot \overline{RL_3} \cdot \overline{RL_2} \cdot \overline{RL_1} \cdot \overline{RL_0})$

Addressing Modes, Execution Time, and Machine Code (hexadecimal/octal/decimal):

Addressing Modes	Execution Time (No. of cycles)	Number of bytes of machine code	Coding of First (or only) byte of machine code		
			HEX.	OCT.	DEC.
INHERENT	4	1	08	010	008

JMP

Jump

Operation: PC ← numerical address

Description: A jump occurs to the instruction stored at the numerical address. The numerical address is obtained according to the rules for EXTended or INDexed addressing.

Condition Codes: Not affected.

Addressing Formats:

Addressing Modes, Execution Time, and Machine Code (hexadecimal/octal/decimal):

Addressing Modes	Execution Time (No. of cycles)	Number of bytes of machine code	Coding of First (or only) byte of machine code		
			HEX.	OCT.	DEC.
EXT	3	3	7E	176	126
IND	4	2	6E	156	110

JSR

Jump to Subroutine

Operation:
Either: PC ← (PC) + 0003 (for EXTended addressing)
or: PC ← (PC) + 0002 (for INDexed addressing)
Then: ↓ (PCL)
SP ← (SP) − 0001
↓ (PCH)
SP ← (SP) − 0001
PC ← numerical address

Description: The program counter is incremented by 3 or by 2, depending on the addressing mode, and is then pushed onto the stack, eight bits at a time. The stack pointer points to the next empty location in the stack. A jump occurs to the instruction stored at the numerical address. The numerical address is obtained according to the rules for EXTended or INDexed addressing.

Condition Codes: Not affected.

Addressing Formats:

Addressing Modes, Execution Time, and Machine Code (hexadecimal/ octal/ decimal):

Addressing Modes	Execution Time (No. of cycles)	Number of bytes of machine code	Coding of First (or only) byte of machine code		
			HEX.	OCT.	DEC.
EXT	9	3	BD	275	189
IND	8	2	AD	255	173

JUMP TO SUBROUTINE EXAMPLE (extended mode)

			Memory Location	Machine Code (Hex)	Assembler Language		
					Label	Operator	Operand
A.	Before:						
	PC	→	$0FFF	BD		JSR	CHARLI
			$1000	20			
			$1001	77			
	SP	←	$EFFF				
B.	After:						
	PC	→	$2077	**	CHARLI	***	*****
	SP	→	$EFFD				
			$EFFE	10			
			$EFFF	02			

320

LDA

Load Accumulator

Operation: ACCX ← (M)

Description: Loads the contents of memory into the accumulator. The condition codes are set according to the data.

Condition Codes:
- H: Not affected.
- I: Not affected.
- N: Set if most significant bit of the result is set; cleared otherwise.
- Z: Set if all bits of the result are cleared; cleared otherwise.
- V: Cleared.
- C: Not affected.

Boolean Formulae for Condition Codes:

$N = R_7$

$Z = \overline{R_7} \cdot \overline{R_6} \cdot \overline{R_5} \cdot \overline{R_4} \cdot \overline{R_3} \cdot \overline{R_2} \cdot \overline{R_1} \cdot \overline{R_0}$

$V = 0$

Addressing Formats:

Addressing Modes, Execution Time, and Machine Code (hexadecimal/octal/decimal):
(DUAL OPERAND)

Addressing Modes	Execution Time (No. of cycles)	Number of bytes of machine code	Coding of First (or only) byte of machine code		
			HEX.	OCT.	DEC.
A IMM	2	2	86	206	134
A DIR	3	2	96	226	150
A EXT	4	3	B6	266	182
A IND	5	2	A6	246	166
B IMM	2	2	C6	306	198
B DIR	3	2	D6	326	214
B EXT	4	3	F6	366	246
B IND	5	2	E6	346	230

LDS

Load Stack Pointer

Operation: SPH ← (M)
SPL ← (M+1)

Description: Loads the more significant byte of the stack pointer from the byte of memory at the address specified by the program, and loads the less significant byte of the stack pointer from the next byte of memory, at one plus the address specified by the program.

Condition Codes:
- H: Not affected.
- I: Not affected.
- N: Set if the most significant bit of the stack pointer is set by the operation; cleared otherwise.
- Z: Set if all bits of the stack pointer are cleared by the operation; cleared otherwise.
- V: Cleared.
- C: Not affected.

Boolean Formulae for Condition Codes:
$N = RH_7$
$Z = (\overline{RH_7} \cdot \overline{RH_6} \cdot \overline{RH_5} \cdot \overline{RH_4} \cdot \overline{RH_3} \cdot \overline{RH_2} \cdot \overline{RH_1} \cdot \overline{RH_0}) \cdot$
$\quad (\overline{RL_7} \cdot \overline{RL_6} \cdot \overline{RL_5} \cdot \overline{RL_4} \cdot \overline{RL_3} \cdot \overline{RL_2} \cdot \overline{RL_1} \cdot \overline{RL_0})$
$V = 0$

Addressing Formats:
See Table A-5.

Addressing Modes, Execution Time, and Machine Code (hexadecimal/octal/decimal):

Addressing Modes	Execution Time (No. of cycles)	Number of bytes of machine code	Coding of First (or only) byte of machine code		
			HEX.	OCT.	DEC.
IMM	3	3	8E	216	142
DIR	4	2	9E	236	158
EXT	5	3	BE	276	190
IND	6	2	AE	256	174

LDX

Load Index Register

Operation: IXH ← (M)
IXL ← (M + 1)

Description: Loads the more significant byte of the index register from the byte of memory at the address specified by the program, and loads the less significant byte of the index register from the next byte of memory, at one plus the address specified by the program.

Condition Codes:
H: Not affected.
I: Not affected.
N: Set if the most significant bit of the index register is set by the operation; cleared otherwise.
Z: Set if all bits of the index register are cleared by the operation; cleared otherwise.
V: Cleared.
C: Not affected.

Boolean Formulae for Condition Codes:
$N = RH_7$
$Z = (\overline{RH_7} \cdot \overline{RH_6} \cdot \overline{RH_5} \cdot \overline{RH_4} \cdot \overline{RH_3} \cdot \overline{RH_2} \cdot \overline{RH_1} \cdot \overline{RH_0}) \cdot$
$\quad (\overline{RL_7} \cdot \overline{RL_6} \cdot \overline{RL_5} \cdot \overline{RL_4} \cdot \overline{RL_3} \cdot \overline{RL_2} \cdot \overline{RL_1} \cdot \overline{RL_0})$
$V = 0$

Addressing Formats:
See Table A-5.

Addressing Modes, Execution Time, and Machine Code (hexadecimal/octal/decimal):

Addressing Modes	Execution Time (No. of cycles)	Number of bytes of machine code	Coding of First (or only) byte of machine code		
			HEX.	OCT.	DEC.
IMM	3	3	CE	316	206
DIR	4	2	DE	336	222
EXT	5	3	FE	376	254
IND	6	2	EE	356	238

Logical Shift Right   LSR

Operation: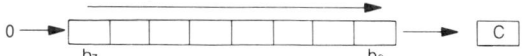

Description: Shifts all bits of ACCX or M one place to the right. Bit 7 is loaded with a zero. The C bit is loaded from the least significant bit of ACCX or M.

Condition Codes:
- H: Not affected.
- I: Not affected.
- N: Cleared.
- Z: Set if all bits of the result are cleared; cleared otherwise.
- V: Set if, after the completion of the shift operation, EITHER (N is set and C is cleared) OR (N is cleared and C is set); cleared otherwise.
- C: Set if, before the operation, the least significant bit of the ACCX or M was set; cleared otherwise.

Boolean Formulae for Condition Codes:

$N = 0$
$Z = \bar{R}_7 \cdot \bar{R}_6 \cdot \bar{R}_5 \cdot \bar{R}_4 \cdot \bar{R}_3 \cdot \bar{R}_2 \cdot \bar{R}_1 \cdot \bar{R}_0$
$V = N \oplus C = [N \cdot \bar{C}] \odot [\bar{N} \cdot C]$
(the foregoing formula assumes values of N and C after the shift operation).
$C = M_0$

Addressing Formats:

Addressing Modes, Execution Time, and Machine Code (hexadecimal/octal/decimal):

Addressing Modes	Execution Time (No. of cycles)	Number of bytes of machine code	Coding of First (or only) byte of machine code		
			HEX.	OCT.	DEC.
A	2	1	44	104	068
B	2	1	54	124	084
EXT	6	3	74	164	116
IND	7	2	64	144	100

Negate   NEG

Operation: $ACCX \leftarrow -(ACCX) = 00 - (ACCX)$
or: $M \leftarrow -(M) = 00 - (M)$

Description: Replaces the contents of ACCX or M with its two's complement. Note that 80 is left unchanged.

Condition Codes:
- H: Not affected.
- I: Not affected.
- N: Set if most significant bit of the result is set; cleared otherwise.
- Z: Set if all bits of the result are cleared; cleared otherwise.
- V: Set if there would be two's complement overflow as a result of the implied subtraction from zero; this will occur if and only if the contents of ACCX or M is 80.
- C: Set if there would be a borrow in the implied subtraction from zero; the C bit will be set in all cases except when the contents of ACCX or M is 00.

Boolean Formulae for Condition Codes:

$N = R_7$
$Z = \bar{R}_7 \cdot \bar{R}_6 \cdot \bar{R}_5 \cdot \bar{R}_4 \cdot \bar{R}_3 \cdot \bar{R}_2 \cdot \bar{R}_1 \cdot \bar{R}_0$
$V = R_7 \cdot \bar{R}_6 \cdot \bar{R}_5 \cdot \bar{R}_4 \cdot \bar{R}_3 \cdot \bar{R}_2 \cdot \bar{R}_1 \cdot \bar{R}_0$
$C = R_7 + R_6 + R_5 + R_4 + R_3 + R_2 + R_1 + R_0$

Addressing Formats:

Addressing Modes, Execution Time, and Machine Code (hexadecimal/octal/decimal):

Addressing Modes	Execution Time (No. of cycles)	Number of bytes of machine code	Coding of First (or only) byte of machine code		
			HEX.	OCT.	DEC.
A	2	1	40	100	064
B	2	1	50	120	080
EXT	6	3	70	160	112
IND	7	2	60	140	096

NOP

No Operation

Description: This is a single-word instruction which causes only the program counter to be incremented. No other registers are affected.

Condition Codes: Not affected.

Addressing Modes, Execution Time, and Machine Code (hexadecimal/octal/decimal):

Addressing Modes	Execution Time (No. of cycles)	Number of bytes of machine code	Coding of First (or only) byte of machine code		
			HEX.	OCT.	DEC.
INHERENT	2	1	01	001	001

ORA

Inclusive OR

Operation: ACCX ← (ACCX)⊙(M)

Description: Perform logical "OR" between the contents of ACCX and the contents of M and places the result in ACCX. (Each bit of ACCX after the operation will be the logical "OR" of the corresponding bits of M and of ACCX before the operation).

Condition Codes:
H: Not affected.
I: Not affected.
N: Set if most significant bit of the result is set; cleared otherwise.
Z: Set if all bits of the result are cleared; cleared otherwise.
V: Cleared.
C: Not affected.

Boolean Formulae for Condition Codes:

$N = R_7$
$Z = \overline{R_7} \cdot \overline{R_6} \cdot \overline{R_5} \cdot \overline{R_4} \cdot \overline{R_3} \cdot \overline{R_2} \cdot \overline{R_1} \cdot \overline{R_0}$
$V = 0$

Addressing Formats:

Addressing Modes, Execution Time, and Machine Code (hexadecimal/octal/decimal):

(DUAL OPERAND)

Addressing Modes	Execution Time (No. of cycles)	Number of bytes of machine code	Coding of First (or only) byte of machine code		
			HEX.	OCT.	DEC.
A IMM	2	2	8A	212	138
A DIR	3	2	9A	232	154
A EXT	4	3	BA	272	186
A IND	5	2	AA	252	170
B IMM	2	2	CA	312	202
B DIR	3	2	DA	332	218
B EXT	4	3	FA	372	250
B IND	5	2	EA	352	234

Push Data Onto Stack **PSH**

Operation: ↓ (ACCX)
SP ← (SP) − 0001

Description: The contents of ACCX is stored in the stack at the address contained in the stack pointer. The stack pointer is then decremented.

Condition Codes: Not affected.

Addressing Formats:

Addressing Modes, Execution Time, and Machine Code (hexadecimal/octal/decimal):

Addressing Modes	Execution Time (No. of cycles)	Number of bytes of machine code	Coding of First (or only) byte of machine code		
			HEX.	OCT.	DEC.
A	4	1	36	066	054
B	4	1	37	067	055

Pull Data from Stack **PUL**

Operation: SP ← (SP) + 0001
↑ ACCX

Description: The stack pointer is incremented. The ACCX is then loaded from the stack, from the address which is contained in the stack pointer.

Condition Codes: Not affected.

Addressing Formats:

Addressing Modes, Execution Time, and Machine Code (hexadecimal/octal/decimal):

Addressing Modes	Execution Time (No. of cycles)	Number of bytes of machine code	Coding of First (or only) byte of machine code		
			HEX.	OCT.	DEC.
A	4	1	32	062	050
B	4	1	33	063	051

ROL
Rotate Left

Operation:

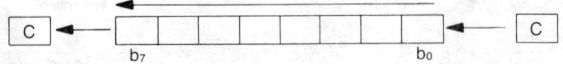

Description: Shifts all bits of ACCX or M one place to the left. Bit 0 is loaded from the C bit. The C bit is loaded from the most significant bit of ACCX or M.

Condition Codes:
- H: Not affected.
- I: Not affected.
- N: Set if most significant bit of the result is set; cleared otherwise.
- Z: Set if all bits of the result are cleared; cleared otherwise.
- V: Set if, after the completion of the operation, EITHER (N is set and C is cleared) OR (N is cleared and C is set); cleared otherwise.
- C: Set if, before the operation, the most significant bit of the ACCX or M was set; cleared otherwise.

Boolean Formulae for Condition Codes:

$N = R_7$
$Z = \bar{R}_7 \cdot \bar{R}_6 \cdot \bar{R}_5 \cdot \bar{R}_4 \cdot \bar{R}_3 \cdot \bar{R}_2 \cdot \bar{R}_1 \cdot \bar{R}_0$
$V = N \oplus C = [N \cdot \bar{C}] \odot [\bar{N} \cdot C]$
(the foregoing formula assumes values of N and C after the rotation)
$C = M_7$

Addressing Formats:

Addressing Modes, Execution Time, and Machine Code (hexadecimal/octal/decimal):

Addressing Modes	Execution Time (No. of cycles)	Number of bytes of machine code	Coding of First (or only) byte of machine code		
			HEX.	OCT.	DEC.
A	2	1	49	111	073
B	2	1	59	131	089
EXT	6	3	79	171	121
IND	7	2	69	151	105

Rotate Right
ROR

Operation:

Description: Shifts all bits of ACCX or M one place to the right. Bit 7 is loaded from the C bit. The C bit is loaded from the least significant bit of ACCX or M.

Condition Codes:
- H: Not affected.
- I: Not affected.
- N: Set if most significant bit of the result is set; cleared otherwise.
- Z: Set if all bits of the result are cleared; cleared otherwise.
- V: Set if, after the completion of the operation, EITHER (N is set and C is cleared) OR (N is cleared and C is set); cleared otherwise.
- C: Set if, before the operation, the least significant bit of the ACCX or M was set; cleared otherwise.

Boolean Formulae for Condition Codes:

$N = R_7$
$Z = \bar{R}_7 \cdot \bar{R}_6 \cdot \bar{R}_5 \cdot \bar{R}_4 \cdot \bar{R}_3 \cdot \bar{R}_2 \cdot \bar{R}_1 \cdot \bar{R}_0$
$V = N \oplus C = [N \cdot \bar{C}] \odot [\bar{N} \cdot C]$
(the foregoing formula assumes values of N and C after the rotation)
$C = M_0$

Addressing Formats:
Addressing Modes, Execution Time, and Machine Code (hexadecimal/octal/decimal):

Addressing Modes	Execution Time (No. of cycles)	Number of bytes of machine code	Coding of First (or only) byte of machine code		
			HEX.	OCT.	DEC.
A	2	1	46	106	070
B	2	1	56	126	086
EXT	6	3	76	166	118
IND	7	2	66	146	102

Return from Interrupt   RTI

Operation: SP ← (SP) + 0001 , ↑CC
                SP ← (SP) + 0001 , ↑ACCB
                SP ← (SP) + 0001 , ↑ACCA
                SP ← (SP) + 0001 , ↑IXH
                SP ← (SP) + 0001 , ↑IXL
                SP ← (SP) + 0001 , ↑PCH
                SP ← (SP) + 0001 , ↑PCL

Description: The condition codes, accumulators B and A, the index register, and the program counter, will be restored to a state pulled from the stack. Note that the interrupt mask bit will be reset if and only if the corresponding bit stored in the stack is zero.

Condition Codes: Restored to the states pulled from the stack.

Addressing Modes, Execution Time, and Machine Code (hexadecimal/octal/decimal):

Addressing Modes	Execution Time (No. of cycles)	Number of bytes of machine code	Coding of First (or only) byte of machine code		
			HEX.	OCT.	DEC.
INHERENT	10	1	3B	073	059

Return from Interrupt
Example

			Memory Location	Machine Code (Hex)	Label	Assembler Language Operator	Operand
A.	Before						
	PC	→	$D066	3B		RTI	
	SP	→	$EFF8				
			$EFF9	11HINZVC	(binary)		
			$EFFA	12			
			$EFFB	34			
			$EFFC	56			
			$EFFD	78			
			$EFFE	55			
			$EFFF	67			

B. *After*

PC	→	$5567	**		***	*****
		$EFF8				
		$EFF9	11HINZVC	(binary)		
		$EFFA	12			
		$EFFB	34			
		$EFFC	56			
		$EFFD	78			
		$EFFE	55			
SP	→	$EFFF	67			

CC = HINZVC (binary)
ACCB = 12 (Hex)   IXH = 56 (Hex)
ACCA = 34 (Hex)   IXL = 78 (Hex)

RTS
Return from Subroutine

Operation: SP ← (SP) + 0001
↑ PCH
SP ← (SP) + 0001
↑ PCL

Description: The stack pointer is incremented (by 1). The contents of the byte of memory, at the address now contained in the stack pointer, are loaded into the 8 bits of highest significance in the program counter. The stack pointer is again incremented (by 1). The contents of the byte of memory, at the address now contained in the stack pointer, are loaded into the 8 bits of lowest signifficance in the program counter.

Condition Codes: Not affected.

Addressing Modes, Execution Time, and Machine Code (hexadecimal/octal/decimal):

Addressing Modes	Execution Time (No. of cycles)	Number of bytes of machine code	Coding of First (or only) byte of machine code		
			HEX.	OCT.	DEC.
INHERENT	5	1	39	071	057

Return from Subroutine

EXAMPLE

		Memory Location	Machine Code (Hex)	Label	Assembler Language Operator	Operand
A.	*Before*					
	PC	$30A2	39		RTS	
	SP	$EFFD				
		$EFFE	10			
		$EFFF	02			
B.	*After*					
	PC	$1002	**		***	*****
		$EFFD				
		$EFFE	10			
	SP	$EFFF	02			

Subtract Accumulators SBA

Operation: ACCA ← (ACCA) − (ACCB)

Description: Subtracts the contents of ACCB from the contents of ACCA and places the result in ACCA. The contents of ACCB are not affected.

Condition Codes:
- H: Not affected.
- I: Not affected.
- N: Set if most significant bit of the result is set; cleared otherwise.
- Z: Set if all bits of the result are cleared; cleared otherwise.
- V: Set if there was two's complement overflow as a result of the operation.
- C: Carry is set if the absolute value of accumulator B plus previous carry is larger than the absolute value of accumulator A; reset otherwise.

Boolean Formulae for Condition Codes:

$N = R_7$
$Z = \overline{R_7} \cdot \overline{R_6} \cdot \overline{R_5} \cdot \overline{R_4} \cdot \overline{R_3} \cdot \overline{R_2} \cdot \overline{R_1} \cdot \overline{R_0}$
$V = A_7 \cdot \overline{B_7} \cdot \overline{R_7} + \overline{A_7} \cdot B_7 \cdot R_7$
$C = \overline{A_7} \cdot B_7 + B_7 \cdot R_7 + R_7 \cdot \overline{A_7}$

Addressing Modes, Execution Time, and Machine Code (hexadecimal/octal/decimal):

Addressing Modes	Execution Time (No. of cycles)	Number of bytes of machine code	Coding of First (or only) byte of machine code		
			HEX.	OCT.	DEC.
INHERENT	2	1	10	020	016

Subtract with Carry SBC

Operation: ACCX ← (ACCX) − (M) − (C)

Description: Subtracts the contents of M and C from the contents of ACCX and places the result in ACCX.

Condition Codes:
- H: Not affected.
- I: Not affected.
- N: Set if most significant bit of the result is set; cleared otherwise.
- Z: Set if all bits of the result are cleared; cleared otherwise.
- V: Set if there was two's complement overflow as a result of the operation; cleared otherwise.
- C: Carry is set if the absolute value of the contents of memory plus previous carry is larger than the absolute value of the accumulator; reset otherwise.

Boolean Formulae for Condition Codes:

$N = R_7$
$Z = \overline{R_7} \cdot \overline{R_6} \cdot \overline{R_5} \cdot \overline{R_4} \cdot \overline{R_3} \cdot \overline{R_2} \cdot \overline{R_1} \cdot \overline{R_0}$
$V = X_7 \cdot \overline{M_7} \cdot \overline{R_7} + \overline{X_7} \cdot M_7 \cdot R_7$
$C = \overline{X_7} \cdot M_7 + M_7 \cdot R_7 + R_7 \cdot \overline{X_7}$

Addressing Formats:
Addressing Modes, Execution Time, and Machine Code (hexadecimal/ octal/ decimal):
(DUAL OPERAND)

Addressing Modes	Execution Time (No. of cycles)	Number of bytes of machine code	Coding of First (or only) byte of machine code		
			HEX.	OCT.	DEC.
A IMM	2	2	82	202	130
A DIR	3	2	92	222	146
A EXT	4	3	B2	262	178
A IND	5	2	A2	242	162
B IMM	2	2	C2	302	194
B DIR	3	2	D2	322	210
B EXT	4	3	F2	362	242
B IND	5	2	E2	342	226

SEC
Set Carry

Operation: C bit ← 1

Description: Sets the carry bit in the processor condition codes register.

Condition Codes: H: Not affected.
I: Not affected.
N: Not affected.
Z: Not affected.
V: Not affected.
C: Set.

Boolean Formulae for Condition Codes:
C = 1

Addressing Modes, Execution Time, and Machine Code (hexadecimal/ octal/ decimal):

Addressing Modes	Execution Time (No. of cycles)	Number of bytes of machine code	Coding of First (or only) byte of machine code		
			HEX.	OCT.	DEC.
INHERENT	2	1	0D	015	013

SEI
Set Interrupt Mask

Operation: I bit ← 1

Description: Sets the interrupt mask bit in the processor condition codes register. The microprocessor is inhibited from servicing an interrupt from a peripheral device, and will continue with execution of the instructions of the program, until the interrupt mask bit has been cleared.

Condition Codes: H: Not affected.
I: Set.
N: Not affected.
Z: Not affected.
V: Not affected.
C: Not affected.

Boolean Formulae for Condition Codes:
I = 1

Addressing Modes, Execution Time, and Machine Code (hexadecimal/octal/decimal):

Addressing Modes	Execution Time (No. of cycles)	Number of bytes of machine code	Coding of First (or only) byte of machine code		
			HEX.	OCT.	DEC.
INHERENT	2	1	0F	017	015

Set Two's Complement Overflow Bit — SEV

Operation: V bit ← 1

Description: Sets the two's complement overflow bit in the processor condition codes register.

Condition Codes:
- H: Not affected.
- I: Not affected.
- N: Not affected.
- Z: Not affected.
- V: Set.
- C: Not affected.

Boolean Formulae for Condition Codes:
$V = 1$

Addressing Modes, Execution Time, and Machine Code (hexadecimal/octal/decimal):

Addressing Modes	Execution Time (No. of cycles)	Number of bytes of machine code	Coding of First (or only) byte of machine code		
			HEX.	OCT.	DEC.
INHERENT	2	1	0B	013	011

Store Accumulator — STA

Operation: M ← (ACCX)

Description: Stores the contents of ACCX in memory. The contents of ACCX remains unchanged.

Condition Codes:
- H: Not affected.
- I: Not affected.
- N: Set if the most significant bit of the contents of ACCX is set; cleared otherwise.
- Z: Set if all bits of the contents of ACCX are cleared; cleared otherwise.
- V: Cleared.
- C: Not affected.

Boolean Formulae for Condition Codes:

$N = X_7$
$Z = \overline{X_7} \cdot \overline{X_6} \cdot \overline{X_5} \cdot \overline{X_4} \cdot \overline{X_3} \cdot \overline{X_2} \cdot \overline{X_1} \cdot \overline{X_0}$
$V = 0$

Addressing Formats:

Addressing Modes, Execution Time, and Machine Code (hexadecimal/octal/decimal):

Addressing Modes	Execution Time (No. of cycles)	Number of bytes of machine code	Coding of First (or only) byte of machine code		
			HEX.	OCT.	DEC.
A DIR	4	2	97	227	151
A EXT	5	3	B7	267	183
A IND	6	2	A7	247	167
B DIR	4	2	D7	327	215
B EXT	5	3	F7	367	247
B IND	6	2	E7	347	231

STS
Store Stack Pointer

Operation: M ← (SPH)
                 M + 1 ← (SPL)

Description: Stores the more significant byte of the stack pointer in memory at the address specified by the program, and stores the less significant byte of the stack pointer at the next location in memory, at one plus the address specified by the program.

Condition Codes: H: Not affected.
                      I: Not affected.
                     N: Set if the most significant bit of the stack pointer is set; cleared otherwise.
                     Z: Set if all bits of the stack pointer are cleared; cleared otherwise.
                     V: Cleared.
                     C: Not affected.

Boolean Formulae for Condition Codes:

$N = SPH_7$

$Z = (\overline{SPH_7} \cdot \overline{SPH_6} \cdot \overline{SPH_5} \cdot \overline{SPH_4} \cdot \overline{SPH_3} \cdot \overline{SPH_2} \cdot \overline{SPH_1} \cdot \overline{SPH_0}) \cdot$
$\quad\quad (\overline{SPL_7} \cdot \overline{SPL_6} \cdot \overline{SPL_5} \cdot \overline{SPL_4} \cdot \overline{SPL_3} \cdot \overline{SPL_2} \cdot \overline{SPL_1} \cdot \overline{SPL_0})$

$V = 0$

Addressing Formats:

Addressing Modes, Execution Time, and Machine Code (hexadecimal/octal/decimal):

Addressing Modes	Execution Time (No. of cycles)	Number of bytes of machine code	Coding of First (or only) byte of machine code		
			HEX.	OCT.	DEC.
DIR	5	2	9F	237	159
EXT	6	3	BF	277	191
IND	7	2	AF	257	175

STX
Store Index Register

Operation: M ← (IXH)
                 M + 1 ← (IXL)

Description: Stores the more significant byte of the index register in memory at the address specified by the program, and stores the less significant byte of the index register at the next location in memory, at one plus the address specified by the program.

Condition Codes: H: Not affected.
 I: Not affected.
 N: Set if the most significant bite of the index register is set; cleared otherwise.
 Z: Set if all bits of the index register are cleared; cleared otherwise.
 V: Cleared.
 C: Not affected.

Boolean Formulae for Condition Codes:

$N = IXH_7$

$Z = (\overline{IXH_7} \cdot \overline{IXH_6} \cdot \overline{IXH_5} \cdot \overline{IXH_4} \cdot \overline{IXH_3} \cdot \overline{IXH_2} \cdot \overline{IXH_1} \cdot \overline{IXH_0}) \cdot$
$\quad\;\, (\overline{IXL_7} \cdot \overline{IXL_6} \cdot \overline{IXL_5} \cdot \overline{IXL_4} \cdot \overline{IXL_3} \cdot \overline{IXL_2} \cdot \overline{IXL_1} \cdot \overline{IXL_0})$

$V = 0$

Addressing Formats:

Addressing Modes, Execution Time, and Machine Code (hexadecimal / octal / decimal):

Addressing Modes	Execution Time (No. of cycles)	Number of bytes of machine code	Coding of First (or only) byte of machine code		
			HEX.	OCT.	DEC.
DIR	5	2	DF	337	223
EXT	6	3	FF	377	255
IND	7	2	EF	357	239

Subtract

SUB

Operation: ACCX ← (ACCX) − (M)

Description: Subtracts the contents of M from the contents of ACCX and places the result in ACCX.

Condition Codes: H: Not affected.
 I: Not affected.
 N: Set if most significant bit of the result is set; cleared otherwise.
 Z: Set if all bits of the result are cleared; cleared otherwise.
 V: Set if there was two's complement overflow as a result of the operation; cleared otherwise.
 C: Set if the absolute value of the contents of memory are larger than the absolute value of the accumulator; reset otherwise.

Boolean Formulae for Condition Codes:

$N = R_7$

$Z = \overline{R_7} \cdot \overline{R_6} \cdot \overline{R_5} \cdot \overline{R_4} \cdot \overline{R_3} \cdot \overline{R_2} \cdot \overline{R_1} \cdot \overline{R_0}$

$V = X_7 \cdot \overline{M_7} \cdot \overline{R_7} \cdot \overline{X_7} \cdot M_7 \cdot R_7$

$C = \overline{X_7} \cdot M_7 + M_7 \cdot R_7 + R_7 \cdot \overline{X_7}$

Addressing Formats:

Addressing Modes, Execution Time, and Machine Code (hexadecimal/octal/decimal):
(DUAL OPERAND)

Addressing Modes	Execution Time (No. of cycles)	Number of bytes of machine code	Coding of First (or only) byte of machine code		
			HEX.	OCT.	DEC.
A IMM	2	2	80	200	128
A DIR	3	2	90	220	144
A EXT	4	3	B0	260	176
A IND	5	2	A0	240	160
B IMM	2	2	C0	300	192
B DIR	3	2	D0	320	208
B EXT	4	3	F0	360	240
B IND	5	2	E0	340	224

SWI
Software Interrupt

Operation: PC ← (PC) + 0001
↓ (PCL) , SP ← (SP)-0001
↓ (PCH) , SP ← (SP)-0001
↓ (IXL) , SP ← (SP)-0001
↓ (IXH) , SP ← (SP)-0001
↓ (ACCA) , SP ← (SP)-0001
↓ (ACCB) , SP ← (SP)-0001
↓ (CC) , SP ← (SP)-0001
I ← 1
PCH ← (n-0005)
PCL ← (n-0004)

Description: The program counter is incremented (by 1). The program counter, index register, and accumulator A and B, are pushed into the stack. The condition codes register is then pushed into the stack, with condition codes H, I, N, Z, V, C going respectively into bit positions 5 thru 0, and the top two bits (in bit positions 7 and 6) are set (to the 1 state). The stack pointer is decremented (by 1) after each byte of data is stored in the stack.

The interrupt mask bit is then set. The program counter is then loaded with the address stored in the software interrupt pointer at memory locations (n-5) and (n-4), where n is the address corresponding to a high state on all lines of the address bus.

Condition Codes: H: Not affected.
I: Set.
N: Not affected.
Z: Not affected.
V: Not affected.
C: Not affected.

Boolean Formula for Condition Codes:
I = 1

Addressing Modes, Execution Time, and Machine Code (hexadecimal/octal/decimal):

Addressing Modes	Execution Time (No. of cycles)	Number of bytes of machine code	Coding of First (or only) byte of machine code		
			HEX.	OCT.	DEC.
INHERENT	12	1	3F	077	063

334

Software Interrupt
EXAMPLE

A. *Before:*
   CC = HINZVC (binary)
   ACCB = 12 (Hex)   IXH = 56 (Hex)
   ACCA = 34 (Hex)   IXL = 78 (Hex)

		Memory Location	Machine Code (Hex)	Label	Assembler Language Operator	Operand
PC	→	$5566	3F		SWI	
SP	→	$EFFF				
		$FFFA	D0			
		$FFFB	55			

B. *After:*

		Memory Location	Machine Code (Hex)	Label	Operator	Operand
PC	→	$D055				
SP	→	$EFF8				
		$EFF9	11HINZVC	(binary)		
		$EFFA	12			
		$EFFB	34			
		$EFFC	56			
		$EFFD	78			
		$EFFE	55			
		$EFFF	67			

Note: This example assumes that FFFF is the memory location addressed when all lines of the address bus go to the high state.

Transfer from Accumulator A to Accumulator B **TAB**

Operation: ACCB ← (ACCA)

Description: Moves the contents of ACCA to ACCB. The former contents of ACCB are lost. The contents of ACCA are not affected.

Condition Codes:
- H: Not affected.
- I: Not affected.
- N: Set if the most significant bit of the contents of the accumulator is set; cleared otherwise.
- Z: Set if all bits of the contents of the accumulator are cleared; cleared otherwise.
- V: Cleared.
- C: Not affected.

Boolean Formulae for Condition Codes:
$N = R_7$
$Z = \overline{R_7} \cdot \overline{R_6} \cdot \overline{R_5} \cdot \overline{R_4} \cdot \overline{R_3} \cdot \overline{R_2} \cdot \overline{R_1} \cdot \overline{R_0}$
$V = 0$

Addressing Modes, Execution Time, and Machine Code (hexadecimal/octal/decimal):

Addressing Modes	Execution Time (No. of cycles)	Number of bytes of machine code	Coding of First (or only) byte of machine code		
			HEX.	OCT.	DEC.
INHERENT	2	1	16	026	022

TAP

Transfer from Accumulator A to Processor Condition Codes Register

Operation: CC ← (ACCA)

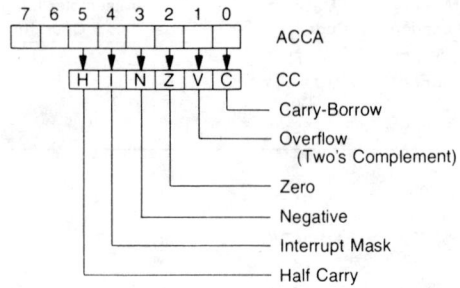

Description: Transfers the contents of bit positions 0 thru 5 of accumulator A to the corresponding bit positions of the processor condition codes register. The contents of accumulator A remain unchanged.

Condition Codes: Set or reset according to the contents of the respective bits 0 thru 5 of accumulator A.

Addressing Modes, Execution Time, and Machine Code (hexadecimal/octal/decimal):

Addressing Modes	Execution Time (No. of cycles)	Number of bytes of machine code	Coding of First (or only) byte of machine code		
			HEX.	OCT.	DEC.
INHERENT	2	1	06	006	006

TBA

Transfer from Accumulator B to Accumulator A

Operation: ACCA ← (ACCB)

Description: Moves the contents of ACCB to ACCA. The former contents of ACCA are lost. The contents of ACCB are not affected.

Condition Codes:
- H: Not affected.
- I: Not affected.
- N: Set if the most significant accumulator bit is set; cleared otherwise.
- Z: Set if all accumulator bits are cleared; cleared otherwise.
- V: Cleared.
- C: Not affected.

Boolean Formulae for Condition Codes:

$N = R_7$
$Z = \overline{R}_7 \cdot \overline{R}_6 \cdot \overline{R}_5 \cdot \overline{R}_4 \cdot \overline{R}_3 \cdot \overline{R}_2 \cdot \overline{R}_1 \cdot \overline{R}_0$
$V = 0$

Addressing Modes, Execution Time, and Machine Code (hexadecimal/octal/decimal):

Addressing Modes	Execution Time (No. of cycles)	Number of bytes of machine code	Coding of First (or only) byte of machine code		
			HEX.	OCT.	DEC.
INHERENT	2	1	17	027	023

Transfer from Processor Condition Codes Register to Accumulator A   **TPA**

Operation: ACCA ← (CC)

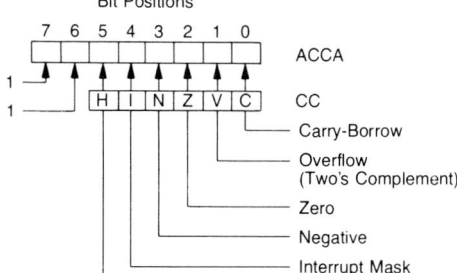

Description: Transfers the contents of the processor condition codes register to corresponding bit positions 0 thru 5 of accumulator A. Bit positions 6 and 7 of accumulator A are set (i.e. go to the "1" state). The processor condition codes register remains unchanged.

Condition Codes: Not affected.

Addressing Modes, Execution Time, and Machine Code (hexadecimal/ octal/ decimal):

Addressing Modes	Execution Time (No. of cycles)	Number of bytes of machine code	Coding of First (or only) byte of machine code		
			HEX.	OCT.	DEC.
INHERENT	2	1	07	007	007

Test   **TST**

Operation: (ACCX) − 00
               (M) − 00

Description: Set condition codes N and Z according to the contents of ACCX or M.

Condition Codes:
- H: Not affected.
- I: Not affected.
- N: Set if most significant bit of the contents of ACCX or M is set; cleared otherwise.
- Z: Set if all bits of the contents of ACCX or M are cleared; cleared otherwise.
- V: Cleared.
- C: Cleared.

Boolean Formulae for Condition Codes:

$N = M_7$
$Z = \overline{M_7} \cdot \overline{M_6} \cdot \overline{M_5} \cdot \overline{M_4} \cdot \overline{M_3} \cdot \overline{M_2} \cdot \overline{M_1} \cdot \overline{M_0}$
$V = 0$
$C = 0$

Addressing Formats:

Addressing Modes, Execution Time, and Machine Code (hexadecimal/octal/decimal):

Addressing Modes	Execution Time (No. of cycles)	Number of bytes of machine code	Coding of First (or only) byte of machine code		
			HEX.	OCT.	DEC.
A	2	1	4D	115	077
B	2	1	5D	135	093
EXT	6	3	7D	175	125
IND	7	2	6D	155	109

TSX

Transfer from Stack Pointer to Index Register

Operation: IX ← (SP) + 0001

Description: Loads the index register with one plus the contents of the stack pointer. The contents of the stack pointer remain unchanged.

Condition Codes: Not affected.

Addressing Modes, Execution Time, and Machine Code (hexadecimal/octal/decimal):

Addressing Modes	Execution Time (No. of cycles)	Number of bytes of machine code	Coding of First (or only) byte of machine code		
			HEX.	OCT.	DEC.
INHERENT	4	1	30	060	048

TXS

Transfer From Index Register to Stack Pointer

Operation: SP ← (IX) − 0001

Description: Loads the stack pointer with the contents of the index register, minus one. The contents of the index register remain unchanged.

Condition Codes: Not affected.

Addressing Modes, Execution Time, and Machine Code (hexadecimal/octal/decimal):

Addressing Modes	Execution Time (No. of cycles)	Number of bytes of machine code	Coding of First (or only) byte of machine code		
			HEX.	OCT.	DEC.
INHERENT	4	1	35	.065	053

Wait for Interrupt   WAI

Operation: PC ← (PC) + 0001
↓ (PCL) , SP ← (SP)-0001
↓ (PCH) , SP ← (SP)-0001
↓ (IXL) , SP ← (SP)-0001
↓ (IXH) , SP ← (SP)-0001
↓ (ACCA) , SP ← (SP)-0001
↓ (ACCB) , SP ← (SP)-0001
↓ (CC) , SP ← (SP)-0001

Condition Codes: Not affected.

Description: The program counter is incremented (by 1). The program counter, index register, and accumulators A and B, are pushed into the stack. The condition codes register is then pushed into the stack, with condition codes H, I, N, Z, V, C going respectively into bit positions 5 thru 0, and the top two bits (in bit positions 7 and 6) are set (to the 1 state). The stack pointer is decremented (by 1) after each byte of data is stored in the stack.

Execution of the program is then suspended until an interrupt from a peripheral device is signalled, by the interrupt request control input going to a low state.

When an interrupt is signalled on the interrupt request line, and provided the I bit is clear, execution proceeds as follows. The interrupt mask bit is set. The program counter is then loaded with the address stored in the internal interrupt pointer at memory locations (n-7) and (n-6), where n is the address corresponding to a high state on all lines of the address bus.

Condition Codes:
- H: Not affected.
- I: Not affected until an interrupt request signal is detected on the interrupt request control line. When the interrupt request is received the I bit is set and further execution takes place, provided the I bit was initially clear.
- N: Not affected.
- Z: Not affected.
- V: Not affected.
- C: Not affected.

Addressing Modes, Execution Time, and Machine Code (hexadecimal/ octal/ decimal):

Addressing Modes	Execution Time (No. of cycles)	Number of bytes of machine code	Coding of First (or only) byte of machine code		
			HEX.	OCT.	DEC.
INHERENT	9	1	3E	076	062

APPENDIX D

Specification Sheets

MC6800
(0 to 70°C; L or P Suffix)

MC6800C
(-40 to 85°C; L Suffix only)

MOS

(N-CHANNEL, SILICON-GATE)

MICROPROCESSOR

MICROPROCESSING UNIT (MPU)

The MC6800 is a monolithic 8-bit microprocessor forming the central control function for Motorola's M6800 family. Compatible with TTL, the MC6800, as with all M6800 system parts, requires only one +5.0-volt power supply, and no external TTL devices for bus interface.

The MC6800 is capable of addressing 65K bytes of memory with its 16-bit address lines. The 8-bit data bus is bidirectional as well as 3-state, making direct memory addressing and multiprocessing applications realizable.

- Eight-Bit Parallel Processing
- Bi-Directional Data Bus
- Sixteen-Bit Address Bus – 65K Bytes of Addressing
- 72 Instructions – Variable Length
- Seven Addressing Modes – Direct, Relative, Immediate, Indexed, Extended, Implied and Accumulator
- Variable Length Stack
- Vectored Restart
- Maskable Interrupt Vector
- Separate Non-Maskable Interrupt – Internal Registers Saved In Stack
- Six Internal Registers – Two Accumulators, Index Register, Program Counter, Stack Pointer and Condition Code Register
- Direct Memory Addressing (DMA) and Multiple Processor Capability
- Clock Rates as High as 1 MHz
- Simple Bus Interface Without TTL
- Halt and Single Instruction Execution Capability

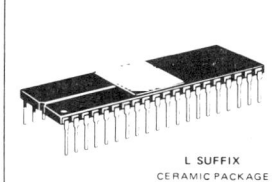

L SUFFIX
CERAMIC PACKAGE
CASE 715

NOT SHOWN P SUFFIX
PLASTIC PACKAGE
CASE 711

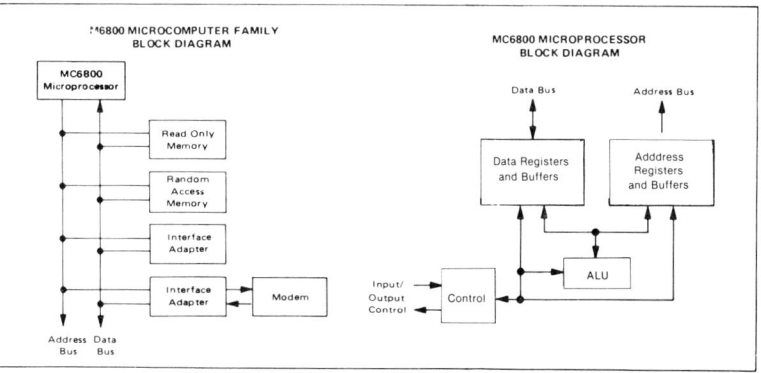

341

MC6800

ELECTRICAL CHARACTERISTICS (V_{CC} = 5.0 V ± 5%, V_{SS} = 0, T_A = 0 to 70°C unless otherwise noted.)

Characteristic		Symbol	Min	Typ	Max	Unit
Input High Voltage	Logic φ1, φ2	V_{IH} V_{IHC}	V_{SS} + 2.0 V_{CC} − 0.3	− −	V_{CC} V_{CC} + 0.1	Vdc
Input Low Voltage	Logic φ1, φ2	V_{IL} V_{ILC}	V_{SS} − 0.3 V_{SS} − 0.1	− −	V_{SS} + 0.8 V_{SS} + 0.3	Vdc
Clock Overshoot/Undershoot − Input High Level − Input Low Level		V_{OS}	V_{CC} − 0.5 V_{SS} − 0.5	− −	V_{CC} + 0.5 V_{SS} + 0.5	Vdc
Input Leakage Current (V_{in} = 0 to 5.25 V, V_{CC} = max) (V_{in} = 0 to 5.25 V, V_{CC} = 0.0 V)	Logic* φ1, φ2	I_{in}	− −	1.0 −	2.5 100	μAdc
Three-State (Off State) Input Current (V_{in} 0.4 to 2.4 V, V_{CC} = max)	D0-D7 A0-A15, R/W	I_{TSI}	− −	2.0 −	10 100	μAdc
Output High Voltage (I_{Load} = −205 μAdc, V_{CC} = min) (I_{Load} = −145 μAdc, V_{CC} = min) (I_{Load} = −100 μAdc, V_{CC} = min)	D0-D7 A0-A15, R/W, VMA BA	V_{OH}	V_{SS} + 2.4 V_{SS} + 2.4 V_{SS} + 2.4	− − −	− − −	Vdc
Output Low Voltage (I_{Load} = 1.6 mAdc, V_{CC} = min)		V_{OL}	−	−	V_{SS} + 0.4	Vdc
Power Dissipation		P_D	−	0.600	1.2	W
Capacitance # (V_{in} = 0, T_A = 25°C, f = 1.0 MHz)	φ1, φ2 TSC DBE D0-D7 Logic Inputs	C_{in}	80 − − − −	120 − 7.0 10 6.5	160 15 10 12.5 8.5	pF
	A0-A15, R/W, VMA	C_{out}	−	−	12	pF
Frequency of Operation		f	0.1	−	1.0	MHz
Clock Timing (Figure 1) Cycle Time		t_{cyc}	1.0	−	10	μs
Clock Pulse Width (Measured at V_{CC} − 0.3 V)	φ1 φ2	$PW_{φH}$	430 450	− −	4500 4500	ns
Total φ1 and φ2 Up Time		t_{ut}	940	−	−	ns
Rise and Fall Times (Measured between V_{SS} + 0.3 V and V_{CC} − 0.3 V)	φ1, φ2	$t_{φr}, t_{φf}$	−	−	50	ns
Delay Time or Clock Separation (Measured at V_{OV} = V_{SS} + 0.5 V)		t_d	0	−	9100	ns
Overshoot Duration		t_{OS}	0	−	40	ns

*Except IRQ and NMI, which require 3 kΩ pullup load resistors for wire-OR capability at optimum operation.
Capacitances are periodically sampled rather than 100% tested.

FIGURE 1 − CLOCK TIMING WAVEFORM

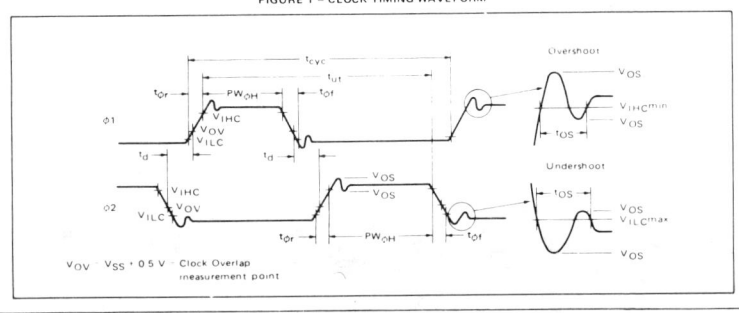

MC6800

MAXIMUM RATINGS

Rating	Symbol	Value	Unit
Supply Voltage	V_{CC}	−0.3 to +7.0	Vdc
Input Voltage	V_{in}	−0.3 to +7.0	Vdc
Operating Temperature Range	T_A	0 to +70	°C
Storage Temperature Range	T_{stg}	−55 to +150	°C
Thermal Resistance	θ_{JA}	70	°C/W

This device contains circuitry to protect the inputs against damage due to high static voltages or electric fields; however, it is advised that normal precautions be taken to avoid application of any voltage higher than maximum rated voltages to this high impedance circuit.

READ/WRITE TIMING Figures 2 and 3, f = 1.0 MHz, Load Circuit of Figure 6.

Characteristic	Symbol	Min	Typ	Max	Unit
Address Delay	t_{AD}	−	220	300	ns
Peripheral Read Access Time $t_{acc} = t_{ut} - (t_{AD} + t_{DSR})$	t_{acc}	−	−	540	ns
Data Setup Time (Read)	t_{DSR}	100	−	−	ns
Input Data Hold Time	t_H	10	−	−	ns
Output Data Hold Time	t_H	10	25	−	ns
Address Hold Time (Address, R/W, VMA)	t_{AH}	50	75	−	ns
Enable High Time for DBE Input	t_{EH}	450	−	−	ns
Data Delay Time (Write)	t_{DDW}	−	165	225	ns
Processor Controls*					
Processor Control Setup Time	t_{PCS}	200	−	−	ns
Processor Control Rise and Fall Time	t_{PCr}, t_{PCf}	−	−	100	ns
Bus Available Delay	t_{BA}	−	−	300	ns
Three State Enable	t_{TSE}	−	−	40	ns
Three State Delay	t_{TSD}	−	−	700	ns
Data Bus Enable Down Time During ϕ1 Up Time (Figure 3)	t_{DBE}	150	−	−	ns
Data Bus Enable Delay (Figure 3)	t_{DBED}	300	−	−	ns
Data Bus Enable Rise and Fall Times (Figure 3)	t_{DBEr}, t_{DBEf}	−	−	25	ns

*Additional information is given in Figures 12 through 16 of the Family Characteristics — see pages 17 through 20.

FIGURE 2 — READ DATA FROM MEMORY OR PERIPHERALS

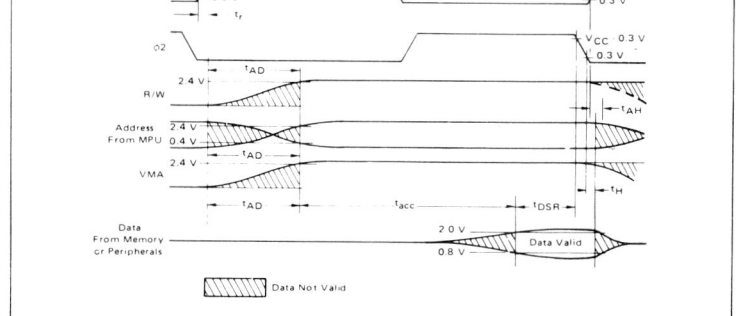

MOTOROLA Semiconductor Products Inc.

343

MC6800

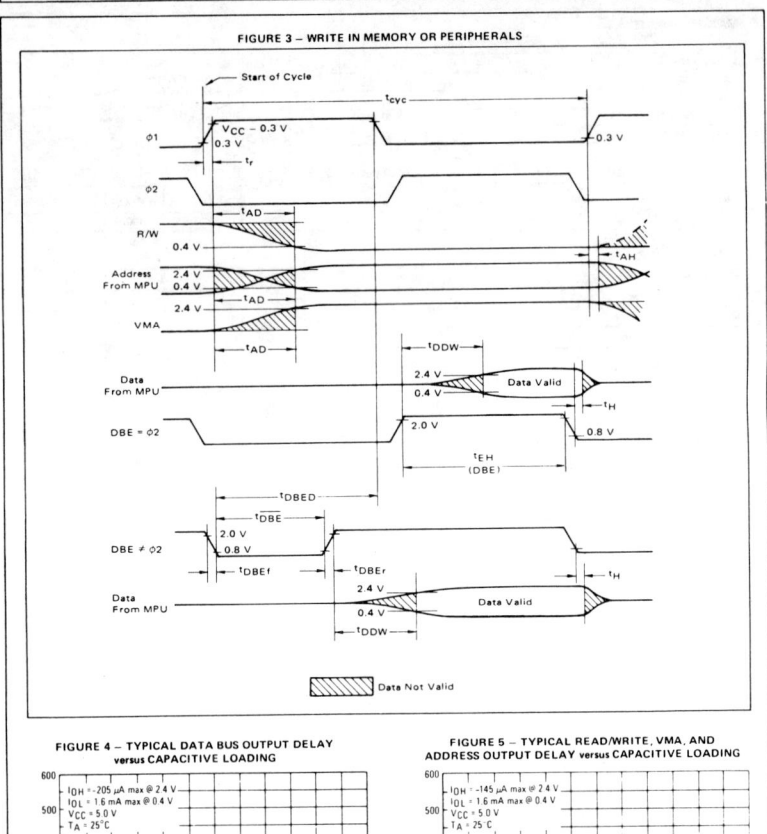

FIGURE 3 — WRITE IN MEMORY OR PERIPHERALS

FIGURE 4 — TYPICAL DATA BUS OUTPUT DELAY versus CAPACITIVE LOADING

FIGURE 5 — TYPICAL READ/WRITE, VMA, AND ADDRESS OUTPUT DELAY versus CAPACITIVE LOADING

MOTOROLA Semiconductor Products Inc.

MC6800

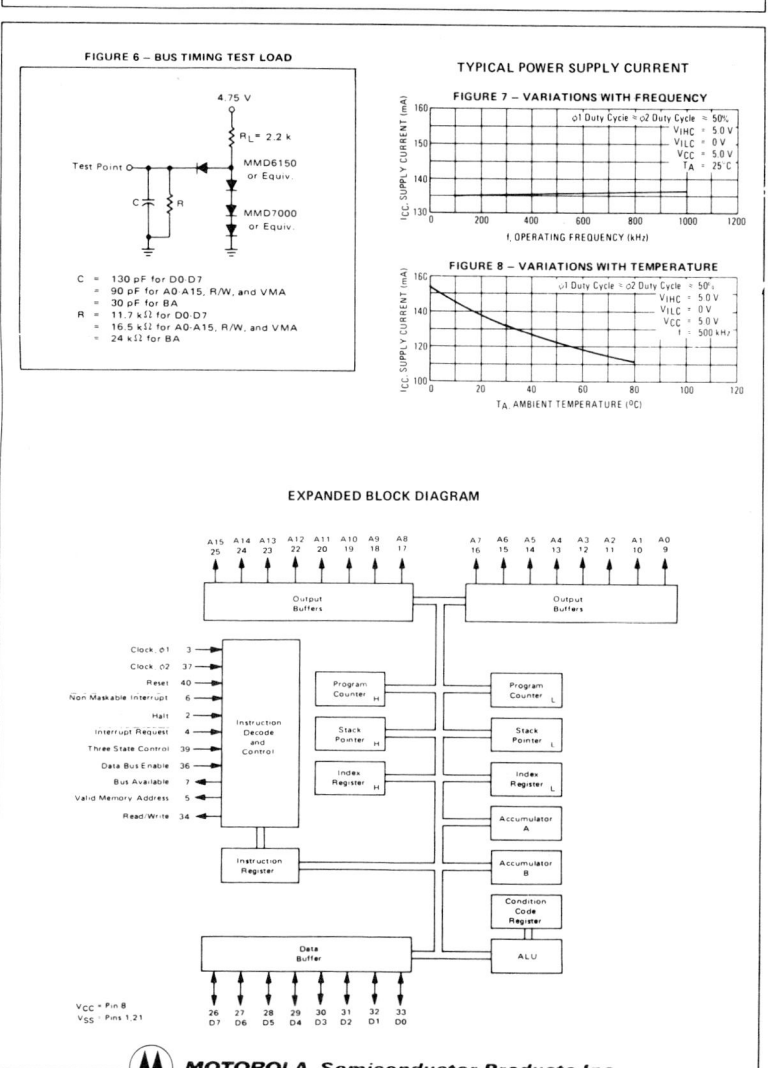

FIGURE 6 – BUS TIMING TEST LOAD

C = 130 pF for D0-D7
  = 90 pF for A0-A15, R/W, and VMA
  = 30 pF for BA
R = 11.7 kΩ for D0-D7
  = 16.5 kΩ for A0-A15, R/W, and VMA
  = 24 kΩ for BA

TYPICAL POWER SUPPLY CURRENT

FIGURE 7 – VARIATIONS WITH FREQUENCY

FIGURE 8 – VARIATIONS WITH TEMPERATURE

EXPANDED BLOCK DIAGRAM

MC6800

MPU SIGNAL DESCRIPTION

Proper operation of the MPU requires that certain control and timing signals be provided to accomplish specific functions and that other signal lines be monitored to determine the state of the processor.

Clocks Phase One and Phase Two ($\phi 1, \phi 2$) — Two pins are used for a two-phase non-overlapping clock that runs at the V_{CC} voltage level.

Address Bus (A0-A15) — Sixteen pins are used for the address bus. The outputs are three-state bus drivers capable of driving one standard TTL load and 130 pF. When the output is turned off, it is essentially an open circuit. This permits the MPU to be used in DMA applications.

Data Bus (D0-D7) — Eight pins are used for the data bus. It is bi-directional, transferring data to and from the memory and peripheral devices. It also has three-state output buffers capable of driving one standard TTL load and 130 pF.

Halt — When this input is in the low state, all activity in the machine will be halted. This input is level sensitive. In the halt mode, the machine will stop at the end of an instruction, Bus Available will be at a one level, Valid Memory Address will be at a zero, and all other three-state lines will be in the three-state mode.

Transition of the Halt line must not occur during the last 250 ns of phase one. To insure single instruction operation, the Halt line must go high for one Clock cycle.

Three-State Control (TSC) — This input causes all of the address lines and the Read/Write line to go into the off or high impedance state. This state will occur 700 ns after TSC = 2.0 V. The Valid Memory Address and Bus Available signals will be forced low. The data bus is not affected by TSC and has its own enable (Data Bus Enable). In DMA applications, the Three-State Control line should be brought high on the leading edge of the Phase One Clock. The $\phi 1$ clock must be held in the high state and the $\phi 2$ in the low state for this function to operate properly. The address bus will then be available for other devices to directly address memory. Since the MPU is a dynamic device, it can be held in this state for only 4.5 μs or destruction of data will occur in the MPU.

Read/Write (R/W) — This TTL compatible output signals the peripherals and memory devices whether the MPU is in a Read (high) or Write (low) state. The normal standby state of this signal is Read (high). Three-State Control going high will turn Read/Write to the off (high impedance) state. Also, when the processor is halted, it will be in the off state. This output is capable of driving one standard TTL load and 90 pF.

Valid Memory Address (VMA) — This output indicates to peripheral devices that there is a valid address on the address bus. In normal operation, this signal should be utilized for enabling peripheral interfaces such as the PIA and ACIA. This signal is not three-state. One standard TTL load and 90 pF may be directly driven by this active high signal.

Data Bus Enable (DBE) — This input is the three-state control signal for the MPU data bus and will enable the bus drivers when in the high state. This input is TTL compatible; however in normal operation, it would be driven by the phase two clock. During an MPU read cycle, the data bus drivers will be disabled internally. When it is desired that another device control the data bus such as in Direct Memory Access (DMA) applications, DBE should be held low.

Bus Available (BA) — The Bus Available signal will normally be in the low state; when activated, it will go to the high state indicating that the microprocessor has stopped and that the address bus is available. This will occur if the Halt line is in the low state or the processor is in the WAIT state as a result of the execution of a WAIT instruction. At such time, all three-state output drivers will go to their off state and other outputs to their normally inactive level. The processor is removed from the WAIT state by the occurrence of a maskable (mask bit I = 0) or nonmaskable interrupt. This output is capable of driving one standard TTL load and 30 pF.

Interrupt Request (IRQ) — This level sensitive input requests that an interrupt sequence be generated within the machine. The processor will wait until it completes the current instruction that is being executed before it recognizes the request. At that time, if the interrupt mask bit in the Condition Code Register is not set, the machine will begin an interrupt sequence. The Index Register, Program Counter, Accumulators, and Condition Code Register are stored away on the stack. Next the MPU will respond to the interrupt request by setting the interrupt mask bit high so that no further interrupts may occur. At the end of the cycle, a 16-bit address will be loaded that points to a vectoring address which is located in memory locations FFF8 and FFF9. An address loaded at these locations causes the MPU to branch to an interrupt routine in memory.

The Halt line must be in the high state for interrupts to be serviced. Interrupts will be latched internally while Halt is low.

The IRQ has a high impedance pullup device internal to the chip; however a 3 kΩ external resistor to V_{CC} should be used for wire-OR and optimum control of interrupts.

Reset — This input is used to reset and start the MPU from a power down condition, resulting from a power failure or an initial start-up of the processor. If a high level is detected on the input, this will signal the MPU to begin the restart sequence. This will start execution of a routine to initialize the processor from its reset condition. All the higher order address lines will be forced high. For the restart, the last two (FFFE, FFFF) locations in memory will be used to load the program that is addressed by the program counter. During the restart routine, the interrupt mask bit is set and must be reset before the MPU can be interrupted by IRQ.

 MOTOROLA *Semiconductor Products Inc.*

Figure 9 shows the initialization of the microprocessor after restart. Reset must be held low for at least eight clock periods after V$_{CC}$ reaches 4.75 volts. If Reset goes high prior to the leading edge of φ2, on the next φ1 the first restart memory vector address (FFFE) will appear on the address lines. This location should contain the higher order eight bits to be stored into the program counter. Following, the next address FFFF should contain the lower order eight bits to be stored into the program counter.

Non-Maskable Interrupt (NMI) — A low-going edge on this input requests that a non-mask-interrupt sequence be generated within the processor. As with the Interrupt Request signal, the processor will complete the current instruction that is being executed before it recognizes the NMI signal. The interrupt mask bit in the Condition Code Register has no effect on NMI.

The Index Register, Program Counter, Accumulators, and Condition Code Register are stored away on the stack. At the end of the cycle, a 16-bit address will be loaded that points to a vectoring address which is located in memory locations FFFC and FFFD. An address loaded at these locations causes the MPU to branch to a non-maskable interrupt routine in memory.

NMI has a high impedance pullup resistor internal to the chip; however a 3 kΩ external resistor to V$_{CC}$ should be used for wire-OR and optimum control of interrupts.

Inputs IRQ and NMI are hardware interrupt lines that are sampled during φ2 and will start the interrupt routine on the φ1 following the completion of an instruction.

Figure 10 is a flow chart describing the major decision paths and interrupt vectors of the microprocessor. Table 1 gives the memory map for interrupt vectors.

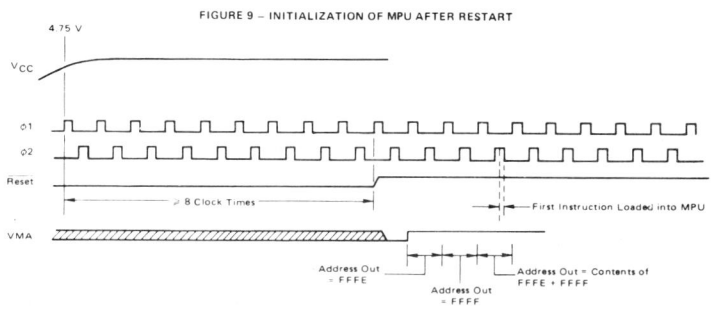

FIGURE 9 – INITIALIZATION OF MPU AFTER RESTART

TABLE 1 – MEMORY MAP FOR INTERRUPT VECTORS

Vector MS	LS	Description
FFFE	FFFF	Restart
FFFC	FFFD	Non-maskable Interrupt
FFFA	FFFB	Software Interrupt
FFF8	FFF9	Interrupt Request

 MOTOROLA *Semiconductor Products Inc.*

MC6800

FIGURE 10 — MPU FLOW CHART

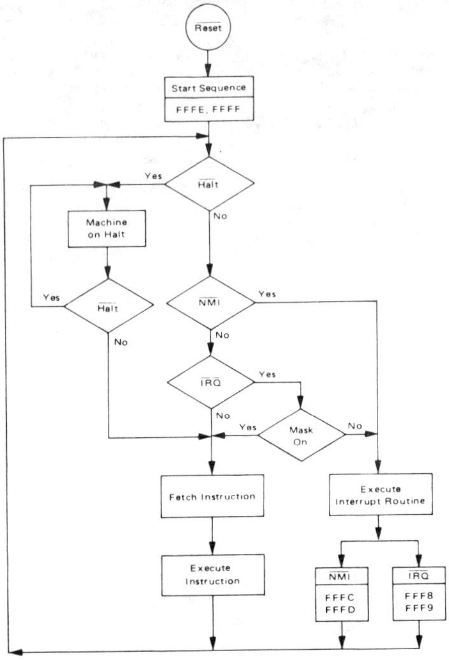

MPU REGISTERS

The MPU has three 16-bit registers and three 8-bit registers available for use by the programmer (Figure 11).

Program Counter — The program counter is a two byte (16-bits) register that points to the current program address.

Stack Pointer — The stack pointer is a two byte register that contains the address of the next available location in an external push-down/pop-up stack. This stack is normally a random access Read/Write memory that may have any location (address) that is convenient. In those applications that require storage of information in the stack when power is lost, the stack must be non-volatile.

Index Register — The index register is a two byte register that is used to store data or a sixteen bit memory address for the Indexed mode of memory addressing.

Accumulators — The MPU contains two 8-bit accumulators that are used to hold operands and results from an arithmetic logic unit (ALU).

 MOTOROLA Semiconductor Products Inc.

MC6800

FIGURE 11 — PROGRAMMING MODEL OF THE MICROPROCESSING UNIT

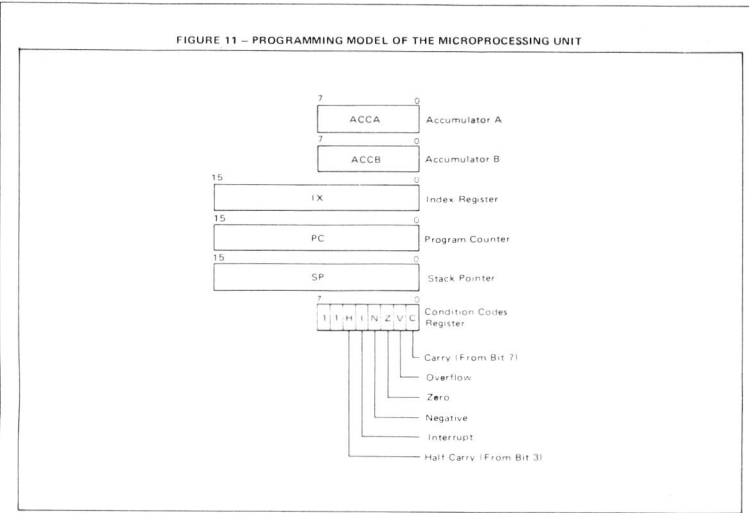

FIGURE 12 — SAVING THE STATUS OF THE MICROPROCESSOR IN THE STACK

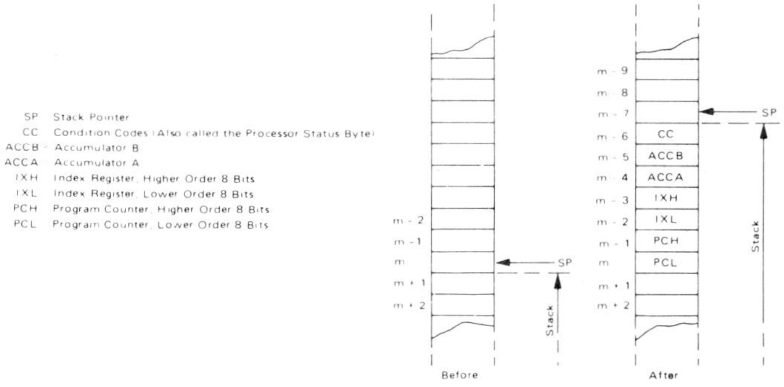

SP   Stack Pointer
CC   Condition Codes (Also called the Processor Status Byte)
ACCB Accumulator B
ACCA Accumulator A
IXH Index Register, Higher Order 8 Bits
IXL Index Register, Lower Order 8 Bits
PCH Program Counter, Higher Order 8 Bits
PCL Program Counter, Lower Order 8 Bits

MOTOROLA *Semiconductor Products Inc.*

MC6800

Condition Code Register — The condition code register indicates the results of an Arithmetic Logic Unit operation: Negative (N), Zero (Z), Overflow (V), Carry from bit 7 (C), and half carry from bit 3 (H). These bits of the Condition Code Register are used as testable conditions for the conditional branch instructions. Bit 4 is the interrupt mask bit (I). The unused bits of the Condition Code Register (b6 and b7) are ones.

Figure 12 shows the order of saving the microprocessor status within the stack.

MPU INSTRUCTION SET

The MC6800 has a set of 72 different instructions. Included are binary and decimal arithmetic, logical, shift, rotate, load, store, conditional or unconditional branch, interrupt and stack manipulation instructions (Tables 2 thru 6).

MPU ADDRESSING MODES

The MC6800 eight-bit microprocessing unit has seven address modes that can be used by a programmer, with the addressing mode a function of both the type of instruction and the coding within the instruction. A summary of the addressing modes for a particular instruction can be found in Table 7 along with the associated instruction execution time that is given in machine cycles. With a clock frequency of 1 MHz, these times would be microseconds.

Accumulator (ACCX) Addressing — In accumulator only addressing, either accumulator A or accumulator B is specified. These are one-byte instructions.

Immediate Addressing — In immediate addressing, the operand is contained in the second byte of the instruction except LDS and LDX which have the operand in the second and third bytes of the instruction. The MPU addresses this location when it fetches the immediate instruction for execution. These are two or three-byte instructions.

Direct Addressing — In direct addressing, the address of the operand is contained in the second byte of the instruction. Direct addressing allows the user to directly address the lowest 256 bytes in the machine i.e., locations zero through 255. Enhanced execution times are achieved by storing data in these locations. In most configurations, it should be a random access memory. These are two-byte instructions.

Extended Addressing — In extended addressing, the address contained in the second byte of the instruction is used as the higher eight-bits of the address of the operand. The third byte of the instruction is used as the lower eight-bits of the address for the operand. This is an absolute address in memory. These are three-byte instructions.

Indexed Addressing — In indexed addressing, the address contained in the second byte of the instruction is added to the index register's lowest eight bits in the MPU. The carry is then added to the higher order eight bits of the index register. This result is then used to address memory. The modified address is held in a temporary address register so there is no change to the index register. These are two-byte instructions.

Implied Addressing — In the implied addressing mode the instruction gives the address (i.e., stack pointer, index register, etc.). These are one-byte instructions.

Relative Addressing — In relative addressing, the address contained in the second byte of the instruction is added to the program counter's lowest eight bits plus two. The carry or borrow is then added to the high eight bits. This allows the user to address data within a range of -125 to +129 bytes of the present instruction. These are two-byte instructions.

TABLE 2 — MICROPROCESSOR INSTRUCTION SET — ALPHABETIC SEQUENCE

ABA	Add Accumulators	CLR	Clear	PUL	Pull Data
ADC	Add with Carry	CLV	Clear Overflow	ROL	Rotate Left
ADD	Add	CMP	Compare	ROR	Rotate Right
AND	Logical And	COM	Complement	RTI	Return from Interrupt
ASL	Arithmetic Shift Left	CPX	Compare Index Register	RTS	Return from Subroutine
ASR	Arithmetic Shift Right	DAA	Decimal Adjust	SBA	Subtract Accumulators
BCC	Branch if Carry Clear	DEC	Decrement	SBC	Subtract with Carry
BCS	Branch if Carry Set	DES	Decrement Stack Pointer	SEC	Set Carry
BEQ	Branch if Equal to Zero	DEX	Decrement Index Register	SEI	Set Interrupt Mask
BGE	Branch if Greater or Equal Zero	EOR	Exclusive OR	SEV	Set Overflow
BGT	Branch if Greater than Zero			STA	Store Accumulator
BHI	Branch if Higher	INC	Increment	STS	Store Stack Register
BIT	Bit Test	INS	Increment Stack Pointer	STX	Store Index Register
BLE	Branch if Less or Equal	INX	Increment Index Register	SUB	Subtract
BLS	Branch if Lower or Same	JMP	Jump	SWI	Software Interrupt
BLT	Branch if Less than Zero	JSR	Jump to Subroutine	TAB	Transfer Accumulators
BMI	Branch if Minus	LDA	Load Accumulator	TAP	Transfer Accumulators to Condition Code Reg.
BNE	Branch if Not Equal to Zero	LDS	Load Stack Pointer	TBA	Transfer Accumulators
BPL	Branch if Plus	LDX	Load Index Register	TPA	Transfer Condition Code Reg. to Accumulator
BRA	Branch Always	LSR	Logical Shift Right	TST	Test
BSR	Branch to Subroutine	NEG	Negate	TSX	Transfer Stack Pointer to Index Register
BVC	Branch if Overflow Clear	NOP	No Operation	TXS	Transfer Index Register to Stack Pointer
BVS	Branch if Overflow Set	ORA	Inclusive OR Accumulator	WAI	Wait for Interrupt
CBA	Compare Accumulators	PSH	Push Data		
CLC	Clear Carry				
CLI	Clear Interrupt Mask				

 MOTOROLA Semiconductor Products Inc.

MC6800

TABLE 3 — ACCUMULATOR AND MEMORY INSTRUCTIONS

OPERATIONS	MNEMONIC	IMMED OP ~ =	DIRECT OP ~ =	INDEX OP ~ =	EXTND OP ~ =	IMPLIED OP ~ =	BOOLEAN/ARITHMETIC OPERATION (All register labels refer to contents)	5 H	4 I	3 N	2 Z	1 V	0 C
Add	ADDA	8B 2 2	9B 3 2	AB 5 2	BB 4 3		A + M → A	●	●	●	●	●	●
	ADDB	CB 2 2	DB 3 2	EB 5 2	FB 4 3		B + M → B	●	●	●	●	●	●
Add Acmltrs	ABA					1B 2 1	A + B → A	●	●	●	●	●	●
Add with Carry	ADCA	89 2 2	99 3 2	A9 5 2	B9 4 3		A + M + C → A	●	●	●	●	●	●
	ADCB	C9 2 2	D9 3 2	E9 5 2	F9 4 3		B + M + C → B	●	●	●	●	●	●
And	ANDA	84 2 2	94 3 2	A4 5 2	B4 4 3		A · M → A	●	●	●	●	R	●
	ANDB	C4 2 2	D4 3 2	E4 5 2	F4 4 3		B · M → B	●	●	●	●	R	●
Bit Test	BITA	85 2 2	95 3 2	A5 5 2	B5 4 3		A · M	●	●	●	●	R	●
	BITB	C5 2 2	D5 3 2	E5 5 2	F5 4 3		B · M	●	●	●	●	R	●
Clear	CLR			6F 7 2	7F 6 3		00 → M	●	●	R	S	R	R
	CLRA					4F 2 1	00 → A	●	●	R	S	R	R
	CLRB					5F 2 1	00 → B	●	●	R	S	R	R
Compare	CMPA	81 2 2	91 3 2	A1 5 2	B1 4 3		A − M	●	●	●	●	●	●
	CMPB	C1 2 2	D1 3 2	E1 5 2	F1 4 3		B − M	●	●	●	●	●	●
Compare Acmltrs	CBA					11 2 1	A − B	●	●	●	●	●	●
Complement, 1's	COM			63 7 2	73 6 3		M̄ → M	●	●	●	●	R	S
	COMA					43 2 1	Ā → A	●	●	●	●	R	S
	COMB					53 2 1	B̄ → B	●	●	●	●	R	S
Complement, 2's (Negate)	NEG			60 7 2	70 6 3		00 − M → M	●	●	●	●	①	②
	NEGA					40 2 1	00 − A → A	●	●	●	●	①	②
	NEGB					50 2 1	00 − B → B	●	●	●	●	①	②
Decimal Adjust, A	DAA					19 2 1	Converts Binary Add of BCD Characters into BCD Format	●	●	●	●	●	③
Decrement	DEC			6A 7 2	7A 6 3		M − 1 → M	●	●	●	●	④	●
	DECA					4A 2 1	A − 1 → A	●	●	●	●	④	●
	DECB					5A 2 1	B − 1 → B	●	●	●	●	④	●
Exclusive OR	EORA	88 2 2	98 3 2	A8 5 2	B8 4 3		A ⊕ M → A	●	●	●	●	R	●
	EORB	C8 2 2	D8 3 2	E8 5 2	F8 4 3		B ⊕ M → B	●	●	●	●	R	●
Increment	INC			6C 7 2	7C 6 3		M + 1 → M	●	●	●	●	⑤	●
	INCA					4C 2 1	A + 1 → A	●	●	●	●	⑤	●
	INCB					5C 2 1	B + 1 → B	●	●	●	●	⑤	●
Load Acmltr	LDAA	86 2 2	96 3 2	A6 5 2	B6 4 3		M → A	●	●	●	●	R	●
	LDAB	C6 2 2	D6 3 2	E6 5 2	F6 4 3		M → B	●	●	●	●	R	●
Or, Inclusive	ORAA	8A 2 2	9A 3 2	AA 5 2	BA 4 3		A + M → A	●	●	●	●	R	●
	ORAB	CA 2 2	DA 3 2	EA 5 2	FA 4 3		B + M → B	●	●	●	●	R	●
Push Data	PSHA					36 4 1	A → M$_{SP}$, SP − 1 → SP	●	●	●	●	●	●
	PSHB					37 4 1	B → M$_{SP}$, SP − 1 → SP	●	●	●	●	●	●
Pull Data	PULA					32 4 1	SP + 1 → SP, M$_{SP}$ → A	●	●	●	●	●	●
	PULB					33 4 1	SP + 1 → SP, M$_{SP}$ → B	●	●	●	●	●	●
Rotate Left	ROL			69 7 2	79 6 3		M ↺	●	●	●	●	⑥	●
	ROLA					49 2 1	A ↺	●	●	●	●	⑥	●
	ROLB					59 2 1	B ↺	●	●	●	●	⑥	●
Rotate Right	ROR			66 7 2	76 6 3		M ↻	●	●	●	●	⑥	●
	RORA					46 2 1	A ↻	●	●	●	●	⑥	●
	RORB					56 2 1	B ↻	●	●	●	●	⑥	●
Shift Left, Arithmetic	ASL			68 7 2	78 6 3		M ←	●	●	●	●	⑥	●
	ASLA					48 2 1	A ←	●	●	●	●	⑥	●
	ASLB					58 2 1	B ←	●	●	●	●	⑥	●
Shift Right, Arithmetic	ASR			67 7 2	77 6 3		M →	●	●	●	●	⑥	●
	ASRA					47 2 1	A →	●	●	●	●	⑥	●
	ASRB					57 2 1	B →	●	●	●	●	⑥	●
Shift Right, Logic	LSR			64 7 2	74 6 3		M →	●	●	R	●	⑥	●
	LSRA					44 2 1	A →	●	●	R	●	⑥	●
	LSRB					54 2 1	B →	●	●	R	●	⑥	●
Store Acmltr	STAA		97 4 2	A7 6 2	B7 5 3		A → M	●	●	●	●	R	●
	STAB		D7 4 2	E7 6 2	F7 5 3		B → M	●	●	●	●	R	●
Subtract	SUBA	80 2 2	90 3 2	A0 5 2	B0 4 3		A − M → A	●	●	●	●	●	●
	SUBB	C0 2 2	D0 3 2	E0 5 2	F0 4 3		B − M → B	●	●	●	●	●	●
Subtract Acmltrs	SBA					10 2 1	A − B → A	●	●	●	●	●	●
Subtr. with Carry	SBCA	82 2 2	92 3 2	A2 5 2	B2 4 3		A − M − C → A	●	●	●	●	●	●
	SBCB	C2 2 2	D2 3 2	E2 5 2	F2 4 3		B − M − C → B	●	●	●	●	●	●
Transfer Acmltrs	TAB					16 2 1	A → B	●	●	●	●	R	●
	TBA					17 2 1	B → A	●	●	●	●	R	●
Test, Zero or Minus	TST			6D 7 2	7D 6 3		M − 00	●	●	●	●	R	R
	TSTA					4D 2 1	A − 00	●	●	●	●	R	R
	TSTB					5D 2 1	B − 00	●	●	●	●	R	R
								H	I	N	Z	V	C

LEGEND

OP Operation Code (Hexadecimal)
~ Number of MPU Cycles
= Number of Program Bytes
+ Arithmetic Plus
− Arithmetic Minus
· Boolean AND
M$_{SP}$ Contents of memory location pointed to be Stack Pointer
+ Boolean Inclusive OR
⊕ Boolean Exclusive OR
M̄ Complement of M
→ Transfer Into
0 Bit = Zero
00 Byte = Zero

Note: Accumulator addressing mode instructions are included in the column for IMPLIED addressing

CONDITION CODE SYMBOLS

H Half-carry from bit 3
I Interrupt mask
N Negative (sign bit)
Z Zero (byte)
V Overflow, 2's complement
C Carry from bit 7
R Reset Always
S Set Always
① Test and set if true, cleared otherwise
● Not Affected

MOTOROLA *Semiconductor Products Inc.*

MC6800

TABLE 4 – INDEX REGISTER AND STACK MANIPULATION INSTRUCTIONS

		IMMED			DIRECT			INDEX			EXTND			IMPLIED				COND. CODE REG.					
																		5	4	3	2	1	0
POINTER OPERATIONS	MNEMONIC	OP	~	=	OP	~	=	OP	~	=	OP	~	=	OP	~	=	BOOLEAN/ARITHMETIC OPERATION	H	I	N	Z	V	C
Compare Index Reg	CPX	8C	3	3	9C	4	2	AC	6	2	BC	5	3				$X_H - M, X_L - (M+1)$	•	•	⑦	:	⑧	•
Decrement Index Reg	DEX													09	4	1	$X - 1 \rightarrow X$	•	•	•	:	•	•
Decrement Stack Pntr	DES													34	4	1	$SP - 1 \rightarrow SP$	•	•	•	•	•	•
Increment Index Reg	INX													08	4	1	$X + 1 \rightarrow X$	•	•	•	:	•	•
Increment Stack Pntr	INS													31	4	1	$SP + 1 \rightarrow SP$	•	•	•	•	•	•
Load Index Reg	LDX	CE	3	3	DE	4	2	EE	6	2	FE	5	3				$M \rightarrow X_H, (M+1) \rightarrow X_L$	•	•	⑨	:	R	•
Load Stack Pntr	LDS	8E	3	3	9E	4	2	AE	6	2	BE	5	3				$M \rightarrow SP_H, (M+1) \rightarrow SP_L$	•	•	⑨	:	R	•
Store Index Reg	STX				DF	5	2	EF	7	2	FF	6	3				$X_H \rightarrow M, X_L \rightarrow (M+1)$	•	•	⑨	:	R	•
Store Stack Pntr	STS				9F	5	2	AF	7	2	BF	6	3				$SP_H \rightarrow M, SP_L \rightarrow (M+1)$	•	•	⑨	:	R	•
Indx Reg → Stack Pntr	TXS													35	4	1	$X - 1 \rightarrow SP$	•	•	•	•	•	•
Stack Pntr → Indx Reg	TSX													30	4	1	$SP + 1 \rightarrow X$	•	•	•	•	•	•

TABLE 5 – JUMP AND BRANCH INSTRUCTIONS

		RELATIVE			INDEX			EXTND			IMPLIED				COND. CODE REG.					
															5	4	3	2	1	0
OPERATIONS	MNEMONIC	OP	~	=	OP	~	=	OP	~	=	OP	~	=	BRANCH TEST	H	I	N	Z	V	C
Branch Always	BRA	20	4	2										None	•	•	•	•	•	•
Branch If Carry Clear	BCC	24	4	2										C = 0	•	•	•	•	•	•
Branch If Carry Set	BCS	25	4	2										C = 1	•	•	•	•	•	•
Branch If = Zero	BEQ	27	4	2										Z = 1	•	•	•	•	•	•
Branch If ≥ Zero	BGE	2C	4	2										N ⊕ V = 0	•	•	•	•	•	•
Branch If > Zero	BGT	2E	4	2										Z + (N ⊕ V) = 0	•	•	•	•	•	•
Branch If Higher	BHI	22	4	2										C + Z = 0	•	•	•	•	•	•
Branch If ≤ Zero	BLE	2F	4	2										Z + (N ⊕ V) = 1	•	•	•	•	•	•
Branch If Lower Or Same	BLS	23	4	2										C + Z = 1	•	•	•	•	•	•
Branch If < Zero	BLT	2D	4	2										N ⊕ V = 1	•	•	•	•	•	•
Branch If Minus	BMI	2B	4	2										N = 1	•	•	•	•	•	•
Branch If Not Equal Zero	BNE	26	4	2										Z = 0	•	•	•	•	•	•
Branch If Overflow Clear	BVC	28	4	2										V = 0	•	•	•	•	•	•
Branch If Overflow Set	BVS	29	4	2										V = 1	•	•	•	•	•	•
Branch If Plus	BPL	2A	4	2										N = 0	•	•	•	•	•	•
Branch To Subroutine	BSR	8D	8	2											•	•	•	•	•	•
Jump	JMP				6E	4	2	7E	3	3				See Special Operations	•	•	•	•	•	•
Jump To Subroutine	JSR				AD	8	2	BD	9	3					•	•	•	•	•	•
No Operation	NOP										01	2	1	Advances Prog. Cntr. Only	•	•	•		•	•
Return From Interrupt	RTI										3B	10	1					⑩		
Return From Subroutine	RTS										39	5	1		•	•	•	•	•	•
Software Interrupt	SWI										3F	12	1	See Special Operations	•	•	•	•	•	•
Wait for Interrupt *	WAI										3E	9	1		•	⑪	•	•	•	•

*WAI puts Address Bus, R/W, and Data Bus in the three state mode while VMA is held low.

MOTOROLA Semiconductor Products Inc.

MC6800

SPECIAL OPERATIONS

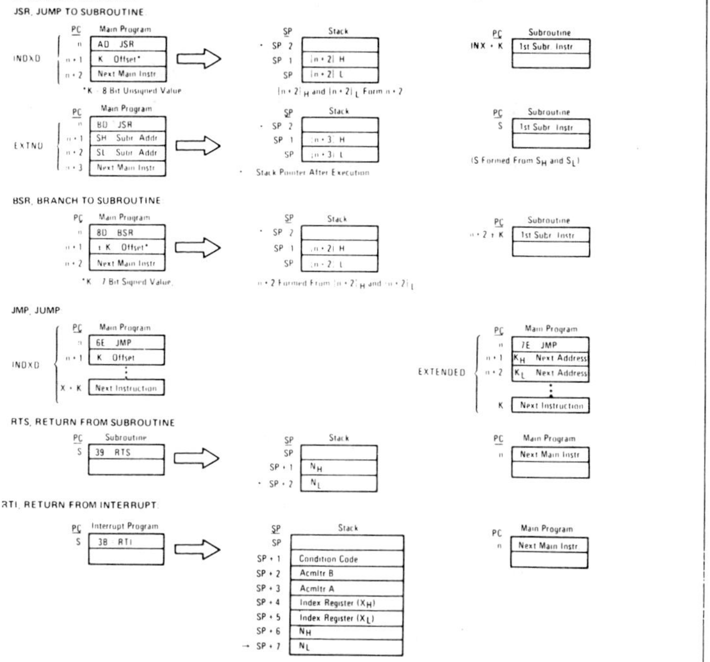

JSR, JUMP TO SUBROUTINE

INDXD:
PC	Main Program
n	AD JSR
n+1	K Offset*
n+2	Next Main Instr

*K = 8 Bit Unsigned Value

SP	Stack
• SP-2	
SP-1	(n+2)H
SP	(n+2)L

(n+2)H and (n+2)L Form n+2

PC	Subroutine
INX+K	1st Subr Instr

EXTND:
PC	Main Program
n	BD JSR
n+1	SH Subr Addr
n+2	SL Subr Addr
n+3	Next Main Instr

SP	Stack
• SP-2	
SP-1	(n+3)H
SP	(n+3)L

• Stack Pointer After Execution

PC	Subroutine
S	1st Subr Instr

(S Formed From SH and SL)

BSR, BRANCH TO SUBROUTINE

PC	Main Program
n	8D BSR
n+1	± K Offset*
n+2	Next Main Instr

*K = 7 Bit Signed Value

SP	Stack
• SP-2	
SP-1	(n+2)H
SP	(n+2)L

n+2 Formed From (n+2)H and (n+2)L

PC	Subroutine
n+2 ± K	1st Subr Instr

JMP, JUMP

INDXD:
PC	Main Program
n	6E JMP
n+1	K Offset
X+K	Next Instruction

EXTENDED:
PC	Main Program
n	7E JMP
n+1	KH Next Address
n+2	KL Next Address
K	Next Instruction

RTS, RETURN FROM SUBROUTINE

PC	Subroutine
S	39 RTS

SP	Stack
SP	
SP+1	NH
• SP+2	NL

PC	Main Program
n	Next Main Instr

RTI, RETURN FROM INTERRUPT

PC	Interrupt Program
S	3B RTI

SP	Stack
SP	
SP+1	Condition Code
SP+2	Acmltr B
SP+3	Acmltr A
SP+4	Index Register (XH)
SP+5	Index Register (XL)
SP+6	NH
→ SP+7	NL

PC	Main Program
n	Next Main Instr

TABLE 6 — CONDITION CODE REGISTER MANIPULATION INSTRUCTIONS

OPERATIONS	MNEMONIC	IMPLIED OP	~	#	BOOLEAN OPERATION	5 H	4 I	3 N	2 Z	1 V	0 C
Clear Carry	CLC	0C	2	1	0 → C	•	•	•	•	•	R
Clear Interrupt Mask	CLI	0E	2	1	0 → I	•	R	•	•	•	•
Clear Overflow	CLV	0A	2	1	0 → V	•	•	•	•	R	•
Set Carry	SEC	0D	2	1	1 → C	•	•	•	•	•	S
Set Interrupt Mask	SEI	0F	2	1	1 → I	•	S	•	•	•	•
Set Overflow	SEV	0B	2	1	1 → V	•	•	•	•	S	•
Acmltr A → CCR	TAP	06	2	1	A → CCR	——(12)——					
CCR → Acmltr A	TPA	07	2	1	CCR → A	•	•	•	•	•	•

CONDITION CODE REGISTER NOTES: (Bit set if test is true and cleared otherwise)

1. (Bit V) Test: Result = 10000000?
2. (Bit C) Test: Result = 00000000?
3. (Bit C) Test: Decimal value of most significant BCD Character greater than nine? (Not cleared if previously set.)
4. (Bit V) Test: Operand = 10000000 prior to execution?
5. (Bit V) Test: Operand = 01111111 prior to execution?
6. (Bit V) Test: Set equal to result of N⊕C after shift has occurred.
7. (Bit N) Test: Sign bit of most significant (MS) byte = 1?
8. (Bit V) Test: 2's complement overflow from subtraction of MS bytes?
9. (Bit N) Test: Result less than zero? (Bit 15 = 1)
10. (All) Load Condition Code Register from Stack. (See Special Operations)
11. (Bit I) Set when interrupt occurs. If previously set, a Non Maskable Interrupt is required to exit the wait state.
12. (All) Set according to the contents of Accumulator A.

 MOTOROLA Semiconductor Products Inc.

TABLE 7 – INSTRUCTION ADDRESSING MODES AND ASSOCIATED EXECUTION TIMES
(Times in Machine Cycles)

	(Dual Operand)	ACC X	Immediate	Direct	Extended	Indexed	Implied	Relative		(Dual Operand)	ACC X	Immediate	Direct	Extended	Indexed	Implied
ABA	•	•	•	•	•	•	2	•	INC	•	2	•	•	6	7	•
ADC	x	•	2	3	4	5	•	•	INS	•	•	•	•	•	•	4
ADD	x	•	2	3	4	5	•	•	INX	•	•	•	•	•	•	4
AND	x	•	2	3	4	5	•	•	JMP	•	•	•	•	3	4	•
ASL	•	2	•	•	6	7	•	•	JSR	•	•	•	•	9	8	•
ASR	•	2	•	•	6	7	•	•	LDA	x	•	2	3	4	5	•
BCC	•	•	•	•	•	•	•	4	LDS	•	•	3	4	5	6	•
BCS	•	•	•	•	•	•	•	4	LDX	•	•	3	4	5	6	•
BEA	•	•	•	•	•	•	•	4	LSR	•	2	•	•	6	7	•
BGE	•	•	•	•	•	•	•	4	NEG	•	2	•	•	6	7	•
BGT	•	•	•	•	•	•	•	4	NOP	•	•	•	•	•	•	2
BHI	•	•	•	•	•	•	•	4	ORA	x	•	2	3	4	5	•
BIT	x	•	2	3	4	5	•	•	PSH	•	•	•	•	•	•	4
BLE	•	•	•	•	•	•	•	4	PUL	•	•	•	•	•	•	4
BLS	•	•	•	•	•	•	•	4	ROL	•	2	•	•	6	7	•
BLT	•	•	•	•	•	•	•	4	ROR	•	2	•	•	6	7	•
BMI	•	•	•	•	•	•	•	4	RTI	•	•	•	•	•	•	10
BNE	•	•	•	•	•	•	•	4	RTS	•	•	•	•	•	•	5
BPL	•	•	•	•	•	•	•	4	SBA	•	•	•	•	•	•	2
BRA	•	•	•	•	•	•	•	4	SBC	x	•	2	3	4	5	•
BSR	•	•	•	•	•	•	•	8	SEC	•	•	•	•	•	•	2
BVC	•	•	•	•	•	•	•	4	SEI	•	•	•	•	•	•	2
BVS	•	•	•	•	•	•	•	4	SEV	•	•	•	•	•	•	2
CBA	•	•	•	•	•	•	2	•	STA	x	•	•	4	5	6	•
CLC	•	•	•	•	•	•	2	•	STS	•	•	•	5	6	7	•
CLI	•	•	•	•	•	•	2	•	STX	•	•	•	5	6	7	•
CLR	•	2	•	•	6	7	•	•	SUB	x	•	2	3	4	5	•
CLV	•	•	•	•	•	•	2	•	SWI	•	•	•	•	•	•	12
CMP	x	•	2	3	4	5	•	•	TAB	•	•	•	•	•	•	2
COM	•	2	•	•	6	7	•	•	TAP	•	•	•	•	•	•	2
CPX	•	•	3	4	5	6	•	•	TBA	•	•	•	•	•	•	2
DAA	•	•	•	•	•	•	2	•	TPA	•	•	•	•	•	•	2
DEC	•	2	•	•	6	7	•	•	TST	•	2	•	•	6	7	•
DES	•	•	•	•	•	•	4	•	TSX	•	•	•	•	•	•	4
DEX	•	•	•	•	•	•	4	•	TSX	•	•	•	•	•	•	4
EOR	x	•	2	3	4	5	•	•	WAI	•	•	•	•	•	•	9

NOTE: Interrupt time is 12 cycles from the end of the instruction being executed, except following a WAI instruction. Then it is 4 cycles.

PIN ASSIGNMENT

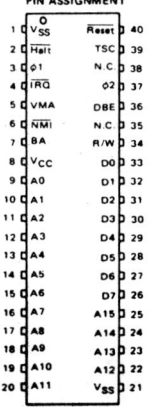

PACKAGE DIMENSIONS
CASE 715-02
(CERAMIC)

See Page 165 for Plastic Package dimensions.

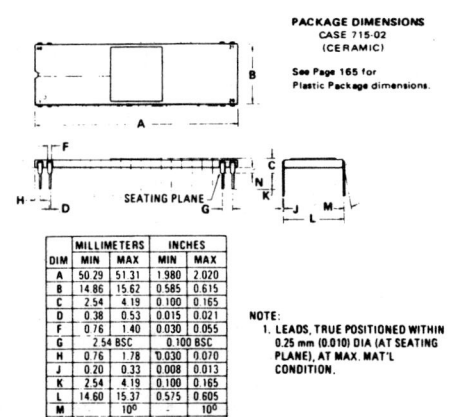

DIM	MILLIMETERS		INCHES	
	MIN	MAX	MIN	MAX
A	50.29	51.31	1.980	2.020
B	14.86	15.62	0.585	0.615
C	2.54	4.19	0.100	0.165
D	0.38	0.53	0.015	0.021
F	0.76	1.40	0.030	0.055
G	2.54 BSC		0.100 BSC	
H	0.76	1.78	0.030	0.070
J	0.20	0.33	0.008	0.013
K	2.54	4.19	0.100	0.165
L	14.60	15.37	0.575	0.605
M		10°		10°
N	0.51	1.52	0.020	0.060

NOTE:
1. LEADS, TRUE POSITIONED WITHIN 0.25 mm (0.010) DIA (AT SEATING PLANE), AT MAX. MAT'L CONDITION.

 MOTOROLA Semiconductor Products Inc.

SUMMARY OF CYCLE BY CYCLE OPERATION

Table 8 provides a detailed description of the information present on the Address Bus, Data Bus, Valid Memory Address line (VMA), and the Read/Write line (R/W) during each cycle for each instruction.

This information is useful in comparing actual with expected results during debug of both software and hardware as the control program is executed. The information is categorized in groups according to Addressing Mode and Number of Cycles per instruction. (In general, instructions with the same Addressing Mode and Number of Cycles execute in the same manner; exceptions are indicated in the table.)

TABLE 8 – OPERATION SUMMARY

Address Mode and Instructions	Cycles	Cycle #	VMA Line	Address Bus	R/W Line	Data Bus
IMMEDIATE						
ADC EOR ADD LDA AND ORA BIT SBC CMP SUB	2	1	1	Op Code Address	1	Op Code
		2	1	Op Code Address + 1	1	Operand Data
CPX LDS LDX	3	1	1	Op Code Address	1	Op Code
		2	1	Op Code Address + 1	1	Operand Data (High Order Byte)
		3	1	Op Code Address + 2	1	Operand Data (Low Order Byte)
DIRECT						
ADC EOR ADD LDA AND ORA BIT SBC CMP SUB	3	1	1	Op Code Address	1	Op Code
		2	1	Op Code Address + 1	1	Address of Operand
		3	1	Address of Operand	1	Operand Data
CPX LDS LDX	4	1	1	Op Code Address	1	Op Code
		2	1	Op Code Address + 1	1	Address of Operand
		3	1	Address of Operand	1	Operand Data (High Order Byte)
		4	1	Operand Address + 1	1	Operand Data (Low Order Byte)
STA	4	1	1	Op Code Address	1	Op Code
		2	1	Op Code Address + 1	1	Destination Address
		3	0	Destination Address	1	Irrelevant Data (Note 1)
		4	1	Destination Address	0	Data from Accumulator
STS STX	5	1	1	Op Code Address	1	Op Code
		2	1	Op Code Address + 1	1	Address of Operand
		3	0	Address of Operand	1	Irrelevant Data (Note 1)
		4	1	Address of Operand	0	Register Data (High Order Byte)
		5	1	Address of Operand + 1	0	Register Data (Low Order Byte)
INDEXED						
JMP	4	1	1	Op Code Address	1	Op Code
		2	1	Op Code Address + 1	1	Offset
		3	0	Index Register	1	Irrelevant Data (Note 1)
		4	0	Index Register Plus Offset (w/o Carry)	1	Irrelevant Data (Note 1)
ADC EOR ADD LDA AND ORA BIT SBC CMP SUB	5	1	1	Op Code Address	1	Op Code
		2	1	Op Code Address + 1	1	Offset
		3	0	Index Register	1	Irrelevant Data (Note 1)
		4	0	Index Register Plus Offset (w/o Carry)	1	Irrelevant Data (Note 1)
		5	1	Index Register Plus Offset	1	Operand Data
CPX LDS LDX	6	1	1	Op Code Address	1	Up Code
		2	1	Op Code Address + 1	1	Offset
		3	0	Index Register	1	Irrelevant Data (Note 1)
		4	0	Index Register Plus Offset (w/o Carry)	1	Irrelevant Data (Note 1)
		5	1	Index Register Plus Offset	1	Operand Data (High Order Byte)
		6	1	Index Register Plus Offset + 1	1	Operand Data (Low Order Byte)

 MOTOROLA *Semiconductor Products Inc.*

MC6800

TABLE 8 — OPERATION SUMMARY (Continued)

Address Mode and Instructions	Cycles	Cycle #	VMA Line	Address Bus	R/W Line	Data Bus
INDEXED (Continued)						
STA	6	1	1	Op Code Address	1	Op Code
		2	1	Op Code Address + 1	1	Offset
		3	0	Index Register	1	Irrelevant Data (Note 1)
		4	0	Index Register Plus Offset (w/o Carry)	1	Irrelevant Data (Note 1)
		5	0	Index Register Plus Offset	1	Irrelevant Data (Note 1)
		6	1	Index Register Plus Offset	0	Operand Data
ASL LSR ASR NEG CLR ROL COM ROR DEC TST INC	7	1	1	Op Code Address	1	Op Code
		2	1	Op Code Address + 1	1	Offset
		3	0	Index Register	1	Irrelevant Data (Note 1)
		4	0	Index Register Plus Offset (w/o Carry)	1	Irrelevant Data (Note 1)
		5	1	Index Register Plus Offset	1	Current Operand Data
		6	0	Index Register Plus Offset	1	Irrelevant Data (Note 1)
		7	1/0 (Note 3)	Index Register Plus Offset	0	New Operand Data (Note 3)
STS STX	7	1	1	Op Code Address	1	Op Code
		2	1	Op Code Address + 1	1	Offset
		3	0	Index Register	1	Irrelevant Data (Note 1)
		4	0	Index Register Plus Offset (w/o Carry)	1	Irrelevant Data (Note 1)
		5	0	Index Register Plus Offset	1	Irrelevant Data (Note 1)
		6	1	Index Register Plus Offset	0	Operand Data (High Order Byte)
		7	1	Index Register Plus Offset + 1	0	Operand Data (Low Order Byte)
JSR	8	1	1	Op Code Address	1	Op Code
		2	1	Op Code Address + 1	1	Offset
		3	0	Index Register	1	Irrelevant Data (Note 1)
		4	1	Stack Pointer	0	Return Address (Low Order Byte)
		5	1	Stack Pointer − 1	0	Return Address (High Order Byte)
		6	0	Stack Pointer − 2	1	Irrelevant Data (Note 1)
		7	0	Index Register	1	Irrelevant Data (Note 1)
		8	0	Index Register Plus Offset (w/o Carry)	1	Irrelevant Data (Note 1)
EXTENDED						
JMP	3	1	1	Op Code Address	1	Op Code
		2	1	Op Code Address + 1	1	Jump Address (High Order Byte)
		3	1	Op Code Address + 2	1	Jump Address (Low Order Byte)
ADC EOR ADD LDA AND ORA BIT SBC CMP SUB	4	1	1	Op Code Address	1	Op Code
		2	1	Op Code Address + 1	1	Address of Operand (High Order Byte)
		3	1	Op Code Address + 2	1	Address of Operand (Low Order Byte)
		4	1	Address of Operand	1	Operand Data
CPX LDS LDX	5	1	1	Op Code Address	1	Op Code
		2	1	Op Code Address + 1	1	Address of Operand (High Order Byte)
		3	1	Op Code Address + 2	1	Address of Operand (Low Order Byte)
		4	1	Address of Operand	1	Operand Data (High Order Byte)
		5	1	Address of Operand + 1	1	Operand Data (Low Order Byte)
STA A STA B	5	1	1	Op Code Address	1	Op Code
		2	1	Op Code Address + 1	1	Destination Address (High Order Byte)
		3	1	Op Code Address + 2	1	Destination Address (Low Order Byte)
		4	0	Operand Destination Address	1	Irrelevant Data (Note 1)
		5	1	Operand Destination Address	0	Data from Accumulator
ASL LSR ASR NEG CLR ROL COM ROR DEC TST INC	6	1	1	Op Code Address	1	Op Code
		2	1	Op Code Address + 1	1	Address of Operand (High Order Byte)
		3	1	Op Code Address + 2	1	Address of Operand (Low Order Byte)
		4	1	Address of Operand	1	Current Operand Data
		5	0	Address of Operand	1	Irrelevant Data (Note 1)
		6	1/0 (Note 3)	Address of Operand	0	New Operand Data (Note 3)

MC6800

TABLE 8 – OPERATION SUMMARY (Continued)

Address Mode and Instructions	Cycles	Cycle #	VMA Line	Address Bus	R/W Line	Data Bus
EXTENDED (Continued)						
STS		1	1	Op Code Address	1	Op Code
STX		2	1	Op Code Address + 1	1	Address of Operand (High Order Byte)
	6	3	1	Op Code Address + 2	1	Address of Operand (Low Order Byte)
		4	0	Address of Operand	1	Irrelevant Data (Note 1)
		5	1	Address of Operand	0	Operand Data (High Order Byte)
		6	1	Address of Operand + 1	0	Operand Data (Low Order Byte)
JSR		1	1	Op Code Address	1	Op Code
		2	1	Op Code Address + 1	1	Address of Subroutine (High Order Byte)
		3	1	Op Code Address + 2	1	Address of Subroutine (Low Order Byte)
		4	1	Subroutine Starting Address	1	Op Code of Next Instruction
	9	5	1	Stack Pointer	0	Return Address (Low Order Byte)
		6	1	Stack Pointer – 1	0	Return Address (High Order Byte)
		7	0	Stack Pointer – 2	1	Irrelevant Data (Note 1)
		8	0	Op Code Address + 2	1	Irrelevant Data (Note 1)
		9	1	Op Code Address + 2	1	Address of Subroutine (Low Order Byte)
INHERENT						
ABA DAA SEC		1	1	Op Code Address	1	Op Code
ASL DEC SEI	2	2	1	Op Code Address + 1	1	Op Code of Next Instruction
ASR INC SEV						
CBA LSR TAB						
CLC NEG TAP						
CLI NOP TBA						
CLR ROL TPA						
CLV ROR TST						
COM SBA						
DES		1	1	Op Code Address	1	Op Code
DEX		2	1	Op Code Address + 1	1	Op Code of Next Instruction
INS	4	3	0	Previous Register Contents	1	Irrelevant Data (Note 1)
INX		4	0	New Register Contents	1	Irrelevant Data (Note 1)
PSH		1	1	Op Code Address	1	Op Code
		2	1	Op Code Address + 1	1	Op Code of Next Instruction
	4	3	1	Stack Pointer	0	Accumulator Data
		4	0	Stack Pointer – 1	1	Accumulator Data
PUL		1	1	Op Code Address	1	Op Code
		2	1	Op Code Address + 1	1	Op Code of Next Instruction
	4	3	0	Stack Pointer	1	Irrelevant Data (Note 1)
		4	1	Stack Pointer + 1	1	Operand Data from Stack
TSX		1	1	Op Code Address	1	Op Code
		2	1	Op Code Address + 1	1	Op Code of Next Instruction
	4	3	0	Stack Pointer	1	Irrelevant Data (Note 1)
		4	0	New Index Register	1	Irrelevant Data (Note 1)
TXS		1	1	Op Code Address	1	Op Code
		2	1	Op Code Address + 1	1	Op Code of Next Instruction
	4	3	0	Index Register	1	Irrelevant Data
		4	0	New Stack Pointer	1	Irrelevant Data
RTS		1	1	Op Code Address	1	Op Code
		2	1	Op Code Address + 1	1	Irrelevant Data (Note 2)
	5	3	0	Stack Pointer	1	Irrelevant Data (Note 1)
		4	1	Stack Pointer + 1	1	Address of Next Instruction (High Order Byte)
		5	1	Stack Pointer + 2	1	Address of Next Instruction (Low Order Byte)

 MOTOROLA Semiconductor Products Inc.

MC6800

TABLE 8 – OPERATION SUMMARY (Continued)

Address Mode and Instructions	Cycles	Cycle #	VMA Line	Address Bus	R/W Line	Data Bus
INHERENT (Continued)						
WAI	9	1	1	Op Code Address	1	Op Code
		2	1	Op Code Address + 1	1	Op Code of Next Instruction
		3	1	Stack Pointer	0	Return Address (Low Order Byte)
		4	1	Stack Pointer – 1	0	Return Address (High Order Byte)
		5	1	Stack Pointer – 2	0	Index Register (Low Order Byte)
		6	1	Stack Pointer – 3	0	Index Register (High Order Byte)
		7	1	Stack Pointer – 4	0	Contents of Accumulator A
		8	1	Stack Pointer – 5	0	Contents of Accumulator B
		9	1	Stack Pointer – 6 (Note 4)	1	Contents of Cond. Code Register
RTI	10	1	1	Op Code Address	1	Op Code
		2	1	Op Code Address + 1	1	Irrelevant Data (Note 2)
		3	0	Stack Pointer	1	Irrelevant Data (Note 1)
		4	1	Stack Pointer + 1	1	Contents of Cond. Code Register from Stack
		5	1	Stack Pointer + 2	1	Contents of Accumulator B from Stack
		6	1	Stack Pointer + 3	1	Contents of Accumulator A from Stack
		7	1	Stack Pointer + 4	1	Index Register from Stack (High Order Byte)
		8	1	Stack Pointer + 5	1	Index Register from Stack (Low Order Byte)
		9	1	Stack Pointer + 6	1	Next Instruction Address from Stack (High Order Byte)
		10	1	Stack Pointer + 7	1	Next Instruction Address from Stack (Low Order Byte)
SWI	12	1	1	Op Code Address	1	Op Code
		2	1	Op Code Address + 1	1	Irrelevant Data (Note 1)
		3	1	Stack Pointer	0	Return Address (Low Order Byte)
		4	1	Stack Pointer – 1	0	Return Address (High Order Byte)
		5	1	Stack Pointer – 2	0	Index Register (Low Order Byte)
		6	1	Stack Pointer – 3	0	Index Register (High Order Byte)
		7	1	Stack Pointer – 4	0	Contents of Accumulator A
		8	1	Stack Pointer – 5	0	Contents of Accumulator B
		9	1	Stack Pointer – 6	0	Contents of Cond. Code Register
		10	0	Stack Pointer – 7	1	Irrelevant Data (Note 1)
		11	1	Vector Address FFFA (Hex)	1	Address of Subroutine (High Order Byte)
		12	1	Vector Address FFFB (Hex)	1	Address of Subroutine (Low Order Byte)
RELATIVE						
BCC BHI BNE BCS BLE BPL BEQ BLS BRA BGE BLT BVC BGT BMI BVS	4	1	1	Op Code Address	1	Op Code
		2	1	Op Code Address + 1	1	Branch Offset
		3	0	Op Code Address + 2	1	Irrelevant Data (Note 1)
		4	0	Branch Address	1	Irrelevant Data (Note 1)
BSR	8	1	1	Op Code Address	1	Op Code
		2	1	Op Code Address + 1	1	Branch Offset
		3	0	Return Address of Main Program	1	Irrelevant Data (Note 1)
		4	1	Stack Pointer	0	Return Address (Low Order Byte)
		5	1	Stack Pointer – 1	0	Return Address (High Order Byte)
		6	0	Stack Pointer – 2	1	Irrelevant Data (Note 1)
		7	0	Return Address of Main Program	1	Irrelevant Data (Note 1)
		8	0	Subroutine Address	1	Irrelevant Data (Note 1)

Note 1. If device which is addressed during this cycle uses VMA, then the Data Bus will go to the high impedance three-state condition. Depending on bus capacitance, data from the previous cycle may be retained on the Data Bus.
Note 2. Data is ignored by the MPU.
Note 3. For TST, VMA = 0 and Operand data does not change.
Note 4. While the MPU is waiting for the interrupt, Bus Available will go high indicating the following states of the control lines: VMA is low; Address Bus, R/W, and Data Bus are all in the high impedance state.

 MOTOROLA *Semiconductor Products Inc.*

MCM6810A
(0 to 70°C, L or P Suffix)

MCM6810AC
(-40 to 85°C, L Suffix only)

MOS
(N-CHANNEL, SILICON-GATE)

128 X 8-BIT STATIC RANDOM ACCESS MEMORY

128 X 8-BIT STATIC RANDOM ACCESS MEMORY

The MCM6810 is a byte-organized memory designed for use in bus-organized systems. It is fabricated with N-channel silicon gate technology. For ease of use, the device operates from a single power supply, has compatibility with TTL and DTL, and needs no clocks or refreshing because of static operation.

The memory is compatible with the M6800 Microcomputer Family, providing random storage in byte increments. Memory expansion is provided through multiple Chip Select inputs.

- Organized as 128 Bytes of 8 Bits
- Static Operation
- Bi-Directional Three State Data Input/Output
- Six Chip Select Inputs (Four Active Low, Two Active High)
- Single 5-Volt Power Supply
- TTL Compatible
- Maximum Access Time = 350 ns — MCM6810AL1
  450 ns — MCM6810AL

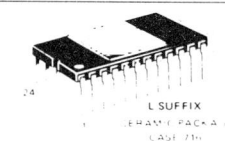

L SUFFIX
CERAMIC PACKAGE
CASE 716

P SUFFIX
NOT SHOWN
PLASTIC PACKAGE
CASE 709

ABSOLUTE MAXIMUM RATINGS See Note 1

Rating	Symbol	Value	Unit
Supply Voltage	V_{CC}	-0.3 to +7.0	Vdc
Input Voltage	V_{in}	-0.3 to +7.0	Vdc
Operating Temperature Range	T_A	0 to +70	°C
Storage Temperature Range	T_{stg}	-65 to +150	°C

NOTE 1: Permanent device damage may occur if ABSOLUTE MAXIMUM RATINGS are exceeded. Functional operation should be restricted to RECOMMENDED OPERATING CONDITIONS. Exposure to higher than recommended voltages for extended periods of time could affect device reliability.

PIN ASSIGNMENT

1	Gnd 0	V_{CC}	24
2	D0	A0	23
3	D1	A1	22
4	D2	A2	21
5	D3	A3	20
6	D4	A4	19
7	D5	A5	18
8	D6	A6	17
9	D7	R/W	16
10	CS0	CS5	15
11	CS1	CS4	14
12	CS2	CS3	13

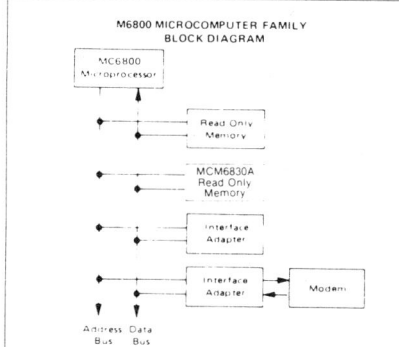

M6800 MICROCOMPUTER FAMILY BLOCK DIAGRAM

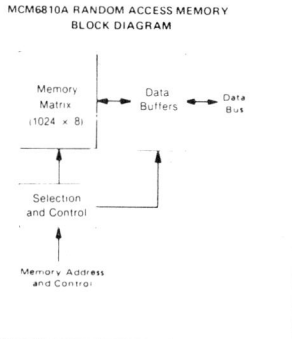

MCM6810A RANDOM ACCESS MEMORY BLOCK DIAGRAM

MCM6810A

DC OPERATING CONDITIONS AND CHARACTERISTICS
(Full operating voltage and temperature range unless otherwise noted.)

RECOMMENDED DC OPERATING CONDITIONS

Parameter	Symbol	Min	Nom	Max	Unit
Supply Voltage	V_{CC}	4.75	5.0	5.25	Vdc
Input High Voltage	V_{IH}	2.0	–	5.25	Vdc
Input Low Voltage	V_{IL}	-0.3		0.8	Vdc

DC CHARACTERISTICS

Characteristic	Symbol	Min	Typ	Max	Unit
Input Current (A_n, R/W, CS_n, $\overline{CS}_n$) (V_{in} 0 to 5.25 V)	I_{in}			2.5	µAdc
Output High Voltage (I_{OH} = -205 µA)	V_{OH}	2.4			Vdc
Output Low Voltage (I_{OL} 1.6 mA)	V_{OL}			0.4	Vdc
Output Leakage Current (Three-State) (CS = 0.8 V or $\overline{CS}$ = 2.0 V, V_{out} = 0.4 V to 2.4 V)	I_{LO}			10	µAdc
Supply Current (V_{CC} = 5.25 V, all other pins grounded, T_A = 0°C) MCM6810AL	I_{CC}			70	mAdc
MCM6810AL1				80	

CAPACITANCE (f = 1.0 MHz, T_A = 25°C, periodically sampled rather than 100% tested.)

Characteristic	Symbol	Max	Unit
Input Capacitance	C_{in}	7.5	pF
Output Capacitance	C_{out}	12.5	pF

This device contains circuitry to protect the inputs against damage due to high static voltages or electric fields, however, it is advised that normal precautions be taken to avoid application of any voltage higher than maximum rated voltages to this high impedance circuit.

BLOCK DIAGRAM

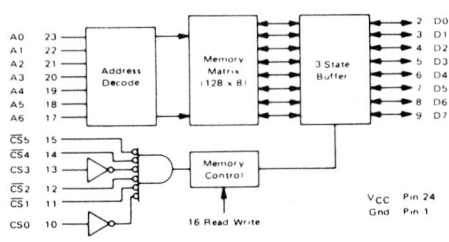

 MOTOROLA Semiconductor Products Inc.

MCM6810A

AC OPERATING CONDITIONS AND CHARACTERISTICS
(Full operating voltage and temperature unless otherwise noted.)

FIGURE 1 – AC TEST LOAD

AC TEST CONDITIONS

Condition	Value
Input Pulse Levels	0.8 V to 2.0 V
Input Rise and Fall Times	20 ns
Output Load	See Figure 1

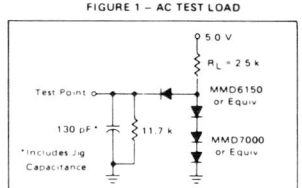

READ CYCLE

Characteristic	Symbol	MCM6810AL Min	MCM6810AL Max	MCM6810AL1 Min	MCM6810AL1 Max	Unit
Read Cycle Time	$t_{cyc(R)}$	450	–	350	–	ns
Access Time	t_{acc}	–	450	–	350	ns
Address Setup Time	t_{AS}	20	–	20	–	ns
Address Hold Time	t_{AH}	0	–	0	–	ns
Data Delay Time (Read)	t_{DDR}	–	230	–	180	ns
Read to Select Delay Time	t_{RCS}	0	–	0	–	ns
Data Hold from Address	t_{DHA}	10	–	10	–	ns
Output Hold Time	t_H	10	–	10	–	ns
Data Hold from Write	t_{DHW}	10	80	10	60	ns

READ CYCLE TIMING

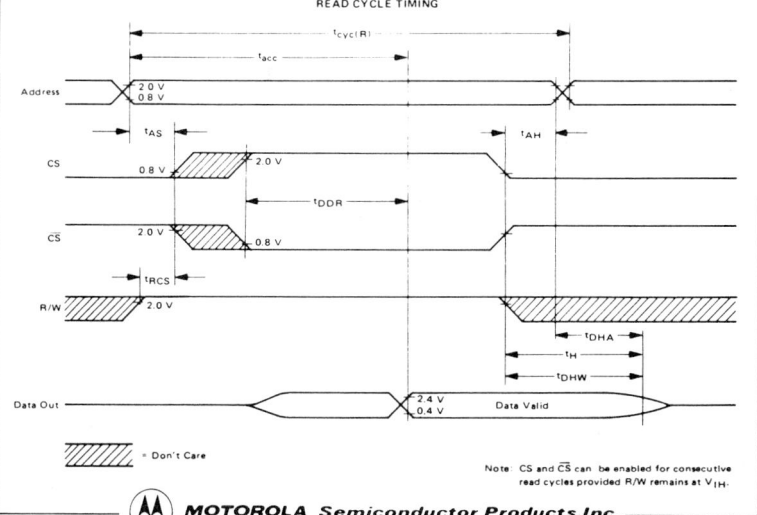

Note: CS and $\overline{CS}$ can be enabled for consecutive read cycles provided R/W remains at V_{IH}.

MOTOROLA Semiconductor Products Inc.

MCM6810A

WRITE CYCLE

Characteristic	Symbol	MCM6810AL Min	MCM6810AL Max	MCM6810AL1 Min	MCM6810AL1 Max	Unit
Write Cycle Time	$t_{cyc(W)}$	450	–	350	–	ns
Address Setup Time	t_{AS}	20	–	20	–	ns
Address Hold Time	t_{AH}	0	–	0	–	ns
Chip Select Pulse Width	t_{CS}	300	–	250	–	ns
Write to Chip Select Delay Time	t_{WCS}	0	–	0	–	ns
Data Setup Time (Write)	t_{DSW}	190	–	150	–	ns
Input Hold Time	t_H	10	–	10	–	ns

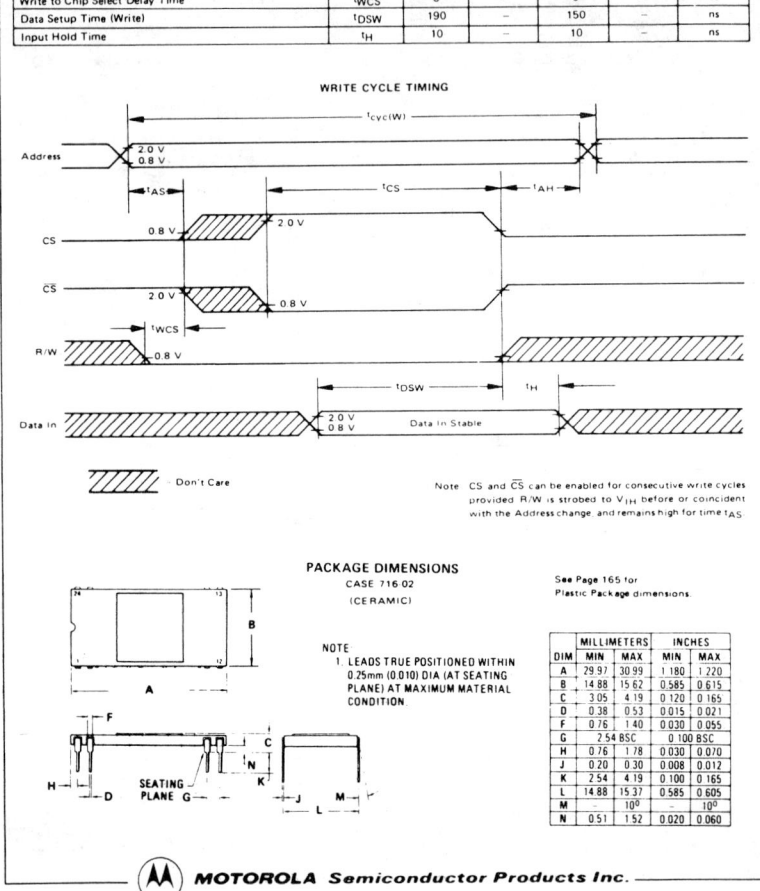

WRITE CYCLE TIMING

Note: CS and $\overline{CS}$ can be enabled for consecutive write cycles provided R/W is strobed to V_{IH} before or coincident with the Address change, and remains high for time t_{AS}.

PACKAGE DIMENSIONS
CASE 716-02
(CERAMIC)

See Page 165 for Plastic Package dimensions.

NOTE
1. LEADS TRUE POSITIONED WITHIN 0.25mm (0.010) DIA (AT SEATING PLANE) AT MAXIMUM MATERIAL CONDITION.

DIM	MILLIMETERS MIN	MILLIMETERS MAX	INCHES MIN	INCHES MAX
A	29.97	30.99	1.180	1.220
B	14.88	15.62	0.585	0.615
C	3.05	4.19	0.120	0.165
D	0.38	0.53	0.015	0.021
F	0.76	1.40	0.030	0.055
G	2.54 BSC		0.100 BSC	
H	0.76	1.78	0.030	0.070
J	0.20	0.30	0.008	0.012
K	2.54	4.19	0.100	0.165
L	14.88	15.37	0.585	0.605
M		10°		10°
N	0.51	1.52	0.020	0.060

MOTOROLA Semiconductor Products Inc.

MC6820
(0 to 70°C, L or P Suffix)

MC6820C
(-40 to 85°C, L Suffix only)

PERIPHERAL INTERFACE ADAPTER (PIA)

The MC6820 Peripheral Interface Adapter provides the universal means of interfacing peripheral equipment to the MC6800 Microprocessing Unit (MPU). This device is capable of interfacing the MPU to peripherals through two 8-bit bidirectional peripheral data buses and four control lines. No external logic is required for interfacing to most peripheral devices.

The functional configuration of the PIA is programmed by the MPU during system initialization. Each of the peripheral data lines can be programmed to act as an input or output, and each of the four control/interrupt lines may be programmed for one of several control modes. This allows a high degree of flexibility in the over-all operation of the interface.

- 8-Bit Bidirectional Data Bus for Communication with the MPU
- Two Bidirectional 8-Bit Buses for Interface to Peripherals
- Two Programmable Control Registers
- Two Programmable Data Direction Registers
- Four Individually-Controlled Interrupt Input Lines; Two Usable as Peripheral Control Outputs
- Handshake Control Logic for Input and Output Peripheral Operation
- High-Impedance 3-State and Direct Transistor Drive Peripheral Lines
- Program Controlled Interrupt and Interrupt Disable Capability
- CMOS Drive Capability on Side A Peripheral Lines

MOS
(N-CHANNEL, SILICON-GATE)

PERIPHERAL INTERFACE ADAPTER

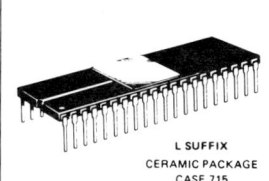

L SUFFIX
CERAMIC PACKAGE
CASE 715

NOT SHOWN: P SUFFIX
PLASTIC PACKAGE
CASE 711

M6800 MICROCOMPUTER FAMILY BLOCK DIAGRAM

MC6820 PERIPHERAL INTERFACE ADAPTER BLOCK DIAGRAM

MC6820

ELECTRICAL CHARACTERISTICS (V_{CC} = 5.0 V ±5%, V_{SS} = 0, T_A = 0 to 70°C unless otherwise noted.)

Characteristic		Symbol	Min	Typ	Max	Unit
Input High Voltage	Enable	V_{IH}	V_{SS} + 2.4	–	V_{CC}	Vdc
	Other Inputs		V_{SS} + 2.0	–	V_{CC}	
Input Low Voltage	Enable	V_{IL}	V_{SS} –0.3	–	V_{SS} + 0.4	Vdc
	Other Inputs		V_{SS} –0.3	–	V_{SS} + 0.8	
Input Leakage Current R/W, Reset, RS0, RS1, CS0, CS1, $\overline{CS2}$, CA1,		I_{in}	–	1.0	2.5	μAdc
(V_{in} = 0 to 5.25 Vdc) CB1, Enable						
Three-State (Off State) Input Current D0-D7, PB0-PB7, CB2		I_{TSI}	–	2.0	10	μAdc
(V_{in} = 0.4 to 2.4 Vdc)						
Input High Current PA0-PA7, CA2		I_{IH}	-100	-250	–	μAdc
(V_{IH} = 2.4 Vdc)						
Input Low Current PA0-PA7, CA2		I_{IL}	–	-1.0	-1.6	mAdc
(V_{IL} = 0.4 Vdc)						
Output High Voltage		V_{OH}				Vdc
(I_{Load} = -205 μAdc, Enable Pulse Width < 25 μs) D0-D7			V_{SS} + 2.4	–	–	
(I_{Load} = -100 μAdc, Enable Pulse Width < 25 μs) Other Outputs			V_{SS} + 2.4	–	–	
Output Low Voltage		V_{OL}	–	–	V_{SS} + 0.4	Vdc
(I_{Load} = 1.6 mAdc, Enable Pulse Width < 25 μs)						
Output High Current (Sourcing)		I_{OH}				
(V_{OH} = 2.4 Vdc) D0-D7			-205	–	–	μAdc
Other Outputs			-100	–	–	μAdc
(V_O = 1.5 Vdc, the current for driving other than TTL, e.g.,						
Darlington Base) PB0-PB7, CB2			-1.0	-2.5	-10	mAdc
Output Low Current (Sinking)		I_{OL}	1.6	–	–	mAdc
(V_{OL} = 0.4 Vdc)						
Output Leakage Current (Off State) $\overline{IRQA}$, $\overline{IRQB}$		I_{LOH}	–	1.0	10	μAdc
(V_{OH} = 2.4 Vdc)						
Power Dissipation		P_D	–	–	650	mW
Input Capacitance Enable		C_{in}	–	–	20	pF
(V_{in} = 0, T_A = 25°C, f = 1.0 MHz) D0-D7			–	–	12.5	
PA0-PA7, PB0-PB7, CA2, CB2			–	–	10	
R/W, Reset, RS0, RS1, CS0, CS1, $\overline{CS2}$, CA1, CB1			–	–	7.5	
Output Capacitance $\overline{IRQA}$, $\overline{IRQB}$		C_{out}	–	–	5.0	pF
(V_{in} = 0, T_A = 25°C, f = 1.0 MHz) PB0-PB7			–	–	10	
Peripheral Data Setup Time (Figure 1)		t_{PDSU}	200	–	–	ns
Delay Time, Enable negative transition to CA2 negative transition		t_{CA2}	–	–	1.0	μs
(Figure 2, 3)						
Delay Time, Enable negative transition to CA2 positive transition		t_{RS1}	–	–	1.0	μs
(Figure 2)						
Rise and Fall Times for CA1 and CA2 input signals (Figure 3)		t_r, t_f	–	–	1.0	μs
Delay Time from CA1 active transition to CA2 positive transition		t_{RS2}	–	–	2.0	μs
(Figure 3)						
Delay Time, Enable negative transition to Peripheral Data valid		t_{PDW}	–	–	1.0	μs
(Figures 4, 5)						
Delay Time, Enable negative transition to Peripheral CMOS Data Valid		t_{CMOS}	–	–	2.0	μs
(V_{CC} – 30% V_{CC}, Figure 4; Figure 12 Load C) PA0-PA7, CA2						
Delay Time, Enable positive transition to CB2 negative transition		t_{CB2}	–	–	1.0	μs
(Figure 6, 7)						
Delay Time, Peripheral Data valid to CB2 negative transition		t_{DC}	20	–	–	ns
(Figure 5)						
Delay Time, Enable positive transition to CB2 positive transition		t_{RS1}	–	–	1.0	μs
(Figure 6)						
Rise and Fall Time for CB1 and CB2 input signals (Figure 7)		t_r, t_f	–	–	1.0	μs
Delay Time, CB1 active transition to CB2 positive transition		t_{RS2}	–	–	2.0	μs
(Figure 7)						
Interrupt Release Time, $\overline{IRQA}$ and $\overline{IRQB}$ (Figure 8)		t_{IR}	–	–	1.6	μs
Reset Low Time* (Figure 9)		t_{RL}	2.0	–	–	μs

*The Reset line must be high a minimum of 1.0 μs before addressing the PIA.

 MOTOROLA Semiconductor Products Inc.

MC6820

MAXIMUM RATINGS

Rating	Symbol	Value	Unit
Supply Voltage	V_{CC}	–0.3 to +7.0	Vdc
Input Voltage	V_{in}	–0.3 to +7.0	Vdc
Operating Temperature Range	T_A	0 to +70	°C
Storage Temperature Range	T_{stg}	–55 to +150	°C
Thermal Resistance	θ_{JA}	82.5	°C/W

This device contains circuitry to protect the inputs against damage due to high static voltages or electric fields; however, it is advised that normal precautions be taken to avoid application of any voltage higher than maximum rated voltages to this high impedance circuit.

BUS TIMING CHARACTERISTICS

READ (Figures 10 and 12)

Characteristic	Symbol	Min	Typ	Max	Unit
Enable Cycle Time	t_{cycE}	1.0	–	–	µs
Enable Pulse Width, High	PW_{EH}	0.45	–	25	µs
Enable Pulse Width, Low	PW_{EL}	0.43	–	–	µs
Setup Time, Address and R/W valid to Enable positive transition	t_{AS}	160	–	–	ns
Data Delay Time	t_{DDR}	–	–	320	ns
Data Hold Time	t_H	10	–	–	ns
Address Hold Time	t_{AH}	10	–	–	ns
Rise and Fall Time for Enable input	t_{Er}, t_{Ef}	–	–	25	ns

WRITE (Figures 11 and 12)

Characteristic	Symbol	Min	Typ	Max	Unit
Enable Cycle Time	t_{cycE}	1.0	–	–	µs
Enable Pulse Width, High	PW_{EH}	0.45	–	25	µs
Enable Pulse Width, Low	PW_{EL}	0.43	–	–	µs
Setup Time, Address and R/W valid to Enable positive transition	t_{AS}	160	–	–	ns
Data Setup Time	t_{DSW}	195	–	–	ns
Data Hold Time	t_H	10	–	–	ns
Address Hold Time	t_{AH}	10	–	–	ns
Rise and Fall Time for Enable input	t_{Er}, t_{Ef}	–	–	25	ns

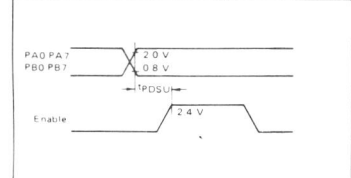

FIGURE 1 – PERIPHERAL DATA SETUP TIME
(Read Mode)

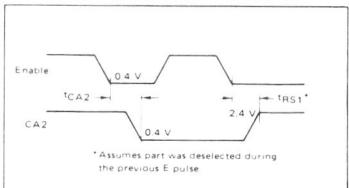

FIGURE 2 – CA2 DELAY TIME
(Read Mode; CRA-5 = CRA-3 = 1, CRA-4 = 0)

*Assumes part was deselected during the previous E pulse.

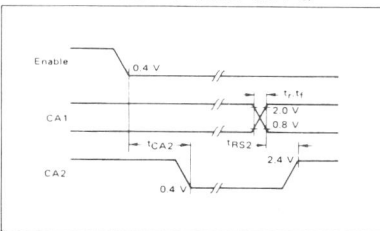

FIGURE 3 – CA2 DELAY TIME
(Read Mode; CRA-5 = 1, CRA-3 = CRA-4 = 0)

MOTOROLA Semiconductor Products Inc.

FIGURE 4 – PERIPHERAL CMOS DATA DELAY TIMES
(Write Mode; CRA-5 = CRA-3 = 1, CRA-4 = 0)

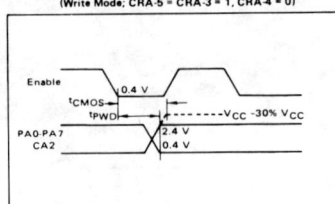

FIGURE 5 – PERIPHERAL DATA AND CB2 DELAY TIMES
(Write Mode; CRB-5 = CRB-3 = 1, CRB-4 = 0)

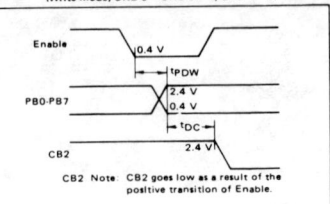

CB2 Note: CB2 goes low as a result of the positive transition of Enable.

FIGURE 6 – CB2 DELAY TIME
(Write Mode; CRB-5 = CRB-3 = 1, CRB-4 = 0)

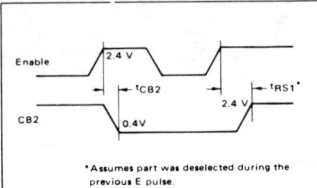

*Assumes part was deselected during the previous E pulse.

FIGURE 7 – CB2 DELAY TIME
(Write Mode; CRB-5 = 1, CRB-3 = CRB-4 = 0)

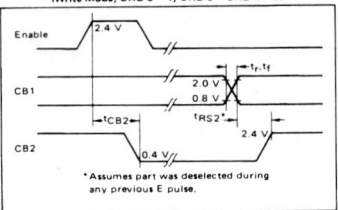

*Assumes part was deselected during any previous E pulse.

FIGURE 8 – IRQ RELEASE TIME

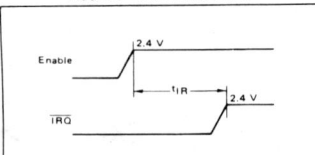

FIGURE 9 – RESET LOW TIME

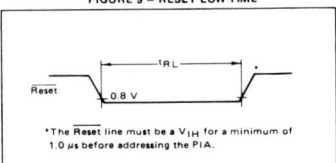

*The Reset line must be a V_{IH} for a minimum of 1.0 µs before addressing the PIA.

FIGURE 10 – BUS READ TIMING CHARACTERISTICS
(Read Information from PIA)

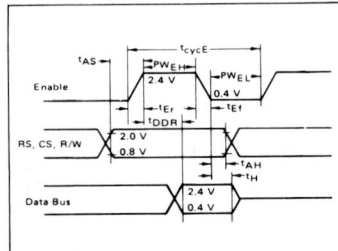

FIGURE 11 – BUS WRITE TIMING CHARACTERISTICS
(Write Information into PIA)

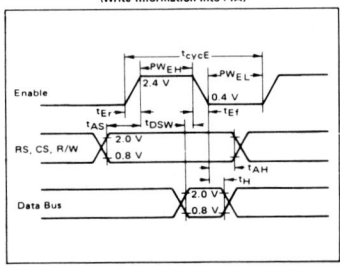

MOTOROLA Semiconductor Products Inc.

MC6820

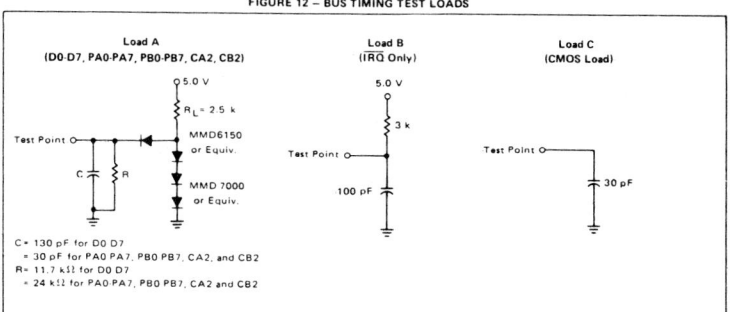

FIGURE 12 – BUS TIMING TEST LOADS

Load A
(D0-D7, PA0-PA7, PB0-PB7, CA2, CB2)

Load B
($\overline{IRQ}$ Only)

Load C
(CMOS Load)

C = 130 pF for D0-D7
= 30 pF for PA0-PA7, PB0-PB7, CA2, and CB2
R = 11.7 kΩ for D0-D7
= 24 kΩ for PA0-PA7, PB0-PB7, CA2 and CB2

PIA INTERFACE SIGNALS FOR MPU

The PIA interfaces to the MC6800 MPU with an eight-bit bi-directional data bus, three chip select lines, two register select lines, two interrupt request lines, read/write line, enable line and reset line. These signals, in conjunction with the MC6800 VMA output, permit the MPU to have complete control over the PIA. VMA should be utilized in conjunction with an MPU address line into a chip select of the PIA.

PIA Bi-Directional Data (D0-D7) – The bi-directional data lines (D0-D7) allow the transfer of data between the MPU and the PIA. The data bus output drivers are three state devices that remain in the high impedance (off) state except when the MPU performs a PIA read operation. The Read/Write line is in the Read (high) state when the PIA is selected for a Read operation.

PIA Enable (E) – The enable pulse, E, is the only timing signal that is supplied to the PIA. Timing of all other signals is referenced to the leading and trailing edges of the E pulse. This signal will normally be a derivative of the MC6800 φ2 Clock.

PIA Read/Write (R/W) – This signal is generated by the MPU to control the direction of data transfers on the Data Bus. A low state on the PIA Read/Write line enables the input buffers and data is transferred from the MPU to the PIA on the E signal if the device has been selected. A high on the Read/Write line sets up the PIA for a transfer of data to the bus. The PIA output buffers are enabled when the proper address and the enable pulse E are present.

$\overline{Reset}$ – The active low $\overline{Reset}$ line is used to reset all register bits in the PIA to a logical zero (low). This line can be used as a power-on reset and as a master reset during system operation.

PIA Chip Select (CS0, CS1 and $\overline{CS2}$) – These three input signals are used to select the PIA. CS0 and CS1 must be high and $\overline{CS2}$ must be low for selection of the device. Data transfers are then performed under the control of the Enable and Read/Write signals. The chip select lines must be stable for the duration of the E pulse. The device is deselected when any of the chip selects are in the inactive state.

PIA Register Select (RS0 and RS1) – The two register select lines are used to select the various registers inside the PIA. These two lines are used in conjunction with internal Control Registers to select a particular register that is to be written or read.

The register and chip select lines should be stable for the duration of the E pulse while in the read or write cycle.

Interrupt Request ($\overline{IRQA}$ and $\overline{IRQB}$) – The active low Interrupt Request lines ($\overline{IRQA}$ and $\overline{IRQB}$) act to interrupt the MPU either directly or through interrupt priority circuitry. These lines are "open drain" (no load device on the chip). This permits all interrupt request lines to be tied together in a wire-OR configuration.

Each Interrupt Request line has two internal interrupt flag bits that can cause the Interrupt Request line to go low. Each flag bit is associated with a particular peripheral interrupt line. Also four interrupt enable bits are provided in the PIA which may be used to inhibit a particular interrupt from a peripheral device.

Servicing an interrupt by the MPU may be accomplished by a software routine that, on a prioritized basis, sequentially reads and tests the two control registers in each PIA for interrupt flag bits that are set.

The interrupt flags are cleared (zeroed) as a result of an

 MOTOROLA Semiconductor Products Inc.

MC6820

EXPANDED BLOCK DIAGRAM

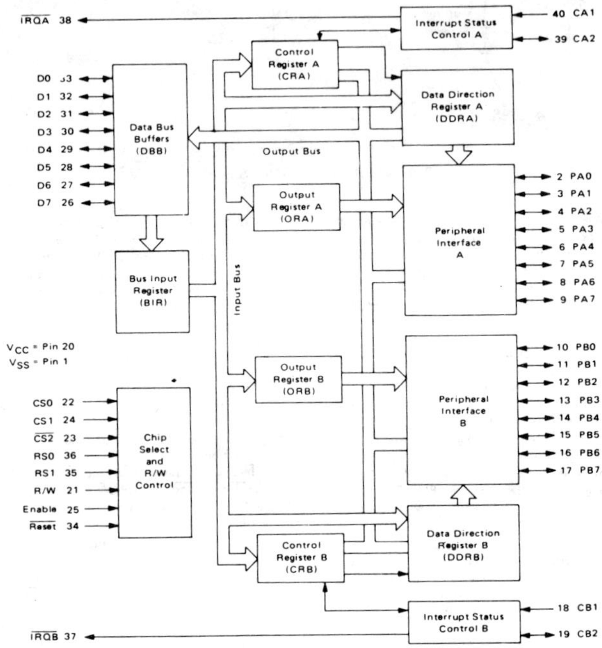

MPU Read Peripheral Data Operation of the corresponding data register. After being cleared, the interrupt flag bit cannot be enabled to be set until the PIA is deselected during an E pulse. The E pulse is used to condition the interrupt control lines (CA1, CA2, CB1, CB2). When these lines are used as interrupt inputs at least one E pulse must occur from the inactive edge to the active edge of the interrupt input signal to condition the edge sense network. If the interrupt flag has been enabled and the edge sense circuit has been properly conditioned, the interrupt flag will be set on the next active transition of the interrupt input pin.

PIA PERIPHERAL INTERFACE LINES

The PIA provides two 8-bit bi-directional data buses and four interrupt control lines for interfacing to peripheral devices.

Section A Peripheral Data (PA0-PA7) — Each of the peripheral data lines can be programmed to act as an input or output. This is accomplished by setting a "1" in the corresponding Data Direction Register bit for those lines which are to be outputs. A "0" in a bit of the Data Direction Register causes the corresponding peripheral data line to act as an input. During an MPU Read Peripheral Data Operation, the data on the peripheral data lines programmed to act as inputs appears directly on the corresponding MPU Data Bus lines. In the input mode the internal pullup resistor on these lines represents a maximum of one standard TTL load.

The data in Output Register A will appear on the data lines that are programmed to be outputs. A logical "1" written into the register will cause a "high" on the corresponding data line while a "0" results in a "low". Data in Output Register A may be read by an MPU "Read Peripheral Data A" operation when the corresponding lines are programmed as outputs. This data will be read properly if the voltage on the peripheral data lines is greater than 2.0 volts for a logic "1" output and less than 0.8 volt for a logic "0" output. Loading the output lines such that the voltage on these lines does not reach full voltage causes the data transferred into the MPU on a Read operation to differ from that contained in the respective bit of Output Register A.

Section B Peripheral Data (PB0-PB7) — The peripheral data lines in the B Section of the PIA can be programmed to act as either inputs or outputs in a similar manner to PA0-PA7. However, the output buffers driving these lines differ from those driving lines PA0-PA7. They have three state capability, allowing them to enter a high impedance state when the peripheral data line is used as an input. In addition, data on the peripheral data lines PB0-PB7 will be read properly from those lines programmed as outputs even if the voltages are below 2.0 volts for a "high". As outputs, these lines are compatible with standard TTL and may also be used as a source of up to 1 milliampere at 1.5 volts to directly drive the base of a transistor switch.

Interrupt Input (CA1 and CB1) — Peripheral Input lines CA1 and CB1 are input only lines that set the interrupt flags of the control registers. The active transition for these signals is also programmed by the two control registers.

Peripheral Control (CA2) — The peripheral control line CA2 can be programmed to act as an interrupt input or as a peripheral control output. As an output, this line is compatible with standard TTL, as an input the internal pullup resistor on this line represents one standard TTL load. The function of this signal line is programmed with Control Register A.

Peripheral Control (CB2) — Peripheral Control line CB2 may also be programmed to act as an interrupt input or peripheral control output. As an input, this line has high input impedance and is compatible with standard TTL. As an output it is compatible with standard TTL and may also be used as a source of up to 1 milliampere at 1.5 volts to directly drive the base of a transistor switch. This line is programmed by Control Register B.

NOTE — It is recommended that the control lines (CA1, CA2, CB1, CB2) should be held in a logic 1 state when Reset is active to prevent setting of corresponding interrupt flags in the control register when Reset goes to an inactive state. Subsequent to Reset going inactive, a read of the data registers may be used to clear any undesired interrupt flags.

 MOTOROLA Semiconductor Products Inc.

MC6820

INTERNAL CONTROLS

There are six locations within the PIA accessible to the MPU data bus: two Peripheral Registers, two Data Direction Registers, and two Control Registers. Selection of these locations is controlled by the RS0 and RS1 inputs together with bit 2 in the Control Register, as shown in Table 1.

TABLE 1 — INTERNAL ADDRESSING

RS1	RS0	Control Register Bit CRA-2	CRB-2	Location Selected
0	0	1	X	Peripheral Register A
0	0	0	X	Data Direction Register A
0	1	X	X	Control Register A
1	0	X	1	Peripheral Register B
1	0	X	0	Data Direction Register B
1	1	X	X	Control Register B

X = Don't Care

INITIALIZATION

A low reset line has the effect of zeroing all PIA registers. This will set PA0-PA7, PB0-PB7, CA2 and CB2 as inputs, and all interrupts disabled. The PIA must be configured during the restart program which follows the reset. Details of possible configurations of the Data Direction and Control Register are as follows.

DATA DIRECTION REGISTERS (DDRA and DDRB)

The two Data Direction Registers allow the MPU to control the direction of data through each corresponding peripheral data line. A Data Direction Register bit set at "0" configures the corresponding peripheral data line as an input; a "1" results in an output.

CONTROL REGISTERS (CRA and CRB)

The two Control Registers (CRA and CRB) allow the MPU to control the operation of the four peripheral control lines CA1, CA2, CB1 and CB2. In addition they allow the MPU to enable the interrupt lines and monitor the status of the interrupt flags. Bits 0 through 5 of the two registers may be written or read by the MPU when the proper chip select and register select signals are applied. Bits 6 and 7 of the two registers are read only and are modified by external interrupts occurring on control lines CA1, CA2, CB1 or CB2. The format of the control words is shown in Table 2.

TABLE 2 — CONTROL WORD FORMAT

CRA	7	6	5 4 3	2	1 0
	IRQA1	IRQA2	CA2 Control	DDRA Access	CA1 Control

CRB	7	6	5 4 3	2	1 0
	IRQB1	IRQB2	CB2 Control	DDRB Access	CB1 Control

Data Direction Access Control Bit (CRA-2 and CRB-2) — Bit 2 in each Control register (CRA and CRB) allows selection of either a Peripheral Interface Register or the Data Direction Register when the proper register select signals are applied to RS0 and RS1.

Interrupt Flags (CRA-6, CRA-7, CRB-6, and CRB-7) — The four interrupt flag bits are set by active transitions of signals on the four Interrupt and Peripheral Control lines when those lines are programmed to be inputs. These bits cannot be set directly from the MPU Data Bus and are reset indirectly by a Read Peripheral Data Operation on the appropriate section.

TABLE 3 — CONTROL OF INTERRUPT INPUTS CA1 AND CB1

CRA-1 (CRB-1)	CRA-0 (CRB-0)	Interrupt Input CA1 (CB1)	Interrupt Flag CRA-7 (CRB-7)	MPU Interrupt Request IRQA (IRQB)
0	0	↓ Active	Set high on ↓ of CA1 (CB1)	Disabled — IRQ remains high
0	1	↓ Active	Set high on ↓ of CA1 (CB1)	Goes low when the interrupt flag bit CRA-7 (CRB-7) goes high
1	0	↑ Active	Set high on ↑ of CA1 (CB1)	Disabled — IRQ remains high
1	1	↑ Active	Set high on ↑ of CA1 (CB1)	Goes low when the interrupt flag bit CRA-7 (CRB-7) goes high

Notes 1 ↑ indicates positive transition (low to high)
        2 ↓ indicates negative transition (high to low)
        3 The Interrupt flag bit CRA-7 is cleared by an MPU Read of the A Data Register and CRB-7 is cleared by an MPU Read of the B Data Register
        4 If CRA-0 (CRB-0) is low when an interrupt occurs (Interrupt disabled) and is later brought high, IRQA (IRQB) occurs after CRA-0 (CRB-0) is written to a "one".

 MOTOROLA Semiconductor Products Inc.

MC6820

Control of CA1 and CB1 Interrupt Input Lines (CRA-0, CRB-0, CRA-1, and CRB-1) — The two lowest order bits of the control registers are used to control the interrupt input lines CA1 and CB1. Bits CRA-0 and CRB-0 are used to enable the MPU interrupt signals $\overline{IRQA}$ and $\overline{IRQB}$, respectively. Bits CRA-1 and CRB-1 determine the active transition of the interrupt input signals CA1 and CB1 (Table 3).

TABLE 4 – CONTROL OF CA2 AND CB2 AS INTERRUPT INPUTS
CRA5 (CRB5) is low

CRA-5 (CRB-5)	CRA-4 (CRB-4)	CRA-3 (CRB-3)	Interrupt Input CA2 (CB2)	Interrupt Flag CRA-6 (CRB-6)	MPU Interrupt Request $\overline{IRQA}$ ($\overline{IRQB}$)
0	0	0	↓ Active	Set high on ↓ of CA2 (CB2)	Disabled — $\overline{IRQ}$ remains high
0	0	1	↓ Active	Set high on ↓ of CA2 (CB2)	Goes low when the interrupt flag bit CRA-6 (CRB-6) goes high
0	1	0	↑ Active	Set high on ↑ of CA2 (CB2)	Disabled — $\overline{IRQ}$ remains high
0	1	1	↑ Active	Set high on ↑ of CA2 (CB2)	Goes low when the interrupt flag bit CRA-6 (CRB-6) goes high

Notes:
1. ↑ indicates positive transition (low to high)
2. ↓ indicates negative transition (high to low)
3. The Interrupt flag bit CRA-6 is cleared by an MPU Read of the A Data Register and CRB-6 is cleared by an MPU Read of the B Data Register.
4. If CRA-3 (CRB-3) is low when an interrupt occurs (Interrupt disabled) and is later brought high, $\overline{IRQA}$ ($\overline{IRQB}$) occurs after CRA-3 (CRB-3) is written to a "one".

TABLE 5 – CONTROL OF CB2 AS AN OUTPUT
CRB-5 is high

CRB-5	CRB-4	CRB-3	CB2	
			Cleared	Set
1	0	0	Low on the positive transition of the first E pulse following an MPU Write "B" Data Register operation.	High when the interrupt flag bit CRB-7 is set by an active transition of the CB1 signal.
1	0	1	Low on the positive transition of the first E pulse after an MPU Write "B" Data Register operation.	High on the positive edge of the first "E" pulse following an "E" pulse which occurred while the part was deselected.
1	1	0	Low when CRB-3 goes low as a result of an MPU Write in Control Register B.	Always low as long as CRB-3 is low. Will go high on an MPU Write in Control Register B that changes CRB-3 to one.
1	1	1	Always high as long as CRB-3 is high. Will be cleared when an MPU Write Control Register B results in clearing CRB-3 to zero.	High when CRB-3 goes high as a result of an MPU Write into Control Register "B".

 MOTOROLA Semiconductor Products Inc.

MC6820

Control of CA2 and CB2 Peripheral Control Lines (CRA-3, CRA-4, CRA-5, CRB-3, CRB-4, and CRB-5) —

Bits 3, 4, and 5 of the two control registers are used to control the CA2 and CB2 Peripheral Control lines. These bits determine if the control lines will be an interrupt input or an output control signal. If bit CRA-5 (CRB-5) is low, CA2 (CB2) is an interrupt input line similar to CA1 (CB1) (Table 4). When CRA-5 (CRB-5) is high, CA2 (CB2) becomes an output signal that may be used to control peripheral data transfers. When in the output mode, CA2 and CB2 have slightly different characteristics (Tables 5 and 6).

TABLE 6 — CONTROL OF CA 2 AS AN OUTPUT
CRA-5 is high

CRA-5	CRA-4	CRA-3	CA2 Cleared	Set
1	0	0	Low on negative transition of E after an MPU Read "A" Data operation.	High when the interrupt flag bit CRA-7 is set by an active transition of the CA1 signal.
1	0	1	Low on negative transition of E after an MPU Read "A" Data operation.	High on the negative edge of the first "E" pulse which occurs during a deselect.
1	1	0	Low when CRA-3 goes low as a result of an MPU Write to Control Register "A".	Always low as long as CRA-3 is low. Will go high on an MPU Write to Control Register "A" that changes CRA-3 to "one".
1	1	1	Always high as long as CRA-3 is high. Will be cleared on an MPU Write to Control Register "A" that clears CRA-3 to a "zero".	High when CRA-3 goes high as a result of an MPU Write to Control Register "A".

PIN ASSIGNMENT

```
 1 [ Vss      CA1 ] 40
 2 [ PA0      CA2 ] 39
 3 [ PA1     IRQA ] 38
 4 [ PA2     IRQB ] 37
 5 [ PA3      RS0 ] 36
 6 [ PA4      RS1 ] 35
 7 [ PA5    Reset ] 34
 8 [ PA6       D0 ] 33
 9 [ PA7       D1 ] 32
10 [ PB0       D2 ] 31
11 [ PB1       D3 ] 30
12 [ PB2       D4 ] 29
13 [ PB3       D5 ] 28
14 [ PB4       D6 ] 27
15 [ PB5       D7 ] 26
16 [ PB6        E ] 25
17 [ PB7      CS1 ] 24
18 [ CB1      CS2 ] 23
19 [ CB2      CS0 ] 22
20 [ Vcc      R/W ] 21
```

PACKAGE DIMENSIONS

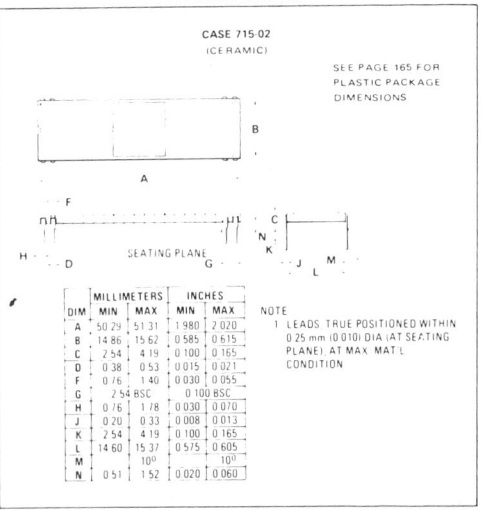

CASE 715-02 (CERAMIC)

SEE PAGE 165 FOR PLASTIC PACKAGE DIMENSIONS

DIM	MILLIMETERS MIN	MILLIMETERS MAX	INCHES MIN	INCHES MAX
A	50.29	51.31	1.980	2.020
B	14.86	15.62	0.585	0.615
C	2.54	4.19	0.100	0.165
D	0.38	0.53	0.015	0.021
F	0.76	1.40	0.030	0.055
G	2.54 BSC		0.100 BSC	
H	0.76	1.78	0.030	0.070
J	0.20	0.33	0.008	0.013
K	2.54	4.19	0.100	0.165
L	14.60	15.37	0.575	0.605
M		10°		10°
N	0.51	1.52	0.020	0.060

NOTE
1. LEADS TRUE POSITIONED WITHIN 0.25 mm (0.010) DIA (AT SEATING PLANE) AT MAX MAT'L CONDITION

 MOTOROLA Semiconductor Products Inc.

MCM6830A

MOS
(N-CHANNEL, SILICON-GATE)

1024 X 8-BIT READ ONLY MEMORY

Advance Information

1024 X 8-BIT READ ONLY MEMORY

The MCM6830A is a mask-programmable byte-organized memory designed for use in bus-organized systems. It is fabricated with N-channel silicon-gate technology. For ease of use, the device operates from a single power supply, has compatibility with TTL and DTL, and needs no clocks or refreshing because of static operation.

The memory is compatible with the M6800 Microcomputer Family, providing read only storage in byte increments. Memory expansion is provided through multiple Chip Select inputs. The active level of the Chip Select inputs and the memory content are defined by the customer.

- Organized as 1024 Bytes of 8 Bits
- Static Operation
- Three-State Data Output
- Four Chip Select Inputs (Programmable)
- Single 5-Volt Power Supply
- TTL Compatible
- Maximum Access Time = 500 ns

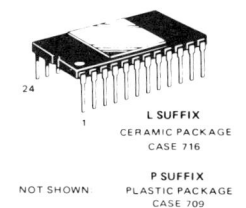

L SUFFIX
CERAMIC PACKAGE
CASE 716

NOT SHOWN

P SUFFIX
PLASTIC PACKAGE
CASE 709

PIN ASSIGNMENT

1	Gnd	A0 24
2	D0	A1 23
3	D1	A2 22
4	D2	A3 21
5	D3	A4 20
6	D4	A5 19
7	D5	A6 18
8	D6	A7 17
9	D7	A8 16
10	CS0	A9 15
11	CS1	CS3 14
12	VCC	CS2 13

ABSOLUTE MAXIMUM RATINGS (See Note 1)

Rating	Symbol	Value	Unit
Supply Voltage	V_{CC}	-0.3 to +7.0	Vdc
Input Voltage	V_{in}	-0.3 to +7.0	Vdc
Operating Temperature Range	T_A	0 to +70	°C
Storage Temperature Range	T_{stg}	-65 to +150	°C

NOTE 1: Permanent device damage may occur if ABSOLUTE MAXIMUM RATINGS are exceeded. Functional operation should be restricted to RECOMMENDED OPERATING CONDITIONS. Exposure to higher than recommended voltages for extended periods of time could affect device reliability.

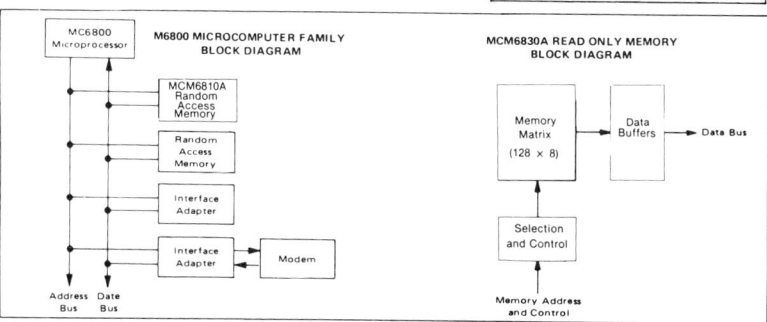

This is advance information and specifications are subject to change without notice.

MCM6830A

DC OPERATING CONDITIONS AND CHARACTERISTICS
(Full operating voltage and temperature range unless otherwise noted.)

RECOMMENDED DC OPERATING CONDITIONS

Parameter	Symbol	Min	Nom	Max	Unit
Supply Voltage	V_{CC}	4.75	5.0	5.25	Vdc
Input High Voltage	V_{IH}	2.0		5.25	Vdc
Input Low Voltage	V_{IL}	-0.3		0.8	Vdc

DC CHARACTERISTICS

Characteristic	Symbol	Min	Typ	Max	Unit
Input Current (V_{in} = 0 to 5.25 V)	I_{in}			2.5	µAdc
Output High Voltage (I_{OH} = -205µA)	V_{OH}	2.4			Vdc
Output Low Voltage (I_{OL} = 1.6 mA)	V_{OL}			0.4	Vdc
Output Leakage Current (Three-State) (CS = 0.8 V or $\overline{CS}$ = 2.0 V, V_{out} = 0.4 V to 2.4 V)	I_{LO}			10	µAdc
Supply Current (V_{CC} = 5.25 V, T_A = 0°C)	I_{CC}			130	mAdc

CAPACITANCE (f = 1.0 MHz, T_A = 25°C, periodically sampled rather than 100% tested.)

Characteristic	Symbol	Max	Unit
Input Capacitance	C_{in}	7.5	pF
Output Capacitance	C_{out}	12.5	pF

This device contains circuitry to protect the inputs against damage due to high static voltages or electric fields; however, it is advised that normal precautions be taken to avoid application of any voltage higher than maximum rated voltages to this high impedance circuit.

BLOCK DIAGRAM

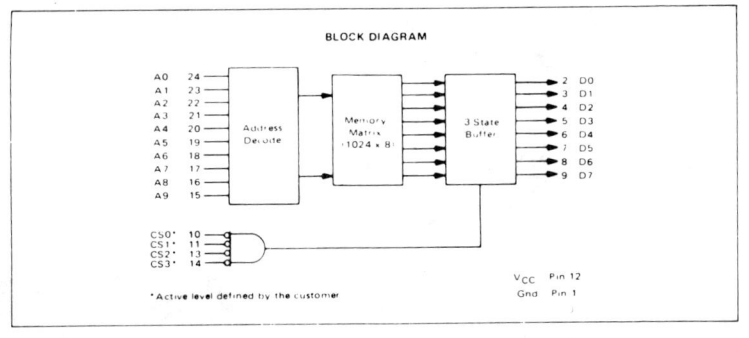

*Active level defined by the customer

V_{CC} Pin 12
Gnd Pin 1

MOTOROLA Semiconductor Products Inc.

MCM6830A

AC OPERATING CONDITIONS AND CHARACTERISTICS
(Full operating voltage and temperature unless otherwise noted.)

(All timing with $t_r = t_f = 20$ ns, Load of Figure 1)

Characteristic	Symbol	Min	Max	Unit
Cycle Time	t_{cyc}	500	–	ns
Access Time	t_{acc}	–	500	ns
Data Delay Time (Read)	t_{DDR}	–	300	ns
Data Hold from Address	t_{DHA}	10	–	ns
Data Hold from Deselection	t_H	10	150	ns

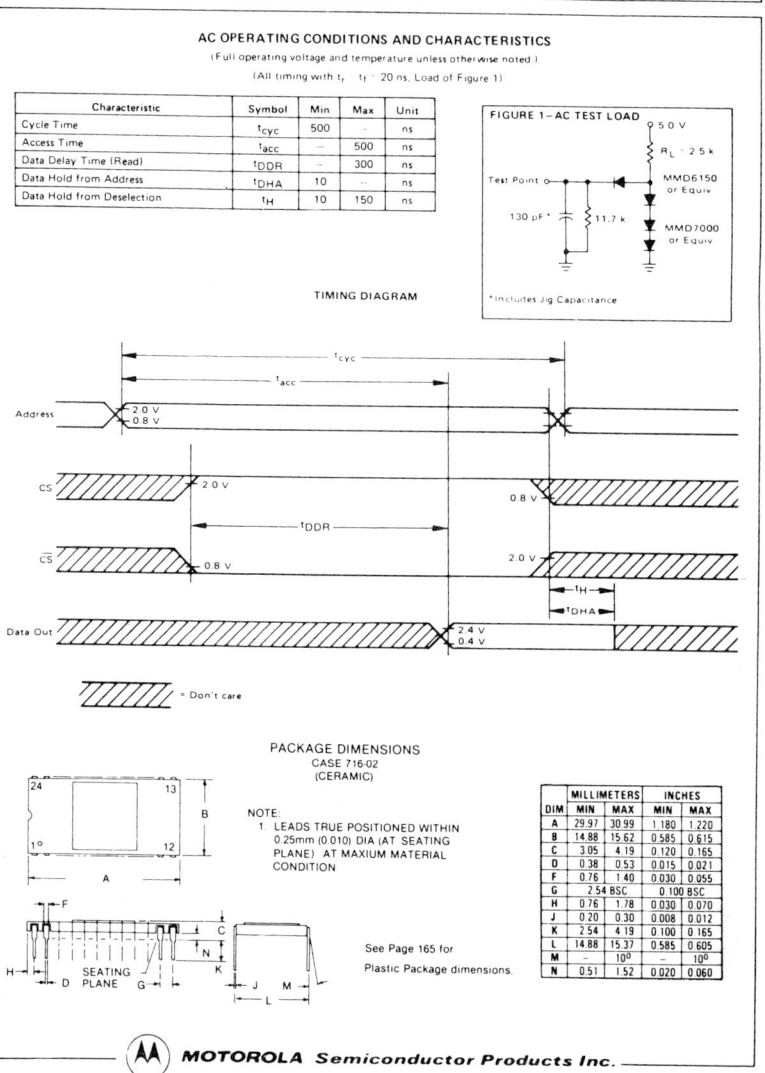

FIGURE 1 – AC TEST LOAD

TIMING DIAGRAM

PACKAGE DIMENSIONS
CASE 716-02
(CERAMIC)

NOTE:
1. LEADS TRUE POSITIONED WITHIN 0.25mm (0.010) DIA (AT SEATING PLANE) AT MAXIUM MATERIAL CONDITION

See Page 165 for Plastic Package dimensions.

DIM	MILLIMETERS		INCHES	
	MIN	MAX	MIN	MAX
A	29.97	30.99	1.180	1.220
B	14.88	15.62	0.585	0.615
C	3.05	4.19	0.120	0.165
D	0.38	0.53	0.015	0.021
F	0.76	1.40	0.030	0.055
G	2.54 BSC		0.100 BSC	
H	0.76	1.78	0.030	0.070
J	0.20	0.30	0.008	0.012
K	2.54	4.19	0.100	0.165
L	14.88	15.37	0.585	0.605
M	–	10°	–	10°
N	0.51	1.52	0.020	0.060

MOTOROLA Semiconductor Products Inc.

MCM6830A

CUSTOM PROGRAMMING

By the programming of a single photomask for the MCM6830A, the customer may specify the content of the memory and the method of enabling the outputs.

Information on the general options of the MCM6830A should be submitted on an Organizational Data form such as that shown in Figure 3.

Information for custom memory content may be sent to Motorola in one of two forms (shown in order of preference):

1. Paper tape output of the Motorola M6800 Software.
2. Hexadecimal coding using IBM Punch Cards.

PAPER TAPE

Included in the software packages developed for the M6800 Micromputer Family is the ability to produce a paper tape output for computerized mask generation. The assembler directives are used to control allocation of memory, to assign values for stored data, and for controlling the assembly process. The paper tape must specify the full 1024 bytes.

Note: Motorola can accept magnetic tape and truth table table formats. For further information, contact your local Motorola sales representative.

FIGURE 2 – BINARY TO HEXADECIMAL CONVERSION

Binary Data				Hexadecimal Character
0	0	0	0	0
0	0	0	1	1
0	0	1	0	2
0	0	1	1	3
0	1	0	0	4
0	1	0	1	5
0	1	1	0	6
0	1	1	1	7
1	0	0	0	8
1	0	0	1	9
1	0	1	0	A
1	0	1	1	B
1	1	0	0	C
1	1	0	1	D
1	1	1	0	E
1	1	1	1	F

IBM PUNCH CARDS

The hexadecimal equivalent (from Figure 2) may be placed on 80 column IBM punch cards as follows

Step	Column	
1	12	Byte "0" Hexadecimal equivalent for outputs D7 thru D4 (D7 = M.S.B.)
2	13	Byte "0" Hexadecimal equivalent for outputs D3 thru D0 (D3 = M.S.B.)
3	14-75	Alternate steps 1 and 2 for consecutive bytes.
4	77-78	Card number (starting 01)
5	79-80	Total number of cards (32)

FIGURE 3 – FORMAT FOR PROGRAMMING GENERAL OPTIONS

ORGANIZATIONAL DATA
MCM6830A MOS READ ONLY MEMORY

Customer:

Company _____

Part No. _____

Originator _____

Phone No. _____

Motorola Use Only

Quote _____

Part No. _____

Specif. No. _____

Enable Options:

	1	0	
CS0	☐	☐	1 is most positive
CS1	☐	☐	0 is most negative
CS2	☐	☐	
CS3	☐	☐	

Ⓜ MOTOROLA *Semiconductor Products Inc.*

MCM68708
MCM68A708

MOS
(N-CHANNEL, SILICON-GATE)

1024 X 8-BIT UV ERASABLE PROM

1024 X 8 ERASABLE PROM

The MCM68708/68A708 is a 8192-bit Erasable and Electrically Reprogrammable PROM designed for system debug usage and similar applications requiring nonvolatile memory that could be reprogrammed periodically. The transparent window on the package allows the memory content to be erased with ultraviolet light. Pin-for-pin mask-programmable ROMs are available for large volume production runs of systems initially using the MCM68708/68A708.

- Organized as 1024 Bytes of 8 Bits
- Fully Static Operation
- Standard Power Supplies of +12 V, +5 V and -5 V
- Maximum Access Time = 300 ns — MCM68A708
  450 ns — MCM68708
- Low Power Dissipation
- Chip-Select Input for Memory Expansion
- TTL Compatible
- Three-State Outputs
- Pin Equivalent to the 2708
- Pin-for-Pin Compatible to MCM65308, MCM68308 or 2308 Mask-Programmable ROMs
- Bus Compatible to the M6800 Family

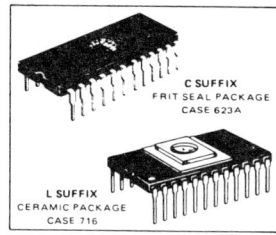

C SUFFIX
FRIT SEAL PACKAGE
CASE 623A

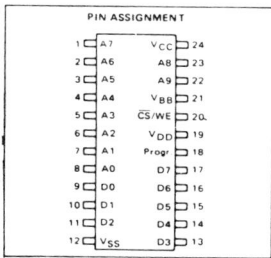

L SUFFIX
CERAMIC PACKAGE
CASE 716

PIN ASSIGNMENT

1	A7	V_{CC}	24
2	A6	A8	23
3	A5	A9	22
4	A4	V_{BB}	21
5	A3	$\overline{CS}/WE$	20
6	A2	V_{DD}	19
7	A1	Progr	18
8	A0	D7	17
9	D0	D6	16
10	D1	D5	15
11	D2	D4	14
12	V_{SS}	D3	13

PIN CONNECTION DURING READ OR PROGRAM

Mode	Pin Number						
	9-11, 13-17	12	18	19	20	21	24
Read	D_{out}	V_{SS}	V_{SS}	V_{DD}	V_{IL}	V_{BB}	V_{CC}
Program	D_{in}	V_{SS}	Pulsed V_{IHP}	V_{DD}	V_{IHW}	V_{BB}	V_{CC}

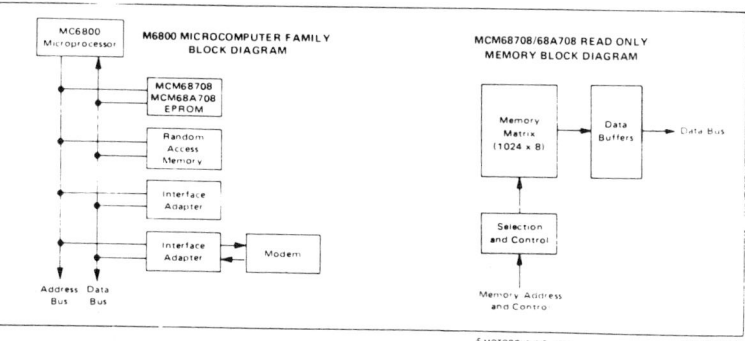

M6800 MICROCOMPUTER FAMILY BLOCK DIAGRAM

MCM68708/68A708 READ ONLY MEMORY BLOCK DIAGRAM

© MOTOROLA INC. 1979   DS 9439 R1

BLOCK DIAGRAM

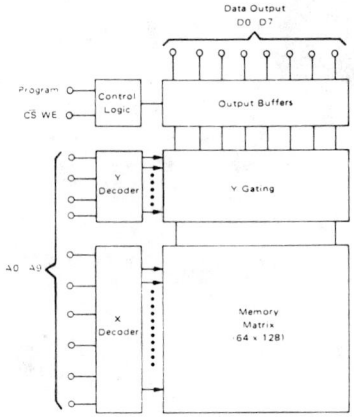

ABSOLUTE MAXIMUM RATINGS[1]

Rating	Value	Unit
Operating Temperature	0 to +70	°C
Storage Temperature	-65 to +125	°C
V_{DD} with Respect to V_{BB}	+20 to -0.3	Vdc
V_{CC} and V_{SS} with Respect to V_{BB}	+15 to -0.3	Vdc
All Input or Output Voltages with Respect to V_{BB} during Read	+15 to -0.3	Vdc
CS/WE Input with Respect to V_{BB} during Programming	+20 to -0.3	Vdc
Program Input with Respect to V_{BB}	+35 to -0.3	Vdc
Power Dissipation	1.8	Watts

Note 1:
Permanent device damage may occur if ABSOLUTE MAXIMUM RATINGS are exceeded. Functional operation should be restricted to RECOMMENDED OPERATING CONDITIONS. Exposure to higher than recommended voltages for extended periods of time could affect device reliability.

DC READ OPERATING CONDITIONS AND CHARACTERISTICS
(Full operating voltage and temperature range unless otherwise noted.)

RECOMMENDED DC READ OPERATING CONDITIONS

Parameter	Symbol	Min	Nom	Max	Unit
Supply Voltage	V_{CC}	4.75	5.0	5.25	Vdc
	V_{DD}	11.4	12	12.6	Vdc
	V_{BB}	-5.25	-5.0	-4.75	Vdc
Input High Voltage	V_{IH}	V_{SS} +2.0	–	V_{CC}	Vdc
Input Low Voltage	V_{IL}	V_{SS} -0.3	–	V_{SS} +0.8	Vdc

READ OPERATION DC CHARACTERISTICS

Characteristic	Condition	Symbol	Min	Typ	Max	Unit
Address and CS Input Sink Current	V_{in} = 5.25 V or V_{in} = V_{IL}	I_{in}	–	1	10	μA
Output Leakage Current	V_{out} = 5.25 V, CS/WE = 5 V	I_{LO}	–	1	10	μA
V_{DD} Supply Current	Worst Case Supply Currents	I_{DD}	–	50	65	mA
V_{CC} Supply Current	(Note 2) All Inputs High	I_{CC}	–	6	10	mA
V_{BB} Supply Current	CS/WE = 5.0 V, T_A = 0°C	I_{BB}	–	30	45	mA
Output Low Voltage	I_{OL} = 1.6 mA	V_{OL}	–	–	V_{SS} +0.4	V
Output High Voltage	I_{OH} = -100 μA	V_{OH}	V_{SS} +2.4	–	–	V
Power Dissipation	(Note 2) T_A = 70°C	P_D	–	–	800	mW

Note 2
The total power dissipation is specified at 800 mW. It is not calculable by summing the various currents (I_{DD}, I_{CC}, and I_{BB}) multiplied by their respective voltages, since current paths exist between the various power supplies and V_{SS}. The I_{DD}, I_{CC}, and I_{BB} currents should be used to determine power supply capacity only.

V_{BB} must be applied prior to V_{CC} and V_{DD}. V_{BB} must also be the last power supply switched off.

 MOTOROLA Semiconductor Products Inc.

AC READ OPERATING CONDITIONS AND CHARACTERISTICS
(Full operating voltage and temperature range unless otherwise noted.)
(All timing with $t_r = t_f = 20$ ns, Load per Note 3)

Characteristic	Symbol	MCM68A708 Min	MCM68A708 Typ	MCM68A708 Max	MCM68708 Min	MCM68708 Typ	MCM68708 Max	Unit
Address to Output Delay	t_{AO}	–	220	300	–	280	450	ns
Chip Select to Output Delay	t_{CO}	–	60	120	–	60	120	ns
Data Hold from Address	t_{DHA}	10	–	–	10	–	–	ns
Data Hold from Deselection	t_{DHD}	10	–	120	10	–	120	ns

CAPACITANCE (periodically sampled rather than 100% tested.)

Characteristic	Condition	Symbol	Typ	Max	Unit
Input Capacitance (f = 1.0 MHz)	$V_{in} = 0$ V, $T_A = 25°C$	C_{in}	4.0	6.0	pF
Output Capacitance (f = 1.0 MHz)	$V_{out} = 0$ V, $T_A = 25°C$	C_{out}	8.0	12	pF

Note 3:
Output Load = 1 TTL Gate and C_L = 100 pF (Includes Jig Capacitance)
Timing Measurement Reference Levels Inputs: 0.8 V and 2.8 V
Outputs: 0.8 V and 2.4 V

AC TEST LOAD

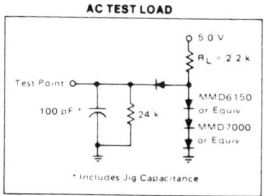

READ OPERATION TIMING DIAGRAM

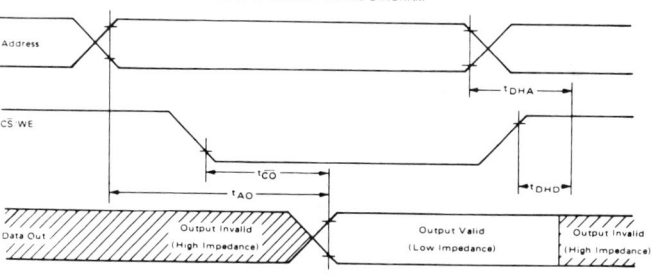

 MOTOROLA Semiconductor Products Inc.

DC PROGRAMMING CONDITIONS AND CHARACTERISTICS
(Full operating voltage and temperature range unless otherwise noted.)

RECOMMENDED PROGRAMMING OPERATING CONDITIONS

Parameter	Symbol	Min	Nom	Max	Unit
Supply Voltage	V_{CC}	4.75	5.0	5.25	Vdc
	V_{DD}	11.4	12	12.6	Vdc
	V_{BB}	-5.25	-5.0	-4.75	Vdc
Input High Voltage for All Addresses and Data	V_{IH}	3.0	—	V_{CC} + 1.0	Vdc
Input Low Voltage (except Program)	V_{IL}	V_{SS}	—	0.65	Vdc
CS/WE Input High Voltage (Note 4)	V_{IHW}	11.4	12	12.6	Vdc
Program Pulse Input High Voltage (Note 4)	V_{IHP}	25	—	27	Vdc
Program Pulse Input Low Voltage (Note 5)	V_{ILP}	V_{SS}	—	1.0	Vdc

Note 4: Referenced to V_{SS}.
Note 5: $V_{IHP} - V_{ILP} = 25$ V min.

PROGRAMMING OPERATION DC CHARACTERISTICS

Characteristic	Condition	Symbol	Min	Typ	Max	Unit
Address and CS/WE Input Sink Current	$V_{in} = 5.25$ V	I_{LI}	—	—	10	µAdc
Program Pulse Source Current		I_{IPL}	—	—	3.0	mAdc
Program Pulse Sink Current		I_{IPH}	—	—	20	mAdc
V_{DD} Supply Current	Worst-Case Supply Currents	I_{DD}	—	50	65	mAdc
V_{CC} Supply Current	All Inputs High	I_{CC}	—	6	10	mAdc
V_{BB} Supply current	CS/WE = 5 V, T_A = 0°C	I_{BB}	—	30	45	mAdc

AC PROGRAMMING OPERATING CONDITIONS AND CHARACTERISTICS
(Full operating voltage and temperature unless otherwise noted.)

Characteristic	Symbol	Min	Max	Unit
Address Setup Time	t_{AS}	10	—	µs
CS/WE Setup Time	t_{CSS}	10	—	µs
Data Setup Time	t_{DS}	10	—	µs
Address Hold Time	t_{AH}	1.0	—	µs
CS/WE Hold Time	t_{CH}	0.5	—	µs
Data Hold Time	t_{DH}	1.0	—	µs
Chip Deselect to Output Float Delay	t_{DF}	0	120	ns
Program to Read Delay	t_{DPR}	—	10	µs
Program Pulse Width	t_{PW}	0.1	1.0	ms
Program Pulse Rise Time	t_{PR}	0.5	2.0	µs
Program Pulse Fall Time	t_{PF}	0.5	2.0	µs

 MOTOROLA *Semiconductor Products Inc.*

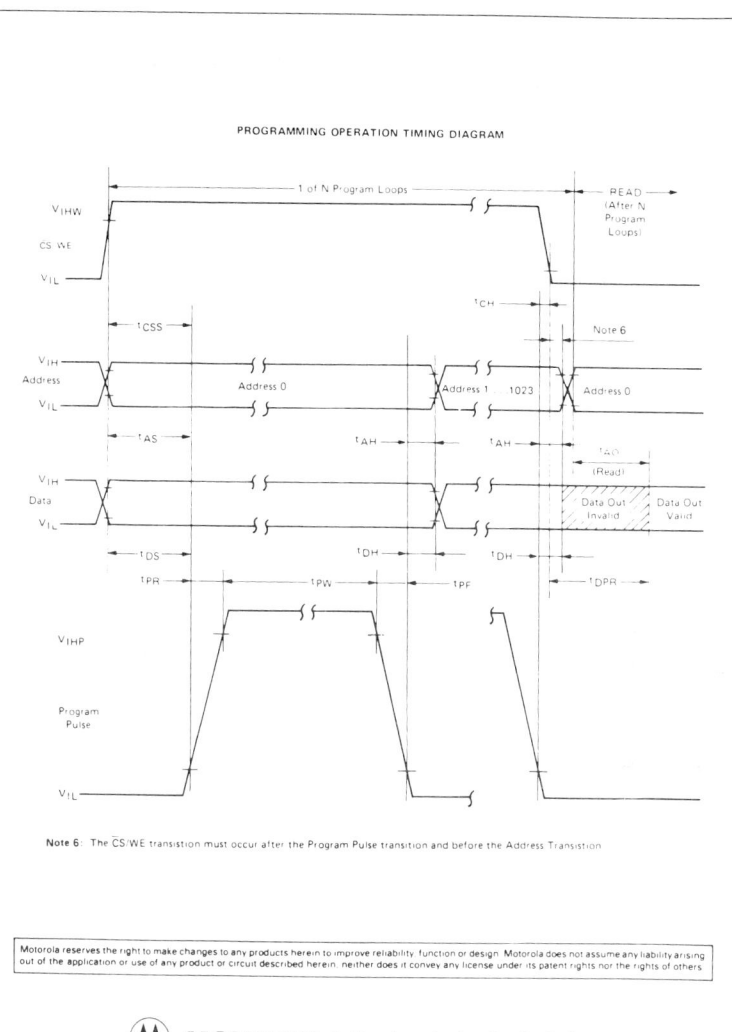

Note 6: The CS/WE transistion must occur after the Program Pulse transition and before the Address Transistion.

Motorola reserves the right to make changes to any products herein to improve reliability, function or design. Motorola does not assume any liability arising out of the application or use of any product or circuit described herein; neither does it convey any license under its patent rights nor the rights of others.

MOTOROLA Semiconductor Products Inc.

PROGRAMMING INSTRUCTIONS

After the completion of an ERASE operation, every bit in the device is in the "1" state (represented by Output High). Data are entered by programming zeros (Output Low) into the required bits. The words are addressed the same way as in the READ operation. A programmed "0" can only be changed to a "1" by ultra-violet light erasure.

To set the memory up for programming mode, the $\overline{CS}/WE$ input (Pin 20) should be raised to +12 V. Programming data is entered in 8-bit words through the data output terminals (D0 to D7).

Logic levels for the data lines and addresses and the supply voltages (V_{CC}, V_{DD}, V_{BB}) are the same as for the READ operation.

After address and data setup one program pulse per address is applied to the program input (Pin 18). A program loop is a full pass through all addresses. Total programming time, $T_{Ptotal} = N \times t_{PW} \geq 100$ ms. The required number of program loops (N) is a function of the program pulse width (t_{PW}), where: 0.1 ms $\leq t_{PW} \leq 1.0$ ms; correspondingly N is: $100 \leq N \leq 1000$. There must be N successive loops through all 1024 addresses. It is not permitted to apply more than one program pulse in succession to the same address (i.e., N program pulses to an address and then change to the next address to be programmed). At the end of a program sequence the $\overline{CS}/WE$ falling edge transition must occur before the first address transition, when changing from a PROGRAM to a READ cycle. The program pin (Pin 18) should be pulled down to V_{ILP} with an active device, because this pin sources a small amount of current (I_{IPL}) when $\overline{CS}/WE$ is at V_{IHW} (12 V) and the program pulse is at V_{ILP}.

EXAMPLES FOR PROGRAMMING

Always use the $T_{Ptotal} = N \times t_{PW} \geq 100$ ms relationship.

1. All 8092 bits should be programmed with a 0.2 ms program pulse width.

   The minimum number of program loops:

   $$N = \frac{T_{Ptotal}}{t_{PW}} = \frac{100 \text{ ms}}{0.2 \text{ ms}} = 500 \text{ . One program loop}$$

   consists of words 0 to 1023.

2. Words 0 to 200 and 300 to 700 are to be programmed. All other bits are "don't care". The program pulse width is 0.5 ms. The minimum number of program loops, $N = \frac{100}{0.5} = 200$. One program loop consists of words 0 to 1023. The data entered into the "don't care" bits should be all 1s.

3. Same requirements as example 2, but the EPROM is now to be updated to include data for words 850 to 880. The minimum number of program loops is the same as in the previous example, N = 200. One program loop consists of words 0 to 1023. The data entered into the "don't care" bits should be all 1s. Addresses 0 to 200 and 300 to 700 must be reprogrammed with their original data pattern.

ERASING INSTRUCTIONS

The MCM68708/68A708 can be erased by exposure to high intensity shortwave ultraviolet light, with a wavelength of 2537 Å. The recommended integrated dose (i.e., UV-intensity x exposure time) is 12.5 Ws/cm^2. As an example, using the "Model 30-000" UV-Eraser (Turner Designs, Mountain View, CA 94043) the ERASE-time is 30 minutes. The lamps should be used without shortwave filters and the MCM68708/68A708 should be positioned about one inch away from the UV-tubes.

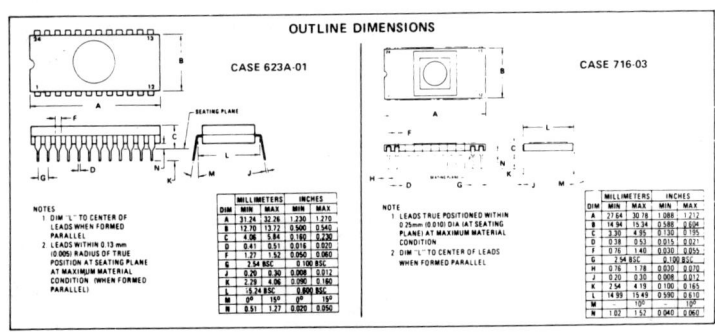

OUTLINE DIMENSIONS

CASE 623A-01

CASE 716-03

MOTOROLA Semiconductor Products Inc.

3501 ED BLUESTEIN BLVD., AUSTIN, TEXAS 78721 • A SUBSIDIARY OF MOTOROLA INC

1024-BIT STATIC MOS RAM (256X4)

2112/2112-1/2112-2

2112-F,N • 2112-1-F,N • 2112-2-F,N

DESCRIPTION

The 2112 series is high performance, low power static read/write RAMs.

The 2112 series is fabricated with n-channel silicon gate technology which allows the design of high performance easy to use MOS circuits and provides a high functional density on a given monolithic chip.

FEATURES

- Fully static
- No refresh operations, sense amps or clocks required
- Directly TTL compatible
- One 5V power supply

PIN CONFIGURATION

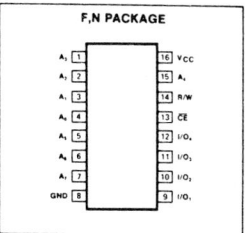

BLOCK DIAGRAM

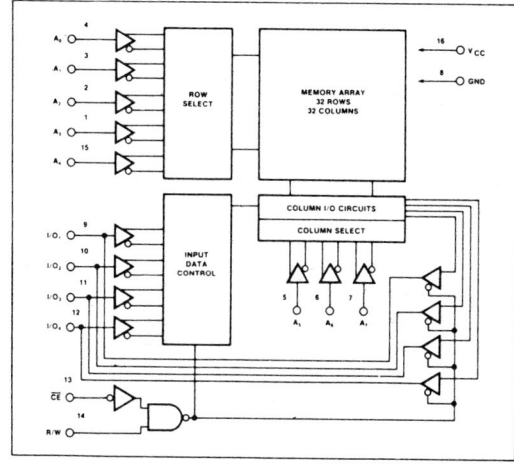

ABSOLUTE MAXIMUM RATINGS[1]

PARAMETER		RATING	UNIT
T_A	Temperature range Operating under bias	0 to 70	°C
T_{STG}	Storage	-65 to 150	
	Voltage on any pin with respect to ground	-0.5 to 7	V
P_D	Power dissipation	1	W

1024-BIT STATIC MOS RAM (256X4)   2112/2112-1/2112-2

2112-F,N • 2112-1-F,N • 2112-2-F,N

DC ELECTRICAL CHARACTERISTICS $T_A = 0°C$ to $70°C$, $V_{CC} = 5V \pm 5\%$ unless otherwise specified.

PARAMETER		TEST CONDITIONS	Min	Typ[2]	Max	UNIT
V_{IL}	Input voltage Low		-0.5		0.65	V
V_{IH}	High		2.2		V_{CC}	
V_{OL}	Output voltage Low	$I_{OL} = 2mA$			0.45	V
V_{OH}	High	$I_{OH} = -150\mu A$	2.2			
I_{LI}	Input current	$V_{IN} = 0$ to $5.25V$			10	μA
	I/O leakage current	$\overline{CE} = 2.2V$				μA
I_{LOH}		$V_{I/O} = 4.0V$			15	
I_{LOL}		$V_{I/O} = 0.45V$			-50	
	Supply current	$V_{IN} = 5.25V$, $I_{I/O} = 0mA$				mA
I_{CC1}		$T_A = 25°C$		30	60	
I_{CC2}		$T_A = 0°C$			70	
	Capacitance[3]	$T_A = 25°C$, $f = 1MHz$				pF
C_{IN}	Input (All pins)	$V_{IN} = 0V$		4	8	
$C_{I/O}$	I/O	$V_{I/O} = 0V$		10	15	

AC ELECTRICAL CHARACTERISTICS $T_A = 0°C$ to $70°C$, $V_{CC} = 5V \pm 5\%$ unless otherwise specified, t_R and $t_F = 20ns$, $V_{IN} = 0.65V$ to $2.2V$, Timing reference = $1.5V$, Load = 1 TTL gate and $C_L = 100pF$

	PARAMETER	TO	FROM	2112 Min	2112 Typ	2112 Max	2112-1 Min	2112-1 Typ	2112-1 Max	2112-2 Min	2112-2 Typ	2112-2 Max	UNIT
	READ CYCLE												
t_{RC}	Read cycle			1000			500			650			ns
t_A	Access time					1000			500			650	ns
t_{CO}		Output	Chip enable			800			150			500	ns
t_{CD}		Output disable	Chip enable	0		200	0		100	0		150	ns
t_{OH}	Previous read data valid after change of address			40			40			40			ns
	WRITE CYCLE #1												
t_{WC1}	Write cycle			850			500			500			ns
	Setup and hold time												ns
t_{AW1}	Setup time	Write	Address	150			100			100			
t_{DW1}	Setup time	R/W high	Data	650			250			280			
t_{CS1}	Setup time	$\overline{CE}$ low	R/W low	0			0			0			
t_{CH1}	Hold time	$\overline{CE}$ high	R/W high	0			0			0			
t_{DH1}	Hold time	Data	R/W high	100			50			50			
t_{CW1}	Setup time	R/W high	$\overline{CE}$ low	650			250			350			
t_{WP1}	Write pulse width			650			250			350			ns
t_{WR1}	Write recovery time			50			50			50			ns
	WRITE CYCLE #2												
t_{WC2}	Write cycle			1050			500			650			ns
	Setup and hold time												ns
t_{AW2}	Setup time	Write	Address	150			100			100			
t_{DW2}	Setup time	R/W high	Data	650			250			280			
t_{CS2}	Setup time	$\overline{CE}$ low	R/W low	0			0			0			
t_{CH2}	Hold time	$\overline{CE}$ high	R/W high	0			0			0			
t_{DH2}	Hold time	Data	R/W high	100			50			50			
t_{WD2}	Disable time	R/W high	Data	200			200			200			ns
t_{WR2}	Write recovery time			50			50			50			ns

NOTES on following page.

1024-BIT STATIC MOS RAM (256X4)   2112/2112-1/2112-2

2112-F,N • 2112-1-F,N • 2112-2-F,N

NOTES

1. Stresses above those listed under Absolute Maximum Ratings may cause permanent damage to the device. This is a stress rating only and functional operation of the device at these or at any other condition above those indicated in the operational sections of this specification is not implied. Exposure to absolute maximum rating conditions for extended periods may affect device reliability.
2. Typical values are for $T_A = 25°C$ and typical supply voltage.
3. This parameter is periodically sampled and is not 100% tested.

4. Output is enabled and t_{CO} commences only with both CE low and WE high.
5. Output is disabled and t_{DF} combined from either the rising edge of CE or the falling edge of WE.
6. Minimum t_{WP} is valid when CE has been high at least t_{DF} before WE goes low. Otherwise $t_{WP(min)} = t_{DW(min)} + t_{DF(max)}$.
7. When WE goes high at the end of the write cycle, it will be possible to turn on the output buffers if CE is still low. The data out will be the same as the data just written and so will not conflict with input data that may still be on the I/O bus.

VOLTAGE WAVEFORMS

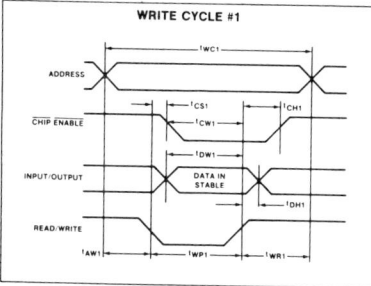

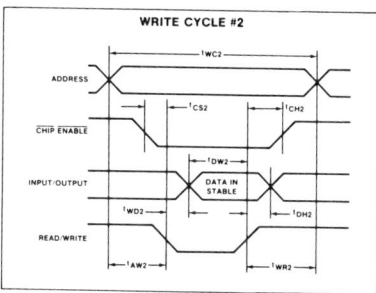

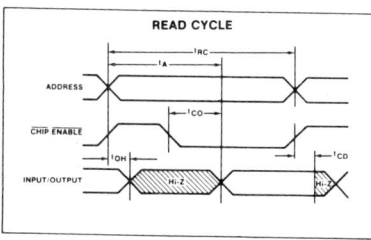

385

8-BIT MULTIPLYING D/A CONVERTER — MC1508-8/1408-8/1408-7

MC1508-8/MC1408-8/MC1408-7 -F,N

DC ELECTRICAL CHARACTERISTICS[1] $V_{CC} = +5.0Vdc$, $V_{EE} = -15Vdc$, $\frac{V_{ref}}{R_{14}} = 2.0mA$ unless otherwise specified.
MC1508: $T_A = -55°C$ to $125°C$. MC1408: $T_A = 0°C$ to $70°C$

PARAMETER		TEST CONDITIONS	MC1508-8			MC1408-8			MC1408-7			UNIT
			Min	Typ	Max	Min	Typ	Max	Min	Typ	Max	
E_r	Relative accuracy	Error relative to full scale I_O, Figure 3			±0.19			±0.19			±0.39	%
t_s	Setting time[1]	To within 1/2 LSB, includes t'PLH. T'A = +25°C. Figure 4		300			300			300		ns
t_{PLH} t_{PHL}	Propagation delay time Low-to-high High-to-low	$T_A = +25°C$. Figure 4		30	100		30	100		30	100	ns
TCI_O	Output full scale current drift			-20			-20			-20		PPM/°C
V_{IH} V_{IL}	Digital input logic level (MSB) High Low	Figure 5	2.0		0.8	2.0		0.8	2.0		0.8	Vdc
I_{IH} I_{IL}	Digital input current (MSB) High Low	Figure 5 $V_{IH} = 5.0V$ $V_{IL} = 0.8V$		0 -0.4	0.04 -0.8		0 -0.4	0.04 -0.8		0 -0.4	0.04 -0.8	mA
I_{15}	Reference input bias current	Pin 15, Figure 5		-1.0	-3.0		-1.0	-3.0		-1.0	-3.0	µA
I_{OR}	Output current range	Figure 5 $V_{EE} = -5.0V$ $V_{EE} = -6.0V$ to -15V	0 0	2.0 2.0	2.1 4.2	0 0	2.0 2.0	2.1 4.2	0 0	2.0 2.0	2.1 4.2	mA
I_O	Output current	Figure 5 $V_{ref} = 2.000V$. $R14 = 1000Ω$	1.9	1.99	2.1	1.9	1.99	2.1	1.9	1.99	2.1	mA
$I_{O(min)}$	Off-state	All bits low		0	4.0		0	4.0		0	4.0	µA
V_O	Output voltage compliance	$E_r \leq 0.19\%$ at $T_A = +25°C$. Figure 5 $V_{EE} = -5V$ V_{EE} below -10V			-0.6, +0.5 -5.0, +0.5			-0.6, +0.5 -5.0, +0.5			-0.6, +0.5 -5.0, +0.5	Vdc
SRI_{ref}	Reference current slew rate	Figure 6		4.0			4.0			4.0		mA/µs
$PSRR_{(-)}$	Output current power supply sensitivity	$I_{ref} = 1mA$		0.5	2.7		0.5	2.7		0.5	2.7	µA/V
I_{CC} I_{EE}	Power supply current Positive Negative	All bits low. Figure 5		+13.5 -7.5	+22 -13		+13.5 -7.5	+22 -13		+13.5 -7.5	+22 -13	mA
V_{CCR} V_{EER}	Power supply voltage range Positive Negative	$T_A = +25°C$. Figure 5	+4.5 -4.5	+5.0 -15	+5.5 -16.5	+4.5 -4.5	+5.0 -15	+5.5 -16.5	+4.5 -4.5	+5.0 -15	+5.5 -16.5	Vdc
P_D	Power dissipation	All bits low, Figure 5 $V_{EE} = -5.0Vdc$ $V_{EE} = -15Vdc$		105 190	170 305		105 190	170 305		105 190	170 305	mW
		All bits high, Figure 5 $V_{EE} = -5.0Vdc$ $V_{EE} = -15Vdc$		90 160			90 160			90 160		

NOTES

1. All bits switched

signetics

8-BIT MULTIPLYING D/A CONVERTER

MC1508-8/1408-8/1408-7

MC1508-8/MC1408-8/MC1408-7 -F,N

DESCRIPTION
The MC1508/MC1408 series of 8-bit monolithic digital-to-analog converters provide high speed performance with low cost. They are designed for use where the output current is a linear product of an 8-bit digital word and an analog reference voltage.

FEATURES
* Fast settling time—300ns (typ)
* Relative accuracy ±0.19% (max error)
* Non-inverting digital inputs are TTL and CMOS compatible
* High speed multiplying rate 4.0mA/μs (input slew)
* Output voltage swing +.5V to -5.0V
* Standard supply voltages + 5.0V and -5.0V to -15V
* Military qualifications pending

APPLICATIONS
* Tracking A-to-D converters
* 2½-digit panel meters and DVM's
* Waveform synthesis
* Sample and hold
* Peak detector
* Programmable gain and attenuation
* CRT character generation
* Audio digitizing and decoding
* Programmable power supplies
* Analog-digital multiplication
* Digital-digital multiplication
* Analog-digital division
* Digital addition and subtraction
* Speech compression and expansion
* Stepping motor drive

CIRCUIT DESCRIPTION
The MC1508/MC1408 consists of a reference current amplifier, and R-2R ladder, and 8 high speed current switches. For many applications, only a reference resistor and reference voltage need be added.

The switches are non-inverting in operation; therefore, a high state on the input turns on the specified output current component.

The switch uses current steering for high speed, and a termination amplifier consisting of an active load gain stage with unity gain feedback. The termination amplifier holds the parasitic capacitance of the ladder at a constant voltage during switching, and provides a low impedance termination of equal voltage for all legs of the ladder.

The R-2R ladder divides the reference amplifier current into binarily-related components, which are fed to the switches. Note that there is always a remainder current which is equal to the least significant bit. This current is shunted to ground, and the maximum output current is 255/256 of the reference amplifier current, or 1.992mA for a 2.0mA reference amplifier current if the NPN current source pair is perfectly matched.

PIN CONFIGURATION

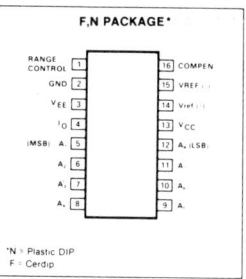

*N = Plastic DIP
F = Cerdip

BLOCK DIAGRAM

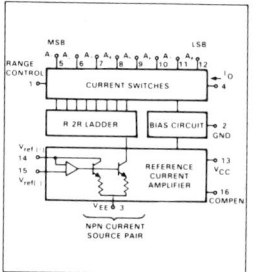

TYPICAL PERFORMANCE CHARACTERISTICS

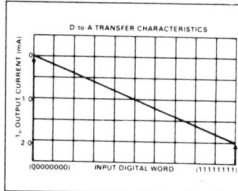

ABSOLUTE MAXIMUM RATNGS T_A = +25°C unless otherwise specified

PARAMETER		RATING	UNIT
V_{CC}	Power supply voltage		V
V_{EE}	Positive	+5.5	
V_5-V_{12}	Negative	-16.5	
V_O	Digital input voltage	+5.5, 0	V
I_{14}	Applied output voltage	+0.5, -5.2	V
V_{14},V_{15}	Reference current	5 0	mA
	Reference amplifier inputs	V_{CC}, V_{EE}	V
P_D	Power dissipation (package limitation)		mW
	Ceramic package	1000	
	Plastic package	800	
T_A	Operating temperature range		°C
	MC1508	-55 to +125	
	MC1408	0 to +75	
T_{stg}	Storage temperature range	-65 to +70	°C

8-BIT MULTIPLYING D/A CONVERTER   MC1508-8/1408-8/1408-7

Output Voltage Range

The voltage on pin 4 is restricted to a range of -0.6 to +0.5V at -24°C, due to the current switching methods employed in the MC1508/MC1408. When a current switch is turned off, the positive voltage on the output terminal can turn on the output diode and increase the output current level. When a current switch is turned on, the negative output voltage range is restricted. The base of the termination circuit Darlington transistor is 1 diode voltage below ground when pin 1 is grounded, so a negative voltage below ground when pin 1 is grounded, so a negative voltage below the specified safe level will drive the low current device of the Darlington into saturation, decreasing the output current level.

The negative output voltage compliance of the MC1508/MC1408 may be extended to -5.0V by opening the circuit at pin 1. The negative supply voltage must be more negative than -10V. Using a full scale current of 1.992mA and load resistor of 2.5kΩ between pin 4 and ground will yield a voltage output of 256 levels between 0 and -4.980V. Floating pin 1 does not affect the converter speed or power dissipation. However, the value of the load resistor determines the switching time due to increased voltage swing. Values of R_L up to 500Ω do not significantly affect performance, but 2.5kΩ load increases worst case settling time to 1.2μs (when all bits are switched on). Refer to the subsequent text section on settling time for more details on output loading.

If a power supply value between -5.0V and -10V is desired, a voltage of between 0 and -5.0V may be applied to pin 1. The value of this voltage will be the maximum allowable negative output swing.

Output Current Range

The output current maximum rating of 4.2mA may be used only for negative supply voltages more negative than -7.0V, due to the increased voltage drop across the 350Ω resistors in the reference current amplifier.

Accuracy

Absolute accuracy is the measure of each output current level with respect to its intended value, and is dependent upon relative accuracy and full scale current drift. Relative accuracy is the measure of each output current level as a fraction of the full scale current. The relative accuracy of the MC1508/MC1408 is essentially constant with temperature due to the excellent temperature tracking of the monolithic resistor ladder. The reference current may drift with temperature, causing a change in the absolute accuracy of output current. However, the MC1508/MC1408 has a very low full scale current drift with temperature.

The MC1508/±MC1408 series is guaranteed accurate to within ±1/2 LSB at +25°C at a full scale output current of 1.992mA. This corresponds to a reference amplifier output current drive to the ladder network of 2.0mA, with the loss of 1 LSB = 8.0μA which is the ladder remainder shunted to ground. The input current to pin 14 has a guaranteed value of between 1.9 and 2.1mA, allowing some mismatch in the NPN current source pair. The accuracy test circuit is shown in Figure 3. The 12-bit converter is calibrated for a full scale output current of 1.992mA. This is an optional step since the MC1508/MC1408 accuracy is essentially the same between 1.5 and 2.5mA. Then the MC1508/MC1408 circuits' full scale current is trimmed to the same value with R14 so that a zero value appears at the error amplifier output. The counter is activated and the error band may be displayed on an oscilloscope, detected by comparators, or stored in a peak detector.

Two 8-bit D-to-A converters may not be used to construct a 16-bit accurate D-to-A converter. Sixteen-bit accuracy implies a total error ±1/2 of 1 part in 65,536, or ±0.00076%, which is much more accurate than the ±0.19% specification provided by the MC1508/MC1408.

Multiplying Accuracy

The MC1508/MC1408 may be used in the multiplying mode with 8-bit accuracy when the reference current is varied over a range of 256:1. The major source of error is the bias current of the termination amplifier. Under worst case conditions, these 8 amplifiers can contribute a total of 1.6μA extra current at the output terminal. If the reference current in the multiplying mode ranges from 16μA to 4.0mA, the 1.6μA contributes an error of 0.1 LSB. This is well within 8-bit accuracy.

A monotonic converter is one which supplies an increase in current for each increment in the binary word. Typically, the MC1508/MC1408 in monotonic for all values of reference current above 0.5mA. The recommended range for operation with a dc reference current is 0.5 to 4.0mA.

Settling Time

The worst case switching condition occurs when all bits are switched on, which corresponds to a low-to-high transition for all bits. This time is typically 300ns for settling to within ±1/2 LSB for 8-bit accuracy and 200ns to 1/2 LSB for 7-bit accuracy. The turnoff is typically under 100ns. These times apply when $R_L \leq 500Ω$ and C_O 25pF.

The slowest single switch is the least significant bit, which turns on and settles in 250ns and truns off in 80ns. In applications where the D-to-A converter functions in a positive going ramp mode, the worst case switching condition does not occur, and a settling time of less than 300ns may be realized. Bit A7 turns on in 200ns and off in 80ns, while bit A6 turns on in 150ns and off in 80ns.

The test circuit of Figure 4 requires a smaller voltage swing for the current switches due to internal voltage clamping in MC1508/MC1408. A 1.0kΩ load resistor from pin 4 to ground gives a typical settling time of 400ns. Thus, it is voltage swing and not the output R_C time constant that determines settling time for most applications.

Extra care must be taken in board layout since this is usually the dominant factor in satisfactory test results when measuring settling time. Short leads, 100μF supply bypassing for low frequencies, and minimum scope lead length are all mandatory.

8-BIT MULTIPLYING D/A CONVERTER

EQUIVALENT CIRCUIT SCHEMATIC

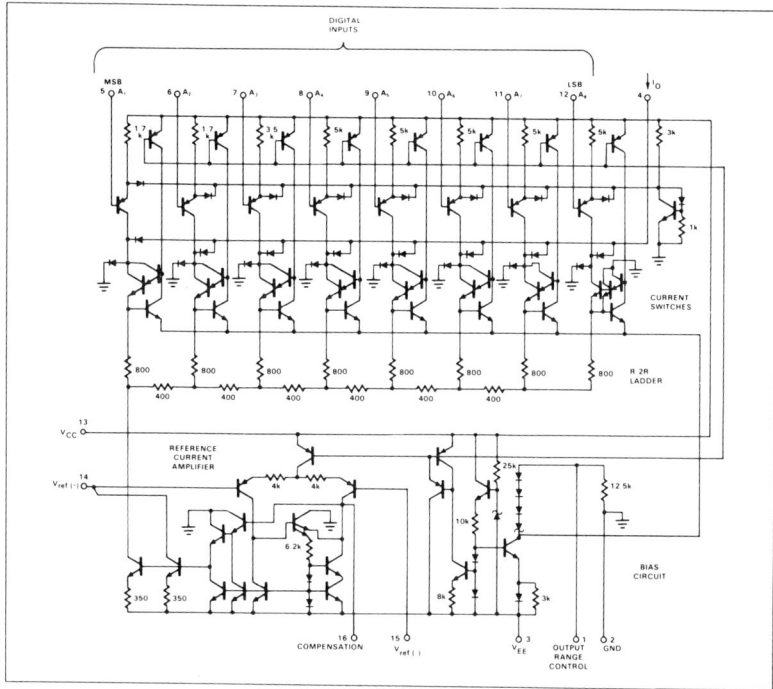

FUNCTIONAL DESCRIPTION

Reference Amplifier Drive and Compensation

The reference amplifier provides a voltage at pin 14 for converting the reference voltage to a current, and a turn-around circuit or current mirror for feeding the ladder. The reference amplifier input current (I_{14}) must always flow into pin 14 regardless of the setup method or reference voltage polarity.

Connections for a positive reference voltage are shown in Figure 1. The reference voltage source supplies the full current I_{14}. For bipolar reference signals, as in the multiplying mode, R_{15} can be tied to a negative voltage corresponding to the minimum input level. It is possible to eliminate R_{15} with only a small sacrifice in accuracy and temperature drift.

The compensation capacitor value must be increased with increases in R_{14} to maintain proper phase margin; for R_{14} values of 1.0, 2.5 and 5.0kΩ, minimum capacitor values are 15, 37, and 75pF. The capacitor may be tied to either V_{EE} or ground, but using V_{EE} increases negative supply rejection.

A negative reference voltage may be used if R_{14} is grounded and the reference voltage is applied to R_{15} as shown in Figure 2. A high input impedance is the main advantage of this method. Compensation involves a capacitor to V_{EE} on pin 16, using the values of the previous paragraph. The negative reference voltage must be at least 3.0V above the V_{EE} supply. Bipolar input signals may be handled by connecting R_{14} to a positive reference voltage equal to the peak positive input level at pin 15.

When a dc reference voltage is used, capacitive bypass to ground is recommended. The 5.0V logic supply is not recommended as a reference voltage. If a well regulated 5.0V supply which drives logic is to be used as the reference, R_{14} should be decoupled by connecting it to +5.0V through another resistor and bypassing the junction of the 2 resistors with 0.1μF to ground. For reference voltages greater than 5.0V, a clamp diode is recommended between pin 14 and ground.

If pin 14 is driven by a high inpedance such as a transistor current source, none of the above compensation methods apply and

389

8-BIT MULTIPLYING D/A CONVERTER

MC1508-8/MC1408-8/MC1408-7

TEST CIRCUITS (Cont'd)

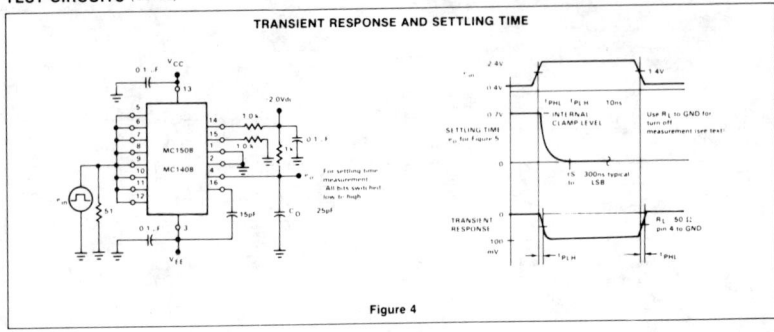

Figure 4 — Transient Response and Settling Time

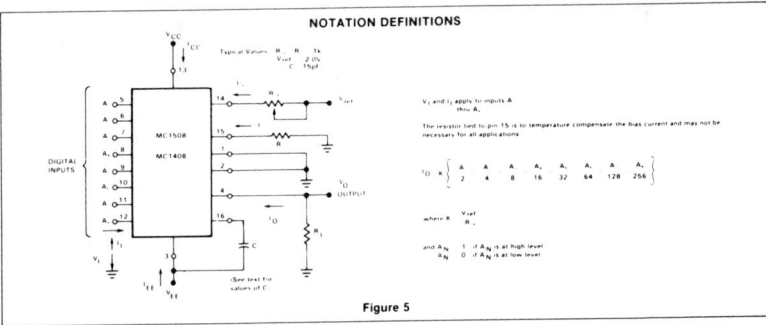

Figure 5 — Notation Definitions

$$I_O = K \left\{ \frac{A_1}{2} + \frac{A_2}{4} + \frac{A_3}{8} + \frac{A_4}{16} + \frac{A_5}{32} + \frac{A_6}{64} + \frac{A_7}{128} + \frac{A_8}{256} \right\}$$

where $K = \dfrac{V_{ref}}{R}$

and $A_N = 1$ if A_N is at high level
$A_N = 0$ if A_N is at low level

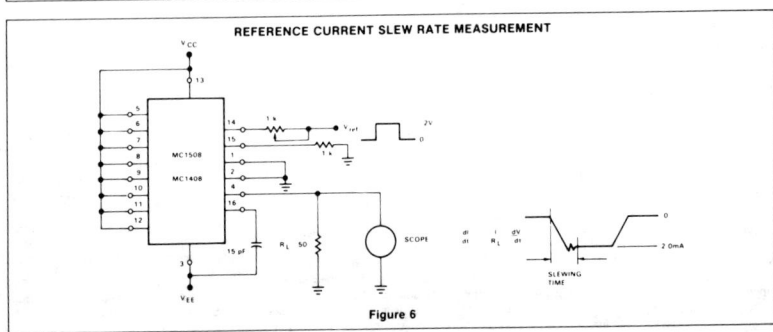

Figure 6 — Reference Current Slew Rate Measurement

8-BIT MULTIPLYING D/A CONVERTER

MC1508-8/1408-8/1408-7

MC1508-8/MC1408-8/MC1408-7 -F,N

TEST CIRCUITS

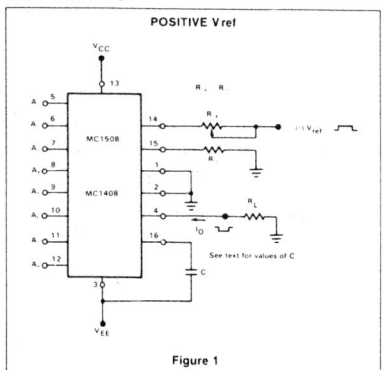

Figure 1 — POSITIVE Vref

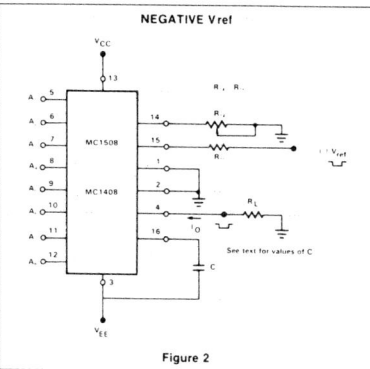

Figure 2 — NEGATIVE Vref

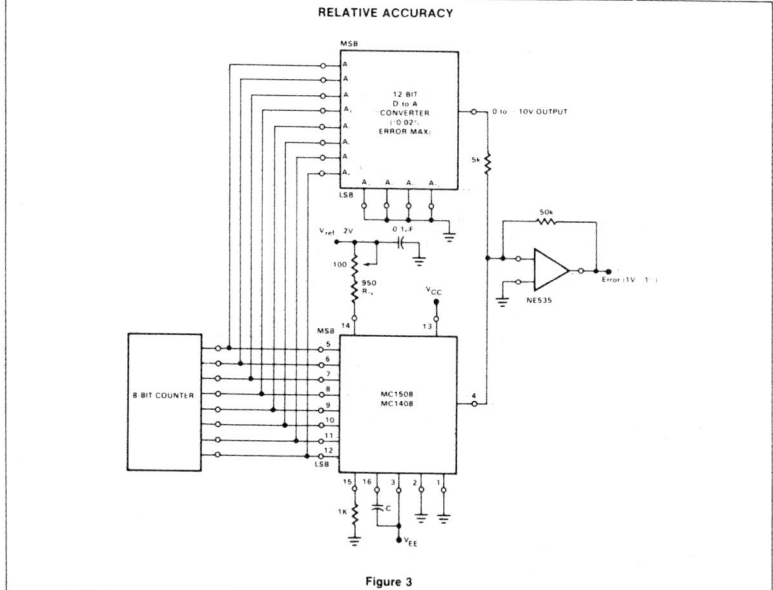

Figure 3 — RELATIVE ACCURACY

Signetics

8-BIT µP-COMPATIBLE D/A CONVERTER

NE5018

NE5018-F,N

PRELIMINARY SPECIFICATION

DESCRIPTION

The NE5018 is a complete 8-bit digital to analog converter subsystem on one monolithic chip. The data inputs have input latches, controlled by a latch enable pin. The data and latch enable inputs are ultra-low loading for easy interfacing with all logic systems. The latches appear transparent when the $\overline{LE}$ input is in the low state. When $\overline{LE}$ goes high, the input data present at the moment of transition is latched and retained until $\overline{LE}$ again goes low. This feature allows easy compatibility with most microprocessors.

The chip also comprises a stable voltage reference (5V nominal) and a high slew rate buffer amplifier. The voltage reference may be externally trimmed with a potentiometer for easy adjustment of full scale, while maintaining a low temperature co-efficient.

The output of the buffer amplifier may be offset so as to provide bipolar as well as unipolar operation.

FEATURES
- 8-bit resolution
- Input latches
- Low-loading data inputs
- On-chip voltage reference
- Output buffer amplifier
- Accurate to ± 1/2 LSB
- Monotonic to 8 bits
- Amplifier and reference both short-circuit protected
- Compatible with 2650, 8080 and many other µP's.

APPLICATIONS
- Precision 8-bit D/A converters
- A/D converters
- Programmable power supplies
- Test equipment
- Measuring instruments
- Analog-digital multiplication

PIN CONFIGURATION

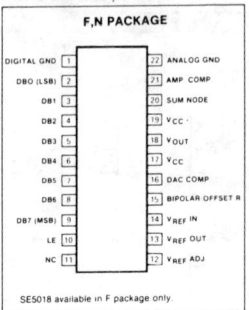

SE5018 available in F package only.

ABSOLUTE MAXIMUM RATINGS

PARAMETER		RATING	UNIT
$V_{CC}+$	Positive supply voltage	18	V
$V_{CC}-$	Negative supply voltage	-18	V
V_{IN}	Logic input voltage	0 to 18	V
$V_{REF}IN$	Voltage at V_{REF} input	12	V
$V_{REF}ADJ$	Voltage at V_{REF} adjust	0 to V_{REF}	V
V_{SUM}	Voltage at sum node	12	V
I_{REFSC}	Short-circuit current to ground at V_{REF} OUT	Continuous	
I_{OUTSC}	Short-circuit current to ground or either supply at V_{OUT}	Continuous	
I_{REF}	Reference input current	5	mA
P_D	Power dissipation*		
	-N package	800	mW
	-F package	1000	mW
T_A	Operating temperature range		
	SE5018	-55 to +125	°C
	NE5018	0 to +70	°C
T_{STG}	Storage temperature range	-65 to +150	°C
T_{SOLD}	Lead soldering temperature (10 seconds)	300	°C

*NOTE
For N package, derate at 120°C/W above 35°C
For F package, derate at 75°C/W above 75°C

8-BIT μP-COMPATIBLE D/A CONVERTER   NE5018

PRELIMINARY SPECIFICATION

NE5018-F,N

DC ELECTRICAL CHARACTERISTICS $V_{CC}+ = 15V$, $V_{CC}- = -15V$, SE5018, $-55°C \leq T_A \leq 125°C$, NE5018, $0°C \leq T_A \leq 70°C$ unless otherwise specified.

PARAMETER		TEST CONDITIONS	SE5018			NE5018			UNITS
			Min	Typ	Max	Min	Typ	Max	
$V_{CC}+$	Positive supply voltage			15			15		V
$V_{CC}-$	Negative supply voltage			-15			-15		V
	Resolution			8			8		bits
	Relative accuracy				±0.19			±0.19	%
T_S	Settling time	To ± 1/2LSB, 10V step		2			2		μs
PSRR	Power supply	$V_{CC}+$ +12 to +18V		±1			±1		mV/V
	Rejection ratio	$V_{CC}-$ -12 to -18V							
$I_{CC}+$	Positive supply current	$V_{CC}+ = 15V$		8			8		mA
$I_{CC}-$	Negative supply current	$V_{CC}- = -15V$		-10			-10		mA
$I_{IN}(0)$	Logic "0" input current	$V_{IN} = 0V$		5			5		μA
$V_{IN}(0)$	Logic "0" input voltage				0.8			0.8	V
$V_{IN}(1)$	Logic "1" input voltage		2.0			2.0			V
T_{PWLE}	Latch enable pulse width			400			400		ns

BLOCK DIAGRAM

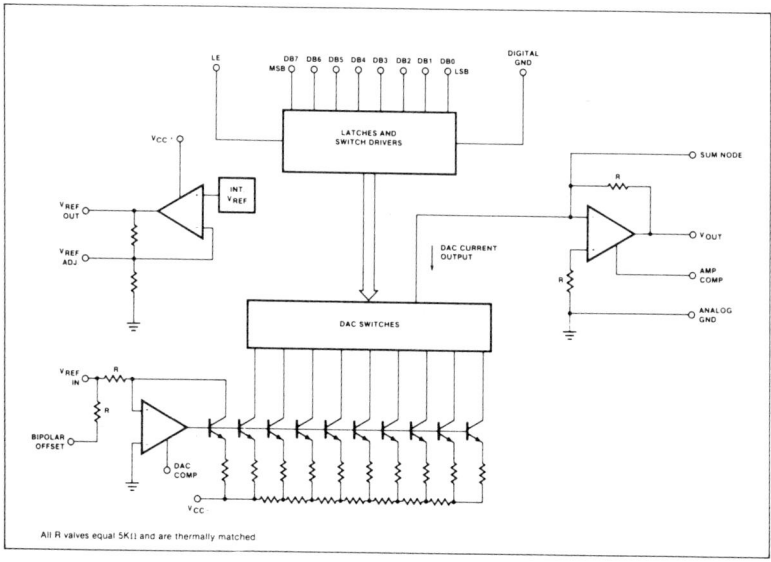

All R values equal 5KΩ and are thermally matched.

8-BIT μP-COMPATIBLE D/A CONVERTER

NE5018

NE5018-F,N

PRELIMINARY SPECIFICATION

EQUIVALENT SCHEMATIC

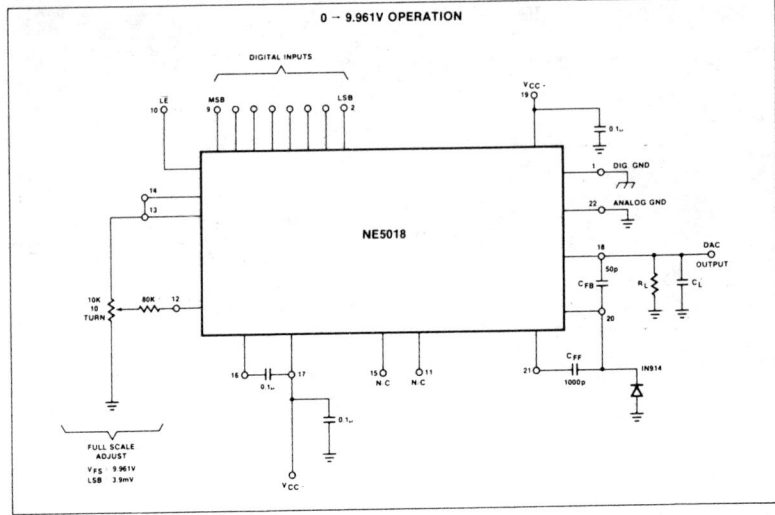

ICL7109 12 Bit Binary A/D Converter for Microprocessor Interfaces

FEATURES
- 12 bit binary (plus polarity and overrange) dual slope integrating analog-to-digital converter.
- Byte-organized TTL-compatible three-state outputs and UART handshake mode for simple parallel or serial interfacing to microprocessor systems.
- RUN/HOLD input and STATUS output can be used to monitor and control conversion timing.
- True differential input and differential reference.
- Low noise-typically 15μV peak-to-peak.
- 1pA typical input current.
- Operates at up to 30 conversions per second.
- On-chip oscillator operates with inexpensive 3.58MHz TV crystal giving 7.5 conversions per second for 60Hz rejection, or may be operated as an RC oscillator for other clock frequencies.
- Fabricated using MAX-CMOS™ technology combining analog and digital functions on a single low power LSI CMOS chip.
- All inputs fully protected against static discharge; no special handling precautions necessary.

GENERAL DESCRIPTION

The ICL7109 is a high performance, low power integrating A/D converter designed to easily interface to microprocessors.

The output data (12 bits, polarity and overrange) may be directly accessed under control of two byte enable inputs and a chip select input for a simple parallel bus interface. A UART handshake mode is provided which allows the ICL7109 to work with industry-standard UARTs to provide serial data transmission, ideal for remote data logging applications. The RUN/HOLD input and STATUS output allow monitoring and control of conversion timing.

The ICL7109 provides the user the high accuracy, low noise, low drift, versatility and economy of the dual-slope integrating A/D converter. Features like true differential input and reference, zero drift of less than 1μV/°C max., input bias current of 10pA max., and typical power consumption of 20mW make the ICL7109 an attractive per-channel alternative to analog multiplexing for many data acquisition applications.

PIN CONFIGURATION AND TEST CIRCUIT:
(See Figure 1 for typical connection to a UART or Microcomputer)

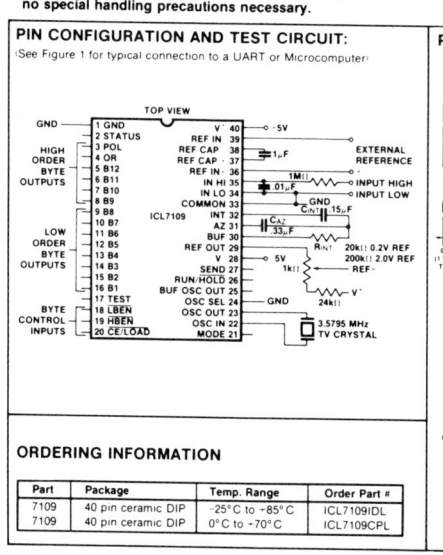

PACKAGE DIMENSIONS

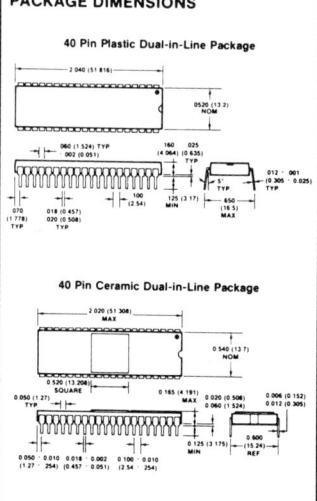

40 Pin Plastic Dual-in-Line Package

40 Pin Ceramic Dual-in-Line Package

ORDERING INFORMATION

Part	Package	Temp. Range	Order Part #
7109	40 pin ceramic DIP	−25°C to +85°C	ICL7109IDL
7109	40 pin ceramic DIP	0°C to +70°C	ICL7109CPL

INTERSIL, INC., 10710 N. TANTAU AVE., CUPERTINO, CA 95014   (408) 996-5000 TWX: 910-338-0171
Printed in U S A

ICL7109
ABSOLUTE MAXIMUM RATINGS

Positive Supply Voltage (GND to V⁺)	+6.2V
Negative Supply Voltage (GND to V⁻)	-9V
Analog Input Voltage (Lo or Hi) (Note 1)	V⁺ to V⁻
Reference Input Voltage (Lo or Hi) (Note 1)	V⁺ to V⁻
Digital Input Voltage (Pins 2-27) (Note 2)	V⁺ + 0.3V GND - 0.3V
Power Dissipation (Note 3)	
Ceramic or Cerdip Package	1W @ 85°C
Plastic Package	500mW @ 70°C
Operating Temperature	
Ceramic or Cerdip Package	$-25°C \leq T_A \leq 85°C$
Plastic Package	$0°C \leq T_A \leq 70°C$
Storage Temperature	$-55°C \leq T_A \leq 125°C$
Lead Temperature (soldering, 60 sec)	300°C

Absolute maximum ratings define stress limitations which if exceeded may permanently damage the device. These ratings are not continuous duty ratings. For continuous operation these devices must be operated under the conditions defined under "Operating Characteristics."

TABLE I OPERATING CHARACTERISTICS
All parameters with V⁺ = +5V, V⁻ = -5V GND = 0V, T_A = 25°C, unless otherwise indicated. Test circuit as shown on page 1.

ANALOG SECTION

PARAMETER	SYMBOL	CONDITIONS	MIN	TYP	MAX	UNITS
Zero Input Reading		V_{IN} = 0.0V Full scale = 409.6mV	-0000_8	$\pm 0000_8$	$+0000_8$	Octal Reading
Ratiometric Reading		$V_{IN} = V_{REF}$ V_{REF} = 204.8mV	3777_8	3777_8 4000_8	4000_8	Octal Reading
Non-Linearity (Max deviation from best straight line fit)		Full scale = 409.6mV or 4.096V	-1	$\pm .2$	+1	Counts
Roll-over Error (difference in reading for equal pos. and neg. inputs near full scale.			-1	$\pm .2$	+1	Counts
Common Mode Rejection Ratio		$V_{CM} \pm 1V$ V_{IN} = 0V Full Scale = 409.6mV		50		$\mu V/V$
Noise (p-p value not exceeded 95% of time)		V_{IN} = 0V Full Scale = 409.6mV		15		μV
Leakage Current at Input		V_{IN} = 0V		1	10	pA
Zero Reading Drift		V_{IN} = 0V		0.2	1	$\mu V/°C$
Scale Factor Temperature Coefficient		V_{IN} = 408.9mV => 7770_8 reading Ext. Ref. 0 ppm/°C		1	5	ppm/°C
Supply Current V⁺ to GND	I_{DL}	V_{IN} = 0, Crystal Osc. 3.58MHz test circuit Pins 2-21, 25, 26, 27, 29, open		700	1500	μA
Supply Current V⁺ to V⁻	I_{DA}			700	1500	μA
Ref Out Voltage		Referred to V⁺, 25kΩ between V⁺ and REF OUT	-2.4	-2.8	-3.2	V
Ref Out Temp. Coefficient		25kΩ between V⁺ and REF OUT		80		ppm/°C

ICL7109

DIGITAL SECTION

PARAMETER		SYMBOL	CONDITIONS	MIN	TYP	MAX	UNITS
Output High Voltage		V_{OH}	$I_{OUT} = 100\mu A$ Pins 2-16, 18, 19, 20	3.5	4.3		V
Output Low Voltage		V_{OL}	$I_{OUT} = 1.6mA$		0.2	0.4	V
Output Leakage Current			Pins 3-16 high impedance		±.01	±1	μA
Control I/O Pullup Current			Pins 18, 19, 20 $V_{OUT} = V^+ -3V$ MODE input at GND		5		μA
Control I/O Loading			$\overline{HBEN}$ Pin 19 $\overline{LBEN}$ Pin 18			50	pF
Input High Voltage		V_{IH}	Pins 18-21, 26, 27 referred to GND	2.5			V
Input Low Voltage		V_{IL}	Pins 18-21, 26, 27 referred to GND			1	V
Input Pull-up Current			Pins 26, 27 $V_{OUT} = V^+ -3V$		5		μA
Input Pull-up Current			Pins 17, 24 $V_{OUT} = V^+ -3V$		25		μA
Input Pull-down Current			Pin 21 $V_{OUT} = GND +3V$		5		μA
Oscillator Output Current	High	O_{OH}	$V_{OUT} = 2.5V$		1		mA
	Low	O_{OL}	$V_{OUT} = 2.5V$		1.5		mA
Buffered Oscillator Output Current	High	BO_{OH}	$V_{OUT} = 2.5V$		2		mA
	Low	BO_{OL}	$V_{OUT} = 2.5V$		5		mA
MODE Input Pulse Width				50			ns

Note 1: Input voltages may exceed the supply voltages provided the input current is limited to ±100μA.
Note 2: Due to the SCR structure inherent in the process used to fabricate these devices, connecting any digital inputs or outputs to voltages greater than V^+ or less than GND may cause destructive device latchup. For this reason it is recommended that no inputs from sources not on the same power supply be applied to the ICL7109 before its power supply is established, and that in multiple supply systems the supply to the ICL7109 be activated first.
Note 3: This limit refers to that of the package and will not be obtained during normal operation.

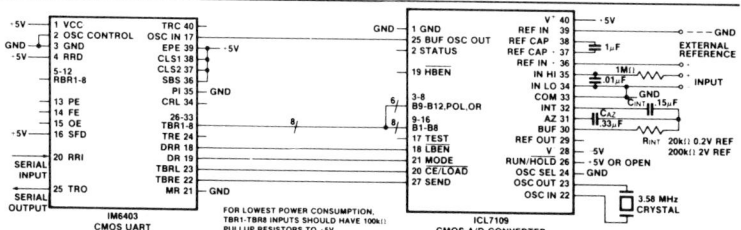

Figure 1A. Typical Connection Diagram UART Interface - Transmits Every Conversion

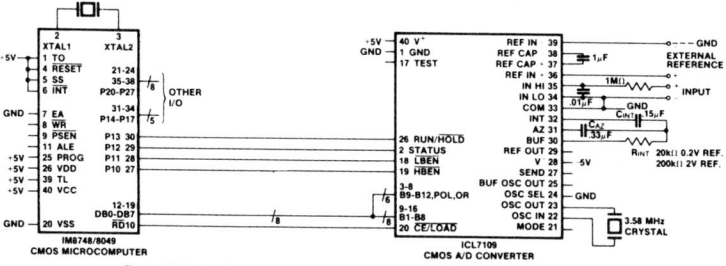

Figure 1B. Typical Connection Diagram Parallel Interface With 8748/8048 Microcomputer

ICL7109

TABLE 2 - Pin Assignment and Function Description

PIN	SYMBOL	DESCRIPTION
1	GND	Digital Ground. 0V. Ground return for all digital logic.
2	STATUS	Output - High during integrate and deintegrate until data is latched. - Low when analog section is in Auto-Zero configuration.
3	POL	Polarity. Three-State Output
4	OR	Over-range. Three-State Output
5	B12	Bit 12 (Most Significant Bit)
6	B11	Bit 11
7	B10	Bit 10
8	B9	Bit 9
9	B8	Bit 8
10	B7	Bit 7
11	B6	Bit 6 — Data Bits, Three-State Output
12	B5	Bit 5
13	B4	Bit 4
14	B3	Bit 3
15	B2	Bit 2
16	B1	Bit 1 (Least Significant Bit)
17	TEST	Input High - Normal Operation. Input Low - Forces all bit outputs high. Note: This input is used for test purposes only.
18	LBEN	Low Byte Enable - With Mode (Pin 21) low, and CE/LOAD (Pin 20) low, taking this pin low activates low order byte outputs B1-B8. - With Mode (Pin 21) high, this pin serves as a low byte flag output used in handshake mode. See Figures 7, 8, 9.
19	HBEN	High Byte Enable - With Mode (Pin 21) low, and CE/LOAD (Pin 20) low, taking this pin low activates high order byte outputs B9-B12, POL, OR. - With Mode (Pin 21) high, this pin serves as a high byte flag output used in handshake mode. See Figures 7, 8, 9.
20	CE/LOAD	Chip Enable Load - With Mode (Pin 21) low, CE/LOAD serves as a master output enable. When high, B1-B12, POL, OR outputs are disabled. - With Mode (Pin 21) high, this pin serves as a load strobe used in handshake mode. See Figures 7, 8, 9.

PIN	SYMBOL	DESCRIPTION
21	MODE	Input Low - Direct output mode where CE/LOAD (Pin 20), HBEN (Pin 19) and LBEN (Pin 18) act as inputs directly controlling byte outputs. Input Pulsed High - Causes immediate entry into handshake mode and output of data as in Figure 9. Input High - Enables CE/LOAD (Pin 20), HBEN (Pin 19), and LBEN (Pin 18) as outputs, handshake mode will be entered and data output as in Figures 7 and 8 at conversion completion.
22	OSC IN	Oscillator Input
23	OSC OUT	Oscillator Output
24	OSC SEL	Oscillator Select - Input high configures OSC IN, OSC OUT, BUF OSC OUT as RC oscillator - clock will be same phase and duty cycle as BUF OSC OUT. - Input low configures OSC IN, OSC OUT for crystal oscillator - clock frequency will be 1/58 of frequency at BUF OSC OUT.
25	BUF OSC OUT	Buffered Oscillator Output
26	RUN/HOLD	Input High - Conversions continuously performed every 8192 clock pulses. Input Low - Conversion in progress completed, converter will stop in Auto-Zero 7 counts before integrate.
27	SEND	Input - Used in handshake mode to indicate ability of an external device to accept data.
28	V⁻	Analog Negative Supply - Nominally -5V with respect to GND (Pin 1).
29	REF OUT	Reference Voltage Output - Nominally 2.8V down from V⁺ (Pin 40).
30	BUFFER	Buffer Amplifier Output
31	AUTO-ZERO	Auto-Zero Node - Inside foil of C_{AZ}
32	INTEGRATOR	Integrator Output - Outside foil of C_{INT}
33	COMMON	Analog Common - System is Auto-Zeroed to COMMON
34	INPUT LO	Differential Input Low Side
35	INPUT HI	Differential Input High Side
36	REF IN +	Differential Reference Input Positive
37	REF CAP +	Reference Capacitor Positive
38	REF CAP -	Reference Capacitor Negative
39	REF IN -	Differential Reference Input Negative
40	V⁺	Positive Supply Voltage - Nominally +5V with respect to GND (Pin 1).

DETAILED DESCRIPTION

Analog Section

Figure 2 shows the equivalent circuit of the Analog Section of the ICL7109. When the RUN/HOLD input is left open or connected to V⁺, the circuit will perform conversions at a rate determined by the clock frequency (8192 clock periods per cycle). Each measurement cycle is divided into three phases as shown in Figure 3. They are (1) Auto-Zero (AZ), (2) Signal Integrate (INT) and (3) Deintegrate (DE).

1. Auto-Zero Phase

During auto-zero three things happen. First, input high and low are disconnected from their pins and internally shorted to analog common. Second, the reference capacitor is charged to the reference voltage. Third, a feedback loop is closed around the system to charge the auto-zero capacitor C_{AZ} to compensate for offset voltages in the buffer amplifier, integrator, and comparator. Since the comparator is included in the loop, the AZ accuracy is limited only by the noise of the system. In any case, the offset referred to the input is less than $10\mu V$.

2. Signal Integrate Phase

During signal integrate the auto-zero loop is opened, the internal short is removed and the internal input high and low are connected to the external pins. The converter then integrates the differential voltage between input high and input low for a fixed time of 2048 clock periods. At the end of this phase, the polarity of the integrated signal is determined.

ICL7109

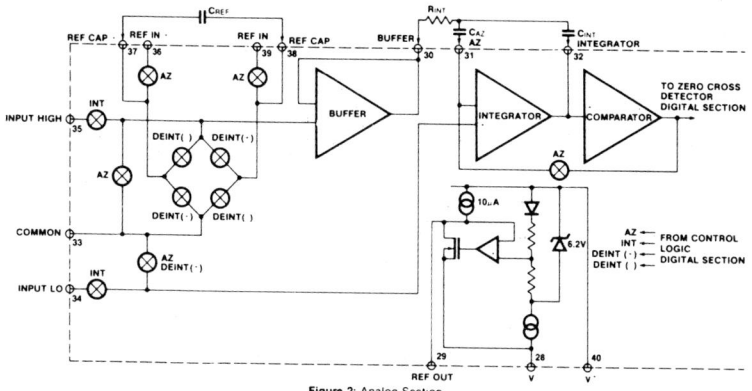

Figure 2: Analog Section

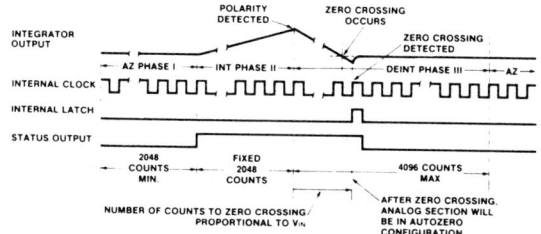

Figure 3: Conversion Timing

3. Deintegrate Phase

The final phase is deintegrate, or reference integrate. Input low is internally connected to analog common and input high is connected across the previously charged (during auto-zero) reference capacitor. Circuitry within the chip ensures that the capacitor will be connected with the correct polarity to cause the integrator output to return to the zero crossing (established in Auto Zero) with a fixed slope. Thus the time for the output to return to zero (represented by the number of clock periods counted) is proportional to the input signal.

Differential Input

The input can accept differential voltages anywhere within the common mode range of the input amplifier; or specifically from 0.5 volts below the positive supply to 1.0 volt above the negative supply. In this range the system has a CMRR of 86dB typical. However, since the integrator also swings with the common mode voltage, care must be exercised to assure the integrator output does not saturate. A worst case condition would be a large positive common mode voltage with a near full-scale negative differential input voltage. The negative input signal drives the integrator positive when most of its swing has been used up by the positive common mode voltage. For these critical applications the integrator swing can be reduced to less than the recommended 4V full scale with some loss of accuracy. The integrator output can swing within 0.3 volts of either supply without loss of linearity.

The ICL7109 has, however, been optimized for operation with analog common near digital ground. With power supplies of +5V and -5V, this allows a 4V full scale integrator swing positive or negative maximizing the performance of the analog section.

Differential Reference

The reference voltage can be generated anywhere within the power supply voltage of the converter. The main source of common mode error is a roll-over voltage caused by the reference capacitor losing or gaining charge to stray capacity on its nodes. If there is a large common mode voltage, the reference capacitor can gain charge (increase voltage) when called up to deintegrate a positive signal but lose charge (decrease voltage) when called up to deintegrate a negative input signal. This difference in reference for (+) or (-) input voltage will give a roll-over error. However, by

ICL7109

selecting the reference capacitor large enough in comparison to the stray capacitance, this error can be held to less than 0.5 count for the worst case condition (see Component Values Selection below).

The roll-over error from these sources is minimized by having the reference common mode voltage near or at analog common.

Component Value Selection

For optimum performance of the analog section, care must be taken in the selection of values for the integrator capacitor and resistor, auto-zero capacity, reference voltage, and conversion rate. These values must be chosen to suit the particular application.

The most important consideration is that the integrator output swing (for full-scale input) be as large as possible. For example, with ±5V supplies and COMMON connected to GND, the nominal integrator output swing at full scale is ±4V. Since the integrator output can go to 0.3V from either supply without significantly affecting linearity, a 4V integrator output swing allows 0.7V for variations in output swing due to component value and oscillator tolerances. With ±5V supplies and a common mode range of ±1V required, the component values should be selected to provide ±3V integrator output swing. Noise and rollover errors will be slightly worse than in the ±4V case. For larger common mode voltage ranges, the integrator output swing must be reduced further. This will increase both noise and rollover errors. To improve the performance, supplies of ±6V may be used.

1. Integrating Resistor

Both the buffer amplifier and the integrator have a class A output stage with 100μA of quiescent current. They supply 20μA of drive current with negligible non-linearity. The integrating resistor should be large enough to remain in this very linear region over the input voltage range, but small enough that undue leakage requirements are not placed on the PC board. For 4.096 volt full scale, 200kΩ is near optimum and similarly a 20kΩ for a 409.6mV scale. For other values of full scale voltage, R_{INT} should be chosen by the relation

$$R_{INT} = \frac{\text{full scale voltage}}{20\mu A}$$

2. Integrating Capacitor

The integrating capacitor C_{INT} should be selected to give the maximum integrator output voltage swing without saturating the integrator (approximately 0.3 volt from either supply). For the ICL7109 with ±5 volt supplies and analog common connected to GND, a ±3.5 to ±4 volt integrator output swing is nominal. For 7-1/2 conversions per second (61.72KHz clock frequency) as provided by the crystal oscillator, nominal values for C_{INT} and C_{AZ} are 0.15μF and 0.33μF, respectively. If different clock frequencies are used, these values should be changed to maintain the integrator output voltage swing. In general, the value of C_{INT} is given by

$$C_{INT} = \frac{(2048 \times \text{clock period}) \; (20\mu A)}{\text{integrator output voltage swing}}$$

An additional requirement of the integrating capacitor is that it have low dielectric absorption to prevent roll-over errors. While other types of capacitors are adequate for this application, polypropylene capacitors give undetectable errors at reasonable cost.

3. Auto-Zero Capacitor

The size of the auto-zero capacitor has some influence on the noise of the system; a big capacitor, giving less noise. However, it cannot be increased without limits since it, in parallel with the integrating capacitor forms an R-C time constant that determines the speed of recovery from overloads and more important the error that exists at the end of an auto-zero cycle. For 409.6mv full scale where noise is very important and the integrating resistor small, a value of C_{AZ} twice C_{INT} is optimum. Similarly for 4.096V full scale where recovery is more important than noise, a value of C_{AZ} equal to half of C_{INT} is recommended.

For optimal rejection of stray pickup, the outer foil of C_{AZ} should be connected to the R-C summing junction and the inner foil to pin 31. Similarly the outer foil of C_{INT} should be connected to pin 32 and the inner foil to the R-C summing junction.

4. Reference Capacitor

A 1μF capacitor gives good results in most applications. However, where a large common mode voltage exists (i.e. the reference low is not at analog common) and a 409.6mV scale is used, a larger value is required to prevent roll-over error. Generally 10μF will hold the roll-over error to 0.5 count in this instance.

5. Reference Voltage

The analog input required to generate a full scale output of 4096 counts is $V_{IN} = 2V_{REF}$. Thus for a normalized scale, a reference of 2.048V should be usd for a 4.096V full scale. However, in many applications where the A/D is sensing the output of a transducer, there will exist a scale factor other than unity between the absolute output voltage to be measured and a desired digital output. For instance, in a weighing system, the designer might like to have a full scale reading when the voltage from the transducer is 0.682V. Instead of dividing the input down to 409.6mV, the input voltage should be measured directly and a reference voltage of 0.341V should be used. Suitable values for integrating resistor and capacitor are 34k and 0.15μF. This avoids a divider on the input. Another advantage of this system occurs when a zero reading is desired for non-zero input. Temperature and weight measurements with an offset or tare are examples. The offset may be introduced by connecting the voltage output of the transducer between common and analog high, and the offset voltage between common and analog low, observing polarities carefully. However, in processor-based systems using the ICL7109, it may be more efficient to perform this type of scaling or tare subtraction digitally using software.

6. Reference Sources

The stability of the reference voltage is a major factor in the overall absolute accuracy of the converter. The resolution of the ICL7109 at 12 bits is one part in 4096, or 244ppm. Thus if the reference has a temperature coefficient of 80ppm/°C (onboard reference) a temperature difference of 3°C will introduce a one-bit absolute error. For this reason, it is recommended that an external high-quality reference be used where the ambient temperature is not controlled or where high-accuracy absolute measurements are being made.

ICL7109

The ICL7109 provides a Reference Output (pin 29) which may be used with a resistive divider to generate a suitable reference voltage. This output will sink up to about 20mA without significant variation in output voltage, and is provided with a pullup bias device which sources about 10µA. The output voltage is nominally 2.8V below V⁺, and has a temperature coefficient of ±80ppm/°C typ. When using the onboard reference, Ref Out (Pin 29) should be connected to Ref− (pin 39), and Ref+ should be connected to the wiper of a precision potentiometer between Ref Out and V⁺. The circuit for a 204.8mV reference is shown in the test circuit. For a 2.048V reference, the fixed resistor should be removed, and a 25kΩ precision potentiometer between Ref Out and V⁺ should be used.

DETAILED DESCRIPTION

Digital Section

The digital section includes the clock oscillator and scaling circuit, a 12-bit binary counter with output latches and TTL-compatible three-state output drivers, polarity, over-range and control logic, and UART handshake logic, as shown in the Block Diagram Figure 4.

Throughout this description, logic levels will be referred to as "low" or "high". The actual logic levels are defined in Table 1 "Operating Characteristics". For minimum power consumption, all inputs should swing from GND (low) to V⁺ (high). Inputs driven from TTL gates should have 3-5kΩ pullup resistors added for maximum noise immunity.

MODE Input

The MODE input is used to control the output mode of the converter. When the MODE pin is connected to GND or left open (this input is provided with a pulldown resistor to ensure a low level when the pin is left open), the converter is in its "Direct" output mode, where the output data is directly accessible under the control of the chip and byte enable inputs. When the MODE input is pulsed high, the converter enters the UART handshake mode and outputs the data in two bytes, then returns to "direct" mode. When the MODE input is left high, the converter will output data in the handshake mode at the end of every conversion cycle. (See section entitled "Handshake Mode" for further details).

STATUS Output

During a conversion cycle, the STATUS output goes high at the beginning of Signal Integrate (Phase II), and goes low one-half clock period after new data from the conversion has been stored in the output latches. See Figure 3 for details of this timing. This signal may be used as a "data valid" flag (data never changes while STATUS is low) to drive interrupts, or for monitoring the status of the converter.

RUN/HOLD Input

When the RUN/HOLD input is connected to V⁺ or left open (this input has a pullup resistor to ensure a high level when the pin is left open), the circuit will continuously perform conversion cycles, updating the output latches at the end of every Deintegrate (Phase III) portion of the conversion cycle (See Figure 3). In this mode of operation, the conversion cycle will be performed in 8192 clock periods, regardless of the resulting value.

If the RUN/HOLD input goes low (and stays there) during Integrate (Phase II) or Deintegrate (Phase III) before the zero crossing is detected, the converter will complete the conversion in progress, update the output latches, and then terminate Phase III, jumping to Auto-Zero (Phase I). If RUN/HOLD stays low, the converter will ensure a minimum Auto-Zero time, and wait in Auto-Zero until the RUN/HOLD input goes high. The converter will begin the Integrate (Phase II) portion of the next conversion (and the STATUS output will go high) seven clock periods after the high level is detected at RUN/HOLD. See Figure 5 for details.

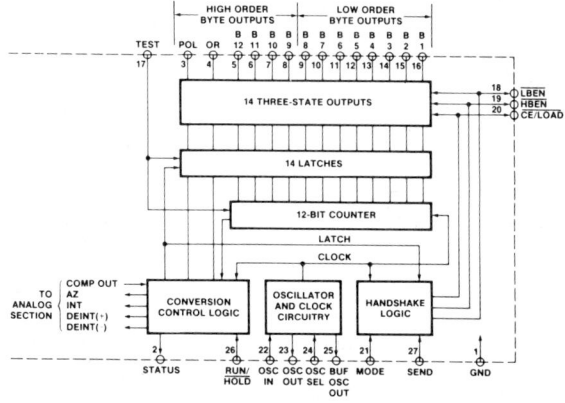

Figure 4: Digital Section

ICL7109

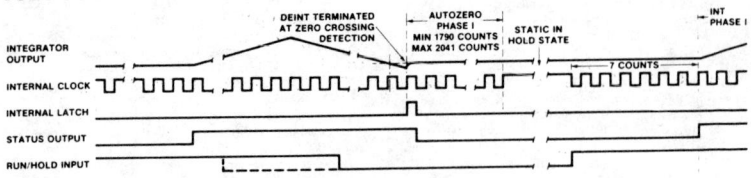

Figure 5: Run/Hold Operation

Using the RUN/HOLD input in this manner allows an easy "convert on demand" interface to be used. The converter may be held at idle in auto-zero with RUN/HOLD low. When RUN/HOLD goes high the conversion is started, and when the STATUS output goes low the new data is valid (or transferred to the UART - see Handshake Mode). RUN/HOLD may now go low terminating Deintegrate and ensuring a minimum Auto-Zero time before stopping to wait for the next conversion.

If RUN/HOLD goes low at any time during Deintegrate (Phase III) after the zero crossing has occurred, the circuit will immediately terminate Deintegrate and jump to Auto-Zero. This feature can be used to "short-cycle" the converter by eliminating the time spent in Deintegrate after the zero crossing. The required activity on the RUN/HOLD input can be provided by connecting it to the Buffered Oscillator Output. In this mode the conversion time is dependent on the input value measured. Also refer to Intersil Application Bulletin A030 for a discussion of the effects this will have on Auto-Zero performance.

If the RUN/HOLD input goes low and stays low during Auto-Zero (Phase I), the converter will simply stop at the end of Auto-Zero and wait for RUN/HOLD to go high. As above, Integrate (Phase II) begins seven clock periods after the high level is detected.

Direct Mode

When the MODE pin is left at a low level, the data outputs (bits 1 through 8 low order byte, bits 9 through 12, polarity and over-range high order byte) are accessible under control of the byte and chip enable terminals as inputs. These three inputs are all active low, and are provided with pullup resistors to ensure an inactive high level when left open. When the chip enable input is low, taking a byte enable input low will allow the outputs of that byte to become active (three-stated on). This allows a variety of parallel data accessing techniques to be used, as shown in the section entitled "Interfacing." The timing requirements for these outputs are shown in Figure 6 and Table 3.

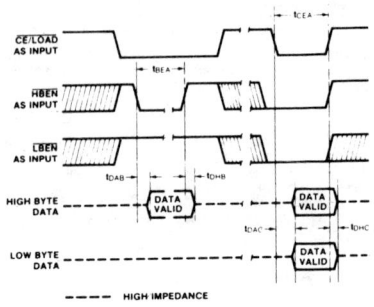

Figure 6: Direct Mode Output Timing

Table 3 - Direct Mode Timing Requirements

SYMBOL	DESCRIPTION	MIN	TYP	MAX	UNITS
t_{BEA}	Byte Enable Width	200	500		ns
t_{DAB}	Data Access Time from Byte Enable		150	300	ns
t_{DHB}	Data Hold Time from Byte Enable		150	300	ns
t_{CEA}	Chip Enable Width	300	500		ns
t_{DAC}	Data Access Time from Chip Enable		200	400	ns
t_{DHC}	Data Hold Time from Chip Enable		200	400	ns

It should be noted that these control inputs are asynchronous with respect to the converter clock - the data may be accessed at any time. Thus it is possible to access the data while it is being updated, which could lead to scrambled data. Synchronizing the access of data with the conversion cycle by monitoring the STATUS output will prevent this. Data is never updated while STATUS is low.

Handshake Mode

The handshake output mode is provided as an alternative means of interfacing the ICL7109 to digital systems, where the A/D converter becomes active in controlling the flow of data instead of passively responding to chip and byte enable inputs. This mode is specifically designed to allow a direct interface between the ICL7109 and industry-standard UARTs (such as the Intersil CMOS UARTs, IM6402/3) with no external logic required. When triggered into the handshake mode, the ICL7109 provides all the control and flag signals necessary to sequence the two bytes of data into the UART and initiate their transmission in serial form. This greatly eases the task and reduces the cost of designing remote data acquisition stations using serial data transmission to minimize the number of lines to the central controlling processor.

Entry into the handshake mode is controlled by the MODE pin. When the MODE terminal is held high, the ICL7109 will enter the handshake mode after new data has been stored in the output latches at the end of every conversion performed (See Figures 7 and 8). The MODE terminal may also be used to trigger entry into the handshake mode on demand. At any time during the conversion cycle, the low to high transition of a short pulse at the MODE input will cause immediate entry

ICL7109

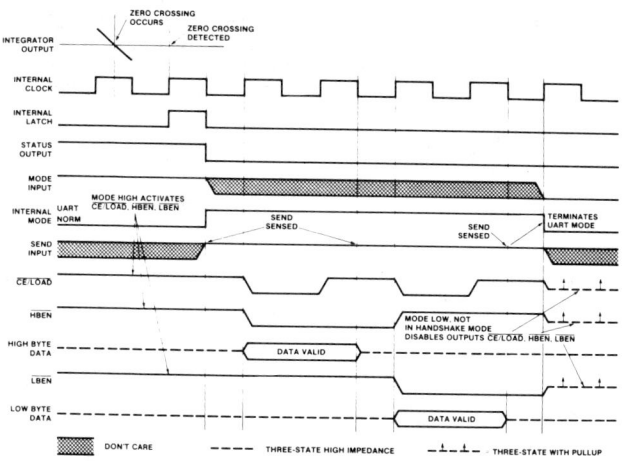

Figure 7: Handshake With Send Held Positive

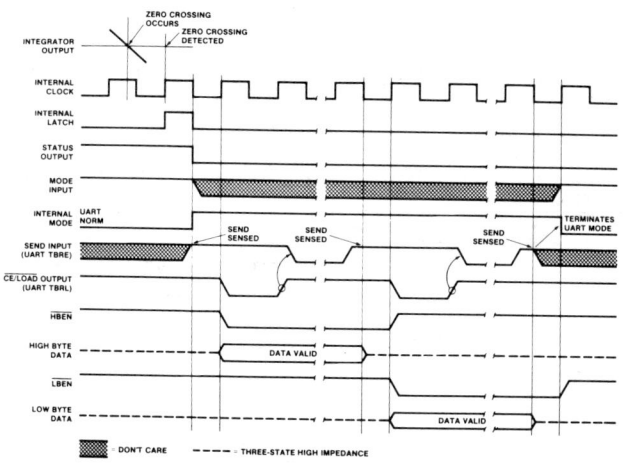

Figure 8: Handshake - Typical UART Interface Timing

ICL7109

into the handshake mode. If this pulse occurs while new data is being stored, the entry into handshake mode is delayed until the data is stable. While the converter is in the handshake mode, the MODE input is ignored, and although conversions will still be performed, data updating will be inhibited (See Figure 9) until the converter completes the output cycle and clears the handshake mode.

When the converter enters the handshake mode, or when the MODE input is high, the chip and byte enable terminals become TTL-compatible outputs which provide the control signals for the output cycle (See Figures 7, 8, and 9).

In handshake mode, the SEND input is used by the converter as an indication of the ability of the receiving device (such as a UART) to accept data.

Figure 7 shows the sequence of the output cycle with SEND held high. The handshake mode (Internal MODE high) is entered after the data latch pulse (since MODE remains high the CE/LOAD, LBEN and HBEN terminals are active as outputs). The high level at the SEND input is sensed on the same high to low internal clock edge. On the next low to high internal clock edge, the CE/LOAD and HBEN outputs assume a low level, and the high-order byte (bits 9 through 12, POL, and OR) outputs are enabled. The CE/LOAD output remains low for one full internal clock period only, the data outputs remain active for 1-1/2 internal clock periods, and the high byte enable remains low for two clock periods. Thus the CE/LOAD output low level or low to high edge may be used as a synchronizing signal to ensure valid data, and the byte enable as an output may be used as a byte identification flag. With SEND remaining high the converter completes the output cycle using CE/LOAD and LBEN while the low order byte outputs (bits 1 through 8) are activated. The handshake mode is terminated when both bytes are sent.

Figure 8 shows an output sequence where the SEND input is used to delay portions of the sequence, or handshake, to ensure correct data transfer. This timing diagram shows the relationships that occur using an industry-standard IM6402/3 CMOS UART to interface to serial data channels. In this interface, the SEND input to the ICL7109 is driven by the TBRE (Transmitter Buffer Register Empty) output of the UART, and the CE/LOAD terminal of the ICL7109 drives the TBRL (Transmitter Buffer Register Load) input to the UART. The data outputs are paralleled into the eight Transmitter Buffer Register inputs.

Assuming the UART Transmitter Buffer Register is empty, the SEND input will be high when the handshake mode is entered after new data is stored. The CE/LOAD and HBEN terminals will go low after SEND is sensed, and the high order byte outputs become active. When CE/LOAD goes high at the end of one clock period, the high order byte data is clocked into the UART Transmitter Buffer Register. The UART TBRE output will now go low, which halts the output cycle with the HBEN output low, and the high order byte outputs active. When the UART has transferred the data to the Transmitter Register and cleared the Transmitter Buffer Register, the TBRE returns high. On the next ICL7109

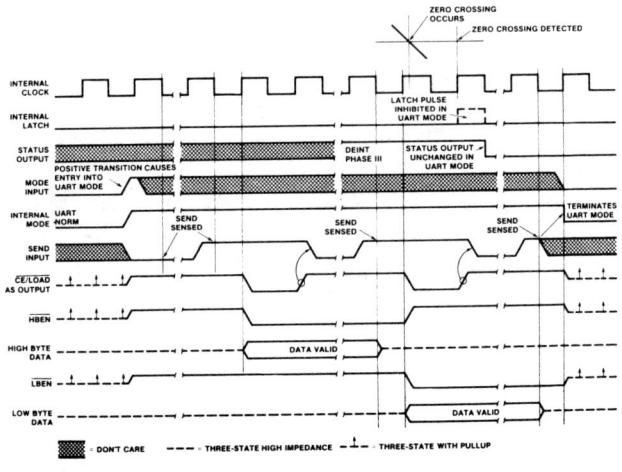

Figure 9: Handshake Triggered By Mode

ICL7109

internal clock high to low edge, the high order byte outputs are disabled, and one-half internal clock later, the HBEN output returns high. At the same time, the CE/LOAD and LBEN outputs go low, and the low order byte outputs become active. Similarly, when the CE/LOAD returns high at the end of one clock period, the low order data is clocked into the UART Transmitter Buffer Register, and TBRE again goes low. When TBRE returns to a high it will be sensed on the next ICL7109 internal clock high to low edge, disabling the data outputs. One-half internal clock later, the handshake mode will be cleared, and the CE/LOAD, HBEN, and LBEN terminals return high and stay active (as long as MODE stays high).

With the MODE input remaining high as in these examples, the converter will output the results of every conversion except those completed during a handshake operation. By triggering the converter into handshake mode with a low to high edge on the MODE input, handshake output sequences may be performed on demand. Figure 9 shows a handshake output sequence triggered by such an edge. In addition, the SEND input is shown as being low when the converter enters handshake mode. In this case, the whole output sequence is controlled by the SEND input, and the sequence for the first (high order) byte is similar to the sequence for the second byte. This diagram also shows the output sequence taking longer than a conversion cycle. Note that the converter still makes conversions, with the STATUS output and RUN/HOLD input functioning normally. The only difference is that new data will not be latched when in handshake mode, and is therefore lost.

Oscillator

The ICL7109 is provided with a versatile three terminal oscillator to generate the internal clock. The oscillator may be overdriven, or may be operated as an RC or crystal oscillator. The OSCILLATOR SELECT input changes the internal configuration of the oscillator to optimize it for RC or crystal operation.

When the OSCILLATOR SELECT input is high or left open (the input is provided with a pullup resistor), the oscillator is configured for RC operation, and the internal clock will be of the same frequency and phase as the signal at the BUFFERED OSCILLATOR OUTPUT. The resistor and capacitor should be connected as in Figure 10. The circuit will oscillate at a frequency given by f = .45/RC. A 100kΩ resistor is recommended for useful ranges of frequency. For optimum 60Hz line rejection, the capacitor value should be chosen such that 2048 clock periods is close to an integral multiple of the 60Hz period.

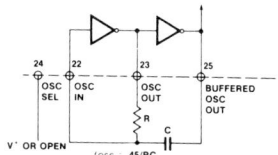

Figure 10: RC Oscillator

When the OSCILLATOR SELECT input is low a feedback device and output and input capacitors are added to the oscillator. In this configuration, as shown in Figure 11, the

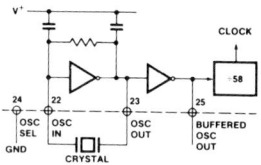

Figure 11: Crystal Oscillator

oscillator will operate with most crystals in the 1 to 5MHz range with no external components. Taking the OSCILLATOR SELECT input low also inserts a fixed ÷58 divider circuit between the BUFFERED OSCILLATOR OUTPUT and the internal clock. Using an inexpensive 3.58MHz TV crystal, this division ratio provides an integration time given by:

$$T = (2048 \text{ clock periods}) \times \left(\frac{58}{3.58\text{MHz}}\right) = 33.18\text{ms}$$

This time is very close to two 60Hz periods or 33.33ms. The error is less than one percent, which will give better than 40dB 60Hz rejection. The converter will operate reliably at conversion rates of up to 30 per second, which corresponds to a clock frequency of 245.8kHz.

If at any time the oscillator is to be overdriven, the overdriving signal should be applied at the OSCILLATOR INPUT, and the OSCILLATOR OUTPUT should be left open. The internal clock will be of the same frequency, duty cycle, and phase as the input signal when OSCILLATOR SELECT is left open. When OSCILLATOR SELECT is at GND, the clock will be a factor of 58 below the input frequency.

When using the ICL7109 with the IM6403 UART, it is possible to use one 3.58MHz crystal for both devices. The BUFFERED OSCILLATOR OUTPUT of the ICL7109 may be used to drive the OSCILLATOR INPUT of the UART, saving the need for a second crystal. However, the BUFFERED OSCILLATOR OUTPUT does not have a great deal of drive, and when driving more than one slave device, external buffering should be used.

Test Input

When the TEST input is taken to a level halfway between V⁺ and GND, the counter output latches are enabled, allowing the counter contents to be examed anytime.

When the TEST input is connected to GND, the counter outputs are all forced into the high state, and the internal clock is disabled. When the input returns to the 1/2 (V⁺ −GND) voltage or to V⁺ and one clock is input, the counter outputs will all be clocked to the negative state. This allows easy testing of the counter and its outputs.

INTERFACING
Direct Mode

Figure 12 shows some of the combinations of chip enable and byte enable control signals which may be used when interfacing the ICL7109 to parallel data lines. The CE/LOAD input may be tied low, allowing either byte to be controlled by its own enable as in Figure 12A. Figure 12B shows a configuration where the two byte enables are connected together. In this configuration, the CE/LOAD serves as a chip enable, and the HBEN and LBEN may be connected to GND or serve as a second chip enable. The 14 data outputs will all be enabled simultaneously. Figure 12C shows the HBEN and LBEN as flag inputs, and CE/LOAD as a master enable, which could be the READ strobe available from most microprocessors.

405

ICL7109

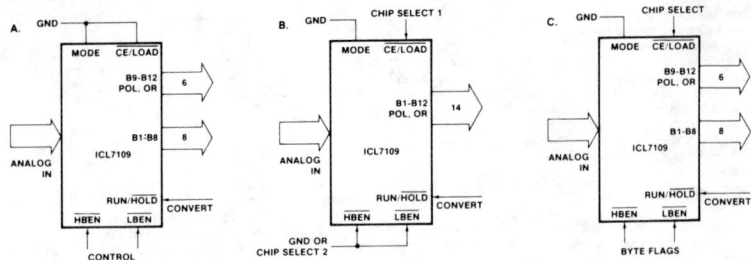

Figure 12: Direct Mode Chip and Byte Enable Combinations

Figure 13 shows an approach to interfacing several ICL7109s to a bus, ganging the HBEN and LBEN signals to several converters together, and using the CE/LOAD inputs (perhaps decoded from an address) to select the desired converter.

Some practical circuits utilizing the parallel three-state output capabilities of the ICL7109 are shown in Figures 14 through 19. Figure 14 shows a straightforward application to the Intel MCS-48, -80 and -85 systems via an 8255PPI, where the ICL7109 data outputs are active at all times. The I/O ports of an 8155 may be used in the same way. This interface can be used in a read-anytime mode, although a read performed while the data latches are being updated will lead to scrambled data. This will occur very rarely, in the proportion of setup-skew times to conversion time. One way to overcome this is to read the STATUS output as well, and if it is high, read the data again after a delay of more than 1/2 converter clock period. If STATUS is now low, the second reading is correct, and if it is still high, the first reading is correct. Alternatively, this timing problem is completely avoided by using a read-after-update sequence, as shown in Figure 15. Here the high to low transition of the STATUS output drives an interrupt to the microprocessor causing it to access the data. This application also shows the RUN/HOLD input being used to initiate conversions under software control.

A similar interface to Motorola MC6800 or MOS Technology MCS650X systems is shown in Figure 16. The high to low transition of the STATUS output generates an interrupt via the Control Register B CB1 line. Note that CB2 controls the RUN/HOLD pin through Control Register B, allowing software-controlled initiation of conversions in this system also.

Figure 17 shows an interface to the Intersil IM6100 CMOS microprocessor family using the IM6101 PIE to control the data transfers. Here the data is read by the microprocessor in an 8-bit and a 6-bit word, directly from the ICL7109 to the microprocessor data bus. Again, the high to low transition of the STATUS output generates an interrupt leading to a software routine controlling the two read operations. As before, the RUN/HOLD input to the ICL7109 is shown as being under software control.

The three-state output capability of the ICL7109 allows direct interfacing to most microprocessor busses. Examples of this are shown in the Typical Connection Diagram on

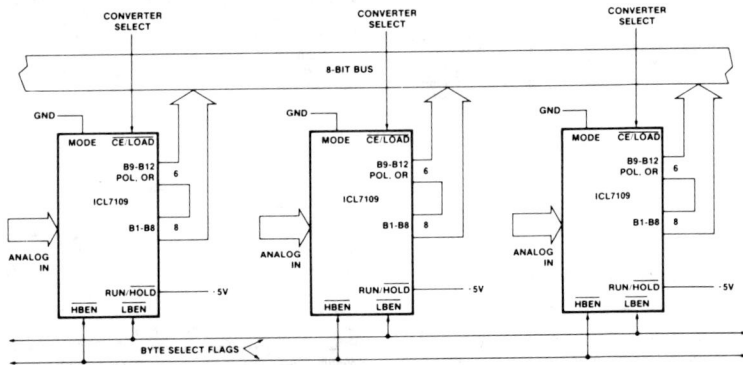

Figure 13: Three-stating Several 7109's to a Small Bus

ICL7109

Page 3 and in Figures 18 and 19. It is necessary to carefully consider the system timing in this type of interface, to be sure that requirements for setup and hold times, and minimum pulse widths are met. Note also the drive limitations on long busses. Generally this type of interface is only favored if the memory peripheral address density is low so that simple address decoding can be used. Interrupt handling can also require many additional components, and using an interface device will usually simplify the system in this case.

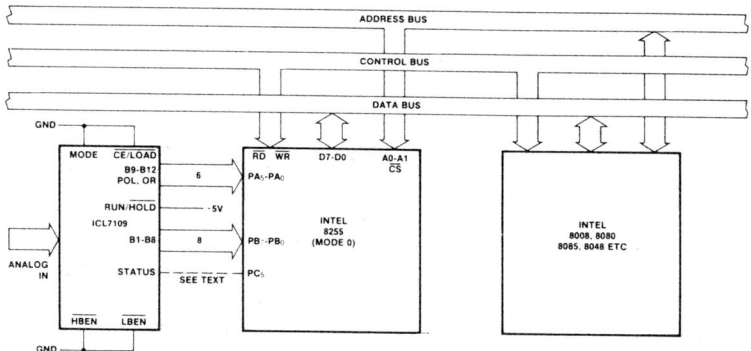

Figure 14: Full-time Parallel Interface to INTEL Microcomputer Systems

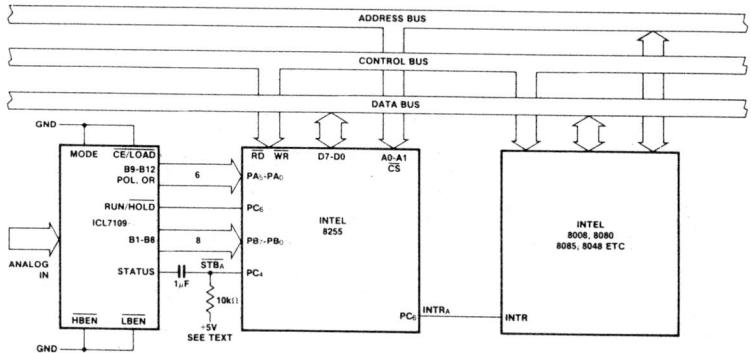

ICL7109

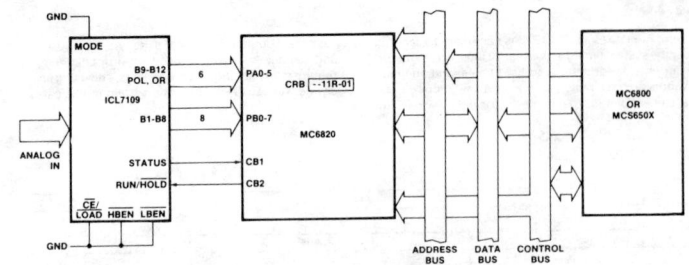

Figure 16: Full-time Parallel Interface to MC6800 or MCS650X Microprocessors

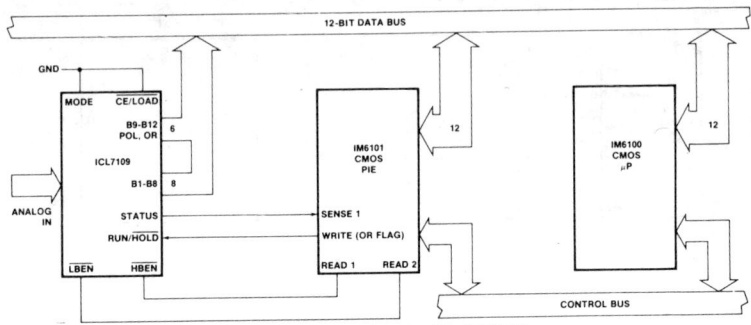

Figure 17: ICL7109-IM6100 Interface Using IM6101 PIE

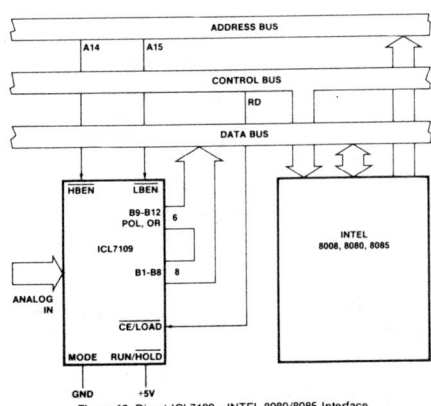

Figure 18: Direct ICL7109 - INTEL 8080/8085 Interface

ICL7109

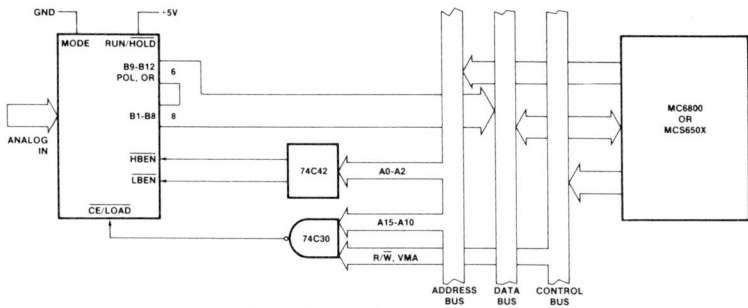

Figure 19: Direct ICL7109 - MC6800 Bus Interface

Handshake Mode

The handshake mode allows ready interface with a wide variety of external devices. For instance, external latches may be clocked by the rising edge of $\overline{CE/LOAD}$, and the byte enables may be used as byte identification flags or as load enables.

Figure 20 shows a handshake interface to Intel microprocessors again using an 8255 PPI. The handshake operation with the 8255 is controlled by inverting its Input Buffer Full (IBF) flag to drive the SEND input to the ICL7109, and using the $\overline{CE/LOAD}$ to drive the 8255 strobe. The internal control register of the PPI should be set in MODE 1 for the port used. If the 7109 is in handshake mode and the 8255 IBF flag is low, the next word will be strobed into the port. The strobe will cause IBF to go high (SEND goes low), which will keep the enabled byte outputs active. The PPI will generate an interrupt which when executed will result in the data being read. When the byte is read, the IBF will be reset low, which causes the ICL7109 to sequence into the next byte. This figure shows the MODE input to the ICL7109 connected to a control line on the PPI. If this output is left high, or tied high

separately, the data from every conversion (provided the data access takes less time than a conversion) will be sequenced in two bytes into the system.

If this output is made to go from low to high, the output sequence can be obtained on demand, and the interrupt may be used to reset the MODE bit. Note that the RUN/$\overline{HOLD}$ input to the ICL7109 may also be driven by a bit of the 8255 so that conversions may be obtained on command under software control. Note that one port of the 8255 is not used, and can service another peripheral device. The same arrangement can also be used with the 8155.

Figure 21 shows a similar arrangement with the MC6800 or MCS650X microprocessors, except that both MODE and RUN/$\overline{HOLD}$ are tied high to save port outputs.

The handshake mode is particularly convenient for directly interfacing to industry standard UARTs (such as the Intersil IM6402/6403 or Western Digital TR1602) providing a minimum component count means of serially transmitting converted data. A typical UART connection is shown on page 3. In this circuit, any word received by the UART causes

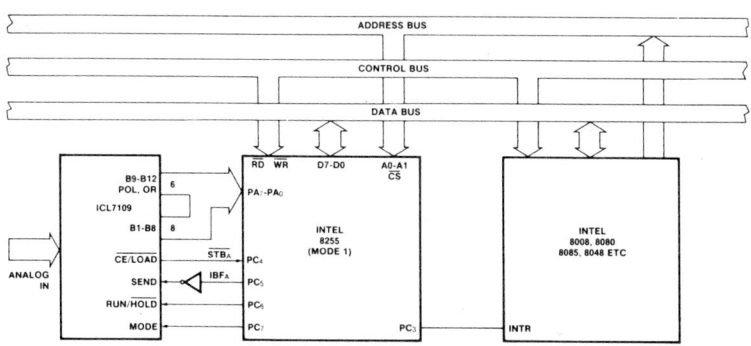

Figure 20: Handshake Interface - ICL7109 to INTEL MCS-48, -80, 85

ICL7109

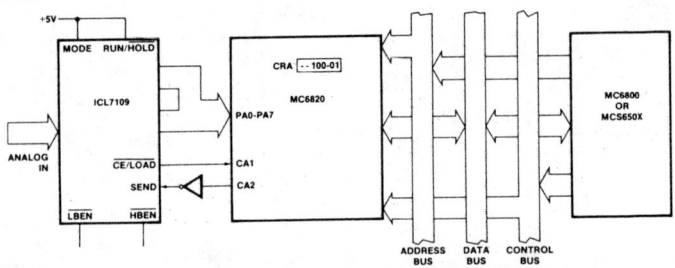

Figure 21: Handshake Interface - ICL7109 to MC6800, MCS650X

the UART DR (Data Ready) output to go high. This drives the MODE input to the ICL7109 high, triggering the ICL7109 into handshake mode. The high order byte is output to the UART first, and when the UART has transferred the data to the Transmitter Register, TBRE (SEND) goes high and the second byte is output. When TBRE (SEND) goes high again, LBEN will go high, driving the UART DRR (Data Ready Reset) which will signal the end of the transfer of data from the ICL7109 to the UART.

Figure 22 shows an extension of the one converter - one UART scheme of the Typical Connection to several ICL7109s with one UART. In this circuit, the word received by the UART (available at the RBR outputs when DR is high) is used to select which converter will handshake with the UART. With no external components, this scheme will allow up to eight ICL7109s to interface with one UART. Using a few more components to decode the received word will allow up to 256 converters to be accessed on one serial line.

The applications of the ICL7109 are not limited to those shown here. The purpose of these examples is to provide a starting point for users to develop useful systems, and to show some of the variety of interfaces and uses of the ICL7109. Many of the ideas suggested here may be used in combination; in particular the uses of the STATUS, RUN/HOLD, and MODE signals may be mixed.

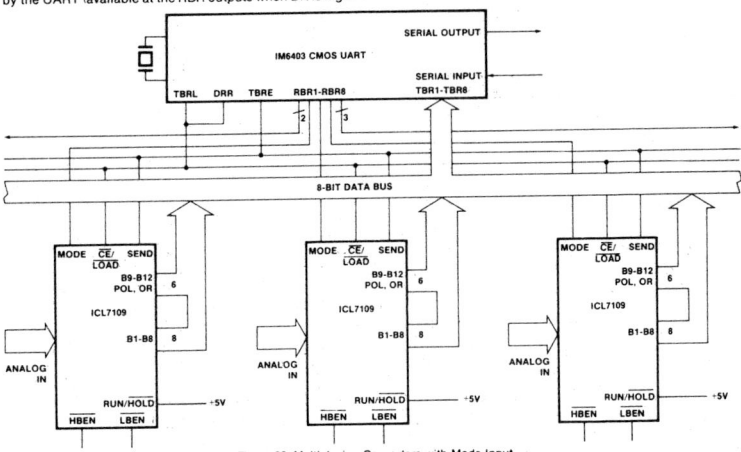

Figure 22: Multiplexing Converters with Mode Input

Index

A

Access
  and breadboarding regions, 32-33
  time, 185
Accumulators, 16
  load, 53-56
  store, 56
  transfer, 56-57
ACIA, 35
Add, 59-60
  accumulators, 60
  and subtract with carry, 94-95
Adding
  numbers immediately, 62
  with the carry bit, 95
Address
  access, 32
  decoder, 150
  map, 149
Addressing
  direct, 54
  extended, 54
  immediate, 54
  indexed, 121-124
AND, 65-66
AND/OR/XOR logic, 294
Arithmetic logic unit, 16

B

Basic(s)
  logic gates, 279-281
  microcomputer/microprocessor, 10-13
  6800 chip structure, 13-16
BGE, 117
BGT, 117
BHI, 118
Binary
  (base 2), 286-287
  coded decimal (bcd), 290-291
    instructions, 100
  switches and displays, 32
Bipolar, 180

Bits, bytes, and nibbles, 289-290
BLE, 118
BLS, 118
BLT, 118
Breadboard console, 32
Branch
  conditional, 116
  instructions, 116-119
  to subroutine (BSR), 131-132
  unconditional, 116
Branching, 115-116
BSR, 118
Buses, 14

C

Carry flag (bit 0), 86
CA2
  input, 222-223
  output, 223-225
Charge-coupled devices, 182-183
Chip structure, 6800, 13-16
Clear accumulator and memory, 57
Clearing accumulators A and B, 59
Clock, 33
CMOS, 181
Comparing index register, immediate addressing, 124
Conclusion of experiments, 38
Conditional branch, 116
Condition code register, 85-90
  operations, 88-89
Controller/sequencer, 16
Control registers, 211
Counter, program, 15
CPU access, 32

D

Data
  access, 32
  comparing, 96-97
  direction registers, 211
  register, 15
  6821, 210-211

Data—cont
    shifting, rotating, comparing, and testing, 90-100
    testing, 97
    transfer, 53-59
Decimal (base 10), 285-286
Decoder, instruction, 16
Decoding, 151-154
Decrement, 62
Decrementing to zero, 64
Destination determination, 116
Determining device
    change of state, 68
    condition, 68
Digital computer arithmetic, 291-292
Direct addressing, 54
Dividing by two, 93-94
DMOS, 182
Dynamic memory, 186

E

EAROM, 194
Encoded keyboard, 248
Equipment for experiments, 37
Executing
    compare instruction, 97
    test instruction, 99
Execution of
    BGT instruction, 119
    BHI instruction, 121
    BNE instruction, 119
Experiment instructions and format, 37-38
Extended addressing, 54
External memory, 15

F

Flip-flops, 282-284
Fully decoded, 152
Functional operating regions, 30-31

G

General i/o concepts, 146-151
Generating
    a last carry, 86
    a twos-complement overflow, 87
    negative result, 88

H

Half-carry flag (bit 5), 88-89
Handshaking, 156
Hardware interrupts, 158

Heath ET3400 microcomputer learning system, 28-33
Hexadecimal (base 16), 288-289
Hex keyboard, 31, 33
High address byte, 54
Hold time, 185-187

I

Immediate addressing, 54
Increment, 61
Indexed addressing, 121-124
Index register and addressing, 119-124
Instruction(s)
    arithmetic, 59-64
    branch, 116-119
    decoder, 16
    logic, 64-68
Interface, 147
Interfacing with
    analog-to-digital converters, 259-262
    digital-to-analog converters, 257-259
    displays, 250-257
    keyboards, 247-250
    read-only memory, 192-196
    read/write memory, 184-187
    switches, 241-247
Interrupt(s), 157-158
    flag (bit 4), 88
    hardware, 158
    nonmaskable, 160-161
    request, 161-162
    software, 159, 162-163
    vector, 158
    vectored, 158
I/O techniques, 154-158

J

JBUG ROM, 33
JSR/RTS, 129-131
Jump (JMP), 128-129

K

Keyboard/display module, 33

L

LED hex display, 31, 33
LIFO, 125
Light-emitting diodes, 150
Load accumulators, 53-56

Loading index register, direct addressing, 123
Look-up table, 252
Low address byte, 54

M

Magnetic bubbles, 183
Maskable interrupt, 157
Mask-programmable ROM, 193
MC6800 CPU, 31, 33
MCM 6830 ROM, 194-196
MCM 68708 (INTEL 2708) EPROM, 196-199
Memory
  address register, 15
  external, 15
  -mapped i/o, 148
  technology, 178-184
Microcomputer, 11
  memory devices, 183-184
  module, 33-36
  system, 11
Microprocessor, 10-11
  /microcomputer basics, 10-13
Minimum requirements for microcomputer system, 147
Module, keyboard/display, 33
MOS, 180-182
Motorola MEK6800D2 evaluation kit, 33-36
Multiplying by two, 93

N

Negative
  logic, 251
  numbers and twos complement, 292-294
  register (bit 3), 88
NMOS, 181
Nonmaskable interrupt, 157, 160-161
Nonvolatile, 147
Number systems, 285-291

O

Octal (base 8), 287-288
Offset address, 121
Ones complement, 64
Operating regions, functional, 30-31
Optional
  RAM, 35
  ROM, 33
OR, 66-67
Overflow (V) flag (bit 1), 86-87

P

Partial decoding, 152
PIA, 36
  control registers, 220-222
  initialization and servicing, 218-225
  interfacing and addressing, 215-217
PMOS, 181
Polling, 154-157
  loop, 156
Positive logic, 251
Procedure for experiments, 38
Program
  counter, 15
  for experiments, 38
Programmed i/o, 154
PROM, 193-194
Pull-up resistors, 150
Purpose of experiments, 37

R

RAM, 30, 35
Read-cycle time, 185
Register
  data, 15
  memory address, 15
  selection, 217-218
Relative address determination
  backward branch, 116
  forward branch, 115
Request, interrupt, 161-162
RESET, 36, 159-160
ROM, 31
Rotate
  left, 92
  right, 92

S

Schematic diagram for experiments, 38
Setting the Z flag
  arithmetic operation, 87
  compare operation, 88
Setup time, 185
Shift left-arithmetic, 90-91
Shift right
  -arithmetic, 91
  -logic, 91-92
Single-bus architecture, 121
6800
  arithmetic instructions, 59-64
  data transfer, 53-59
  fetch and execute, 16-23
  instruction format, 17

6800—cont
 -interrupts, 158-163
  types of, 158
 logic instructions, 64-68
 pin assignments, 164-167
  address, 166
  bus available, 165
  clocks, 164
  data, 166
   bus enable, 166
  ground, 164
  halt, 164
  interrupt request, 164
  nonmaskable interrupt, 165
  +5-volt power, 165
  read/write, 166
  reset, 167
  three-state control, 166
  valid memory address, 164-165
 sample program listing, 17
6810
 pin assignments, 187-190
  address inputs, 188
  chip-select inputs, 187-188
  data, 187
  ground, 187
  read/write, 188
  V_{cc}, 188
 R/W memory, 187-190
6820/6821 pin assignments, 211-215
 chip selects, 213
 data, 214
 enable, 213
 interrupt input, 215
  -port B, 213
 interrupt requests, 214
 peripheral control, 214
  port B, 213
 port A data lines, 212
 port B data lines, 212-213
 read/write, 213
 register selects, 214
 reset, 214
 V_{cc}, 213
 V_{ss}, 211
6821 functional description, 210-211
6830 pin assignments, 194-196
 address, 195-196
 chip-select inputs, 195
 data, 194-195
 ground, 194
 V_{cc}, 195

68708 pin assignments, 197-198
 address, 197
 chip select/write enable, 197
 data, 197
 ground, 197
 program, 197
 V_{BB}, 198
 V_{cc}, 198
 V_{DD}, 197
Software interrupt, 159, 162-163
Stack
 pull operation, 126
 push operation, 126
Stacks and stack pointer, 124-127
Static memory, 186
Store accumulators, 56
Storing index register, indexed addressing, 123
Subroutines, 127-132
Subtract, 60
 accumulators, 61
Subtracting numbers from memory, 63
Swapping accumulator data, 58
Switch, 149

T

Three-state buffers, 150
Transfer accumulators, 56-57
2112 pin assignments, 191-192
 address, 191
 chip enable, 191
 data, 191
 ground, 191
 read/write, 191
 V_{cc}, 191
Twos complement, 65

U

Unconditional branch, 116
Un-encoded keyboard, 248
Using the decimal adjust instruction, 100

V

Vectored interrupt, 158
VMOS, 182
Volatile, 147

W

Wait (WAI), 58-59
Wait for interrupt, 163
Write-cycle time, 185

READER SERVICE CARD

To better serve you, the reader, please take a moment to fill out this card, or a copy of it, for us. Not only will you be kept up to date on the Blacksburg Series books, but as an extra bonus, **we will randomly select five cards every month, from all of the cards sent to us during the previous month. The names that are drawn will win, absolutely free, a book from the Blacksburg Continuing Education Series.** Therefore, make sure to indicate your choice in the space provided below. For a complete listing of all the books to choose from, refer to the inside front cover of this book. Please, one card per person. Give everyone a chance.

In order to find out who has won a book in your area, call (703) 953-1861 anytime during the night or weekend. When you do call, an answering machine will let you know the monthly winners. Too good to be true? Just give us a call. Good luck.

If I win, please send me a copy of:

_____

I understand that this book will be sent to me absolutely free, if my card is selected.

For our information, how about telling us a little about yourself. We are interested in your occupation, how and where you normally purchase books and the books that you would like to see in the Blacksburg Series. We are also interested in finding authors for the series, so if you have a book idea, write to The Blacksburg Group, Inc., P.O. Box 242, Blacksburg, VA 24060 and ask for an Author Packet. We are also interested in TRS-80, APPLE, OSI and PET BASIC programs.

My occupation is _____
I buy books through/from _____
Would you buy books through the mail? _____
I'd like to see a book about _____
Name _____
Address _____
City _____
State _____ Zip _____

MAIL TO: BOOKS, BOX 715, BLACKSBURG, VA 24060
!!!!!PLEASE PRINT!!!!!